3

switch

naked ape : Saki Otoh & Nakamura Tomomi

switch

3

CONTENTS

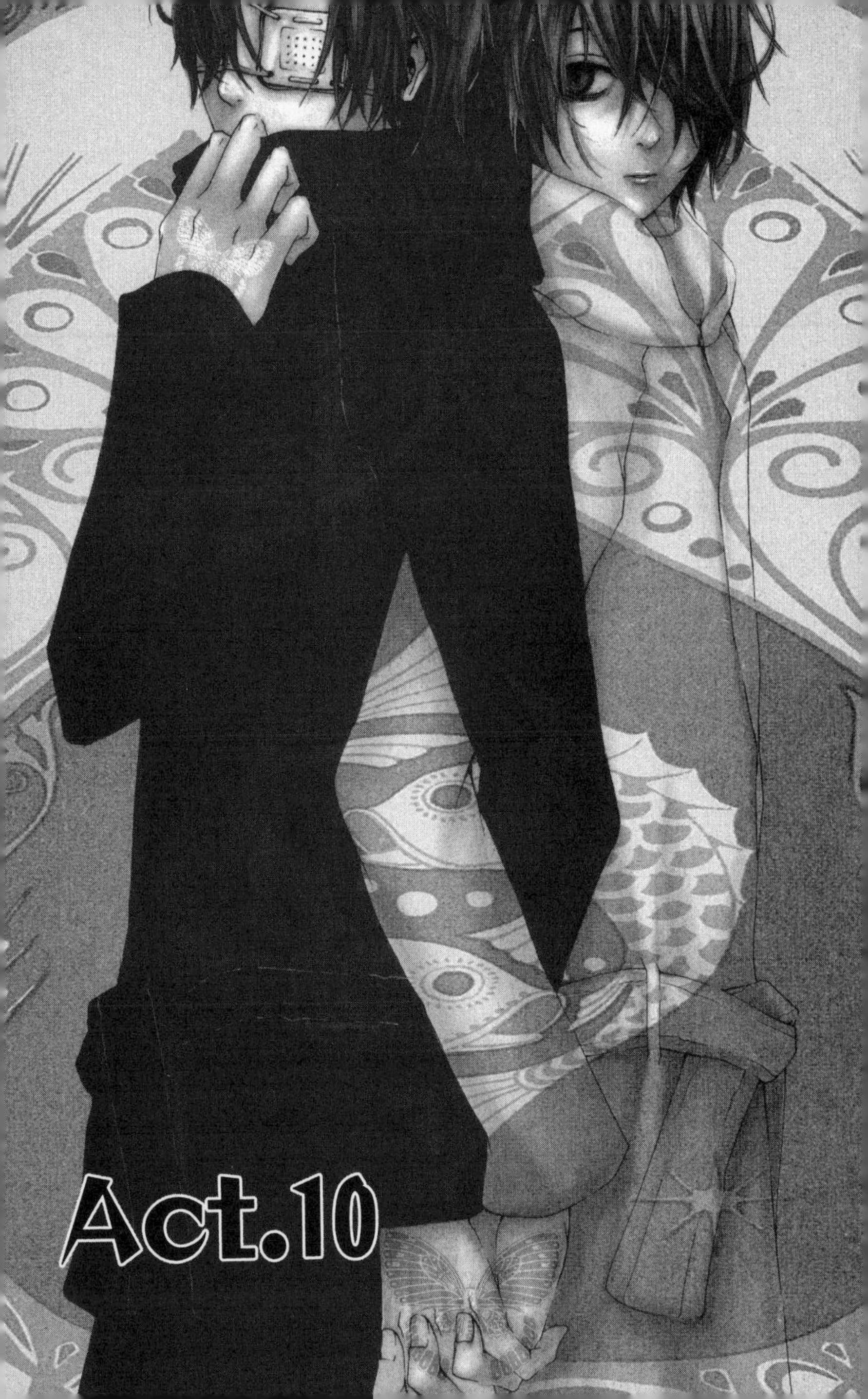
Act.10

[switch]
スイッチ

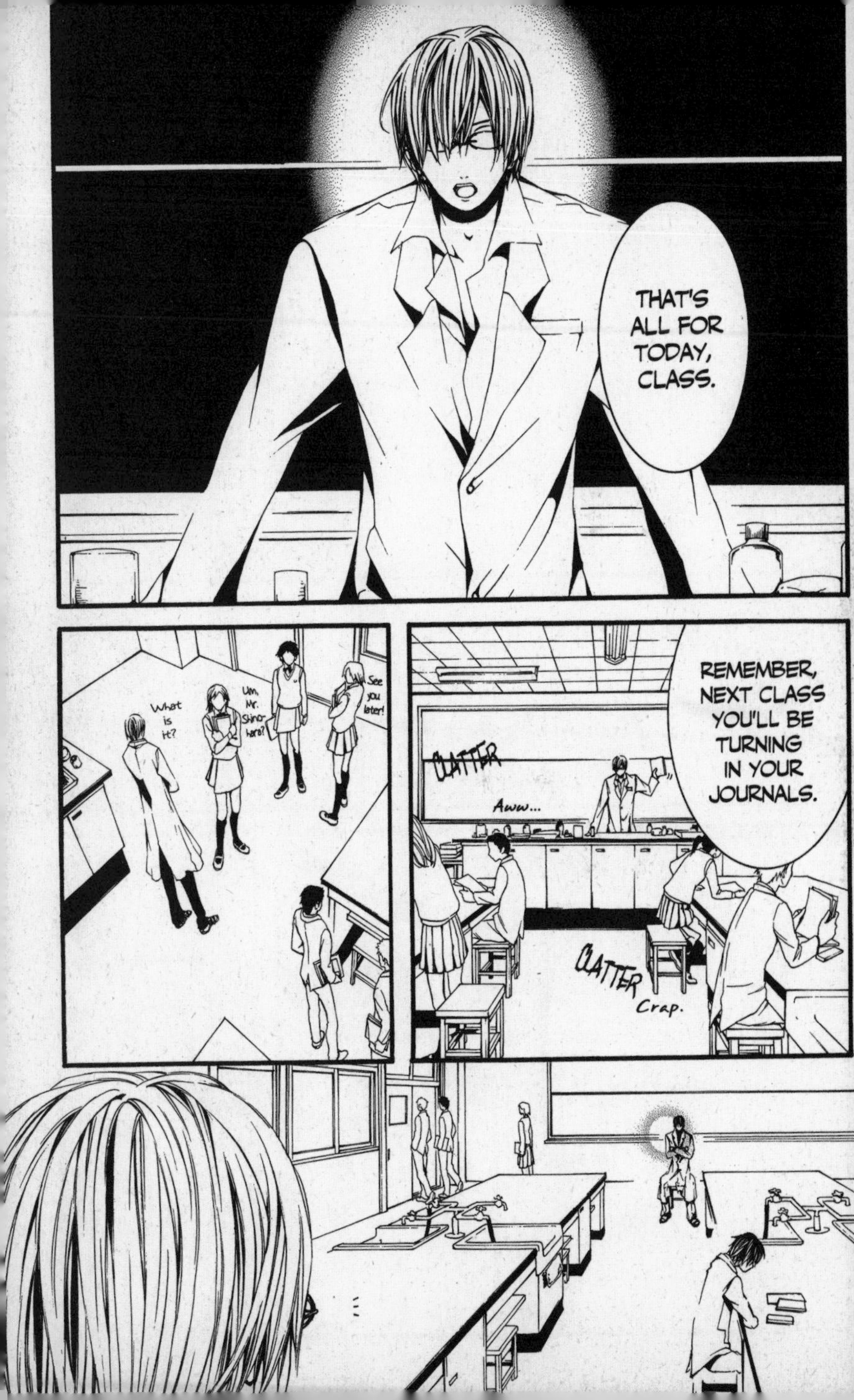
THAT'S ALL FOR TODAY, CLASS.
REMEMBER, NEXT CLASS YOU'LL BE TURNING IN YOUR JOURNALS.
CLATTER
Aww...
CLATTER
Crap.
See you later!
Um, Mr. Shinohara?
What is it?

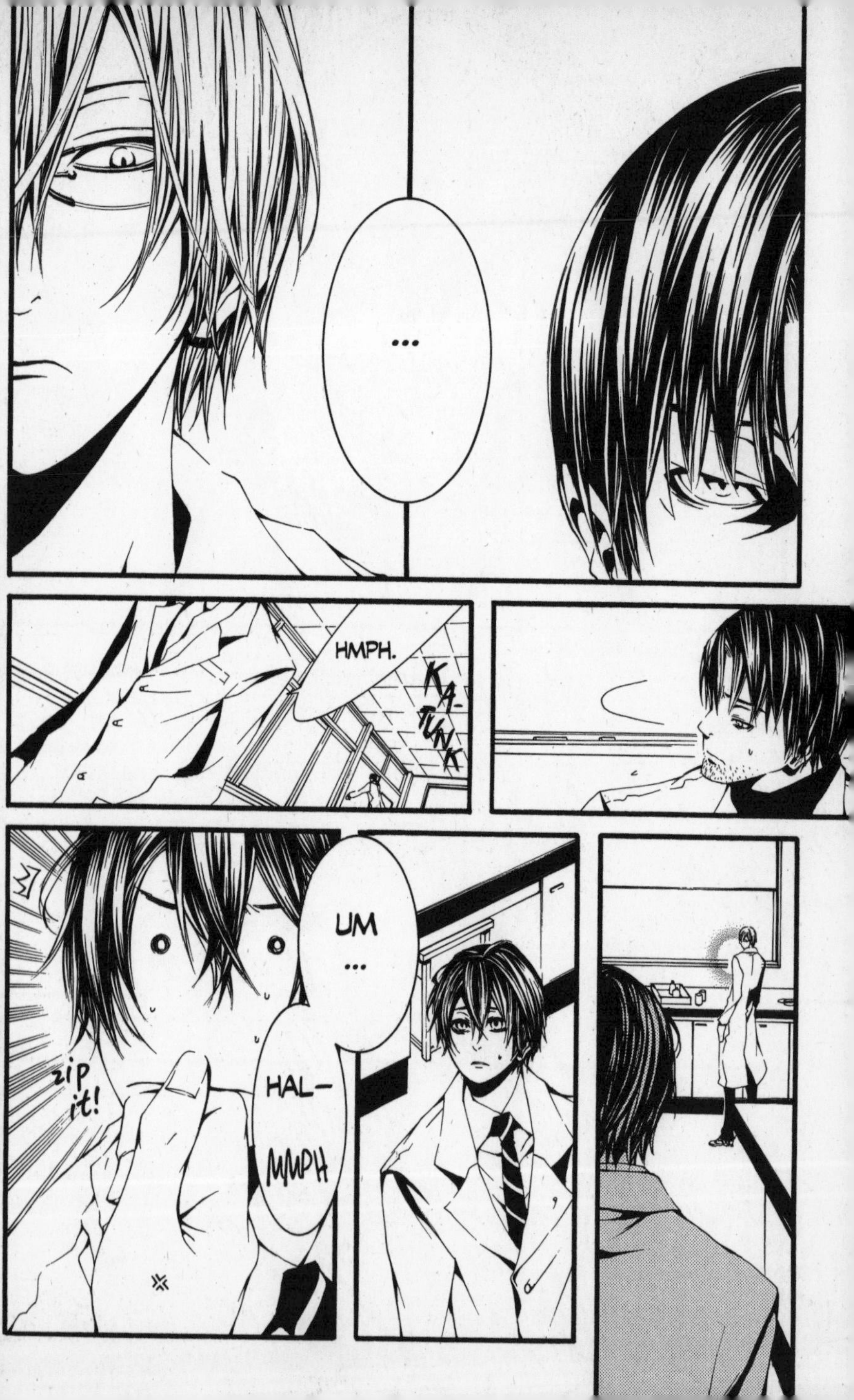
...
HMPH.
KA-TUNK
UM ...
HAL-MMPH
zip it!

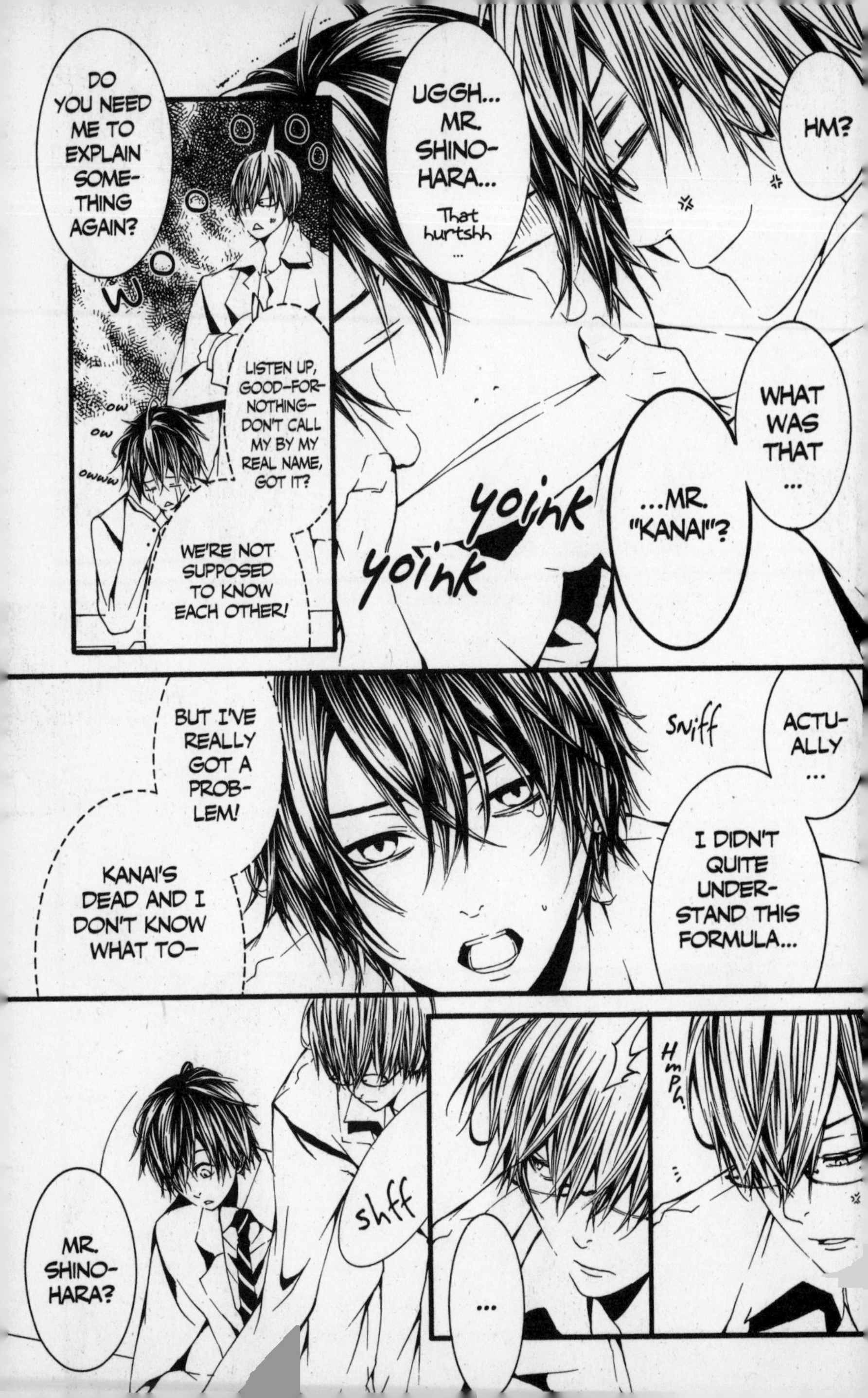
HM?
WHAT WAS THAT ...
...MR. "KANAI"?
UGGH... MR. SHINO-HARA...
That hurtshh ...
yoink
yoink
DO YOU NEED ME TO EXPLAIN SOME-THING AGAIN?
LISTEN UP, GOOD-FOR-NOTHING-DON'T CALL MY BY MY REAL NAME, GOT IT?
WE'RE NOT SUPPOSED TO KNOW EACH OTHER!
ow
ow
owww
ACTU-ALLY ...
Sniff
I DIDN'T QUITE UNDER-STAND THIS FORMULA...
BUT I'VE REALLY GOT A PROB-LEM!
KANAI'S DEAD AND I DON'T KNOW WHAT TO-
Hmph.
...
shff
MR. SHINO-HARA?

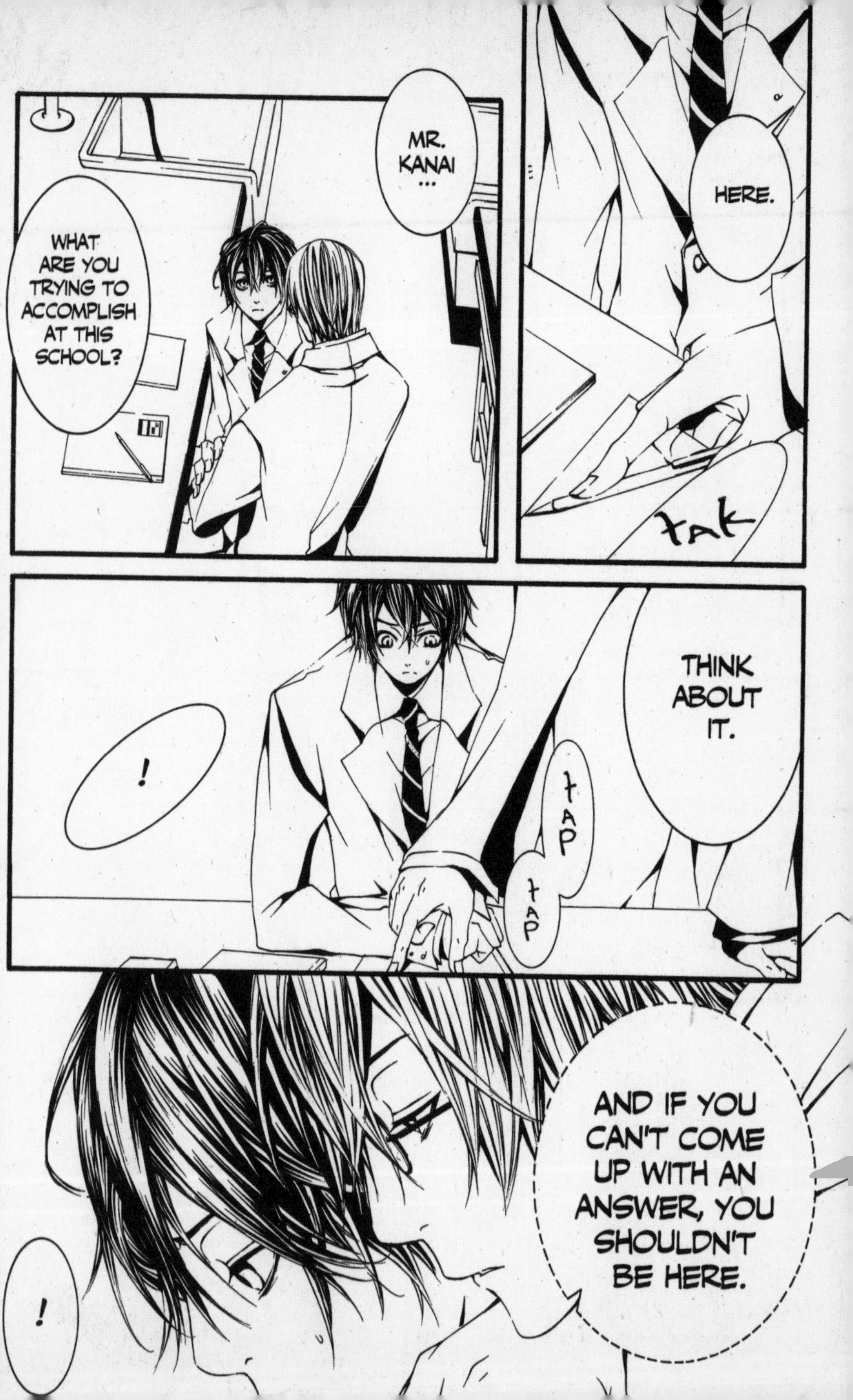
HERE.
tak
MR. KANAI ...
WHAT ARE YOU TRYING TO ACCOMPLISH AT THIS SCHOOL?
THINK ABOUT IT.
tap
tap
!
AND IF YOU CAN'T COME UP WITH AN ANSWER, YOU SHOULDN'T BE HERE.
!

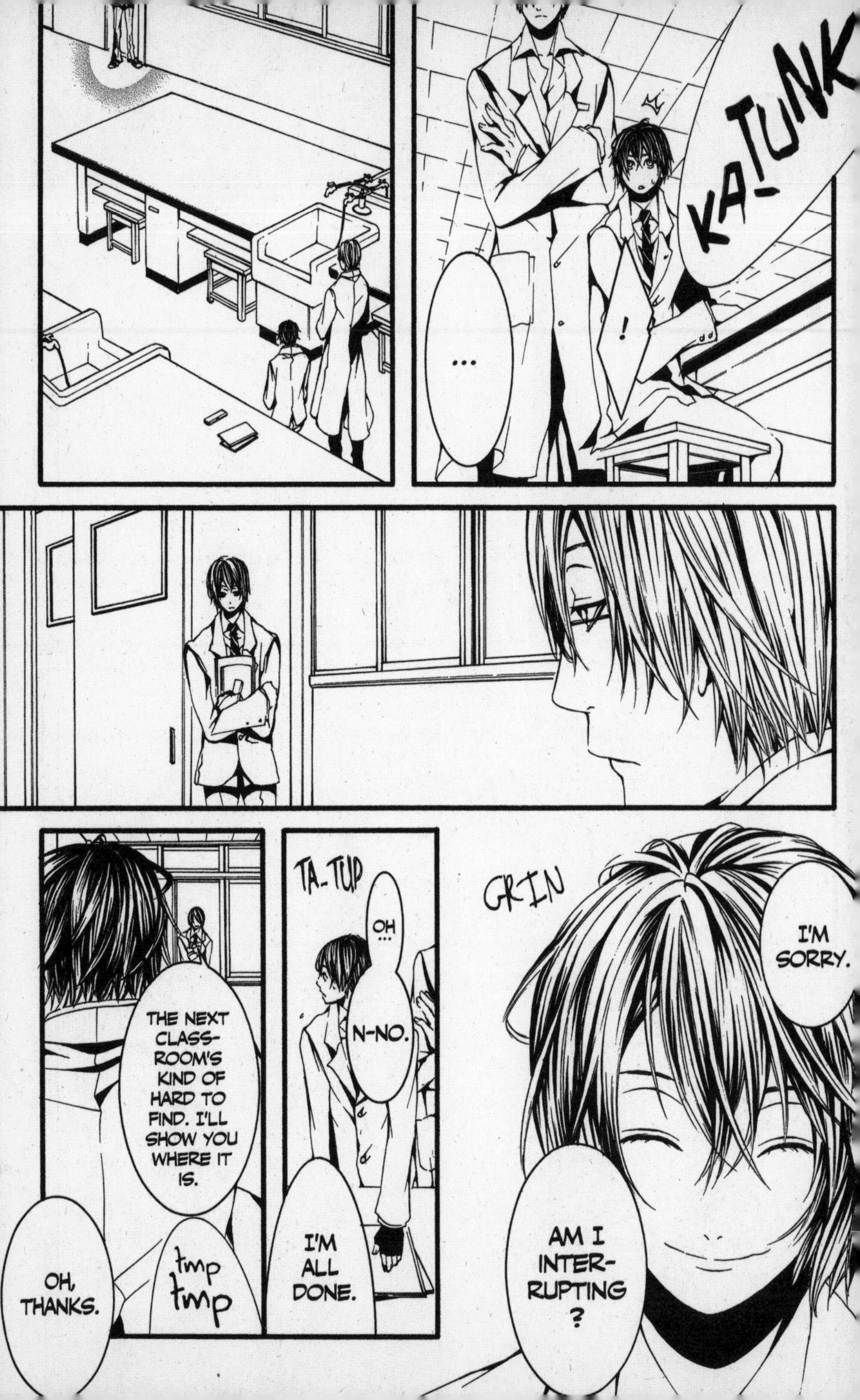
KA-TUNK
...
!
I'M SORRY.
GRIN
AM I INTER-RUPTING?
TA-TUP
OH...
N-NO.
I'M ALL DONE.
THE NEXT CLASS-ROOM'S KIND OF HARD TO FIND. I'LL SHOW YOU WHERE IT IS.
tmp tmp
OH, THANKS.

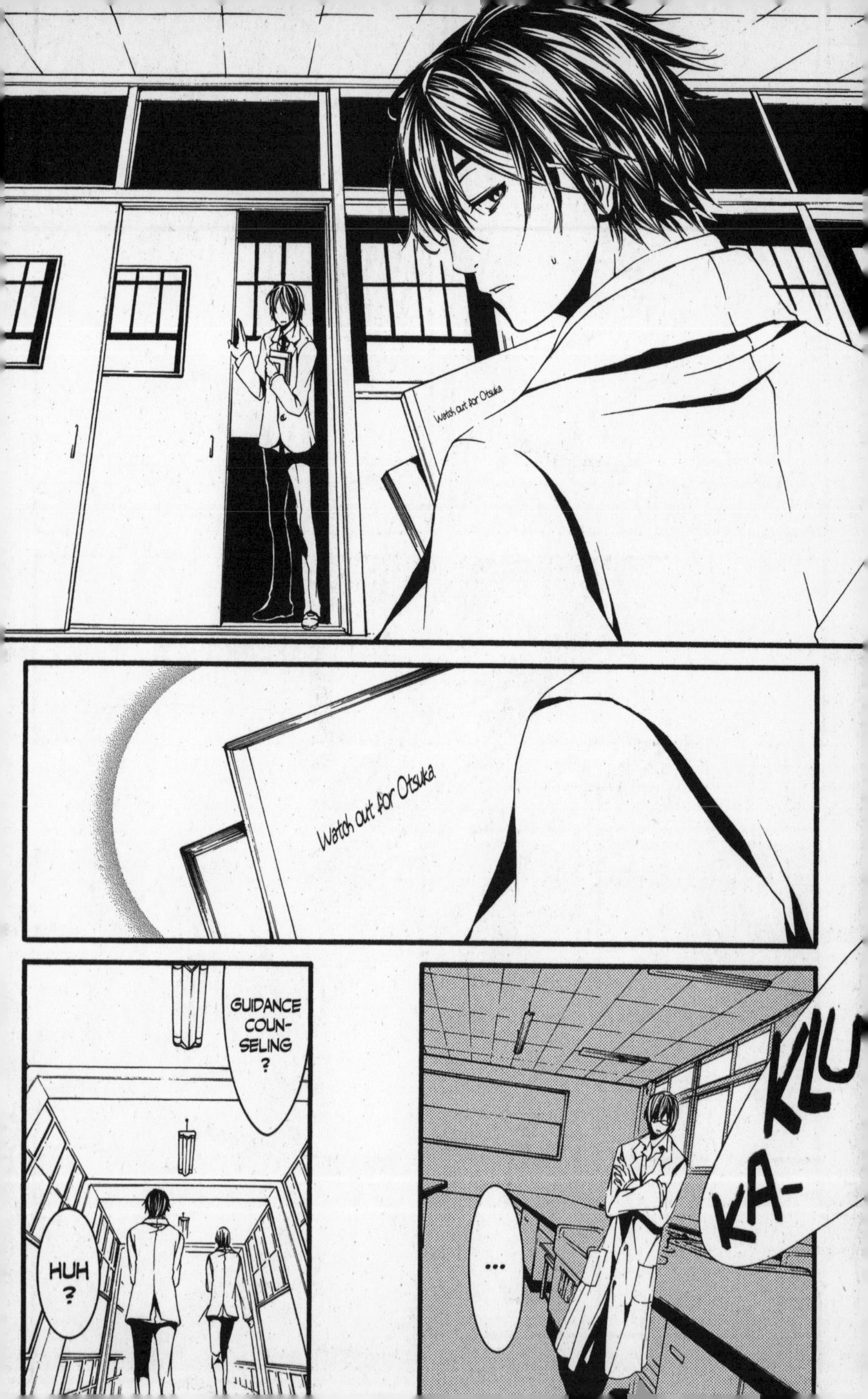
Watch out for Otsuka
Watch out for Otsuka
KA-KLU
...
GUIDANCE COUN-SELING ?
HUH ?

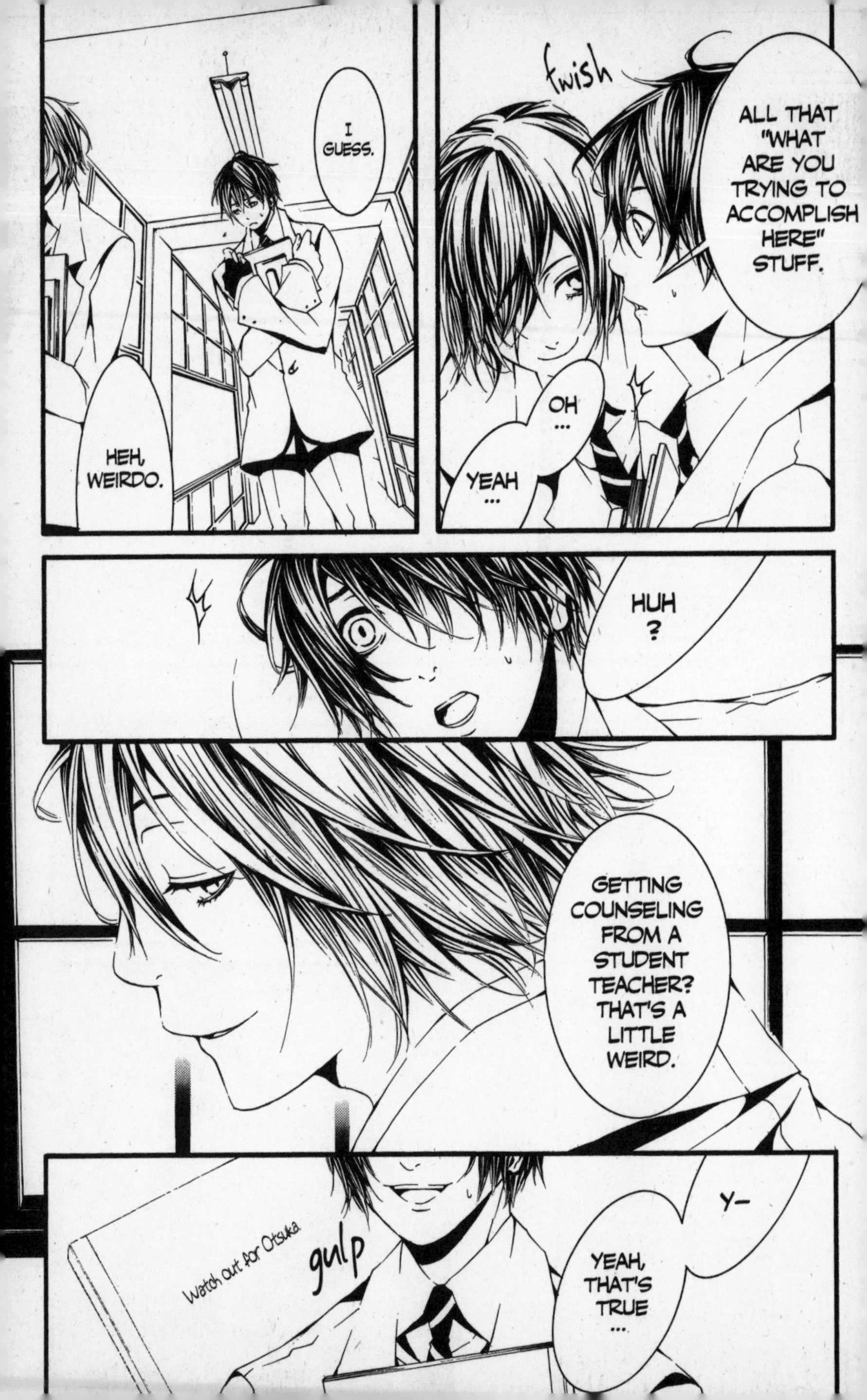
fwish
ALL THAT "WHAT ARE YOU TRYING TO ACCOMPLISH HERE" STUFF.
OH ...
YEAH ...
I GUESS.
HEH, WEIRDO.
HUH ?
GETTING COUNSELING FROM A STUDENT TEACHER? THAT'S A LITTLE WEIRD.
Y-
YEAH, THAT'S TRUE ...
gulp
Watch out for Otsuka

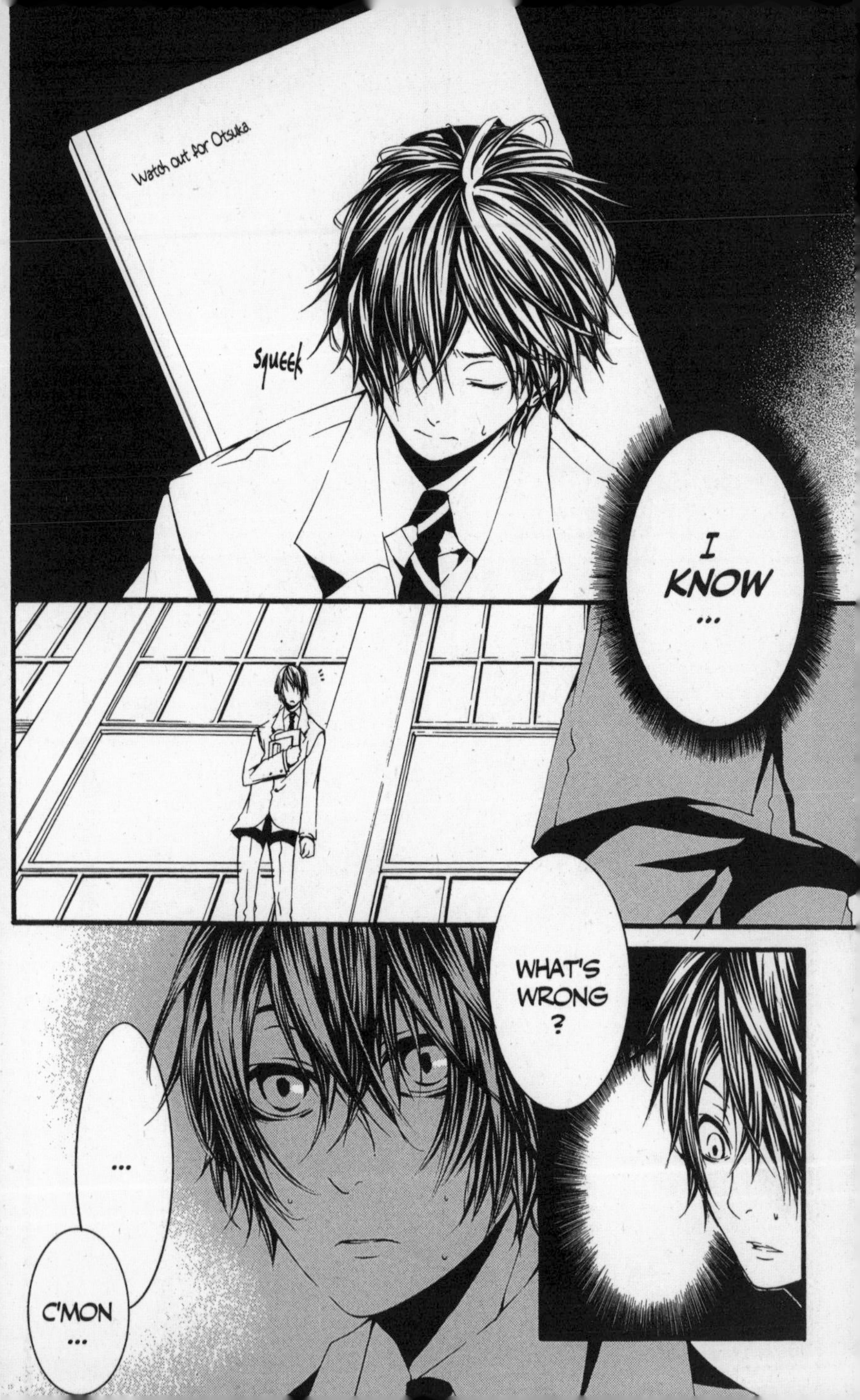
Watch out for Otsuka.
squeek
I KNOW ...
WHAT'S WRONG ?
...
C'MON ...

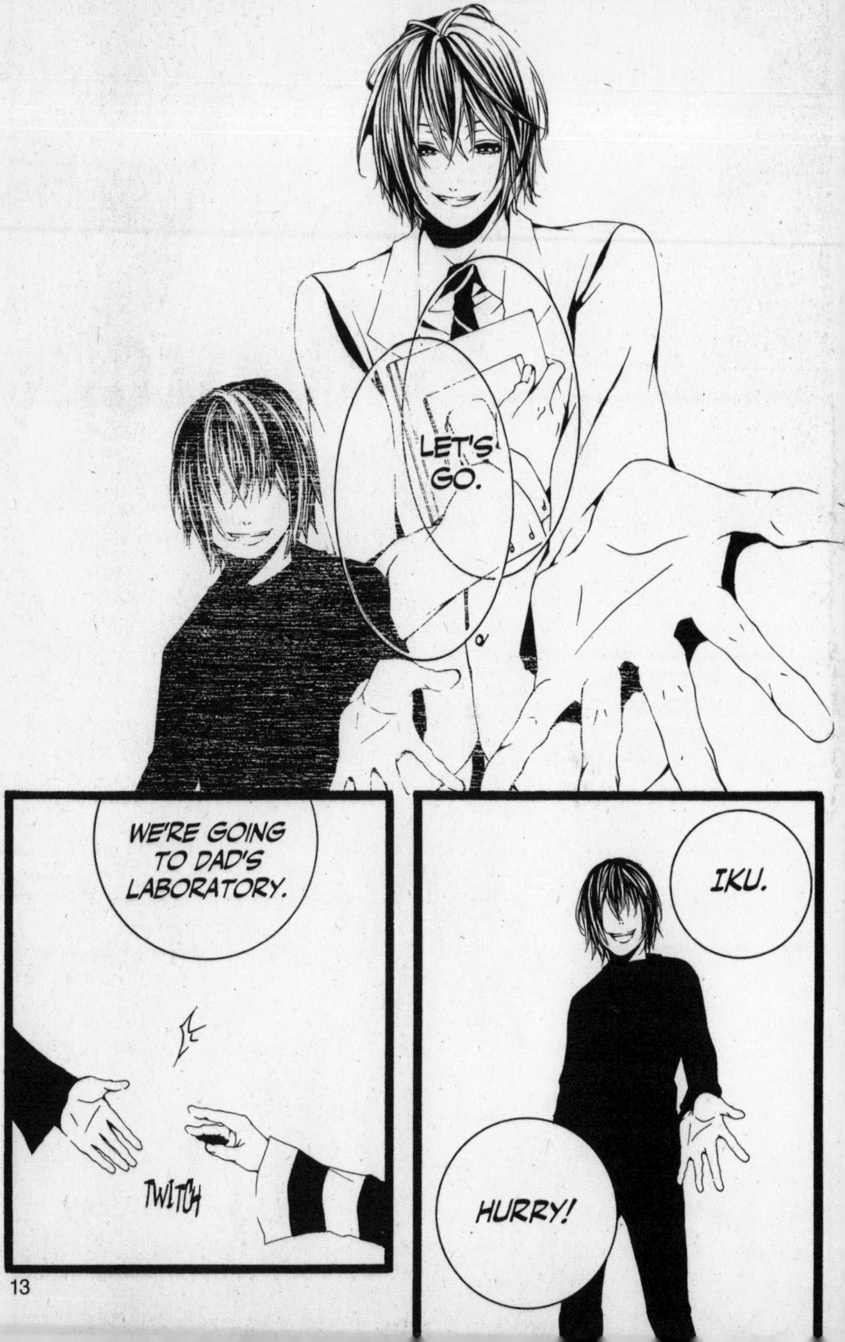
LET'S GO.
IKU.
HURRY!
WE'RE GOING TO DAD'S LABORATORY.
TWITCH

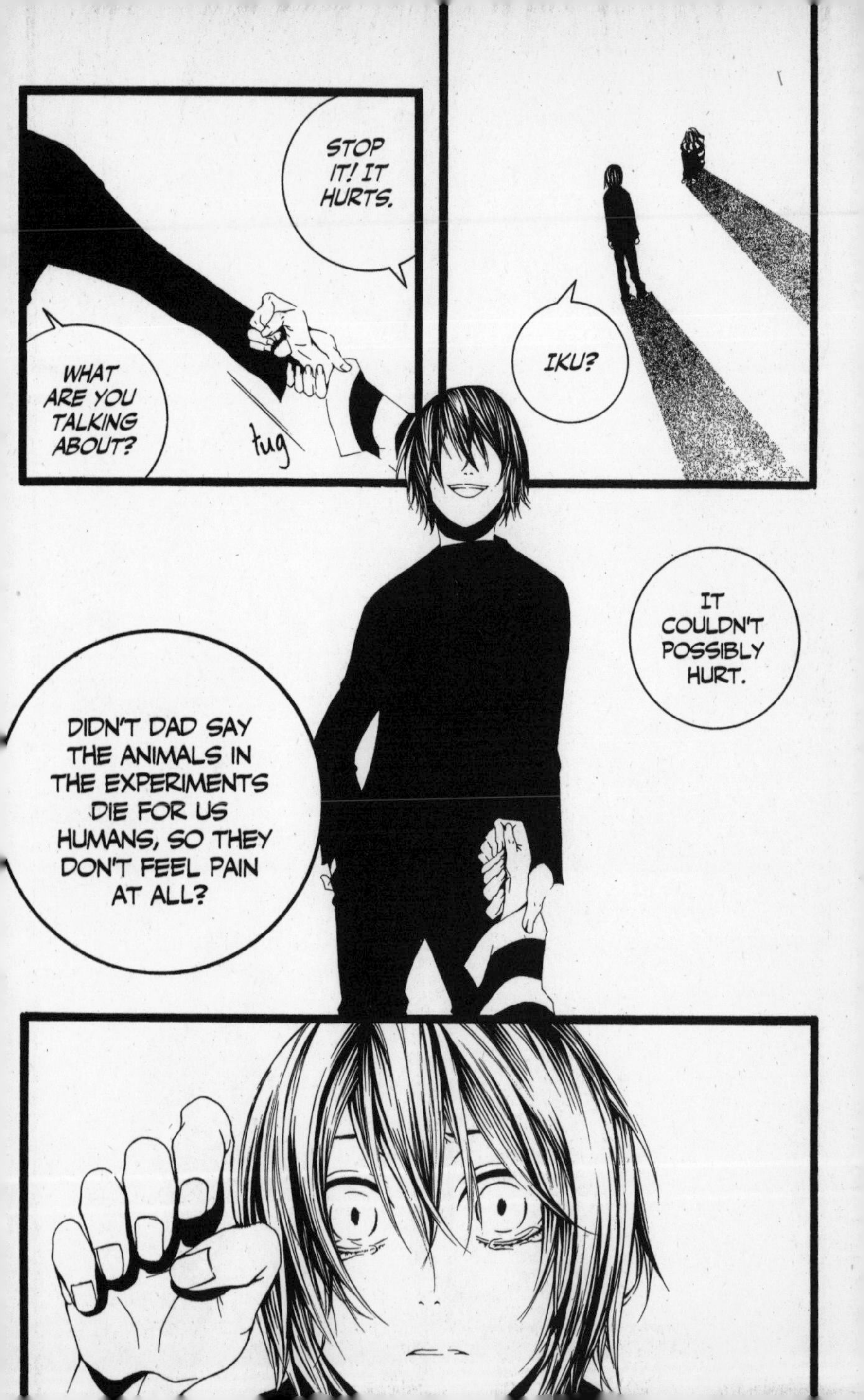
IKU?
STOP IT! IT HURTS.
WHAT ARE YOU TALKING ABOUT?
tug
IT COULDN'T POSSIBLY HURT.
DIDN'T DAD SAY THE ANIMALS IN THE EXPERIMENTS DIE FOR US HUMANS, SO THEY DON'T FEEL PAIN AT ALL?

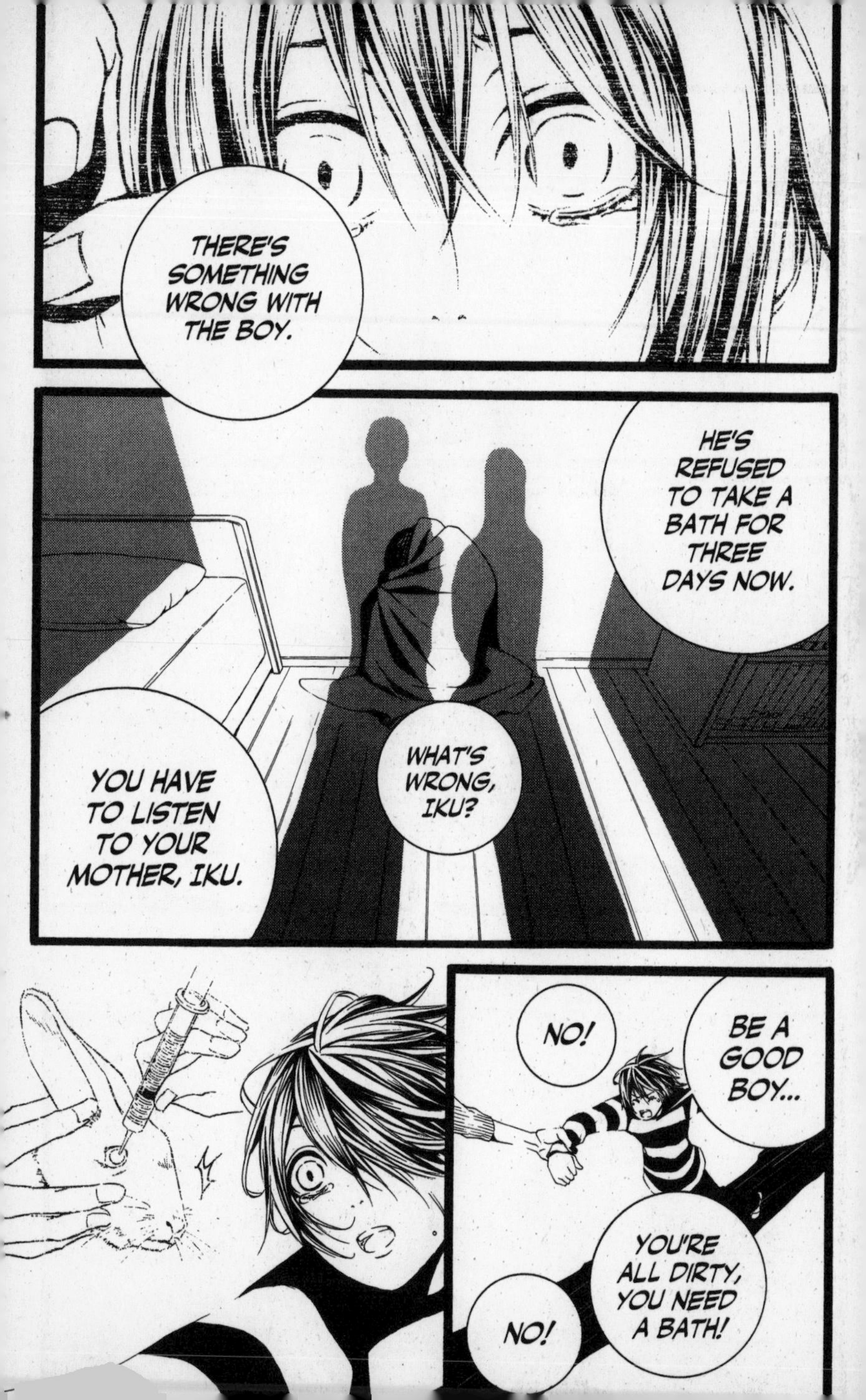
THERE'S SOMETHING WRONG WITH THE BOY.
HE'S REFUSED TO TAKE A BATH FOR THREE DAYS NOW.
WHAT'S WRONG, IKU?
YOU HAVE TO LISTEN TO YOUR MOTHER, IKU.
BE A GOOD BOY...
NO!
YOU'RE ALL DIRTY, YOU NEED A BATH!
NO!

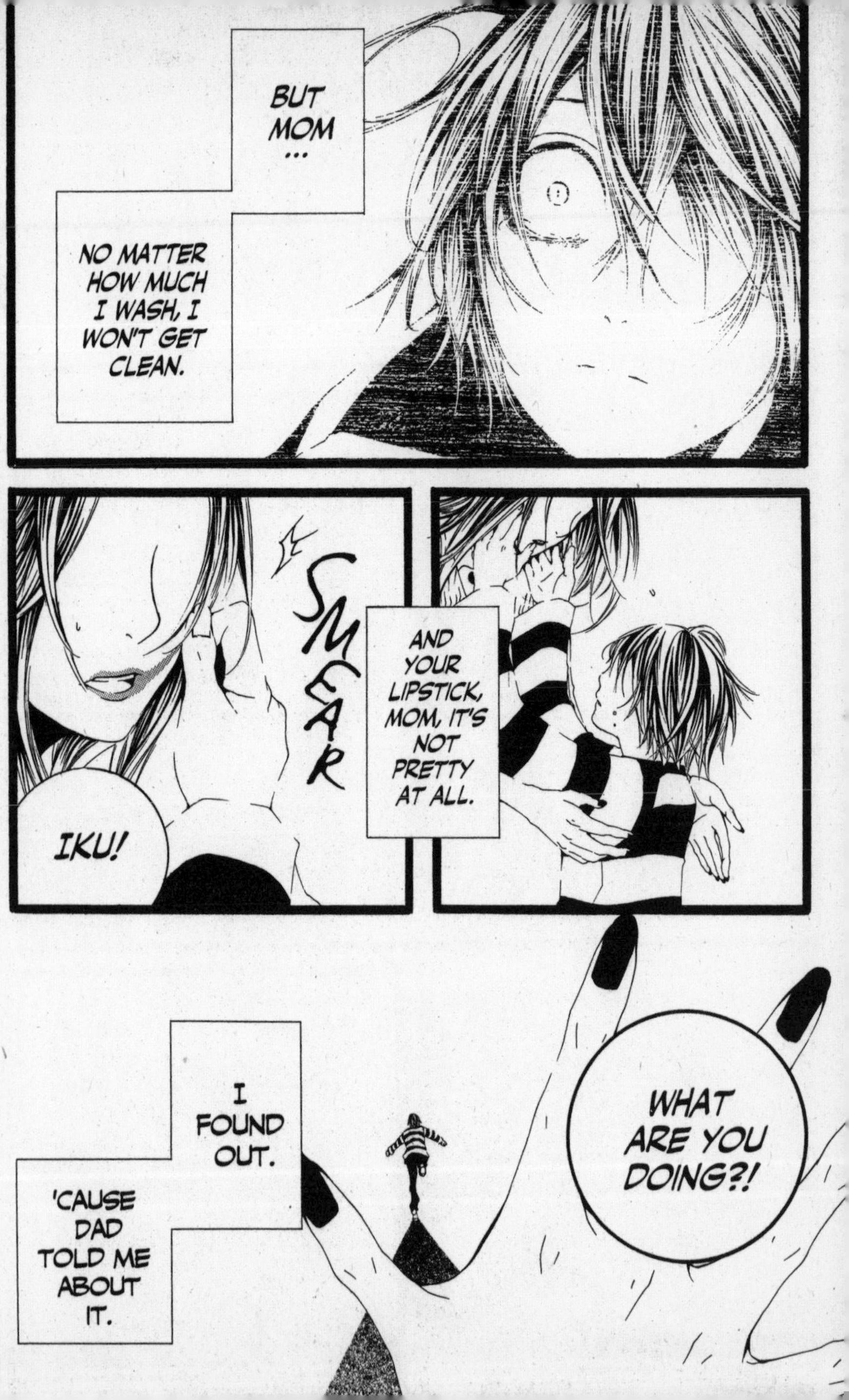
BUT MOM...
NO MATTER HOW MUCH I WASH, I WON'T GET CLEAN.
AND YOUR LIPSTICK, MOM, IT'S NOT PRETTY AT ALL.
SMEAR
IKU!
WHAT ARE YOU DOING?!
I FOUND OUT.
'CAUSE DAD TOLD ME ABOUT IT.

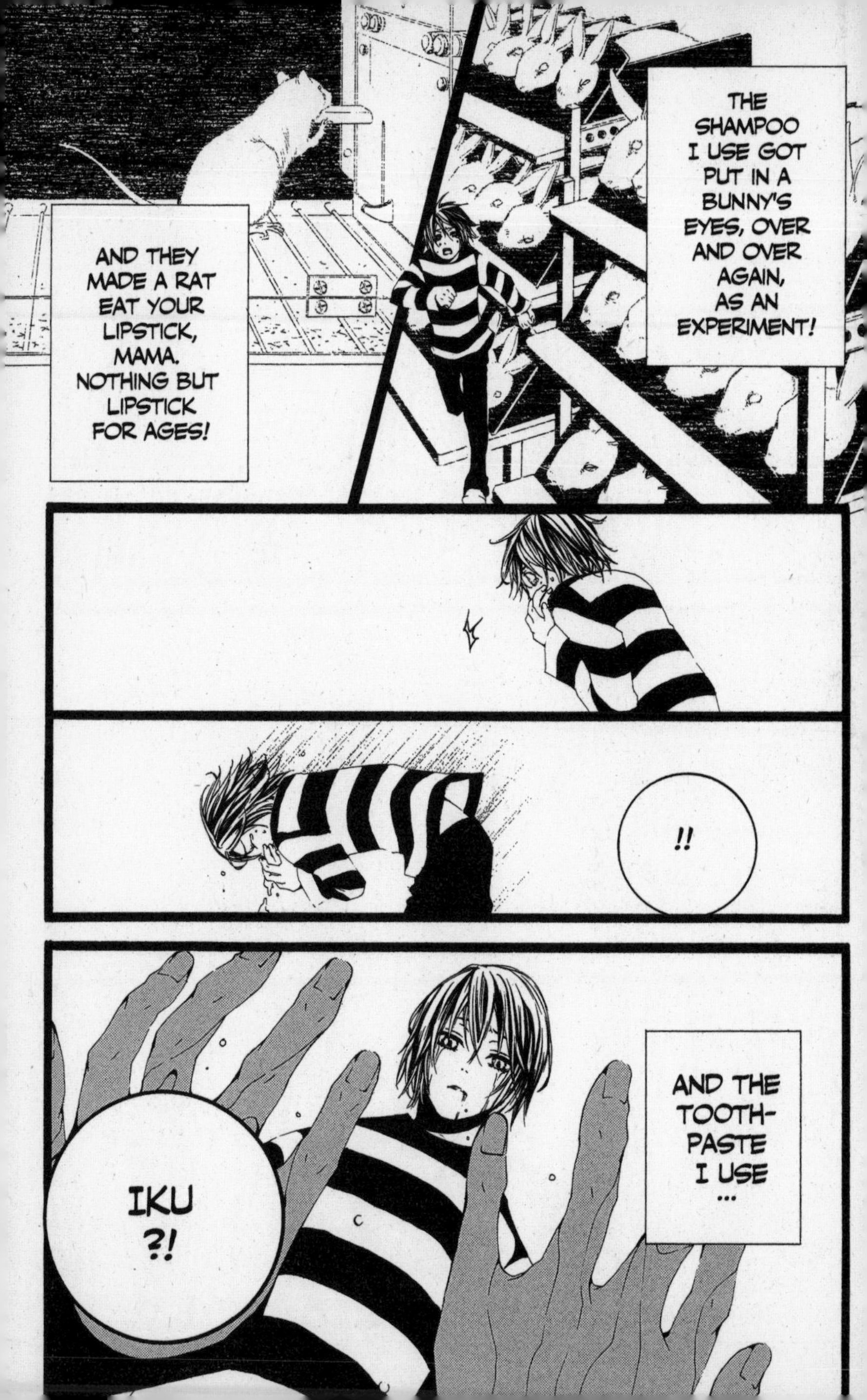
THE SHAMPOO I USE GOT PUT IN A BUNNY'S EYES, OVER AND OVER AGAIN, AS AN EXPERIMENT!
AND THEY MADE A RAT EAT YOUR LIPSTICK, MAMA. NOTHING BUT LIPSTICK FOR AGES!
!!
AND THE TOOTH-PASTE I USE ...
IKU ?!

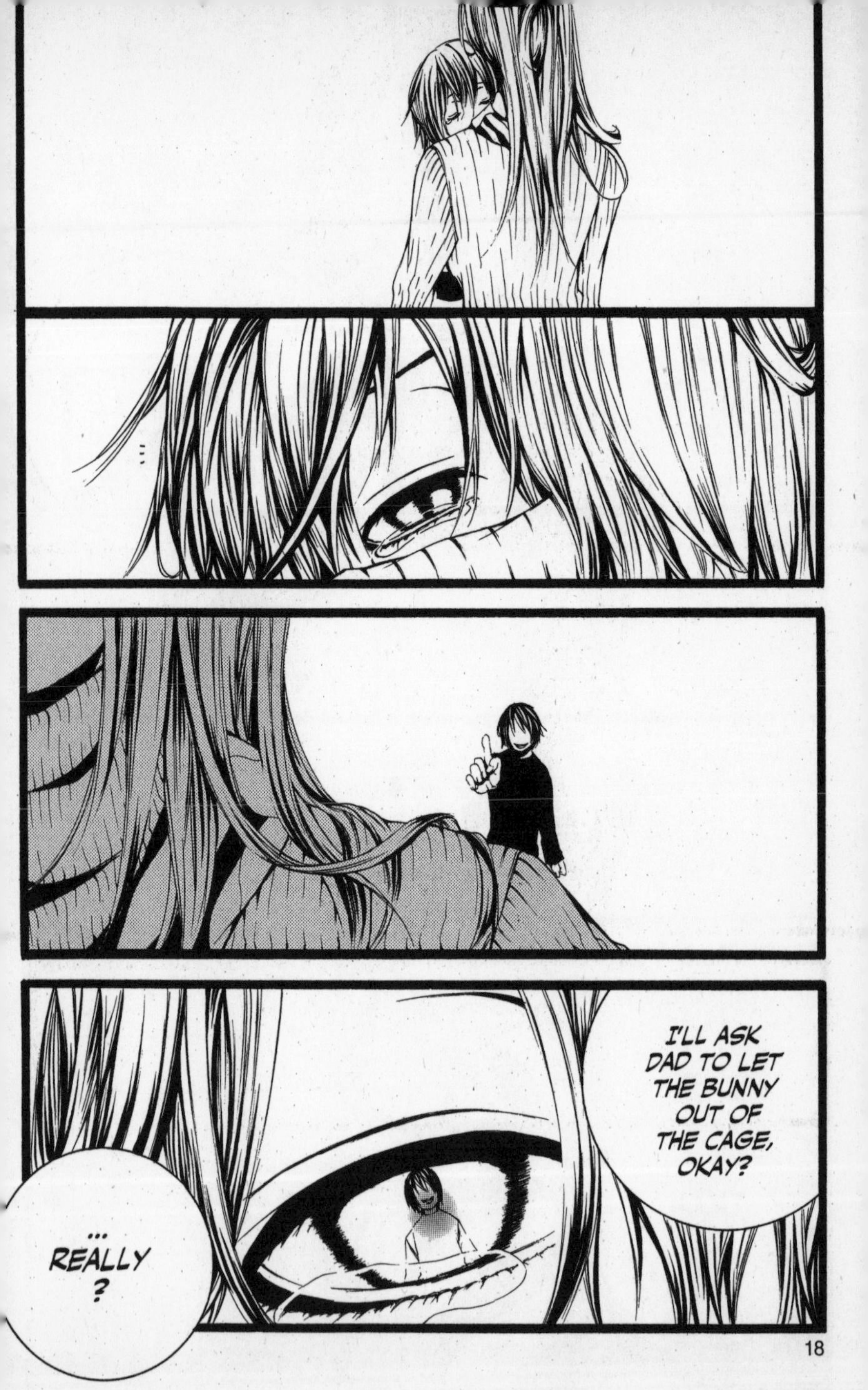
I'LL ASK DAD TO LET THE BUNNY OUT OF THE CAGE, OKAY?
... REALLY ?

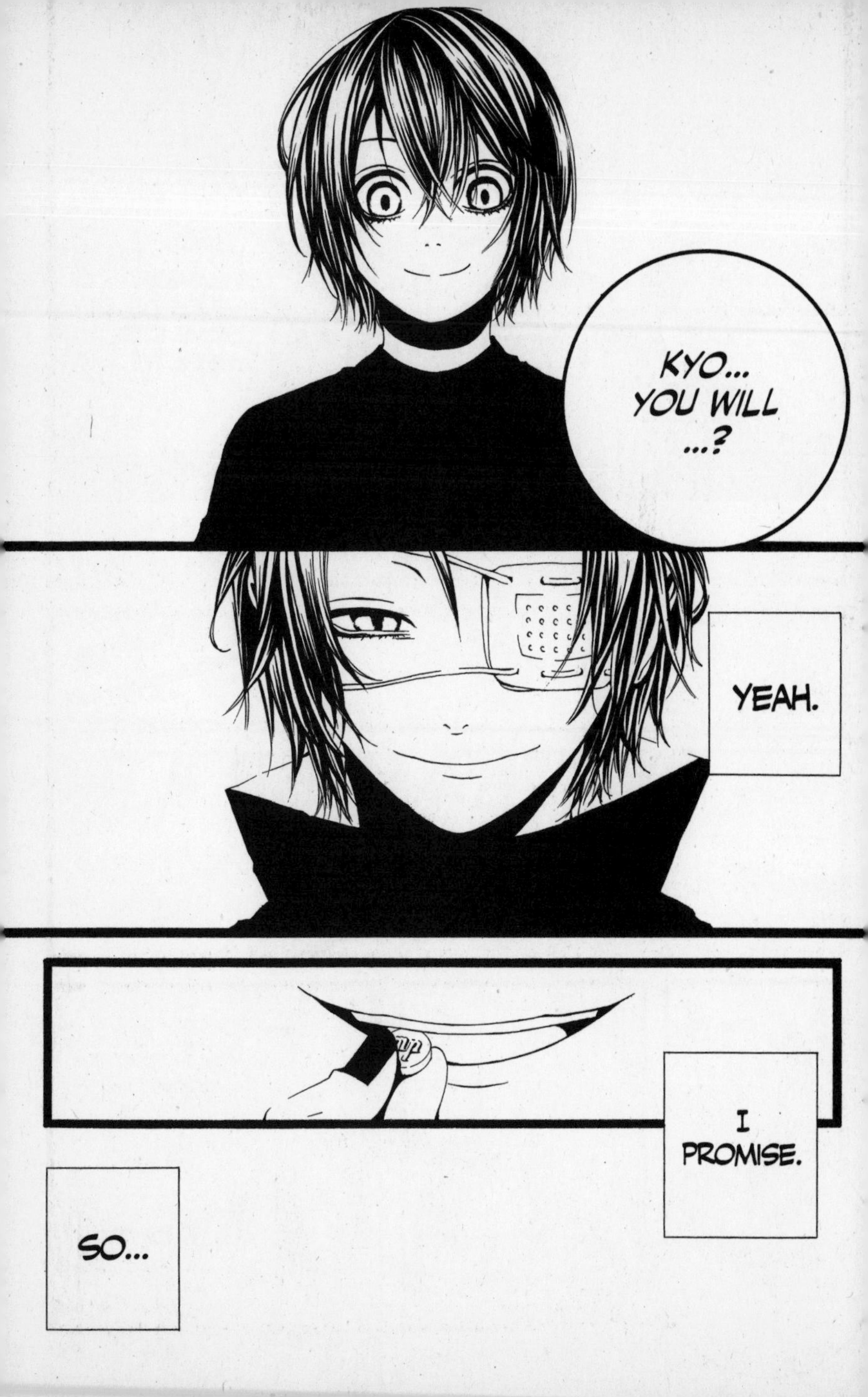
KYO...
YOU WILL
...?
YEAH.
I
PROMISE.
SO...

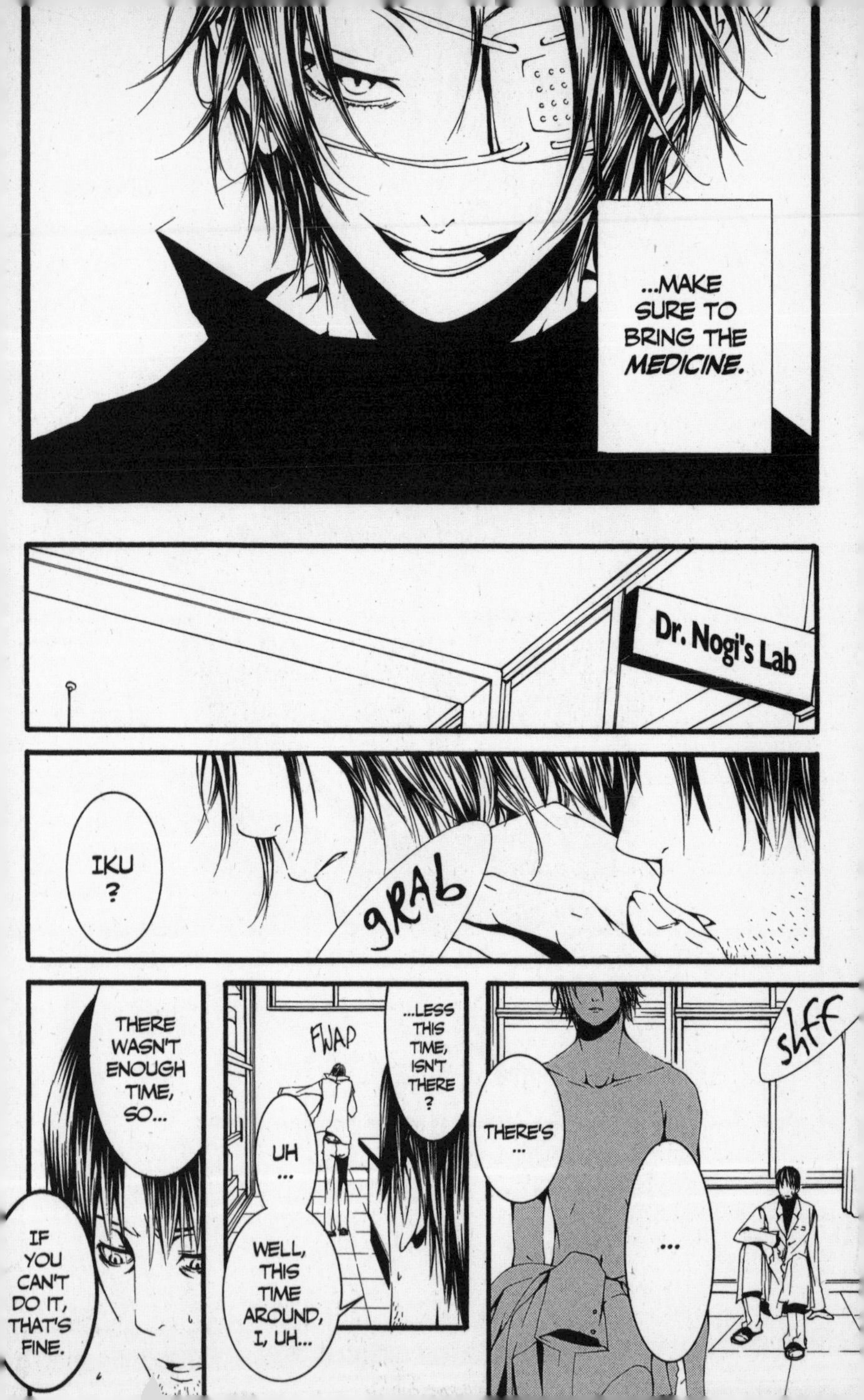
...MAKE SURE TO BRING THE *MEDICINE.*
Dr. Nogi's Lab
GRAB
IKU ?
SHFF
THERE'S ...
...
...LESS THIS TIME, ISN'T THERE ?
FWAP
UH ...
WELL, THIS TIME AROUND, I, UH...
THERE WASN'T ENOUGH TIME, SO...
IF YOU CAN'T DO IT, THAT'S FINE.

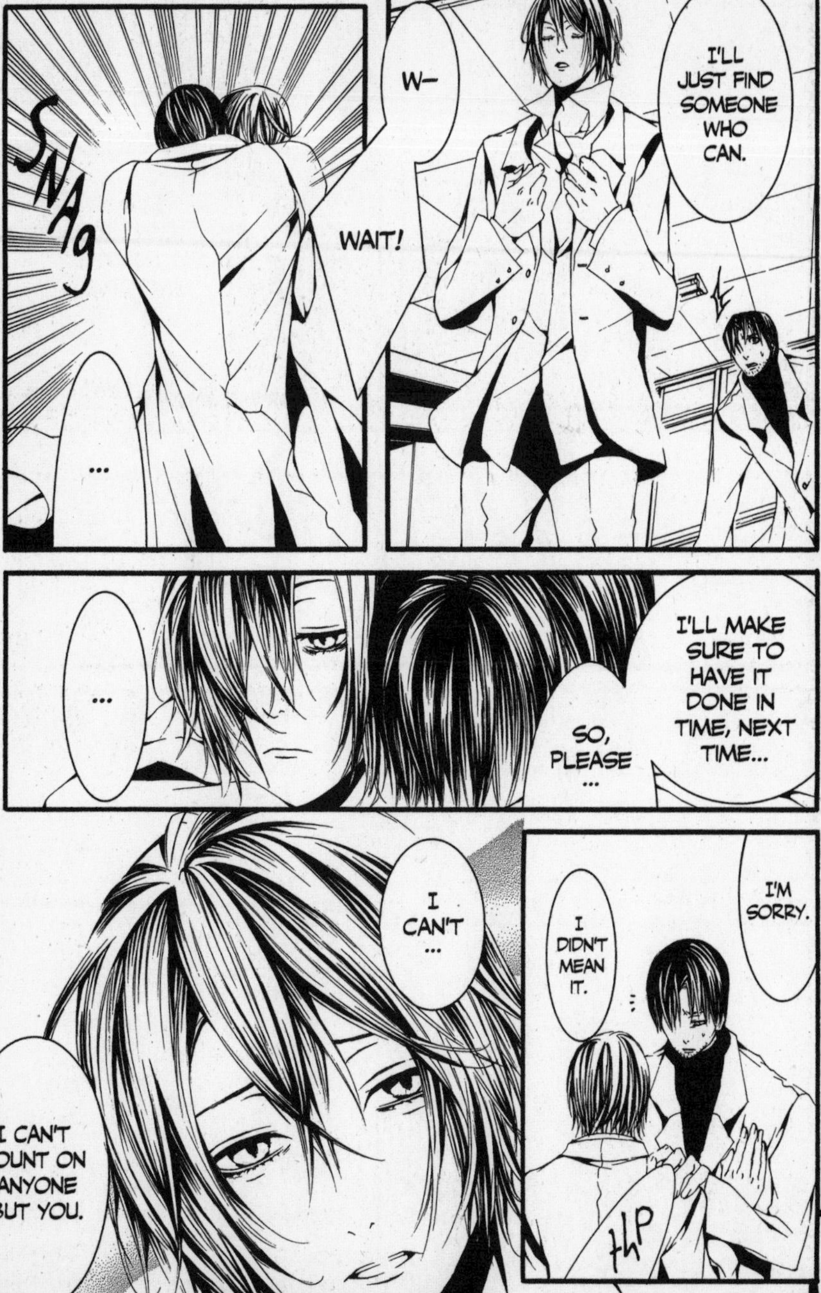
I'LL JUST FIND SOMEONE WHO CAN.
W–
WAIT!
SNAG
...
I'LL MAKE SURE TO HAVE IT DONE IN TIME, NEXT TIME...
SO, PLEASE ...
...
I'M SORRY.
I DIDN'T MEAN IT.
THP
I CAN'T ...
I CAN'T COUNT ON ANYONE BUT YOU.

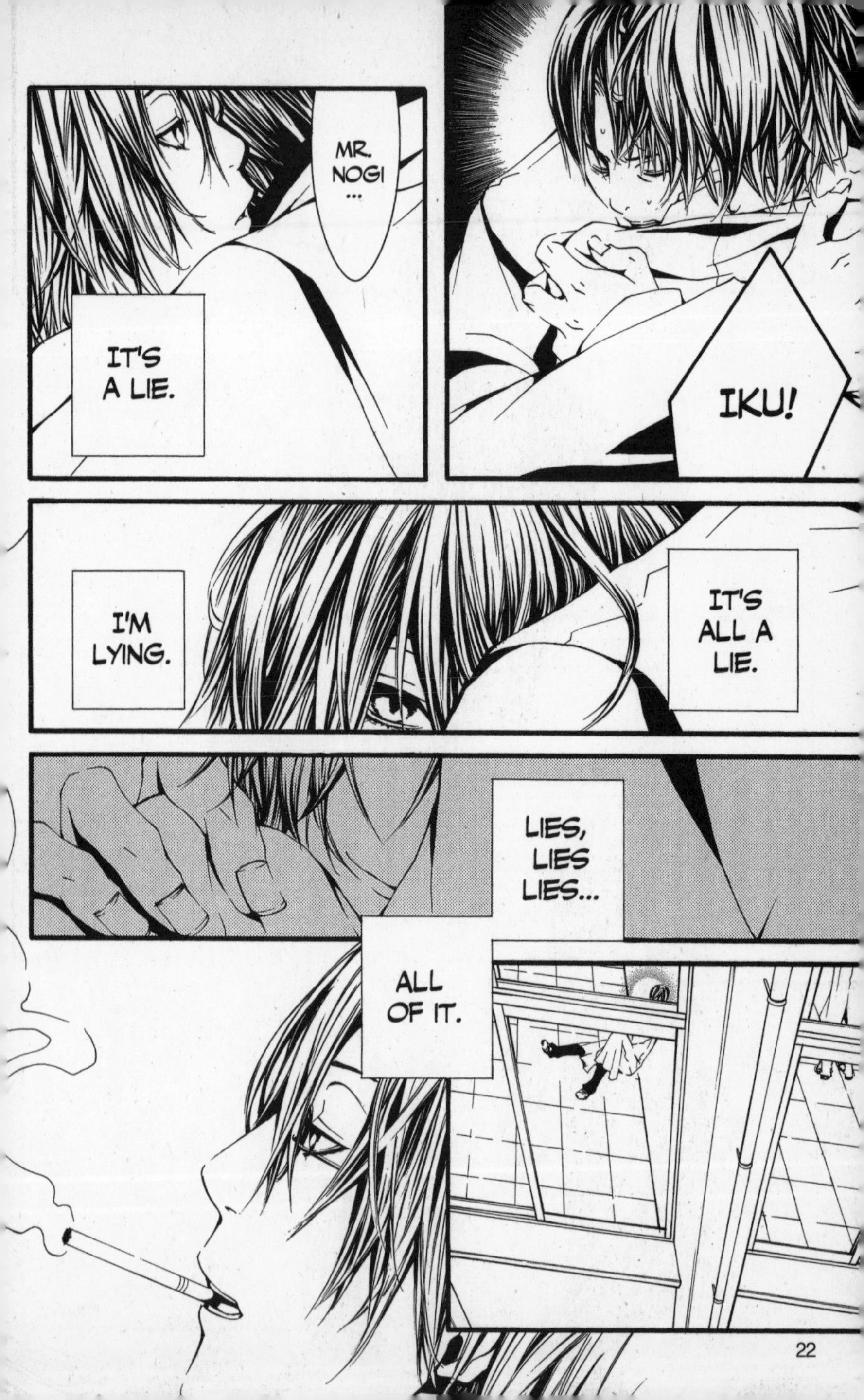
IKU!
MR. NOGI ...
IT'S A LIE.
IT'S ALL A LIE.
I'M LYING.
LIES, LIES LIES...
ALL OF IT.

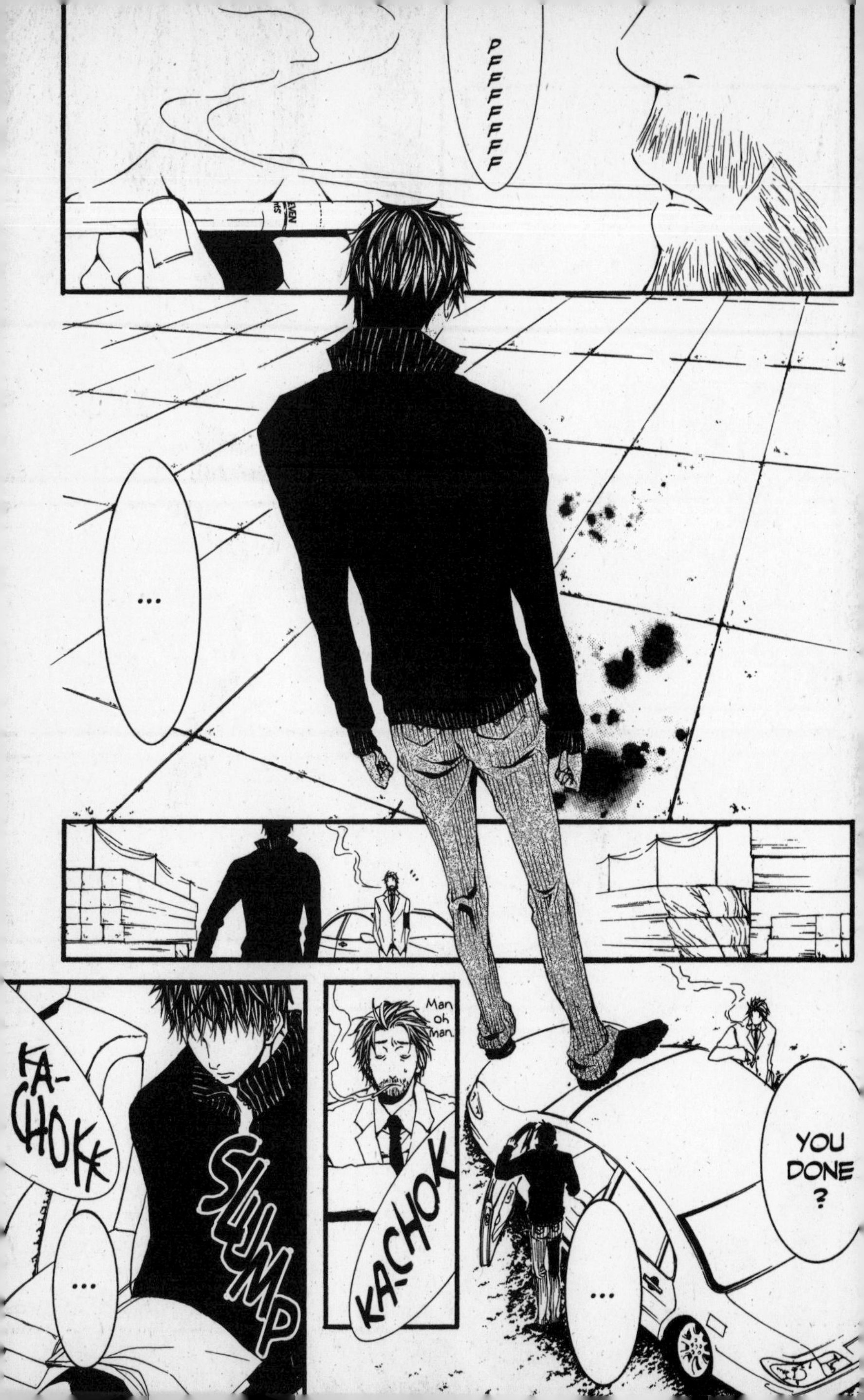
PFFFFFFF
...
YOU DONE ?
...
Man oh man.
KA-CHOK
KA-CHOKK
SLUMP
...

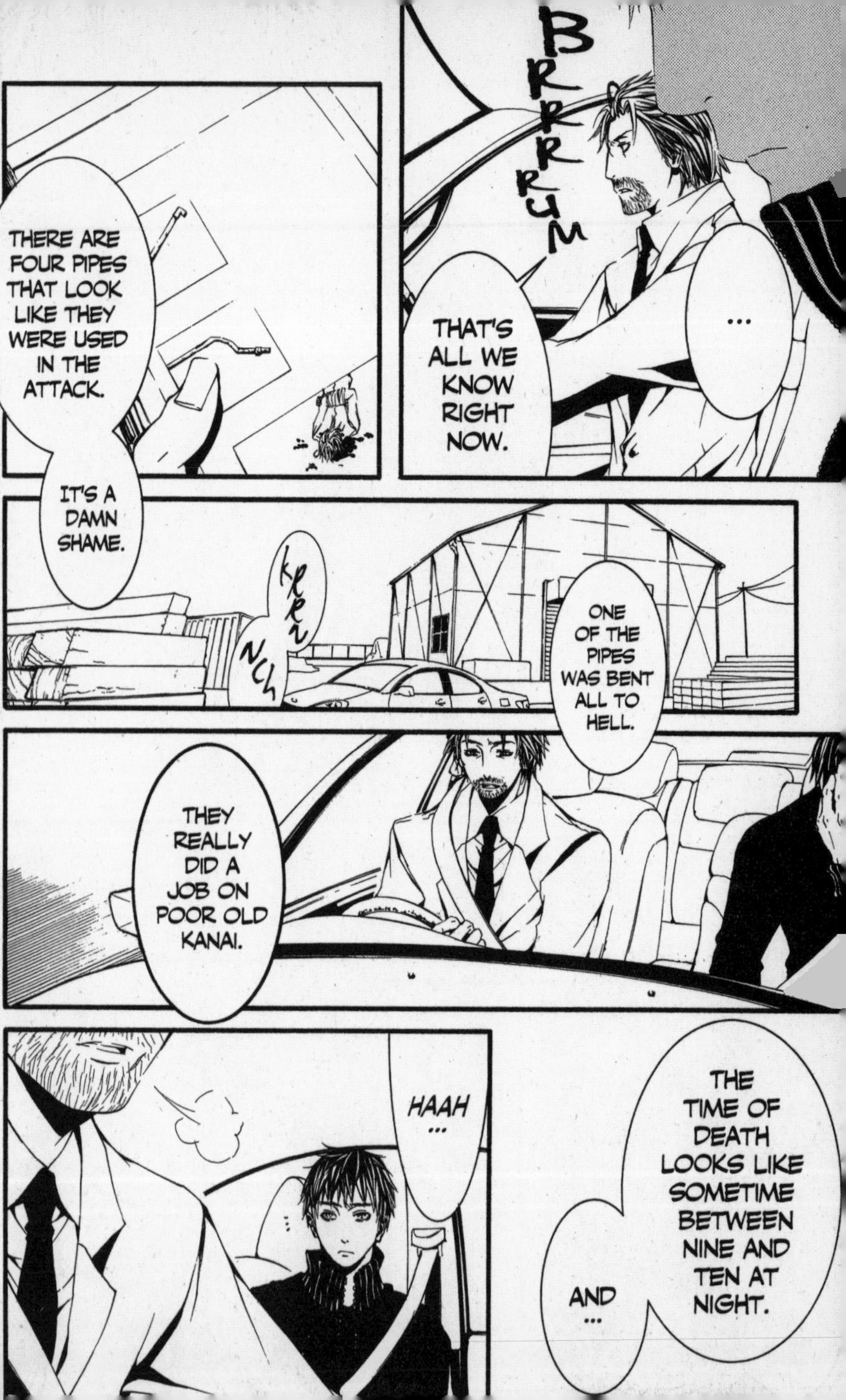
BRRRRUM
...
THAT'S ALL WE KNOW RIGHT NOW.
THERE ARE FOUR PIPES THAT LOOK LIKE THEY WERE USED IN THE ATTACK.
IT'S A DAMN SHAME.
KRRNNCH
ONE OF THE PIPES WAS BENT ALL TO HELL.
THEY REALLY DID A JOB ON POOR OLD KANAI.
THE TIME OF DEATH LOOKS LIKE SOMETIME BETWEEN NINE AND TEN AT NIGHT.
AND ...
HAAH ...

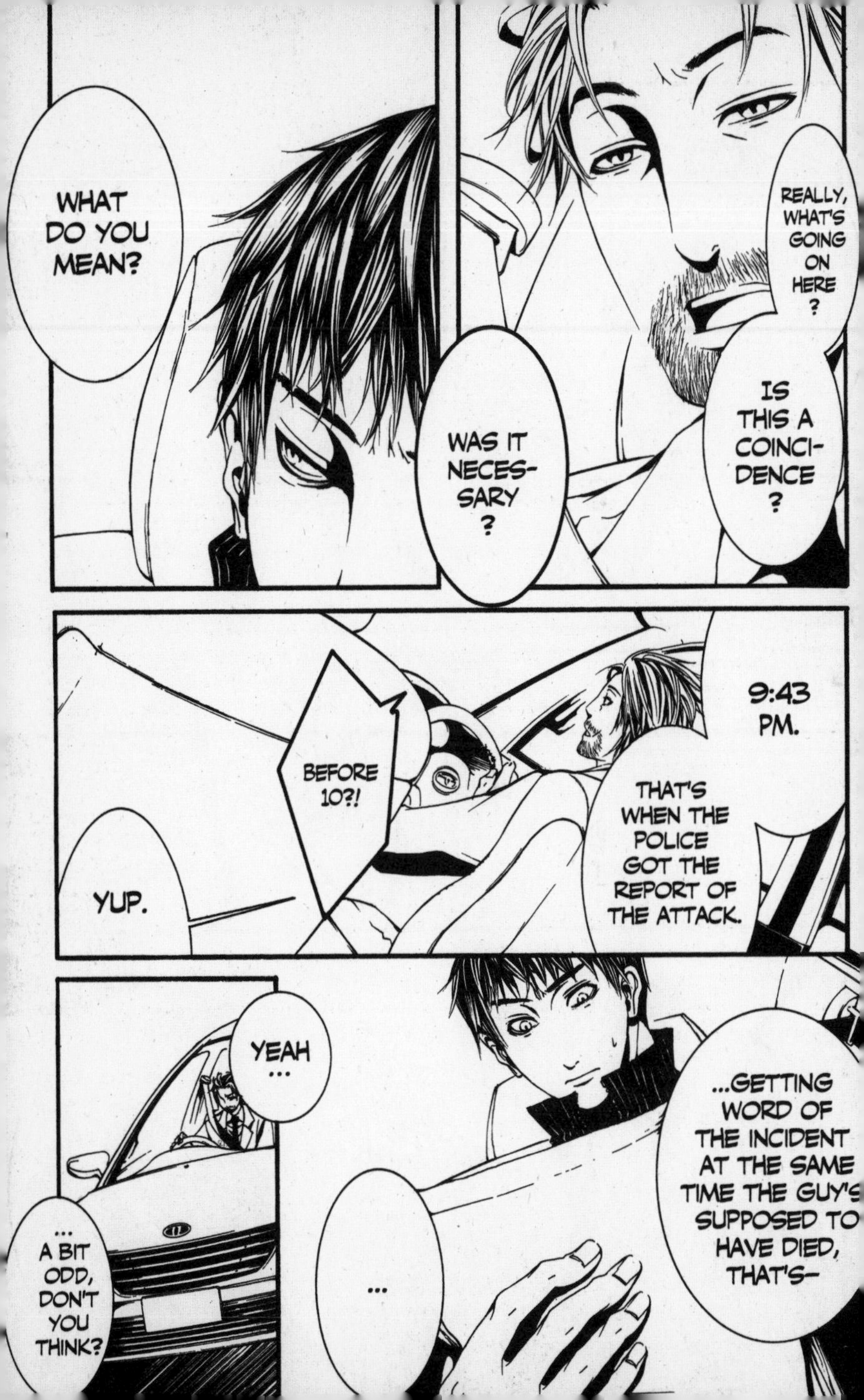
REALLY, WHAT'S GOING ON HERE?
IS THIS A COINCIDENCE?
WAS IT NECESSARY?
WHAT DO YOU MEAN?
9:43 PM.
THAT'S WHEN THE POLICE GOT THE REPORT OF THE ATTACK.
BEFORE 10?!
YUP.
...GETTING WORD OF THE INCIDENT AT THE SAME TIME THE GUY'S SUPPOSED TO HAVE DIED, THAT'S—
...
YEAH...
...A BIT ODD, DON'T YOU THINK?

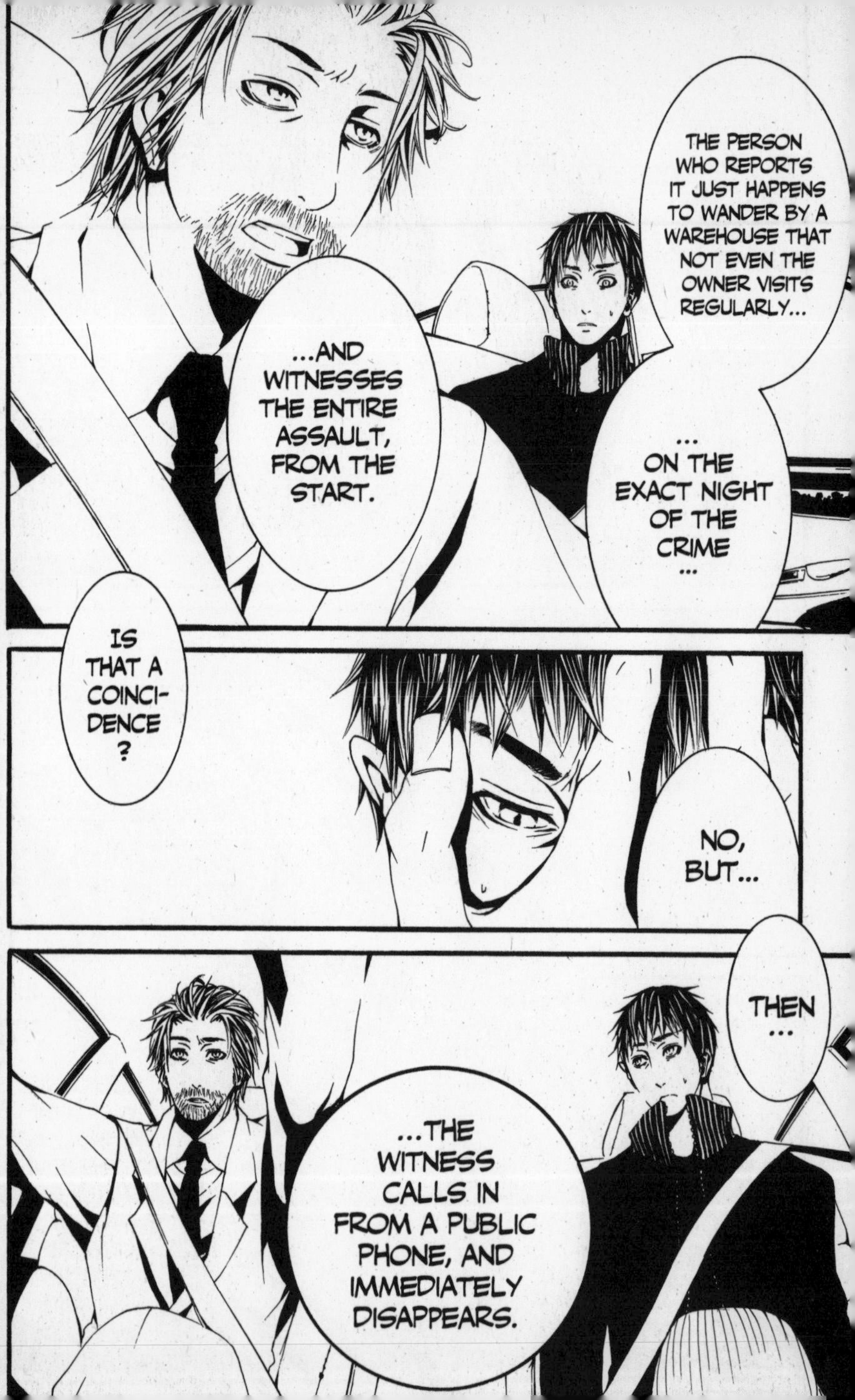
THE PERSON WHO REPORTS IT JUST HAPPENS TO WANDER BY A WAREHOUSE THAT NOT EVEN THE OWNER VISITS REGULARLY...
...ON THE EXACT NIGHT OF THE CRIME...
...AND WITNESSES THE ENTIRE ASSAULT, FROM THE START.
IS THAT A COINCI- DENCE?
NO, BUT...
THEN...
...THE WITNESS CALLS IN FROM A PUBLIC PHONE, AND IMMEDIATELY DISAPPEARS.

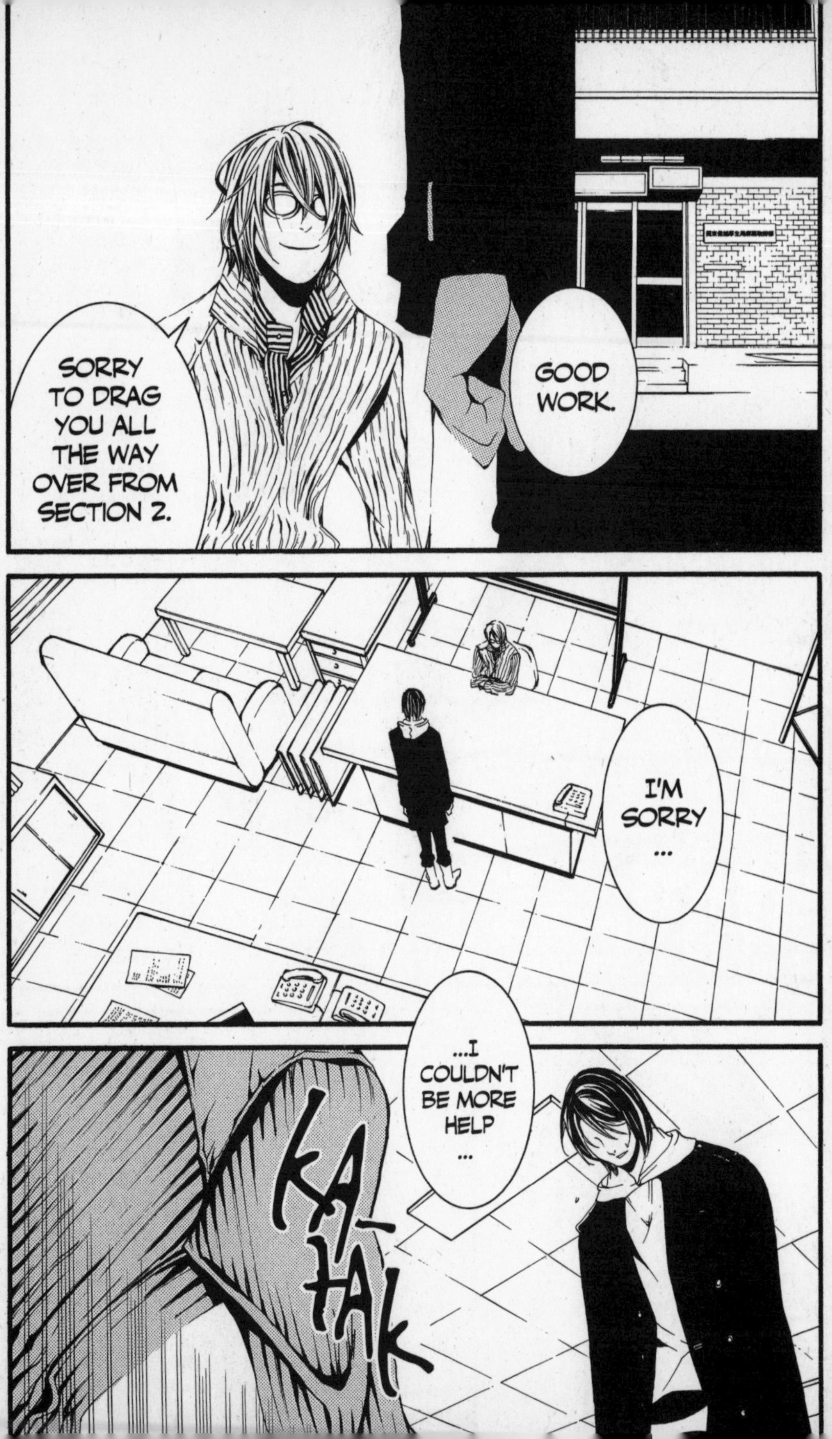
GOOD WORK.
SORRY TO DRAG YOU ALL THE WAY OVER FROM SECTION 2.
I'M SORRY ...
...I COULDN'T BE MORE HELP ...
KA-TAK

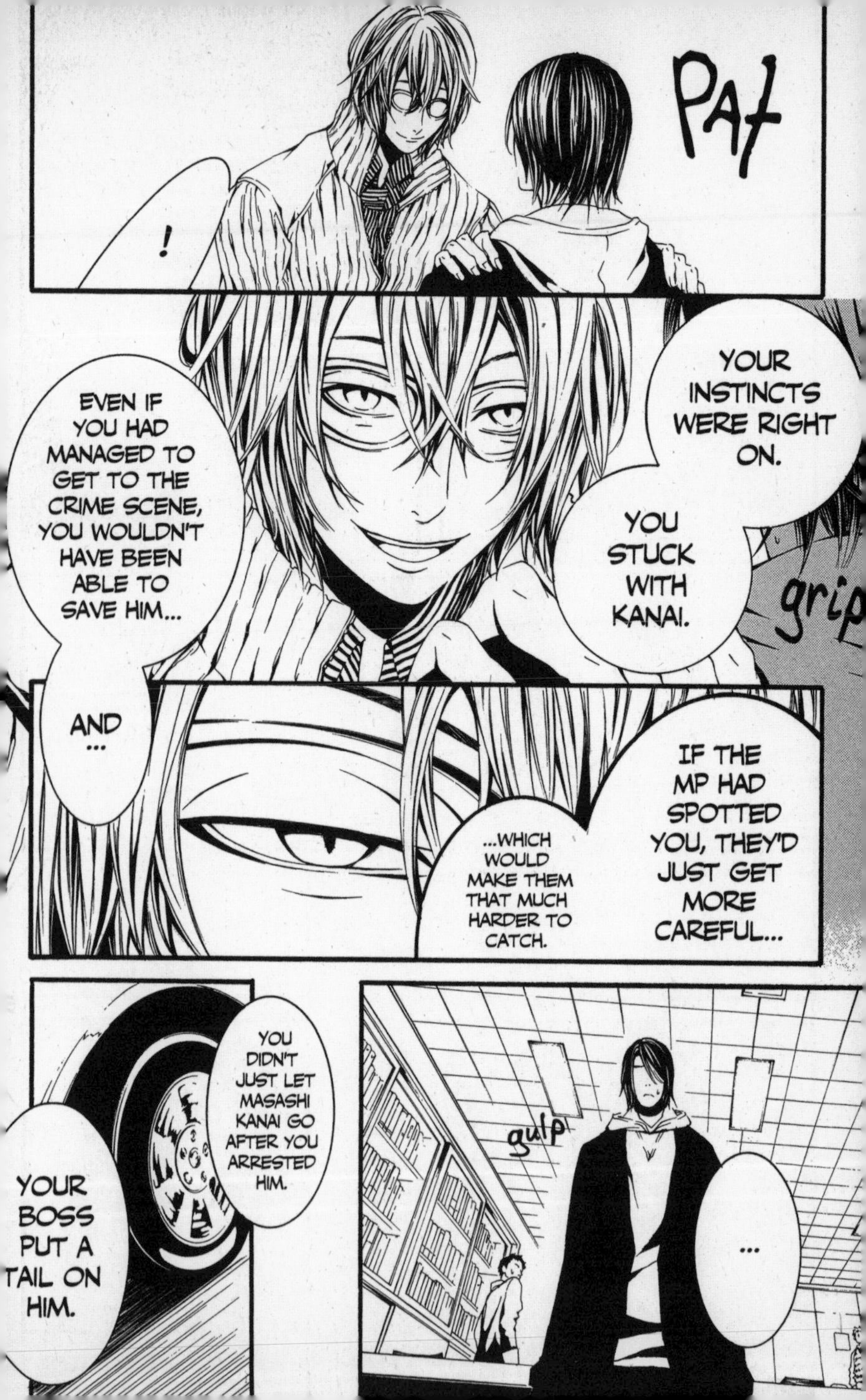
PAT
!
YOUR INSTINCTS WERE RIGHT ON.
YOU STUCK WITH KANAI.
grip
EVEN IF YOU HAD MANAGED TO GET TO THE CRIME SCENE, YOU WOULDN'T HAVE BEEN ABLE TO SAVE HIM...
AND ...
IF THE MP HAD SPOTTED YOU, THEY'D JUST GET MORE CAREFUL...
...WHICH WOULD MAKE THEM THAT MUCH HARDER TO CATCH.
...
gulp
YOU DIDN'T JUST LET MASASHI KANAI GO AFTER YOU ARRESTED HIM.
YOUR BOSS PUT A TAIL ON HIM.

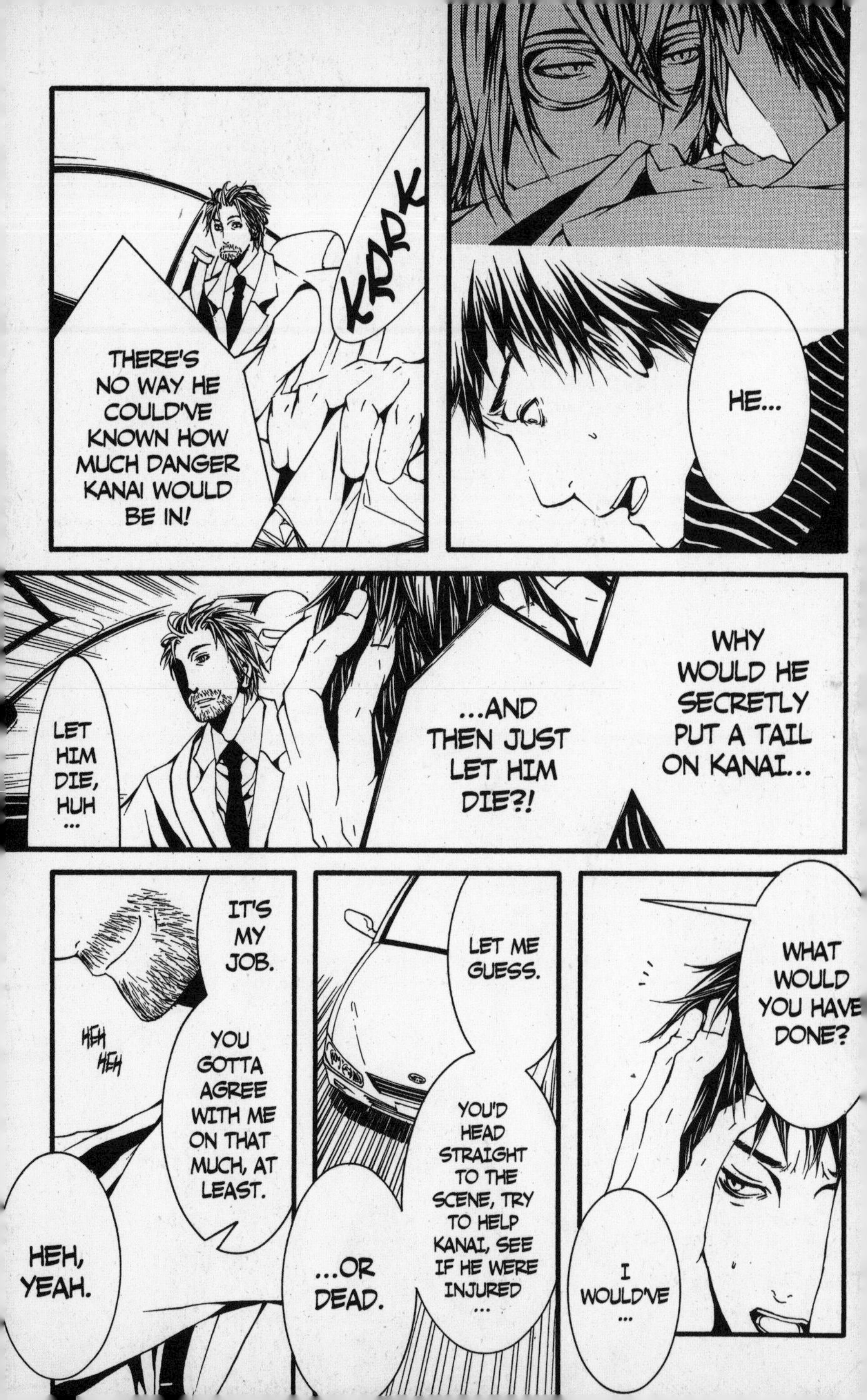
HE...
KRRK
THERE'S NO WAY HE COULD'VE KNOWN HOW MUCH DANGER KANAI WOULD BE IN!
WHY WOULD HE SECRETLY PUT A TAIL ON KANAI...
...AND THEN JUST LET HIM DIE?!
LET HIM DIE, HUH...
WHAT WOULD YOU HAVE DONE?
I WOULD'VE...
LET ME GUESS.
YOU'D HEAD STRAIGHT TO THE SCENE, TRY TO HELP KANAI, SEE IF HE WERE INJURED...
...OR DEAD.
IT'S MY JOB.
HEH HEH
YOU GOTTA AGREE WITH ME ON THAT MUCH, AT LEAST.
HEH, YEAH.

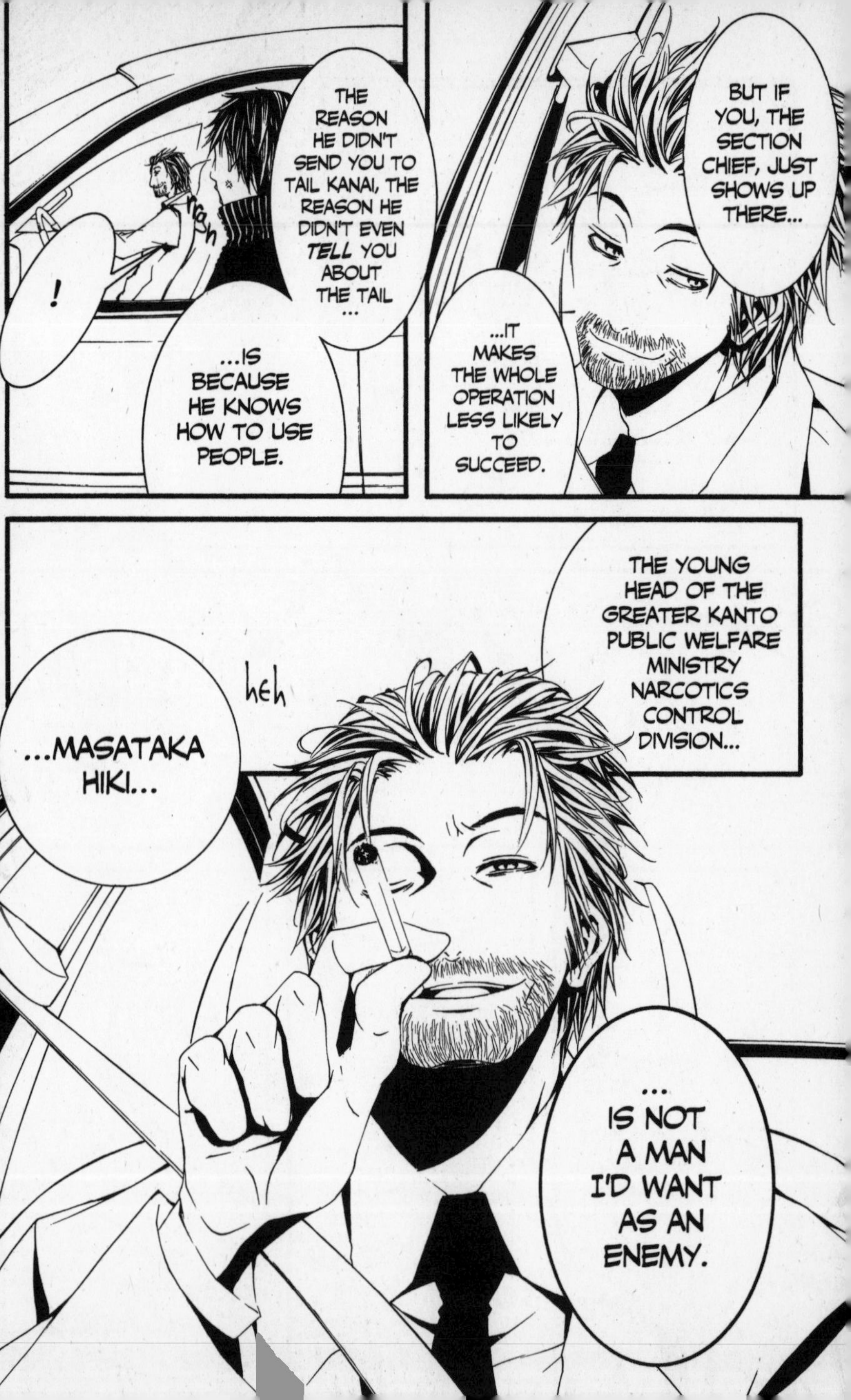
BUT IF YOU, THE SECTION CHIEF, JUST SHOWS UP THERE...
...IT MAKES THE WHOLE OPERATION LESS LIKELY TO SUCCEED.
THE REASON HE DIDN'T SEND YOU TO TAIL KANAI, THE REASON HE DIDN'T EVEN *TELL* YOU ABOUT THE TAIL ...
...IS BECAUSE HE KNOWS HOW TO USE PEOPLE.
!
THE YOUNG HEAD OF THE GREATER KANTO PUBLIC WELFARE MINISTRY NARCOTICS CONTROL DIVISION...
heh
...MASATAKA HIKI...
... IS NOT A MAN I'D WANT AS AN ENEMY.

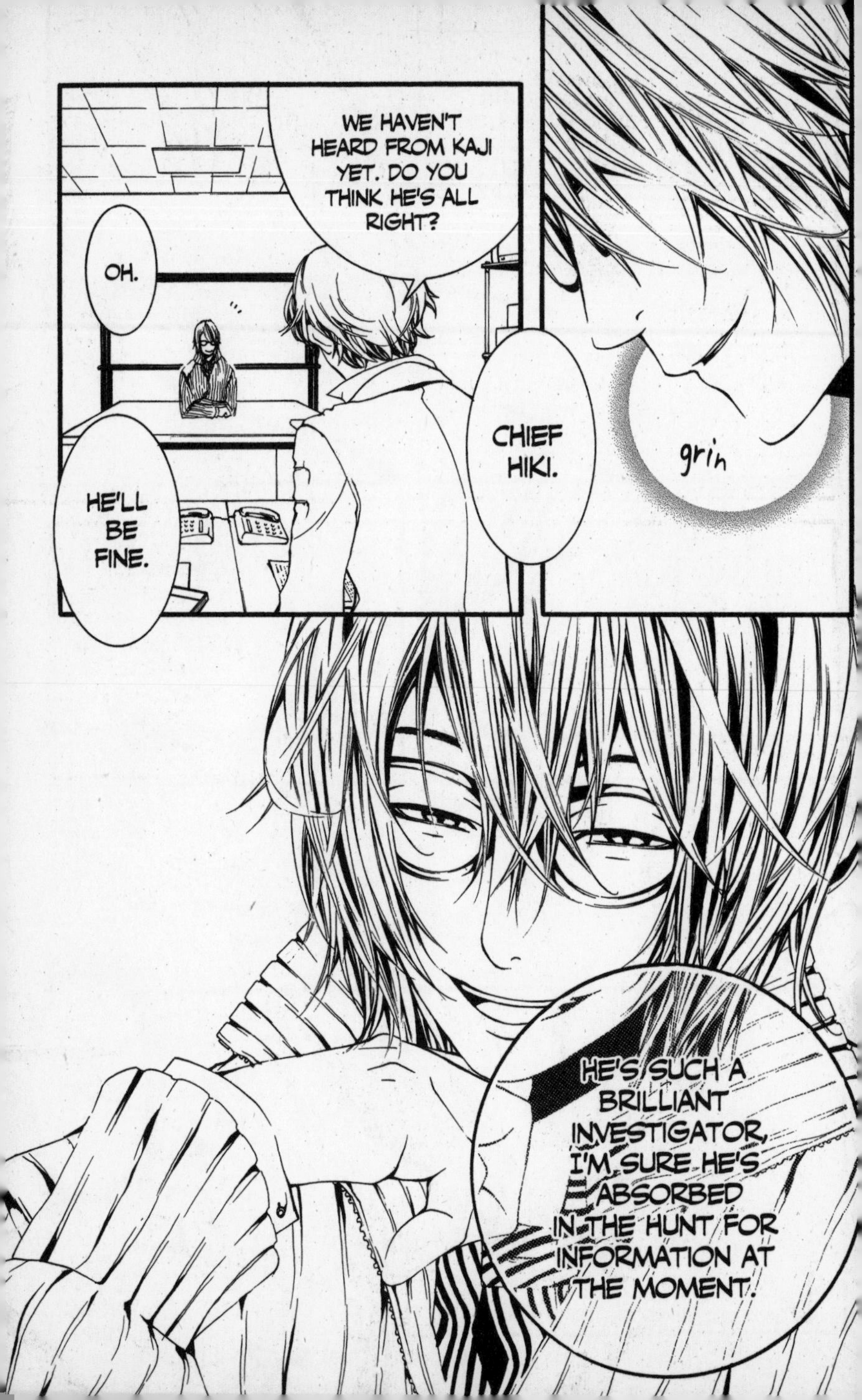
grin
CHIEF HIKI.
WE HAVEN'T HEARD FROM KAJI YET. DO YOU THINK HE'S ALL RIGHT?
OH.
HE'LL BE FINE.
HE'S SUCH A BRILLIANT INVESTIGATOR, I'M SURE HE'S ABSORBED IN THE HUNT FOR INFORMATION AT THE MOMENT.

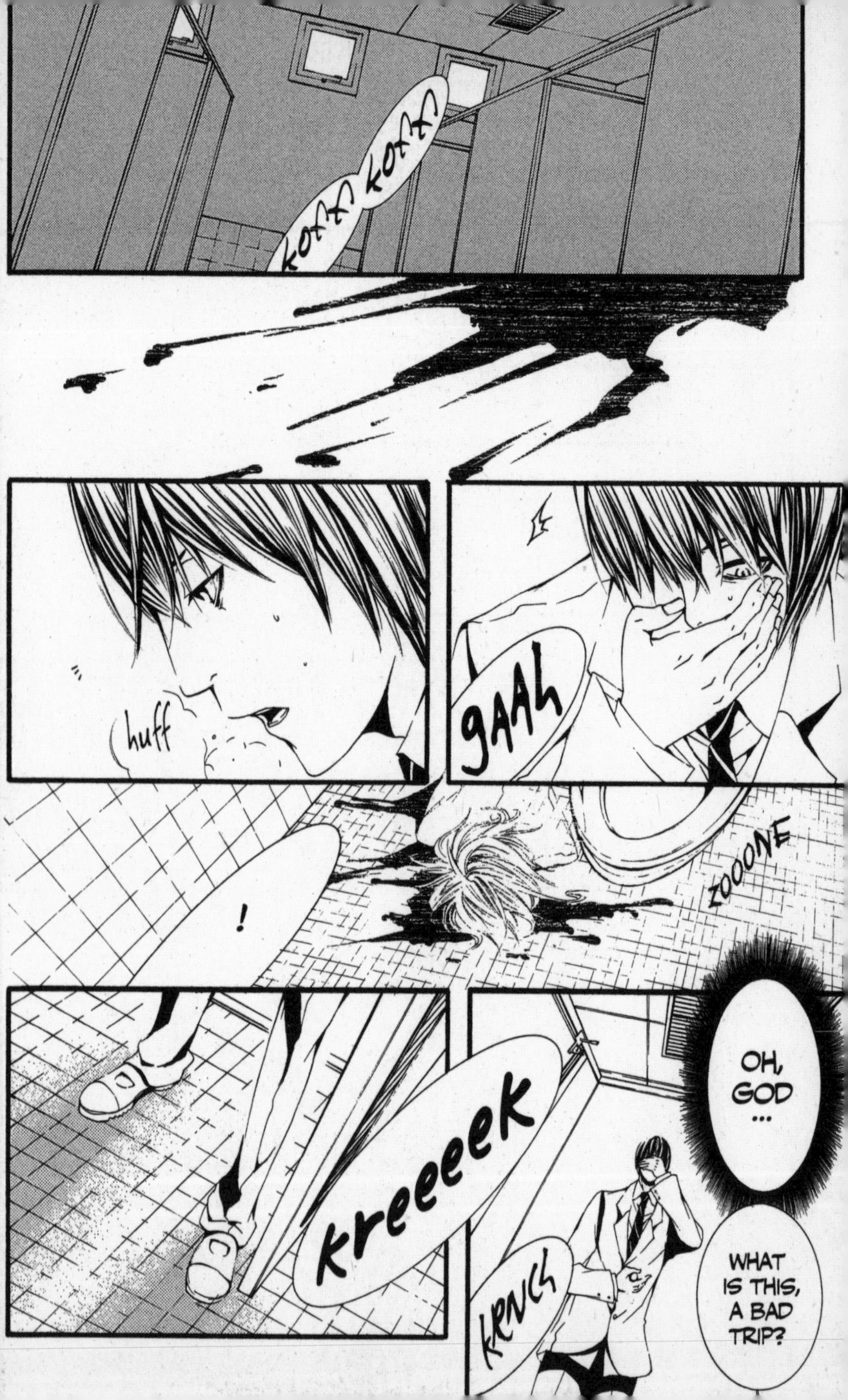
GAAH
huff
ZOOONE
!
OH, GOD ...
WHAT IS THIS, A BAD TRIP?
KRUNCH
kreeeek

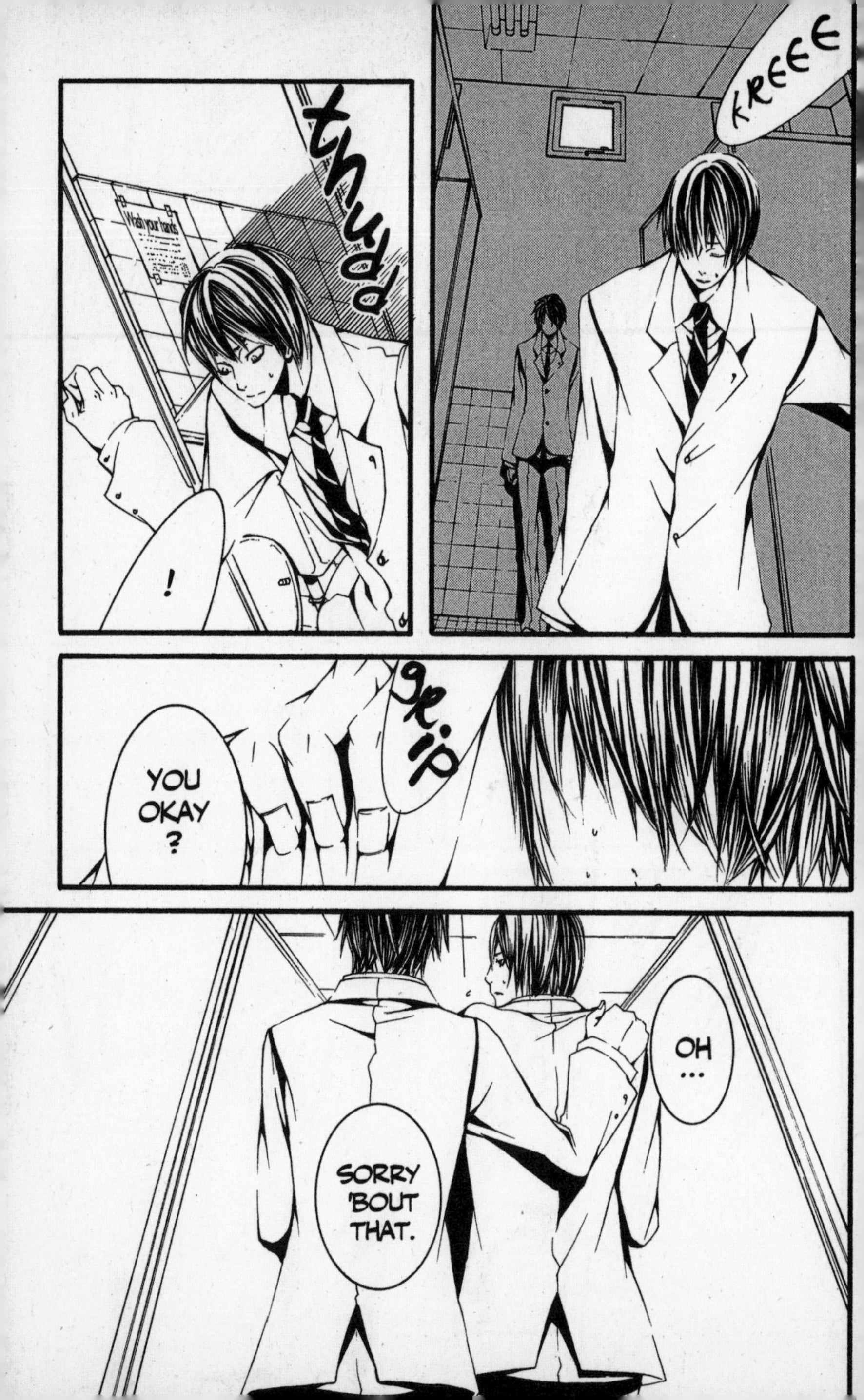
KREEE
thud
Wash your hands
!
grip
YOU OKAY ?
OH ...
SORRY 'BOUT THAT.

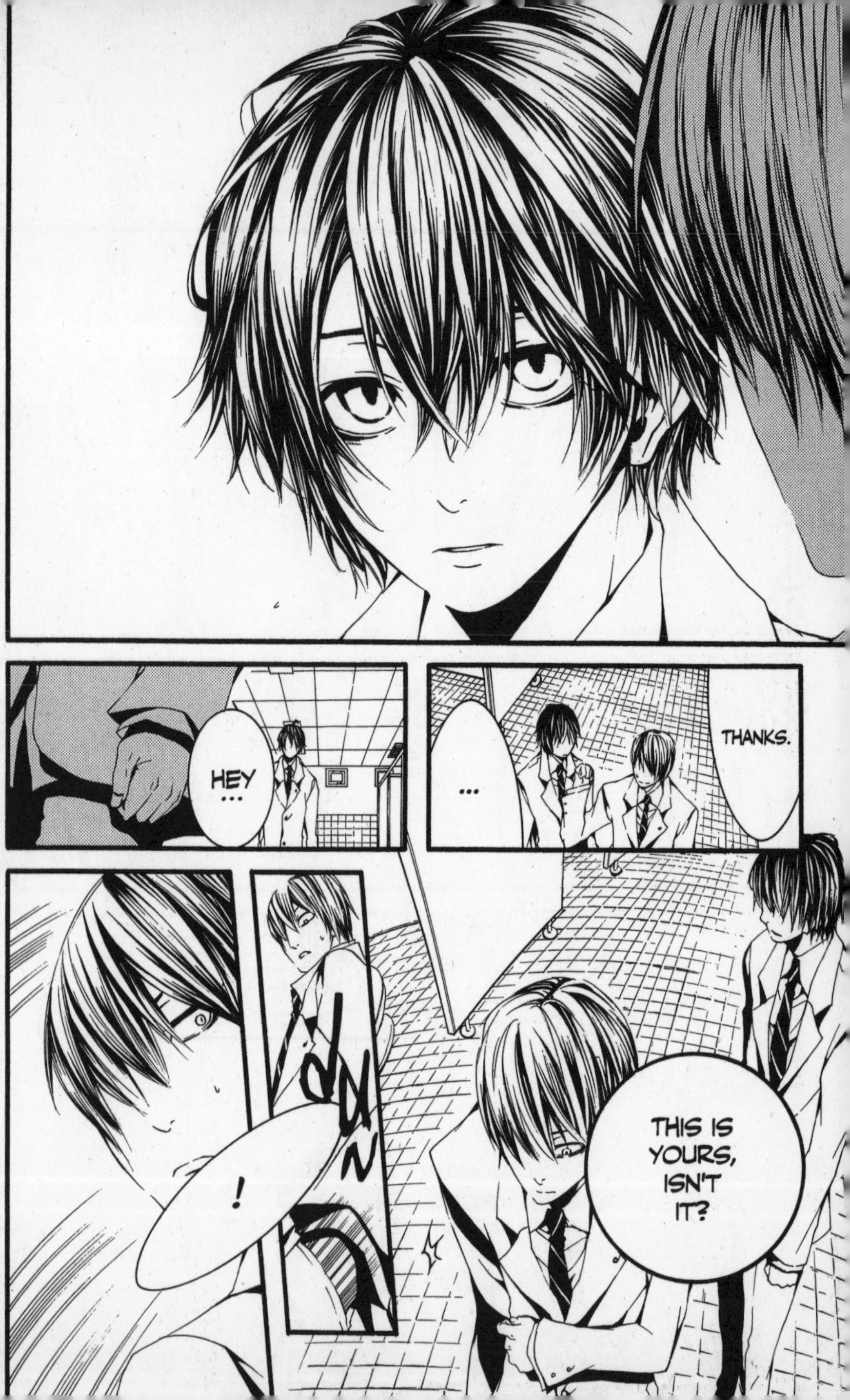
THANKS.
...
HEY ...
THIS IS YOURS, ISN'T IT?
!

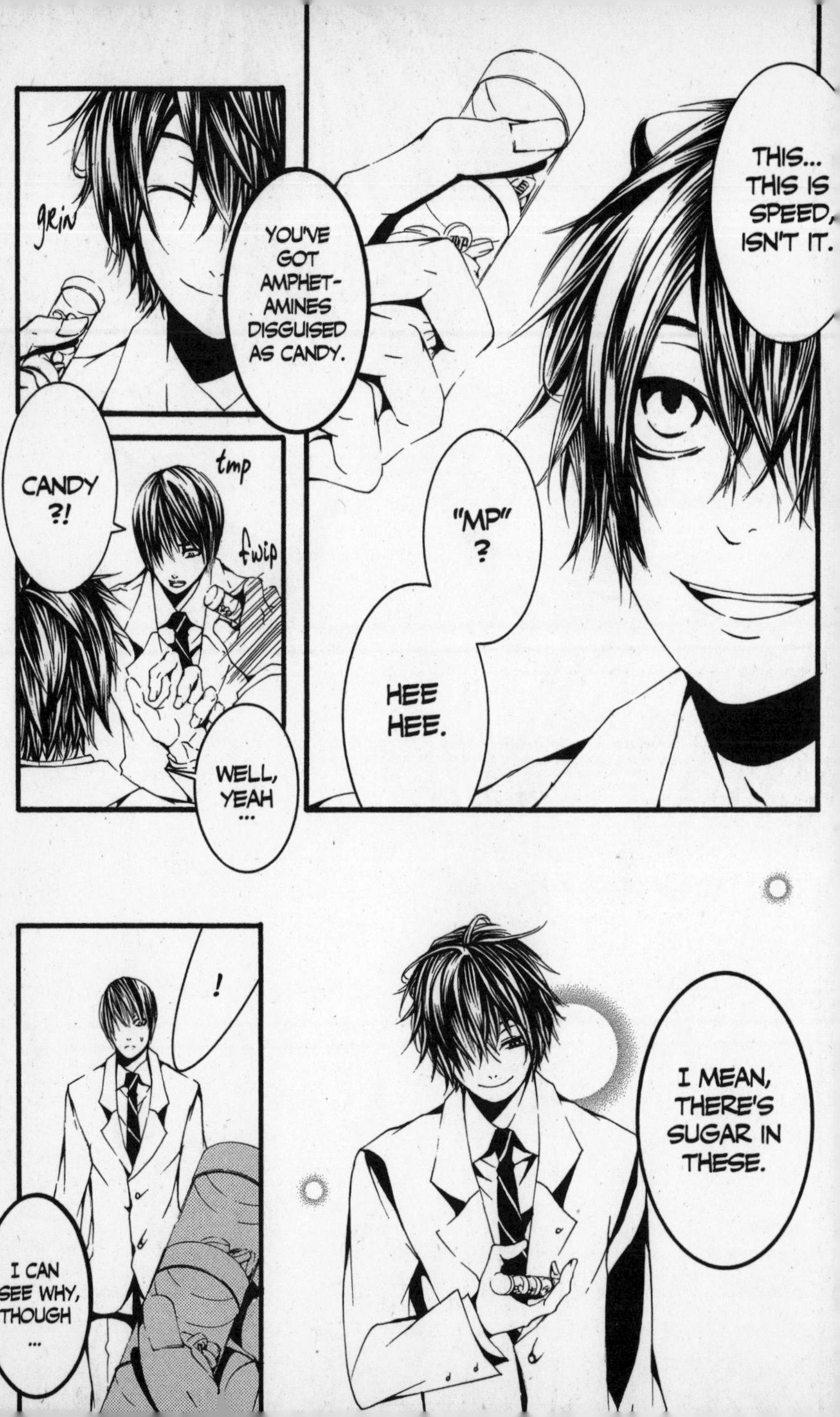
THIS... THIS IS SPEED, ISN'T IT.
"MP"?
HEE HEE.
grin
YOU'VE GOT AMPHET-AMINES DISGUISED AS CANDY.
tmp
fwip
CANDY?!
WELL, YEAH...
I MEAN, THERE'S SUGAR IN THESE.
!
I CAN SEE WHY, THOUGH...

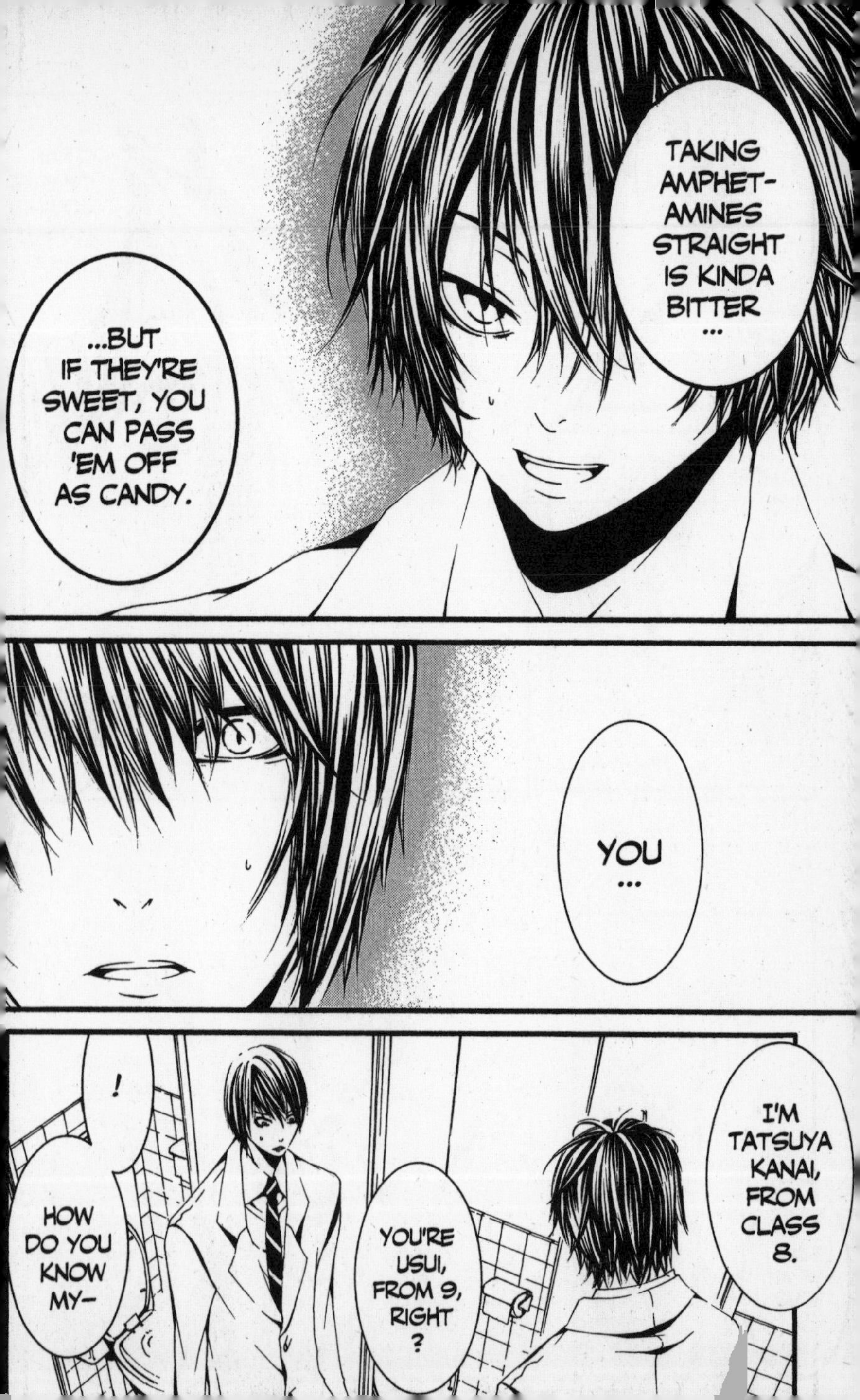
TAKING AMPHET-AMINES STRAIGHT IS KINDA BITTER...
...BUT IF THEY'RE SWEET, YOU CAN PASS 'EM OFF AS CANDY.
YOU...
I'M TATSUYA KANAI, FROM CLASS 8.
YOU'RE USUI, FROM 9, RIGHT?
!
HOW DO YOU KNOW MY-

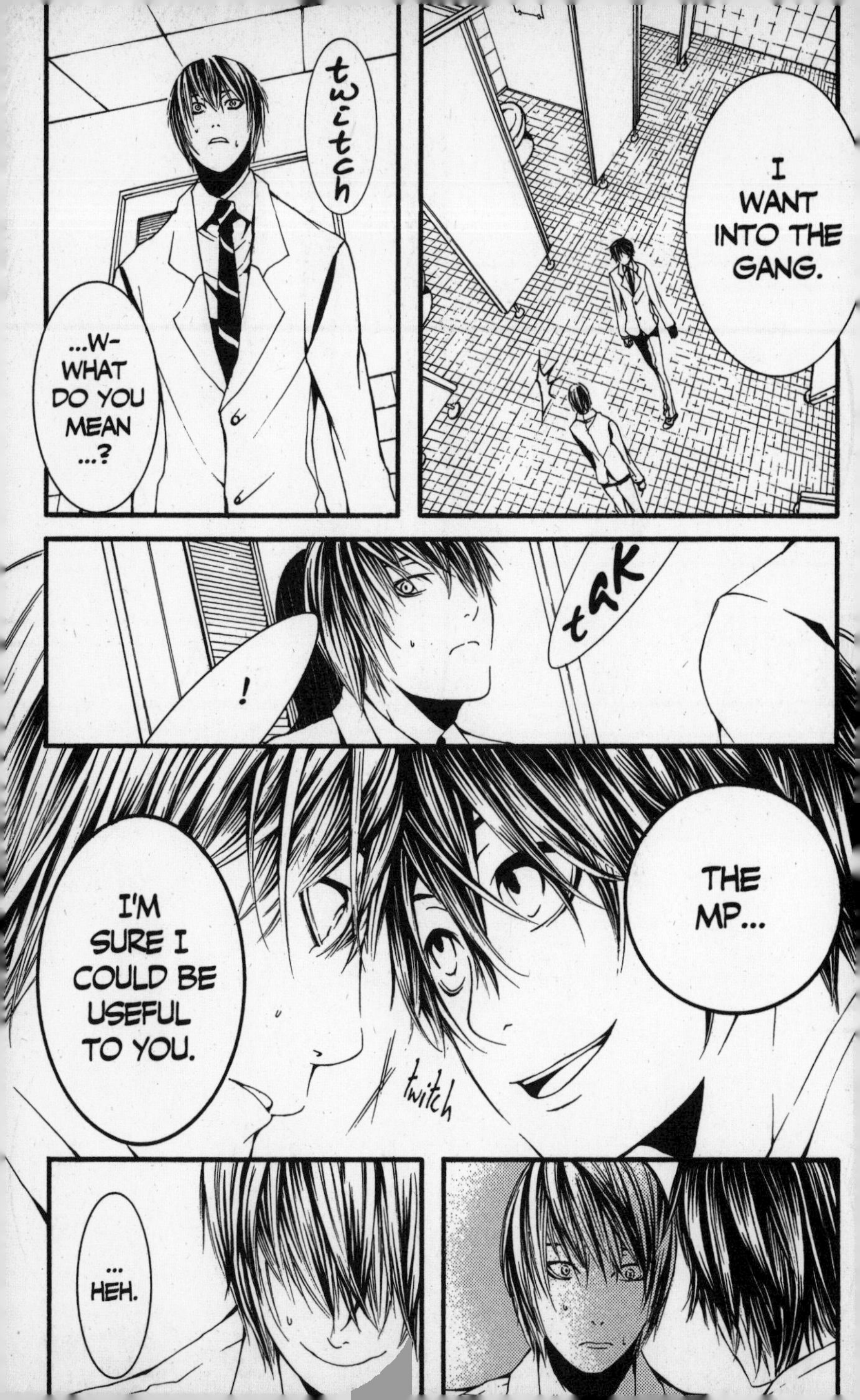
I WANT INTO THE GANG.
twitch
...W-WHAT DO YOU MEAN...?
tak
!
THE MP...
I'M SURE I COULD BE USEFUL TO YOU.
twitch
...HEH.

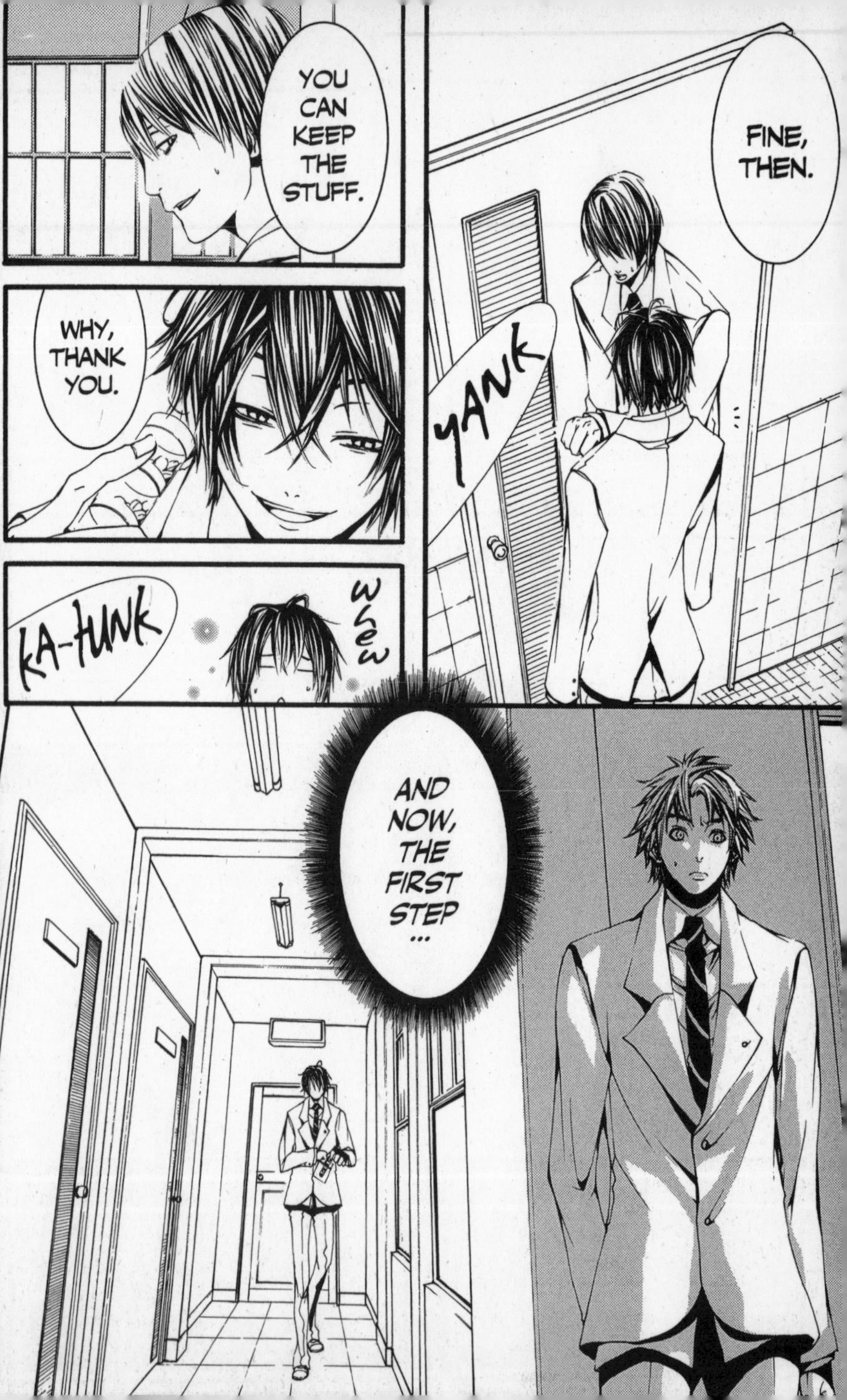
FINE, THEN.
YANK
YOU CAN KEEP THE STUFF.
WHY, THANK YOU.
KA-TUNK
whew
AND NOW, THE FIRST STEP...

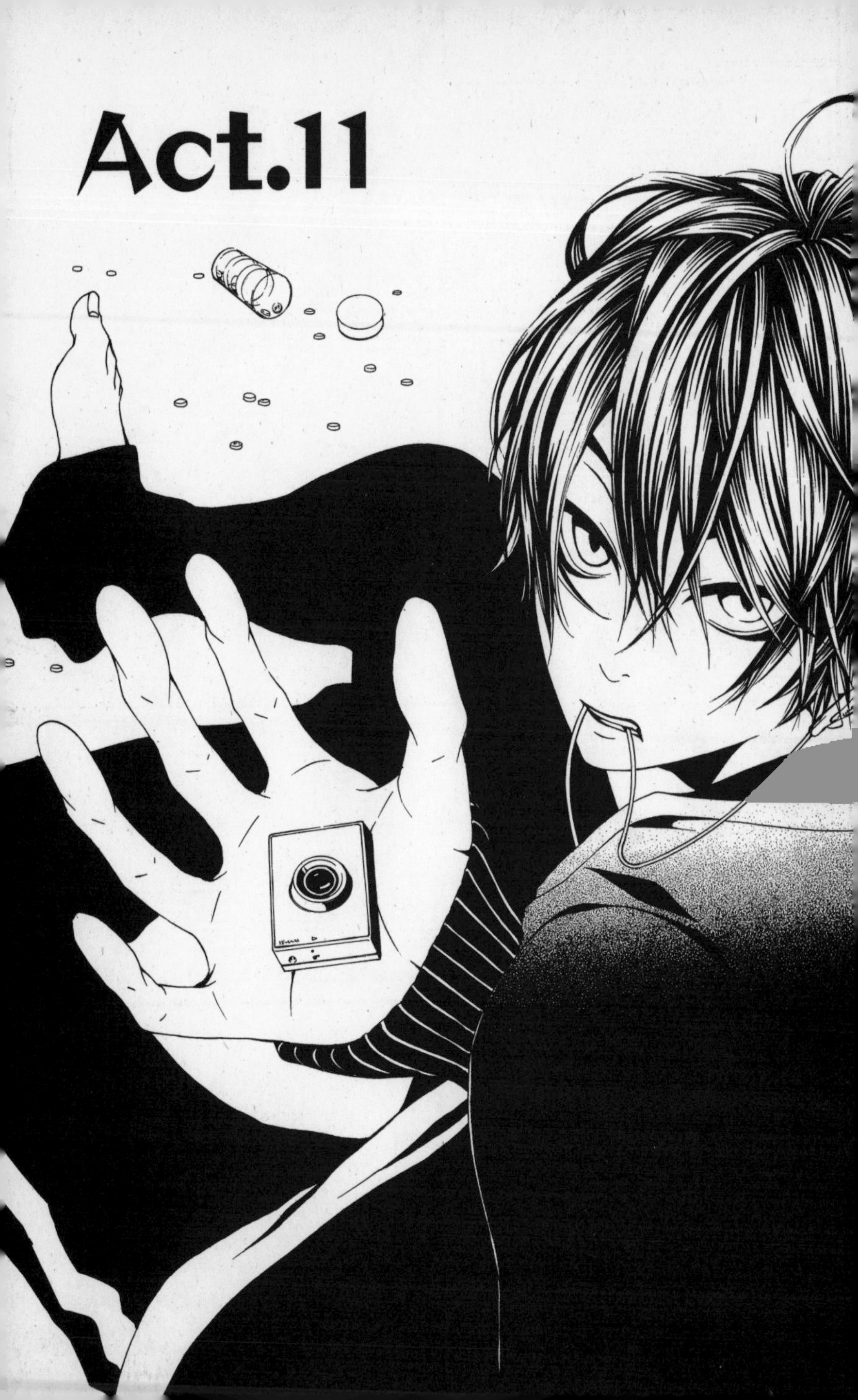
Act.11

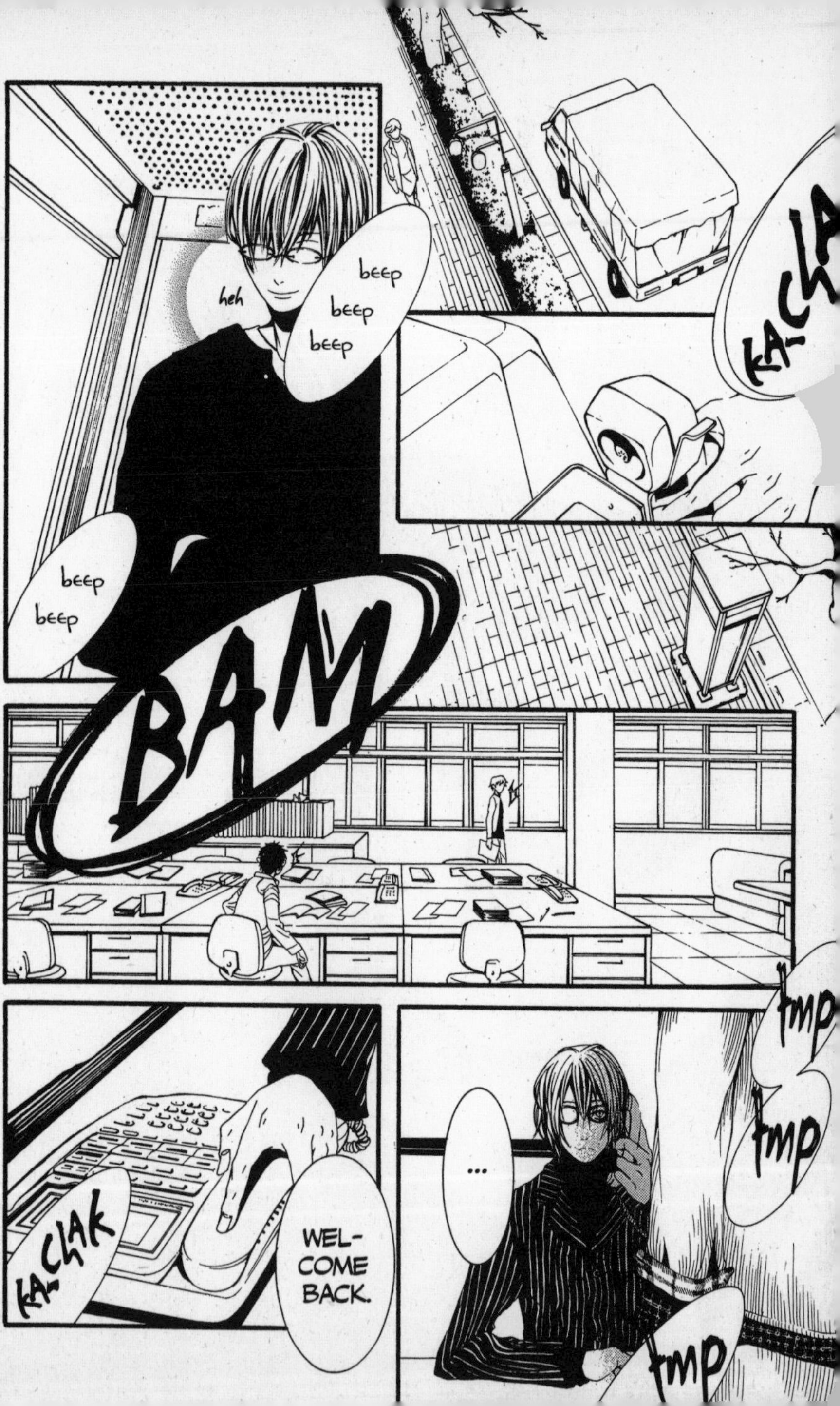
KA-CHA
heh
beep
beep
beep
beep
beep
BAM
tmp
tmp
...
tmp
WEL-
COME
BACK.
KA-CHLAK

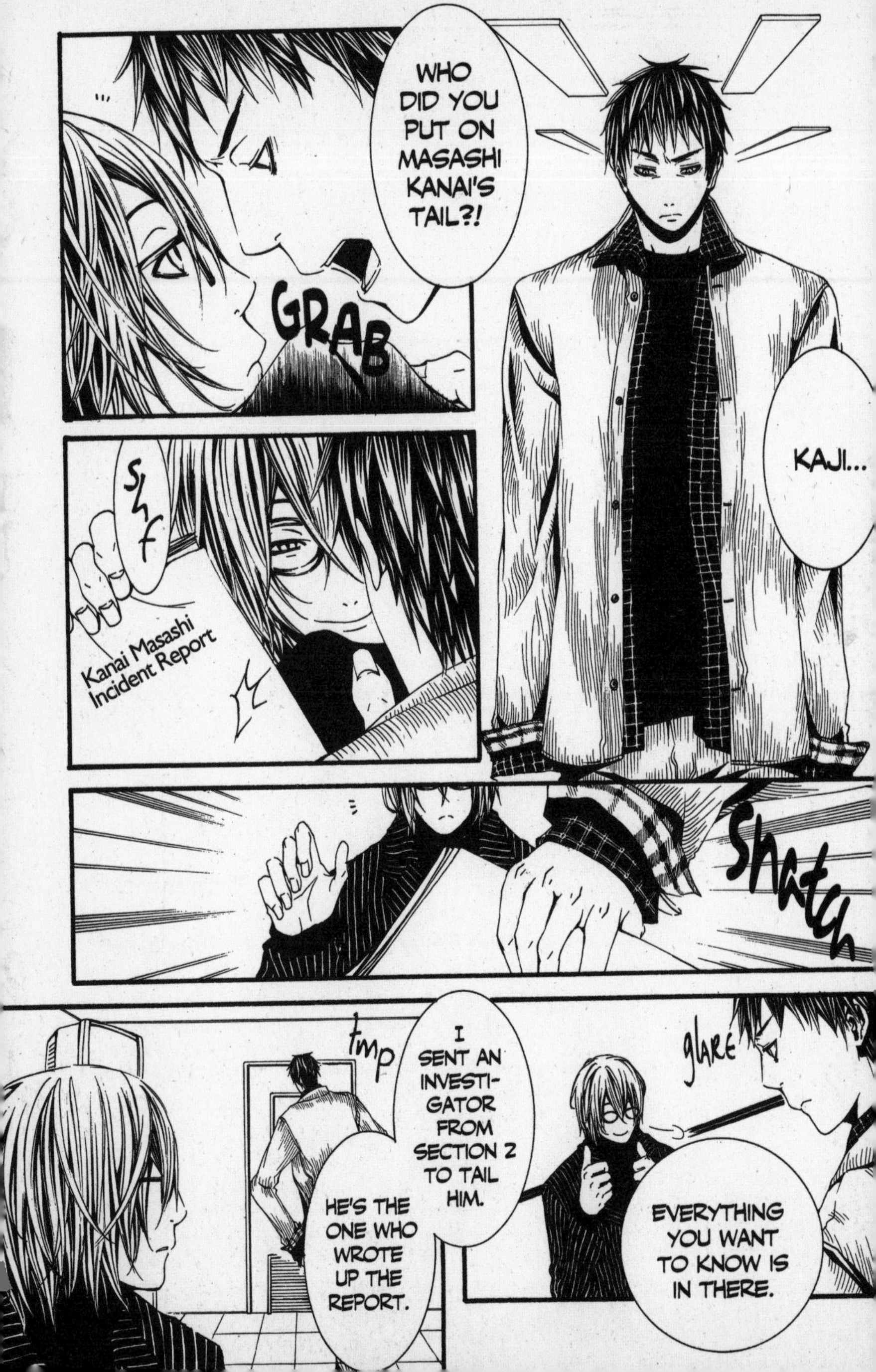
KAJI...
WHO DID YOU PUT ON MASASHI KANAI'S TAIL?!
GRAB
shf
Kanai Masashi Incident Report
Snatch
glare
EVERYTHING YOU WANT TO KNOW IS IN THERE.
tmp
I SENT AN INVESTI-GATOR FROM SECTION 2 TO TAIL HIM.
HE'S THE ONE WHO WROTE UP THE REPORT.

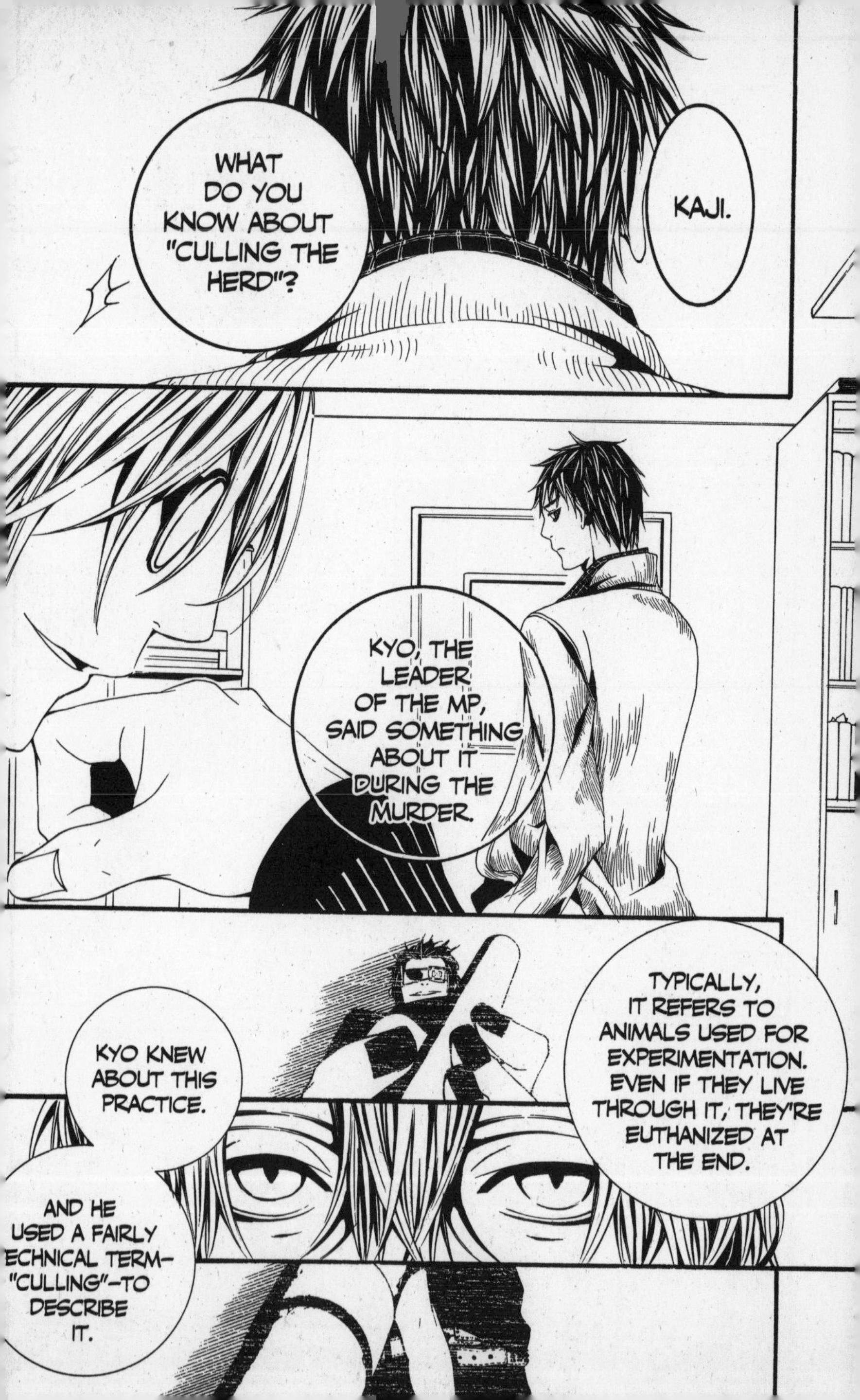
KAJI.
WHAT DO YOU KNOW ABOUT "CULLING THE HERD"?
KYO, THE LEADER OF THE MP, SAID SOMETHING ABOUT IT DURING THE MURDER.
TYPICALLY, IT REFERS TO ANIMALS USED FOR EXPERIMENTATION. EVEN IF THEY LIVE THROUGH IT, THEY'RE EUTHANIZED AT THE END.
KYO KNEW ABOUT THIS PRACTICE.
AND HE USED A FAIRLY ECHNICAL TERM— "CULLING"—TO DESCRIBE IT.

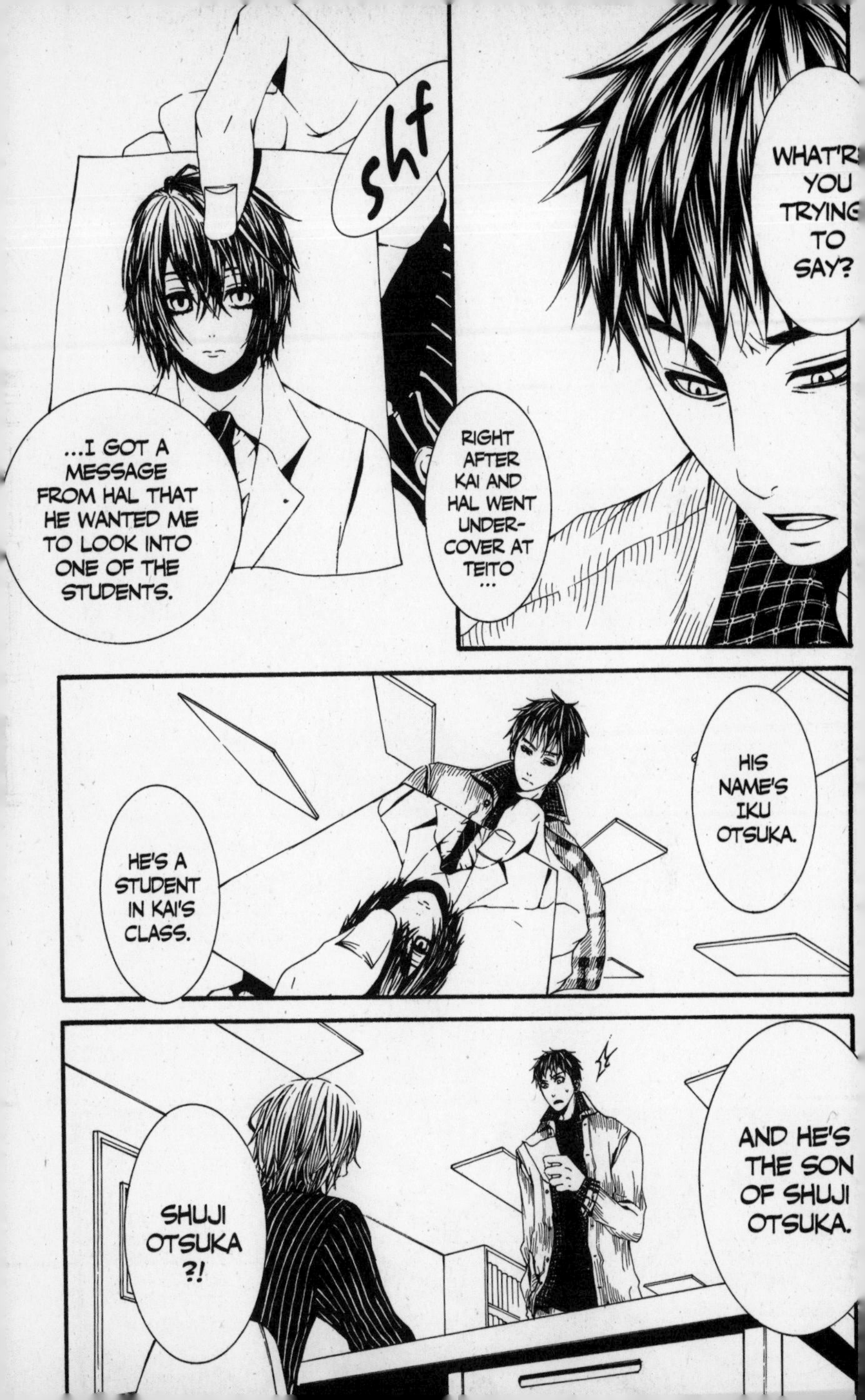
WHAT'RE YOU TRYING TO SAY?
shf
RIGHT AFTER KAI AND HAL WENT UNDER-COVER AT TEITO...
...I GOT A MESSAGE FROM HAL THAT HE WANTED ME TO LOOK INTO ONE OF THE STUDENTS.
HIS NAME'S IKU OTSUKA.
HE'S A STUDENT IN KAI'S CLASS.
AND HE'S THE SON OF SHUJI OTSUKA.
SHUJI OTSUKA?!

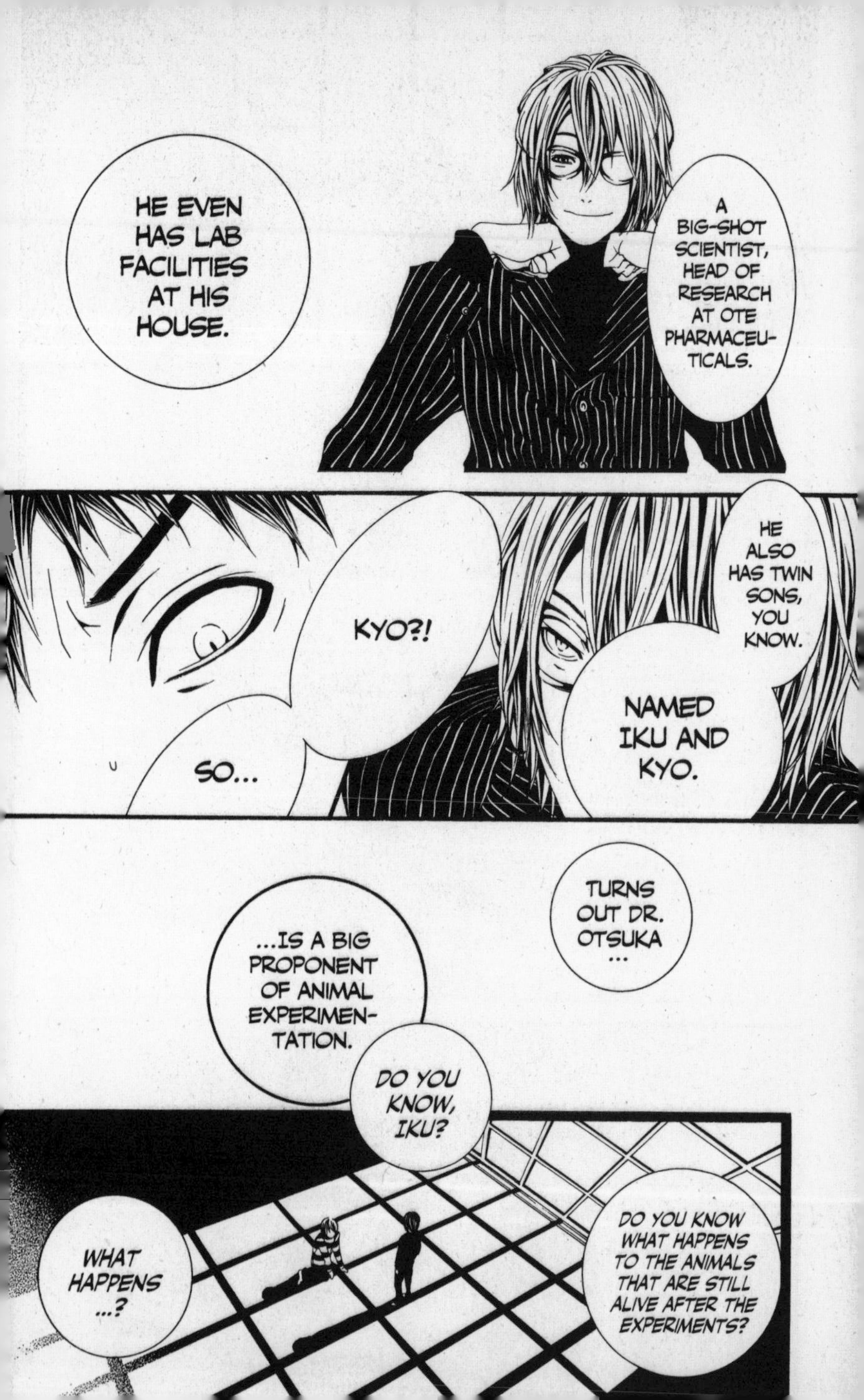
A BIG-SHOT SCIENTIST, HEAD OF RESEARCH AT OTE PHARMACEU-TICALS.
HE EVEN HAS LAB FACILITIES AT HIS HOUSE.
HE ALSO HAS TWIN SONS, YOU KNOW.
NAMED IKU AND KYO.
KYO?!
SO...
TURNS OUT DR. OTSUKA ...
...IS A BIG PROPONENT OF ANIMAL EXPERIMEN-TATION.
DO YOU KNOW, IKU?
DO YOU KNOW WHAT HAPPENS TO THE ANIMALS THAT ARE STILL ALIVE AFTER THE EXPERIMENTS?
WHAT HAPPENS ...?

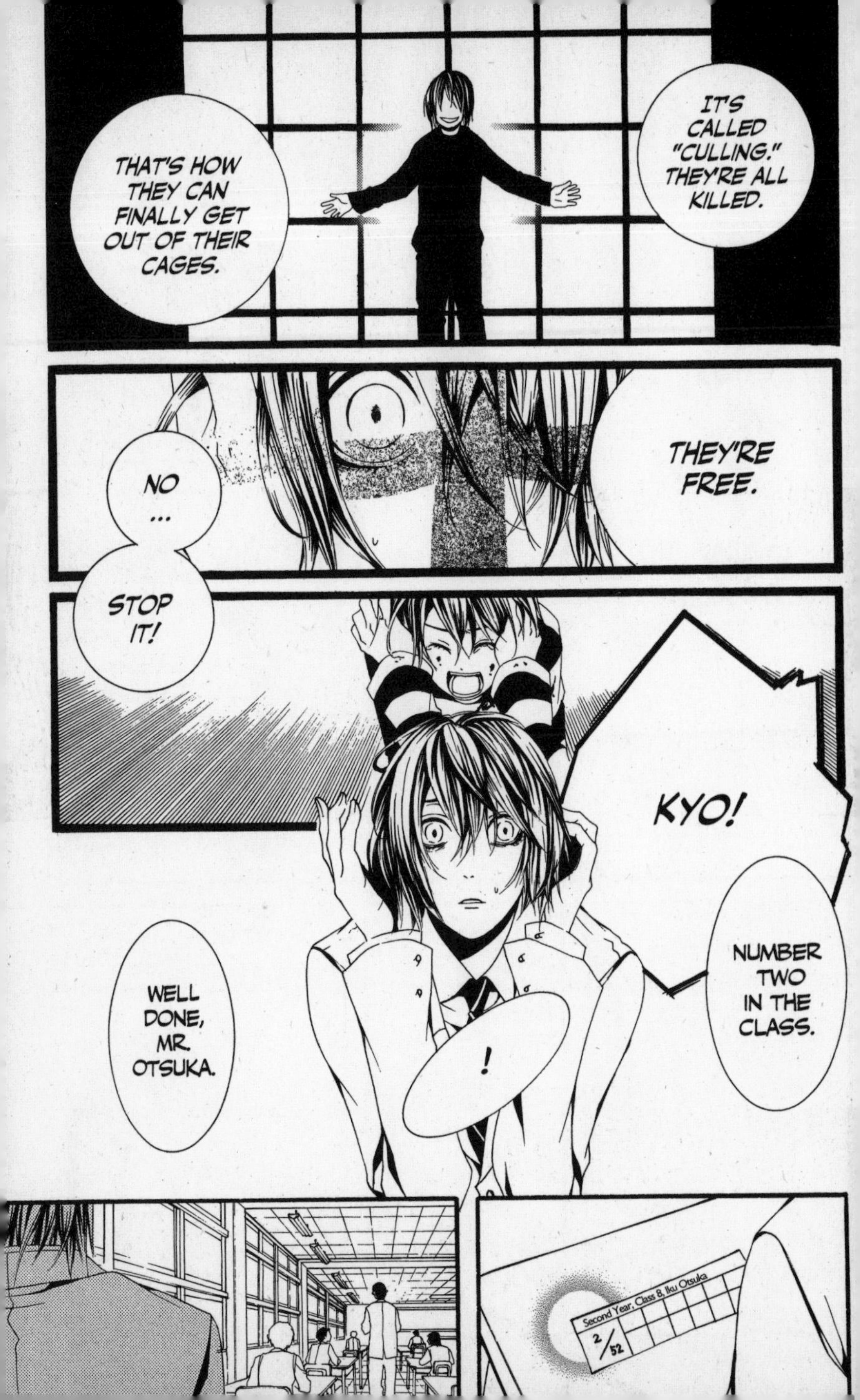
IT'S CALLED "CULLING." THEY'RE ALL KILLED.
THAT'S HOW THEY CAN FINALLY GET OUT OF THEIR CAGES.
THEY'RE FREE.
NO ...
STOP IT!
KYO!
NUMBER TWO IN THE CLASS.
!
WELL DONE, MR. OTSUKA.
Second Year, Class 8, Iku Otsuka
2/52

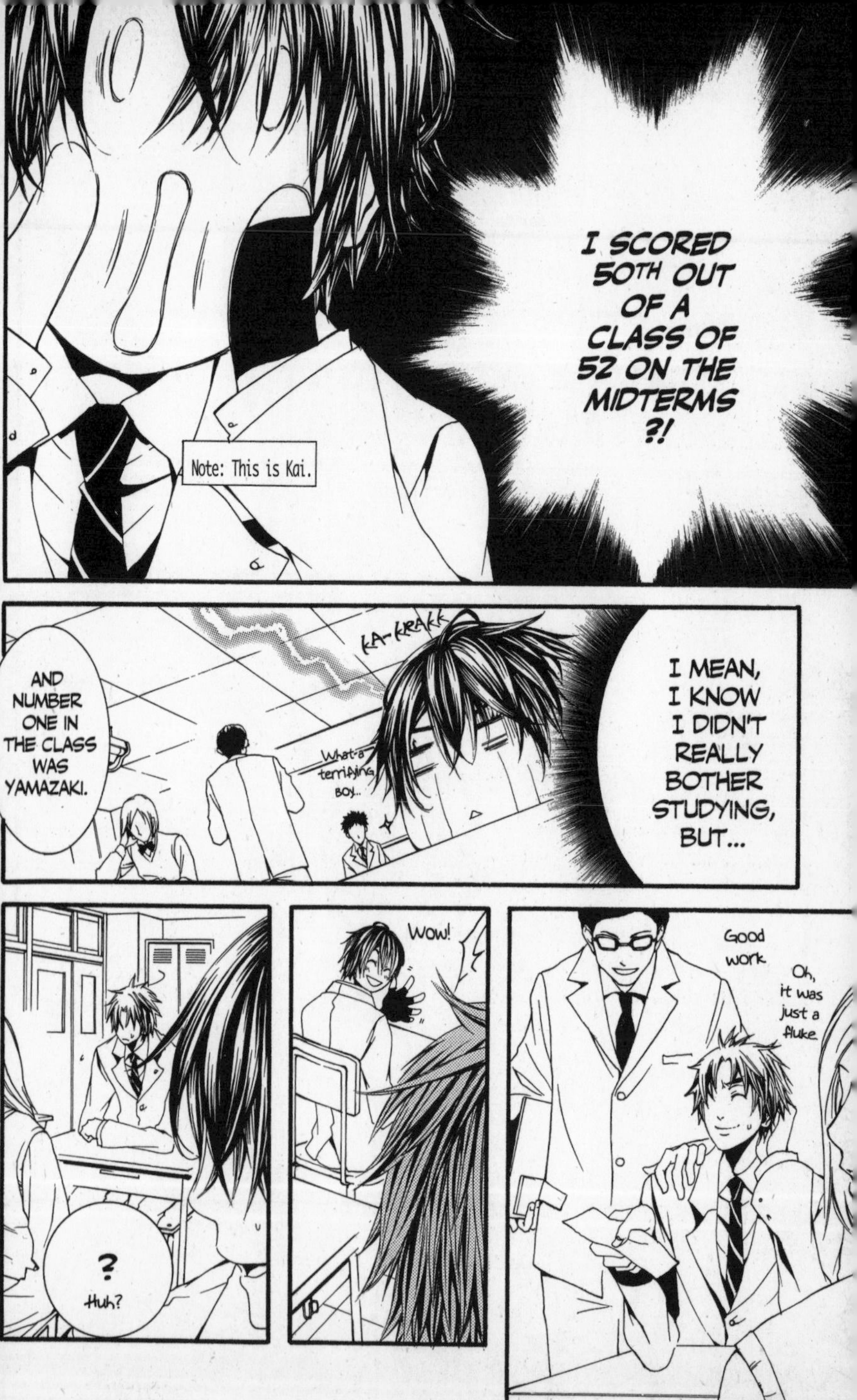
I SCORED 50TH OUT OF A CLASS OF 52 ON THE MIDTERMS ?!
Note: This is Kai.
I MEAN, I KNOW I DIDN'T REALLY BOTHER STUDYING, BUT...
KA-KRAKK
What a terrifying boy...
AND NUMBER ONE IN THE CLASS WAS YAMAZAKI.
Good work.
Oh, it was just a fluke.
Wow!
?
Huh?

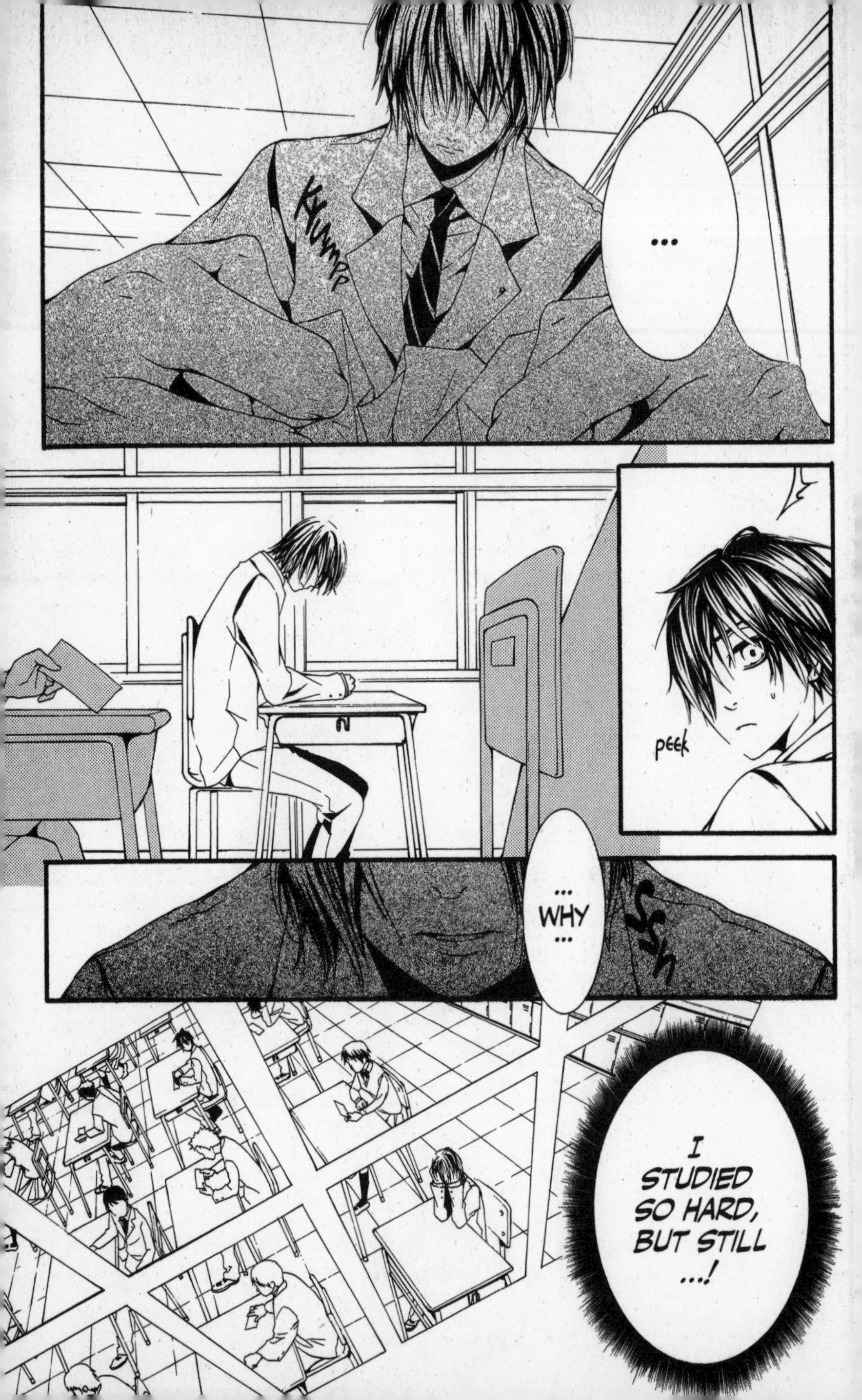
KLUMP
...
peek
...WHY...
I STUDIED SO HARD, BUT STILL ...!

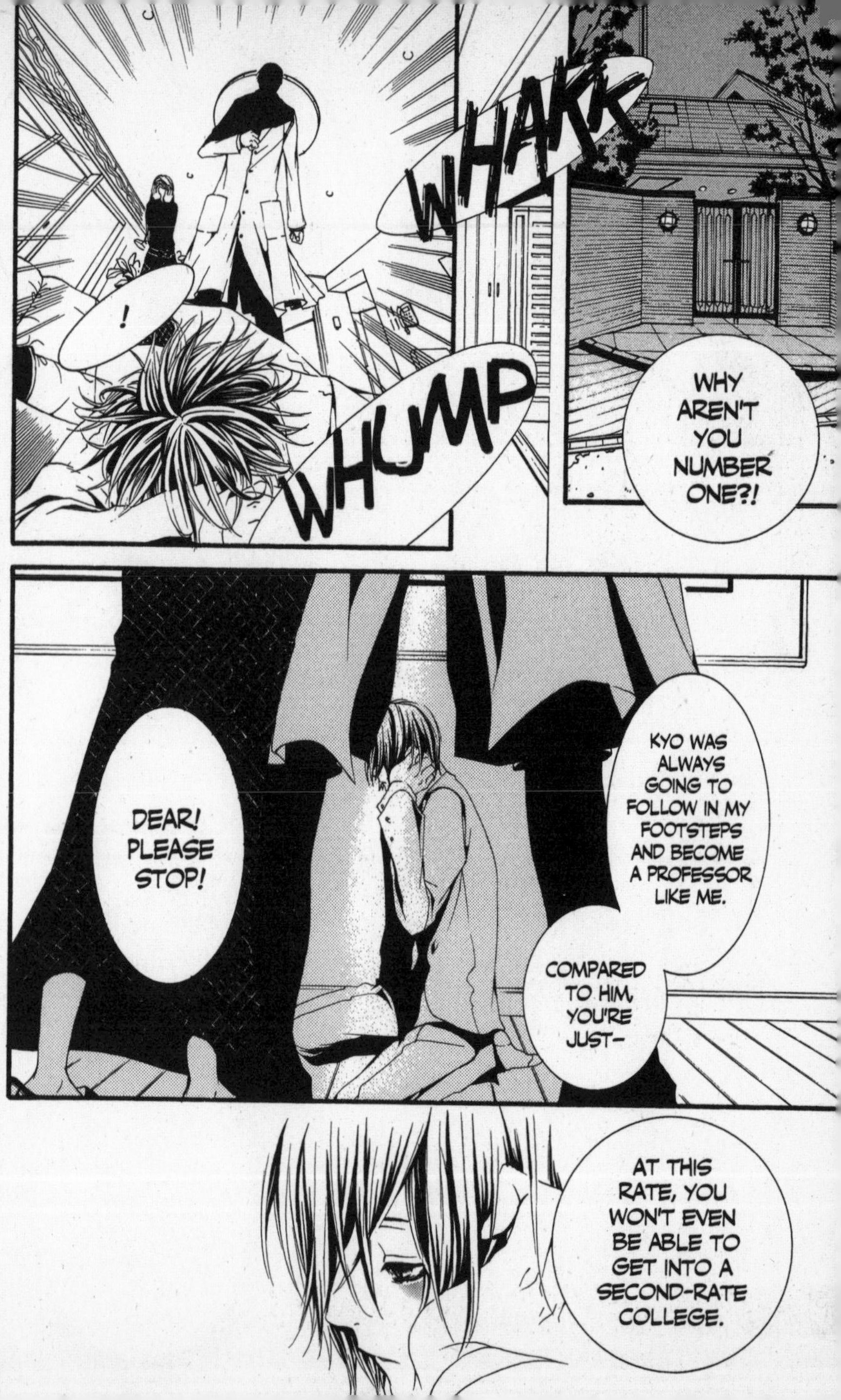
WHY AREN'T YOU NUMBER ONE?!
WHAKK
!
WHUMP
KYO WAS ALWAYS GOING TO FOLLOW IN MY FOOTSTEPS AND BECOME A PROFESSOR LIKE ME.
DEAR! PLEASE STOP!
COMPARED TO HIM, YOU'RE JUST–
AT THIS RATE, YOU WON'T EVEN BE ABLE TO GET INTO A SECOND-RATE COLLEGE.

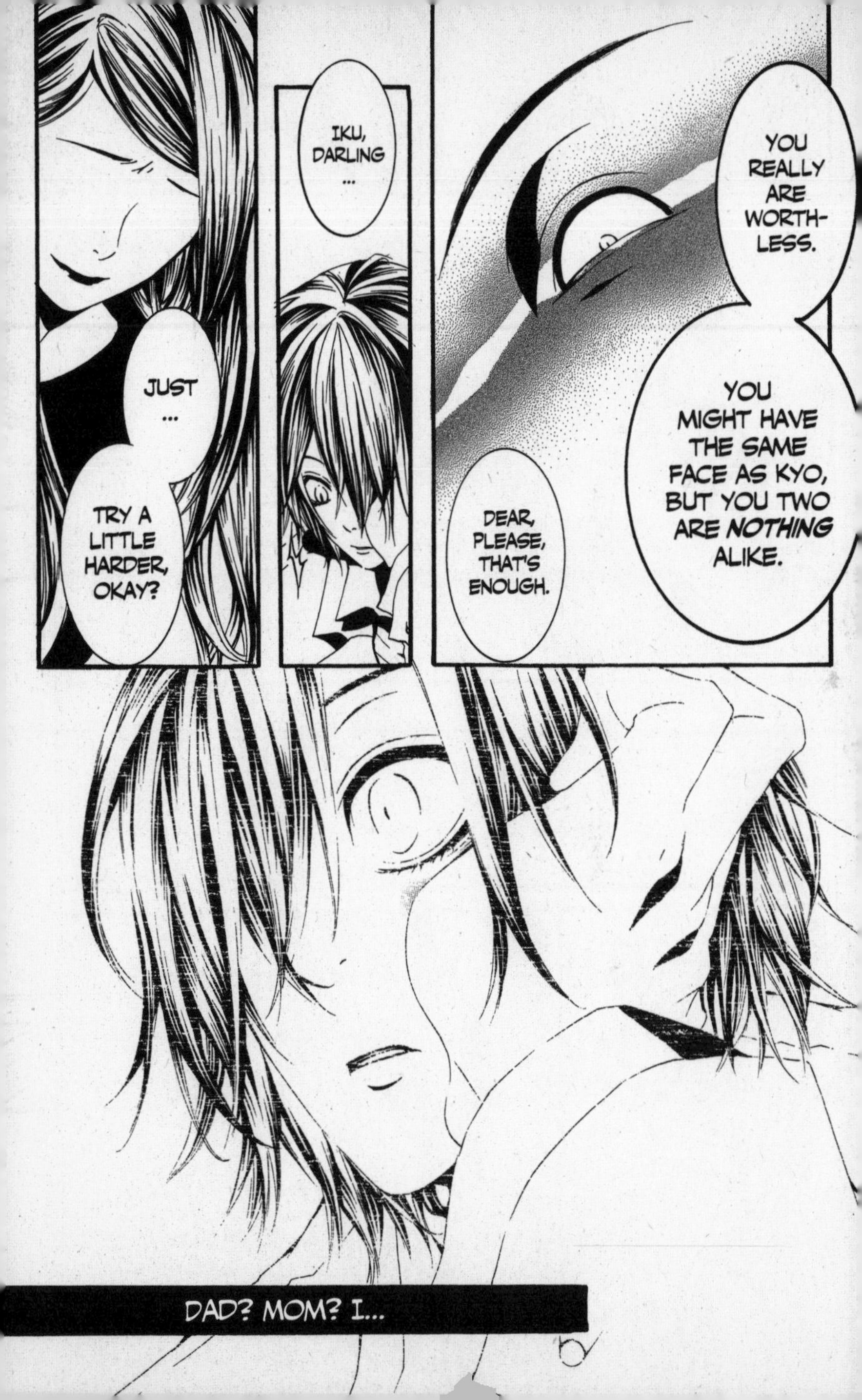
YOU REALLY ARE WORTH-LESS.
YOU MIGHT HAVE THE SAME FACE AS KYO, BUT YOU TWO ARE *NOTHING* ALIKE.
DEAR, PLEASE, THAT'S ENOUGH.
IKU, DARLING ...
JUST ...
TRY A LITTLE HARDER, OKAY?
DAD? MOM? I...

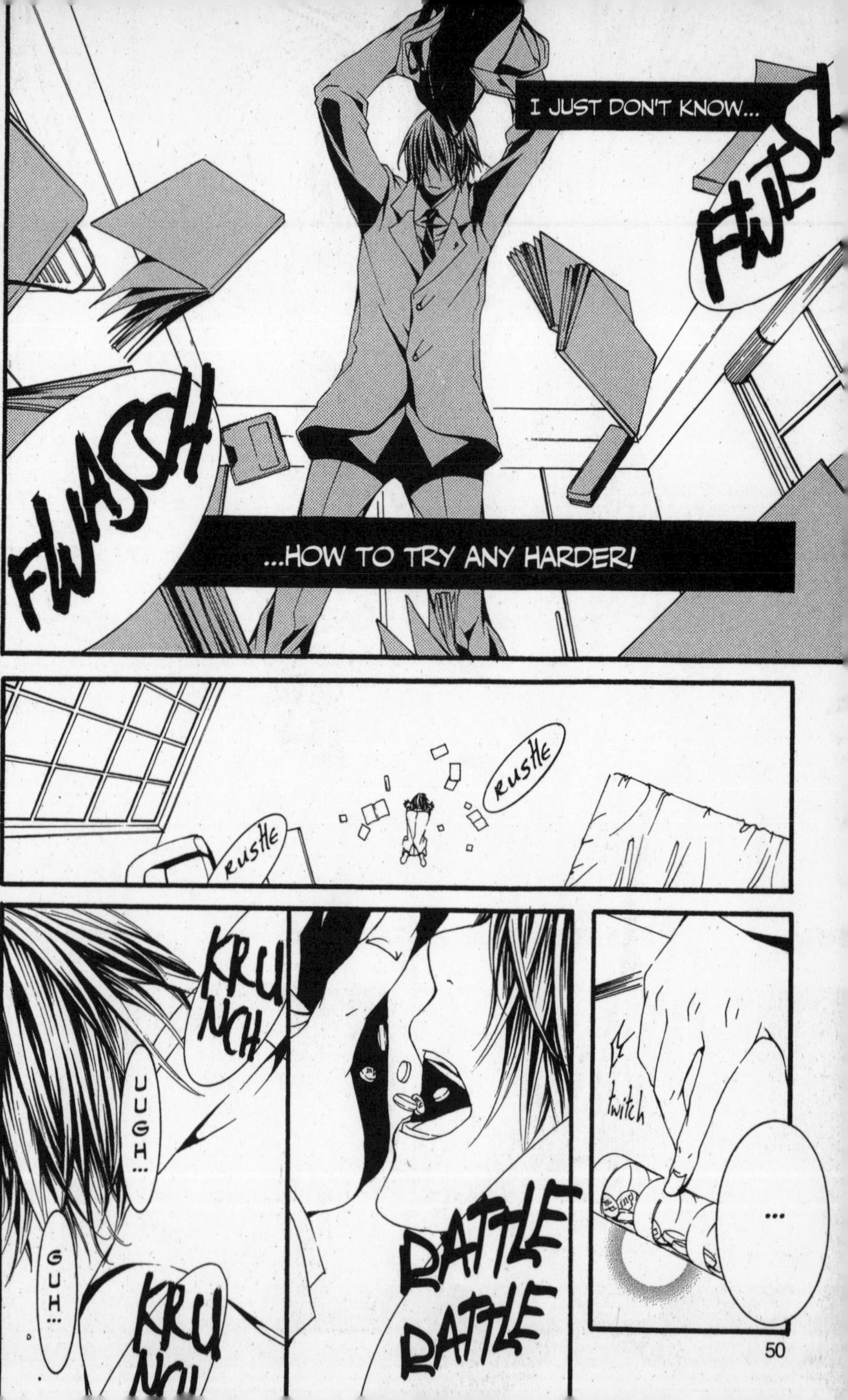
I JUST DON'T KNOW...
FWASCH
...HOW TO TRY ANY HARDER!
rustle
rustle
twitch
...
RATTLE
RATTLE
KRUNCH
UUGH...
GUH...

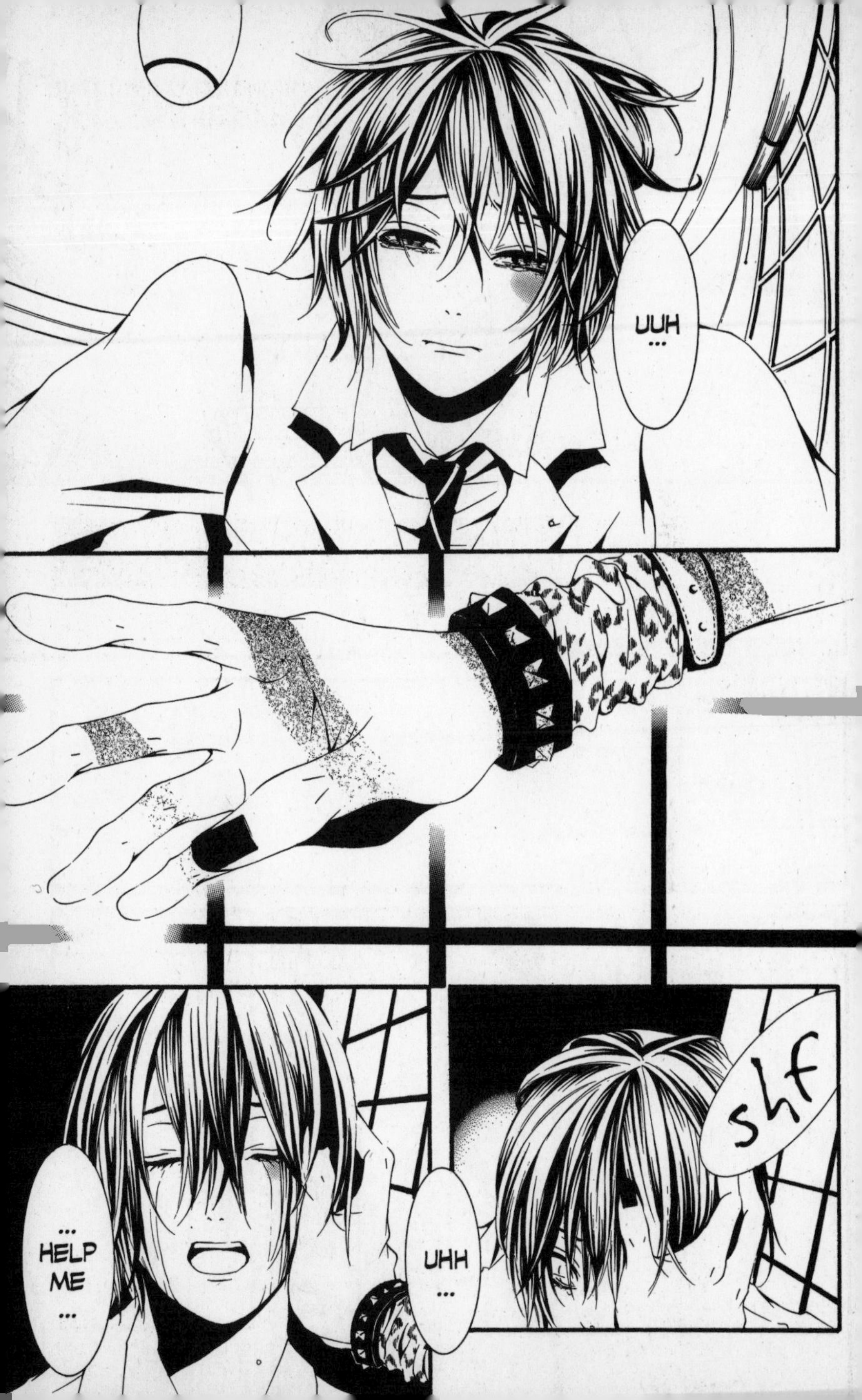
UUH ...
shf
UHH ...
... HELP ME ...

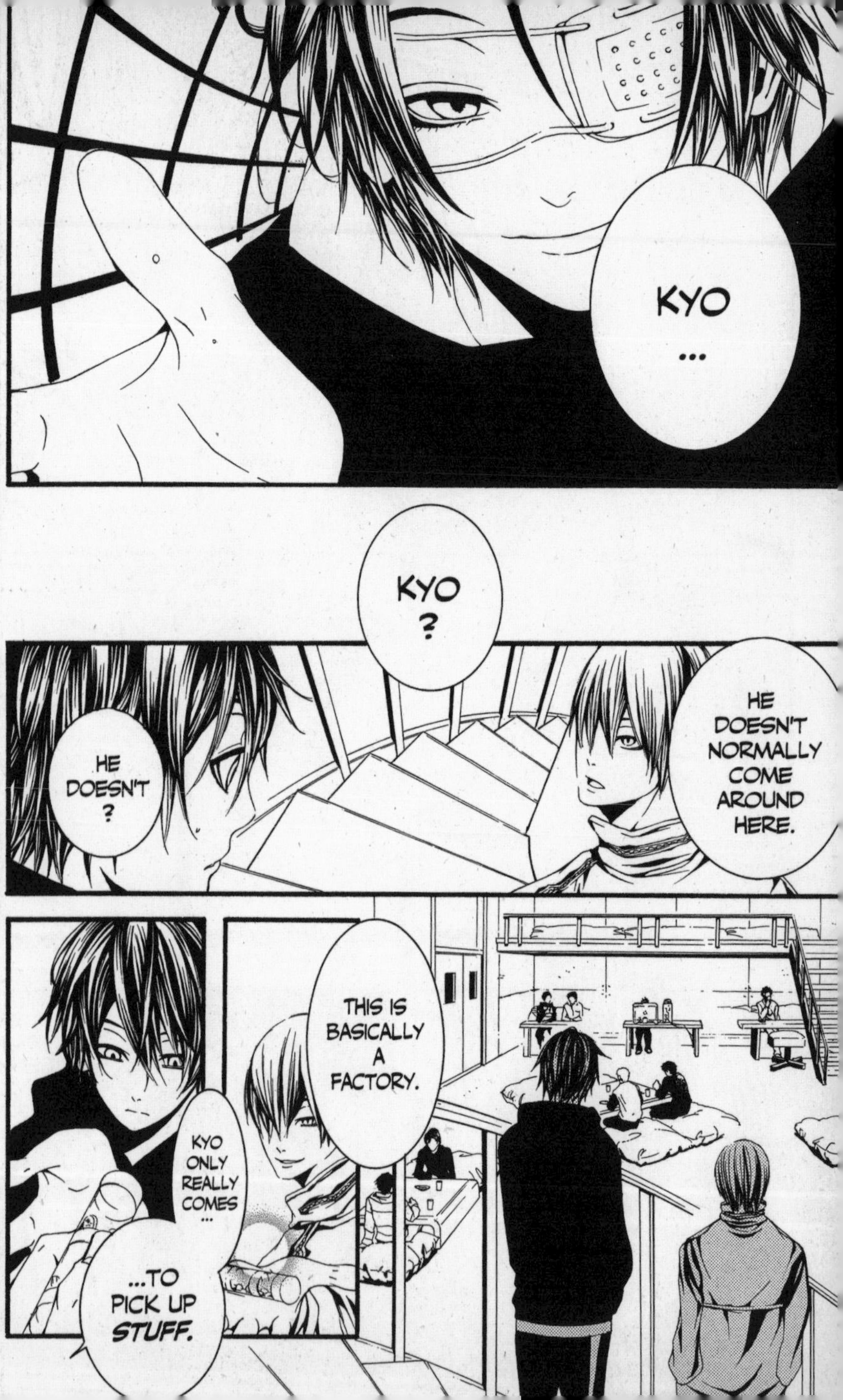
KYO ...
KYO ?
HE DOESN'T NORMALLY COME AROUND HERE.
HE DOESN'T ?
THIS IS BASICALLY A FACTORY.
KYO ONLY REALLY COMES ...
...TO PICK UP *STUFF.*

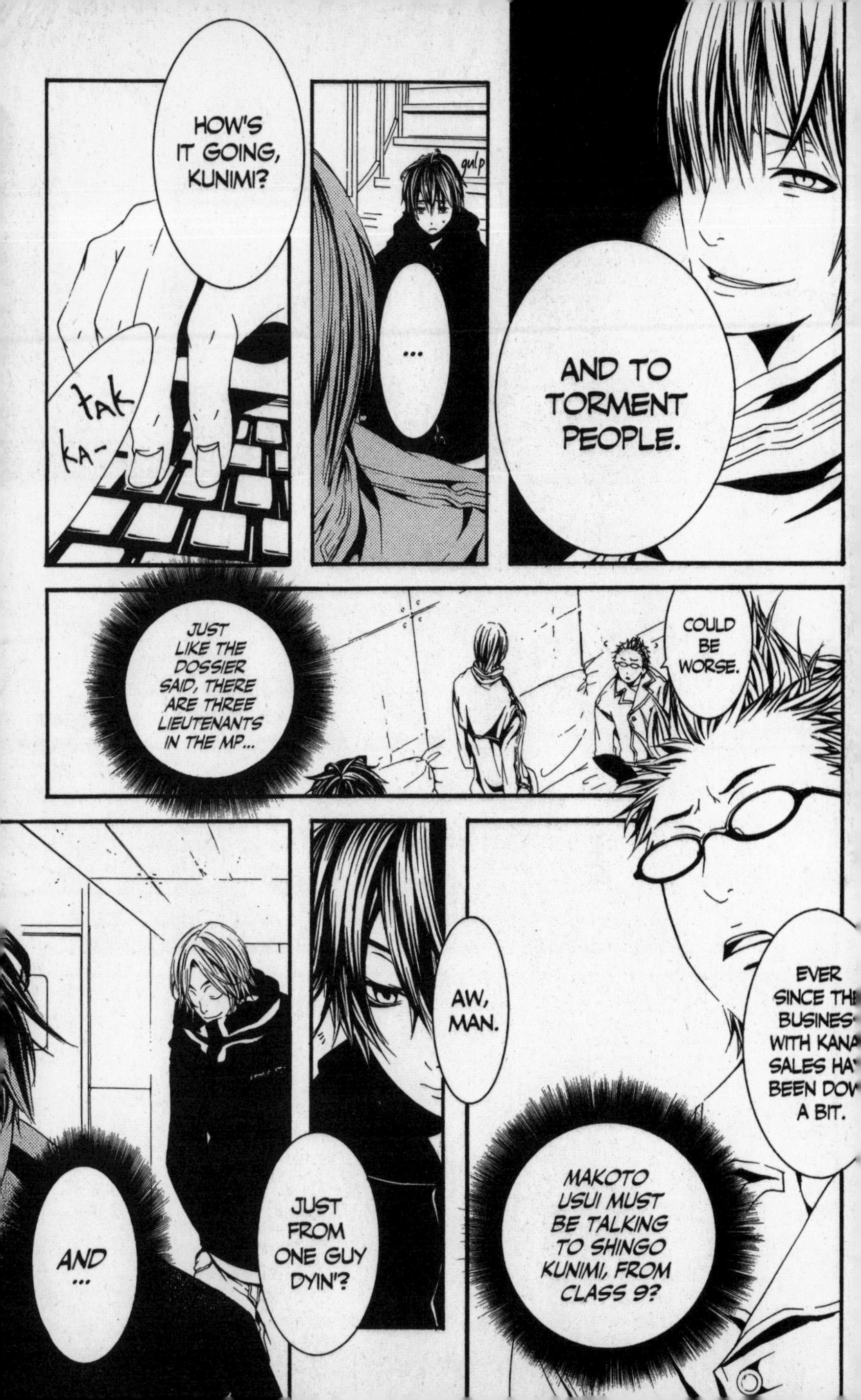
AND TO TORMENT PEOPLE.
gulp
...
HOW'S IT GOING, KUNIMI?
tak ka-
COULD BE WORSE.
JUST LIKE THE DOSSIER SAID, THERE ARE THREE LIEUTENANTS IN THE MP...
EVER SINCE TH BUSINES WITH KANA SALES HA BEEN DOW A BIT.
MAKOTO USUI MUST BE TALKING TO SHINGO KUNIMI, FROM CLASS 9?
AW, MAN.
JUST FROM ONE GUY DYIN'?
AND ...

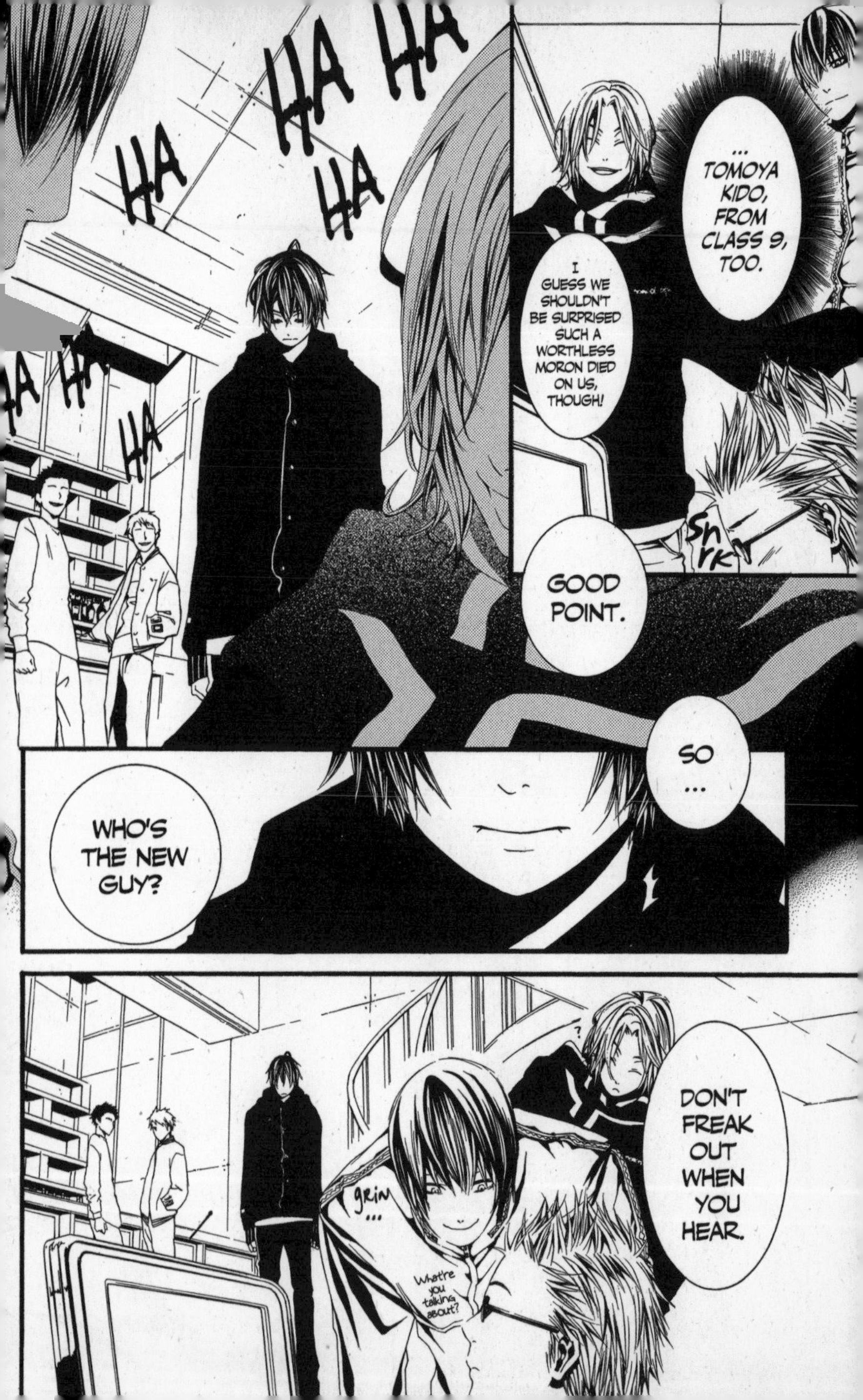

... TOMOYA KIDO, FROM CLASS 9, TOO.
I GUESS WE SHOULDN'T BE SURPRISED SUCH A WORTHLESS MORON DIED ON US, THOUGH!
SHRK
HA HA HA HA
HA
HA HA
HA
GOOD POINT.
SO ...
WHO'S THE NEW GUY?
DON'T FREAK OUT WHEN YOU HEAR.
GRIN ...
What're you talking about?

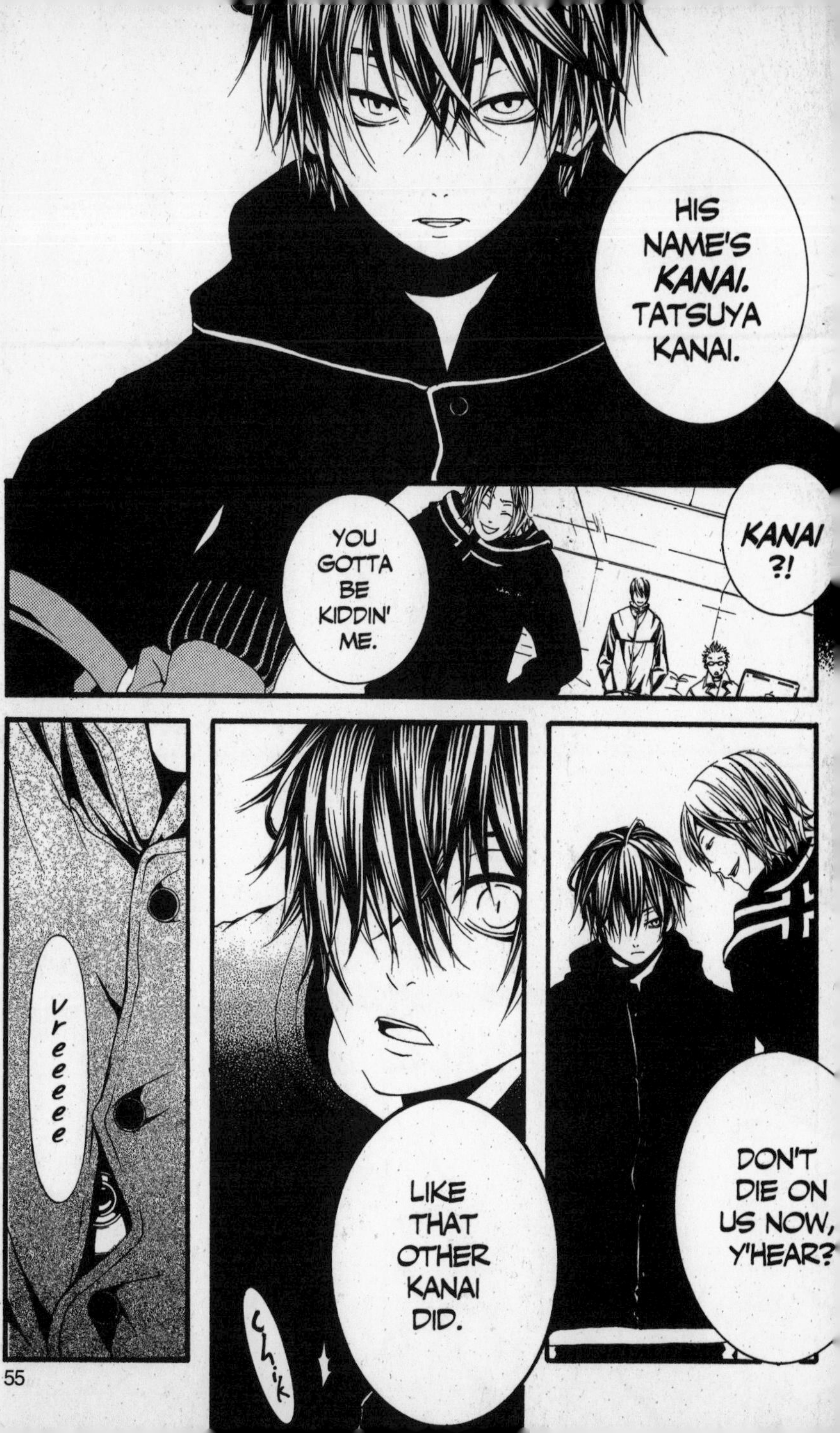
HIS NAME'S *KANAI.* TATSUYA KANAI.
KANAI ?!
YOU GOTTA BE KIDDIN' ME.
DON'T DIE ON US NOW, Y'HEAR?
LIKE THAT OTHER KANAI DID.
Chik
Vreeeeee

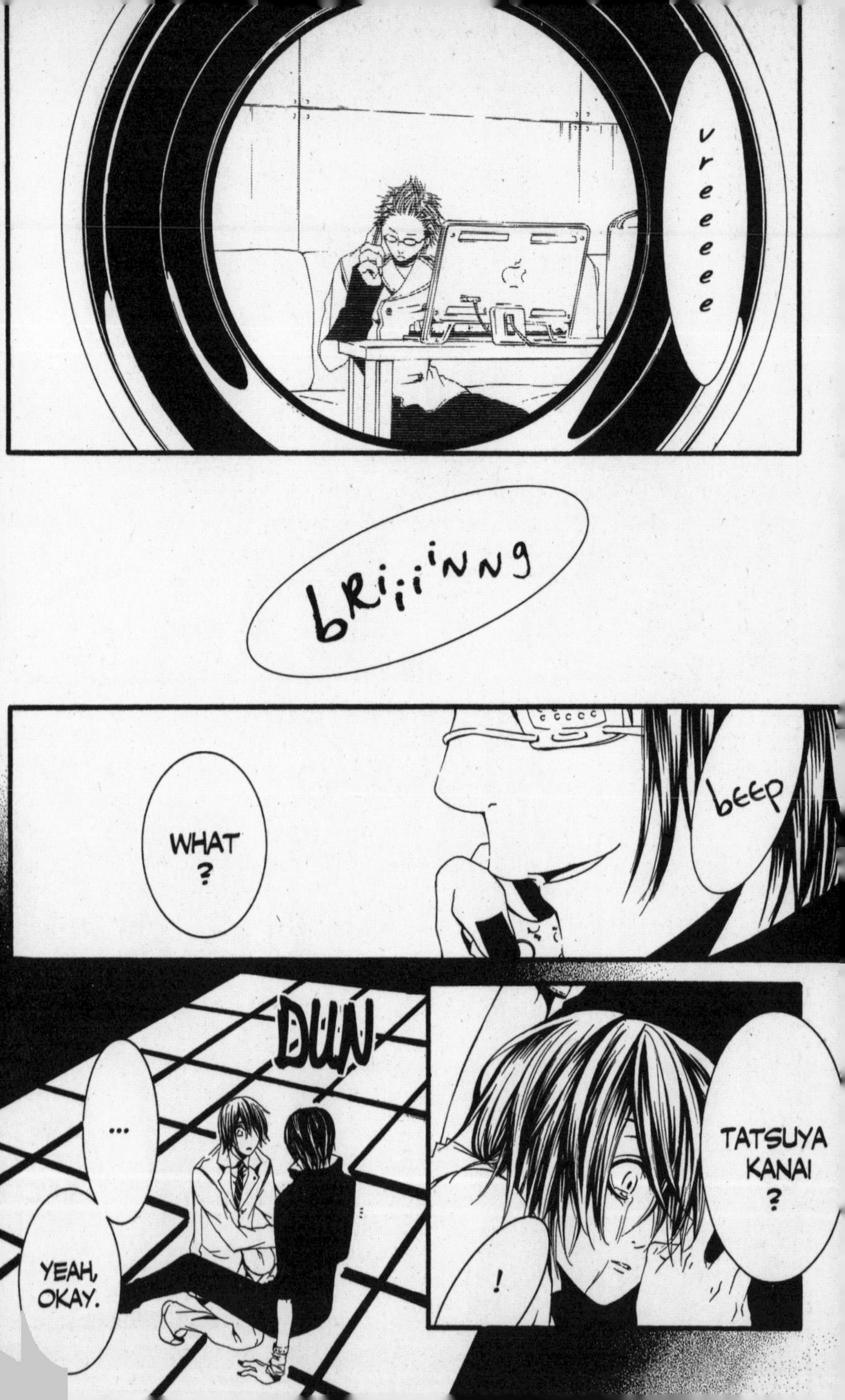
vreeeeee
bRiiiinng
beep
WHAT?
TATSUYA KANAI?
!
DUN
...
YEAH, OKAY.

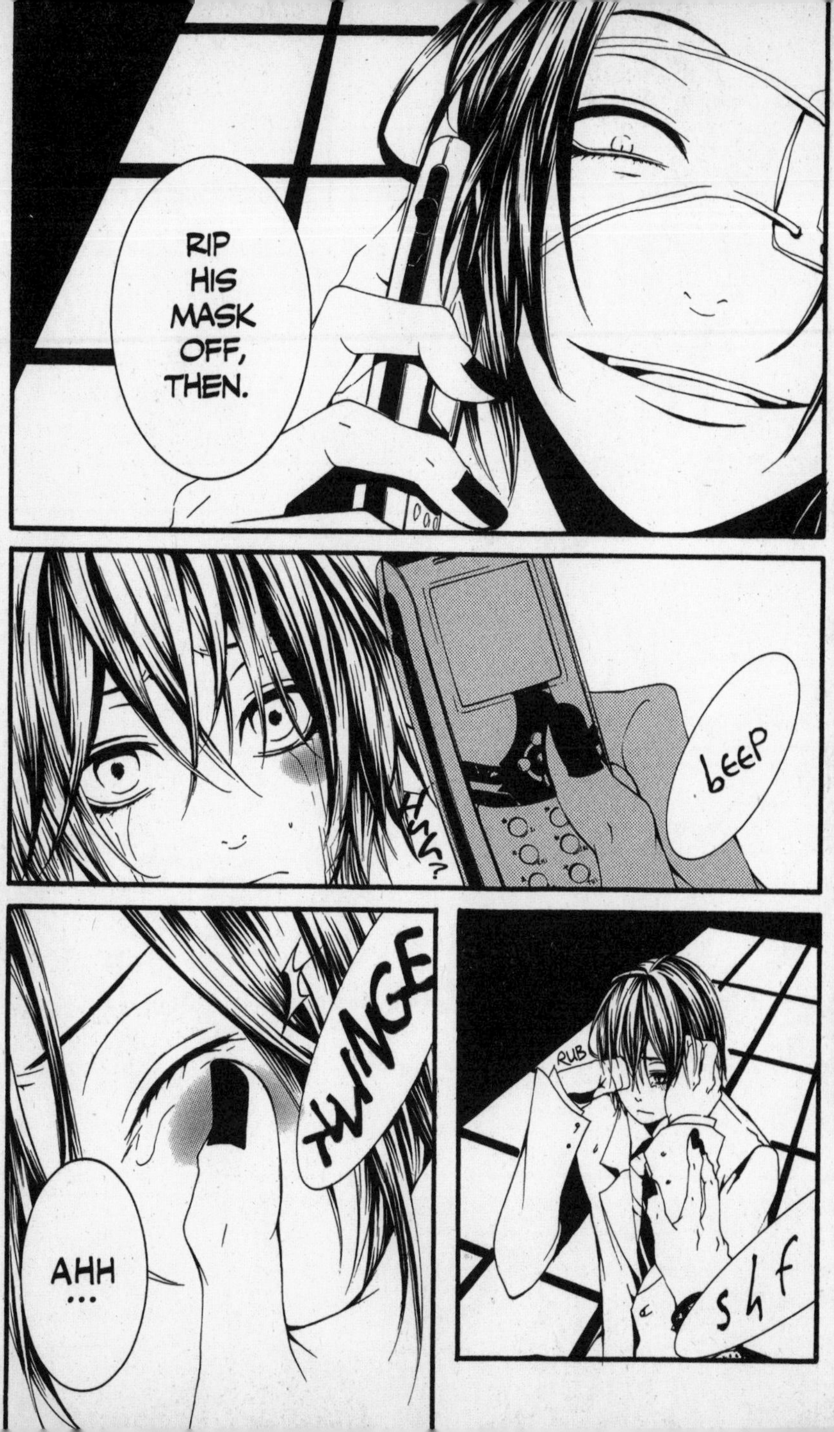
RIP HIS MASK OFF, THEN.
beep
Huh?
RUB
shf
TWINGE
AHH...

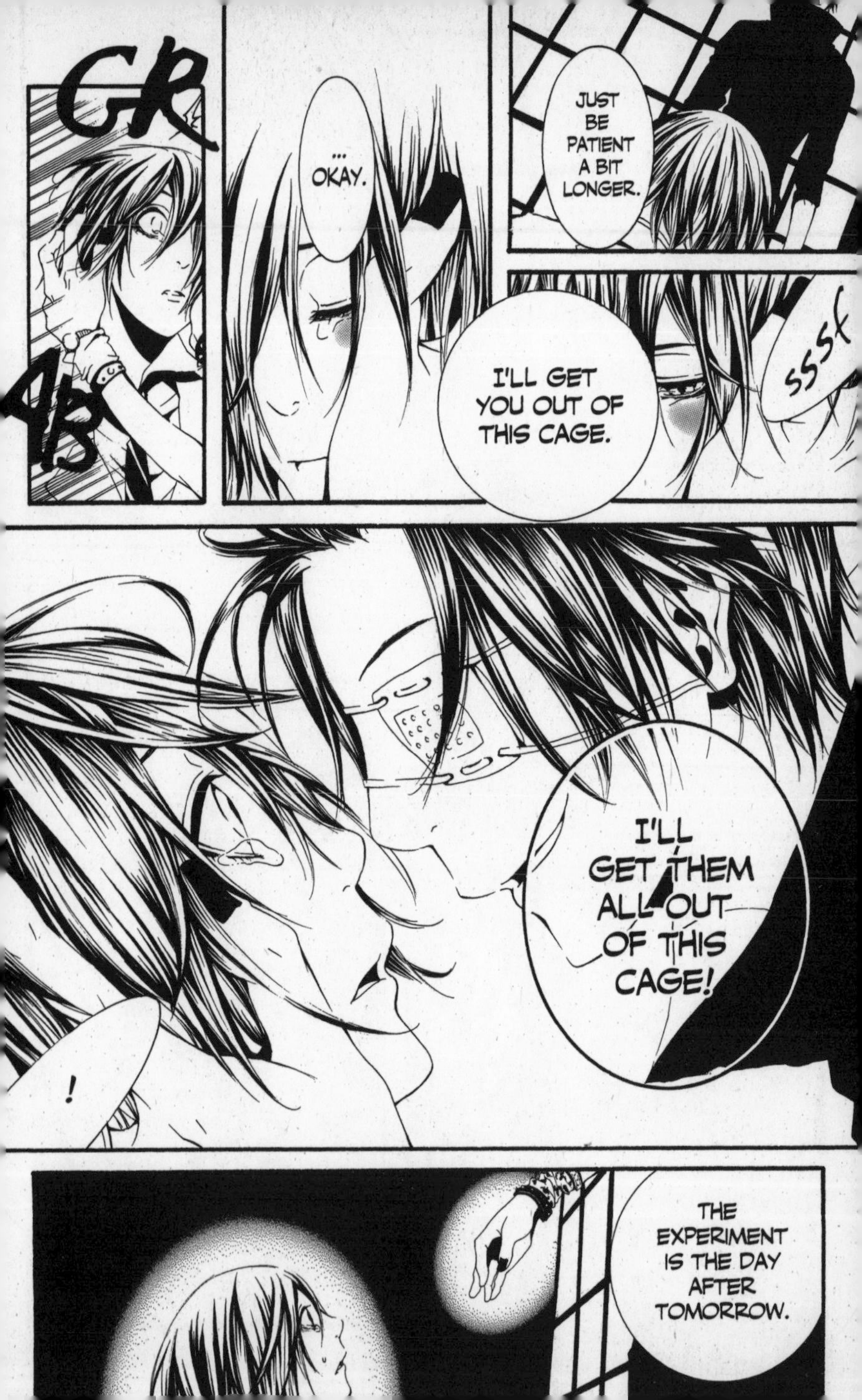
JUST BE PATIENT A BIT LONGER.
I'LL GET YOU OUT OF THIS CAGE.
SSSF
... OKAY.
GR
AB
I'LL GET THEM ALL OUT OF THIS CAGE!
!
THE EXPERIMENT IS THE DAY AFTER TOMORROW.

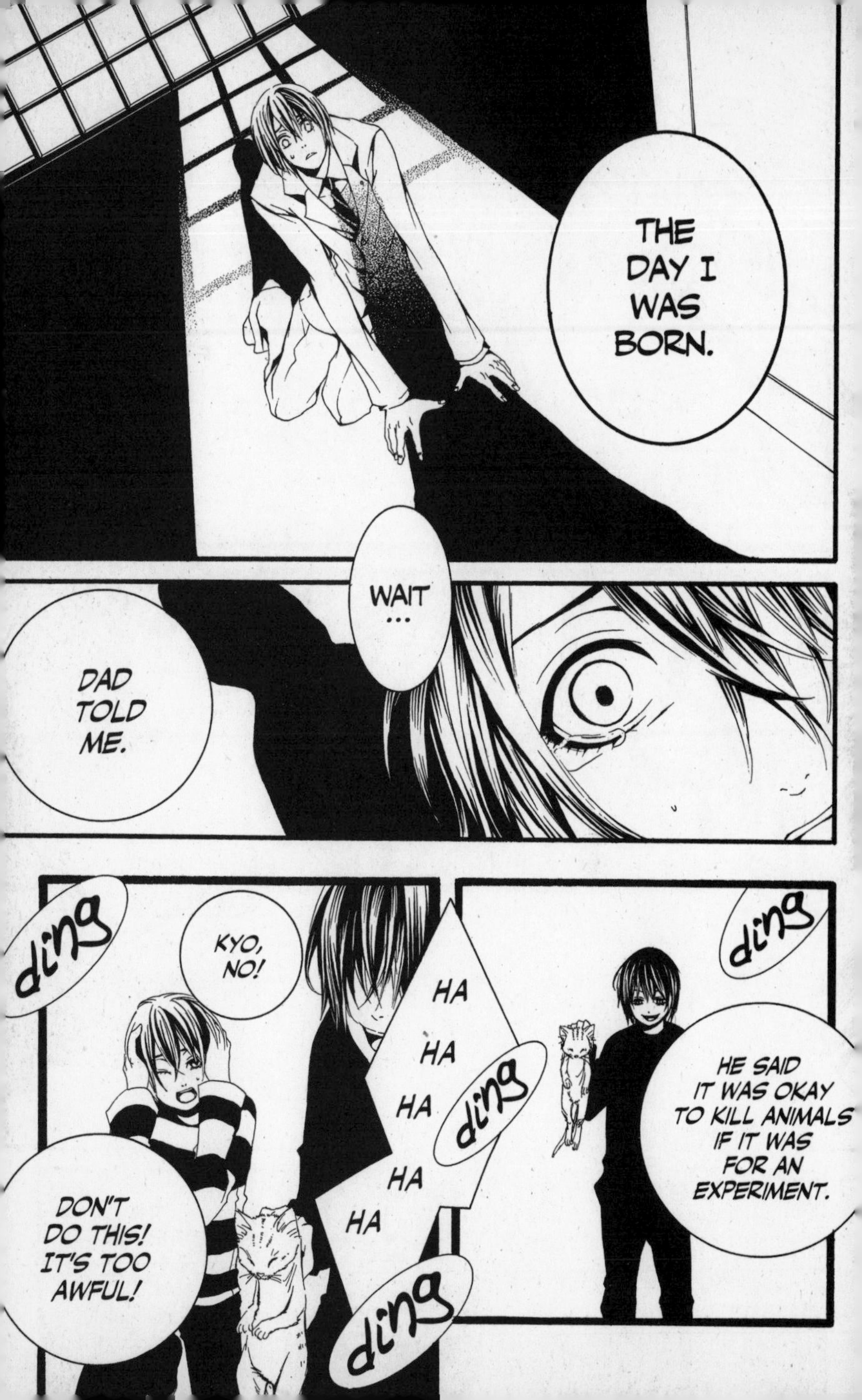
THE DAY I WAS BORN.
WAIT...
DAD TOLD ME.
ding
HE SAID IT WAS OKAY TO KILL ANIMALS IF IT WAS FOR AN EXPERIMENT.
ding
KYO, NO!
HA HA HA HA HA
ding
ding
DON'T DO THIS! IT'S TOO AWFUL!

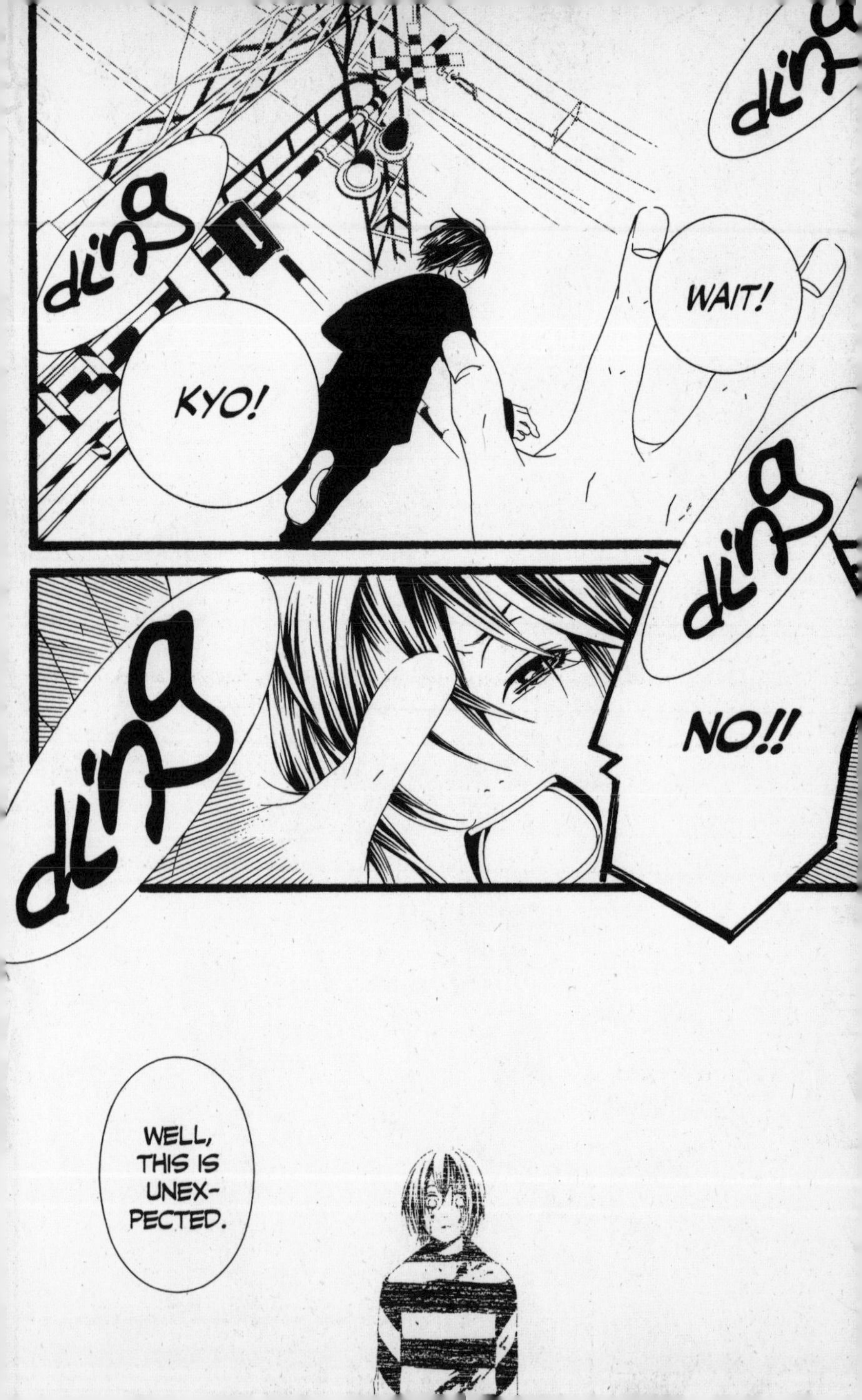
ding
WAIT!
ding
KYO!
ding
NO!!
ding
WELL, THIS IS UNEXPECTED.

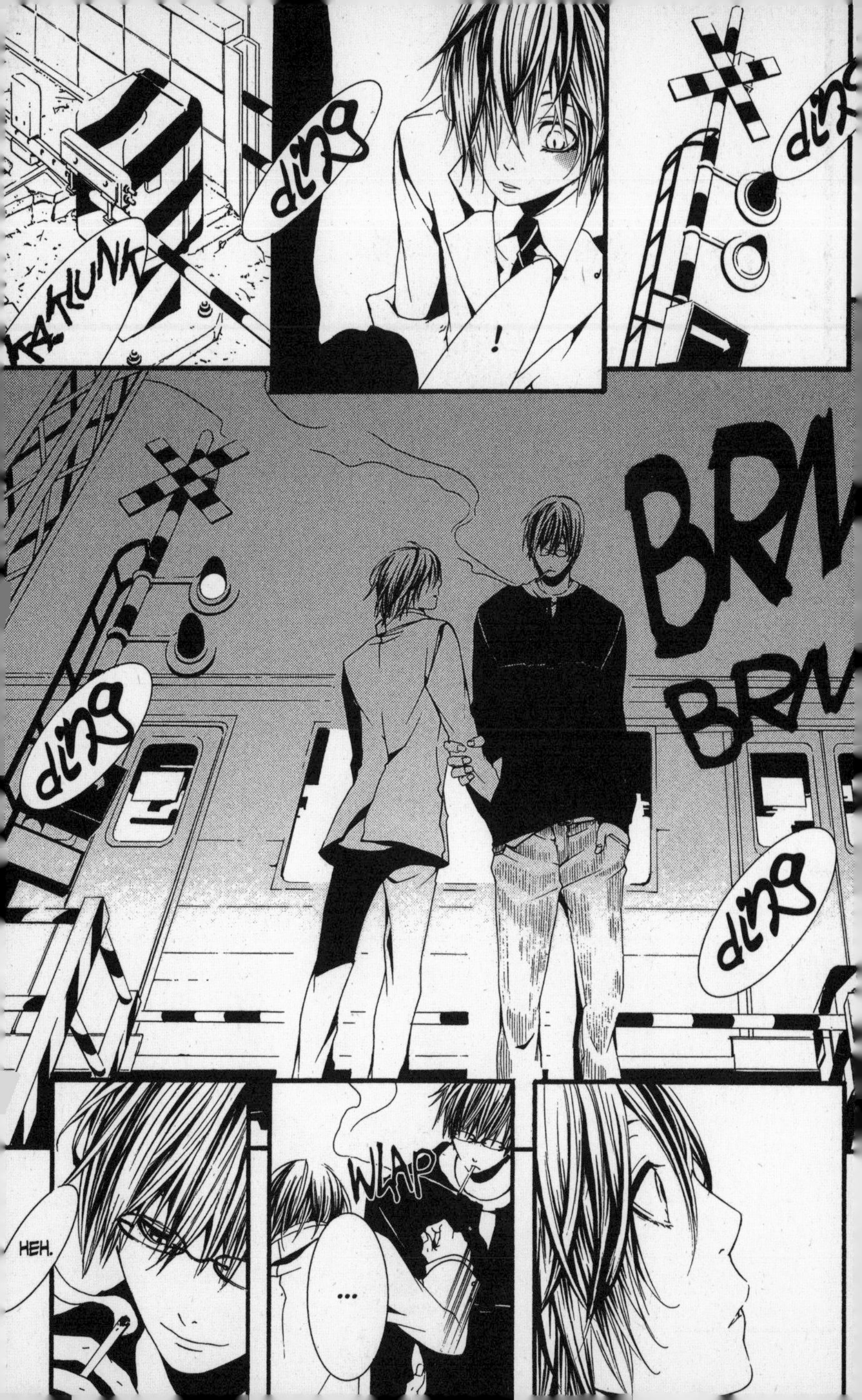
ding
ding
!
KA-KLUNK
BRM
BRM
ding
ding
WLAP
...
HEH.

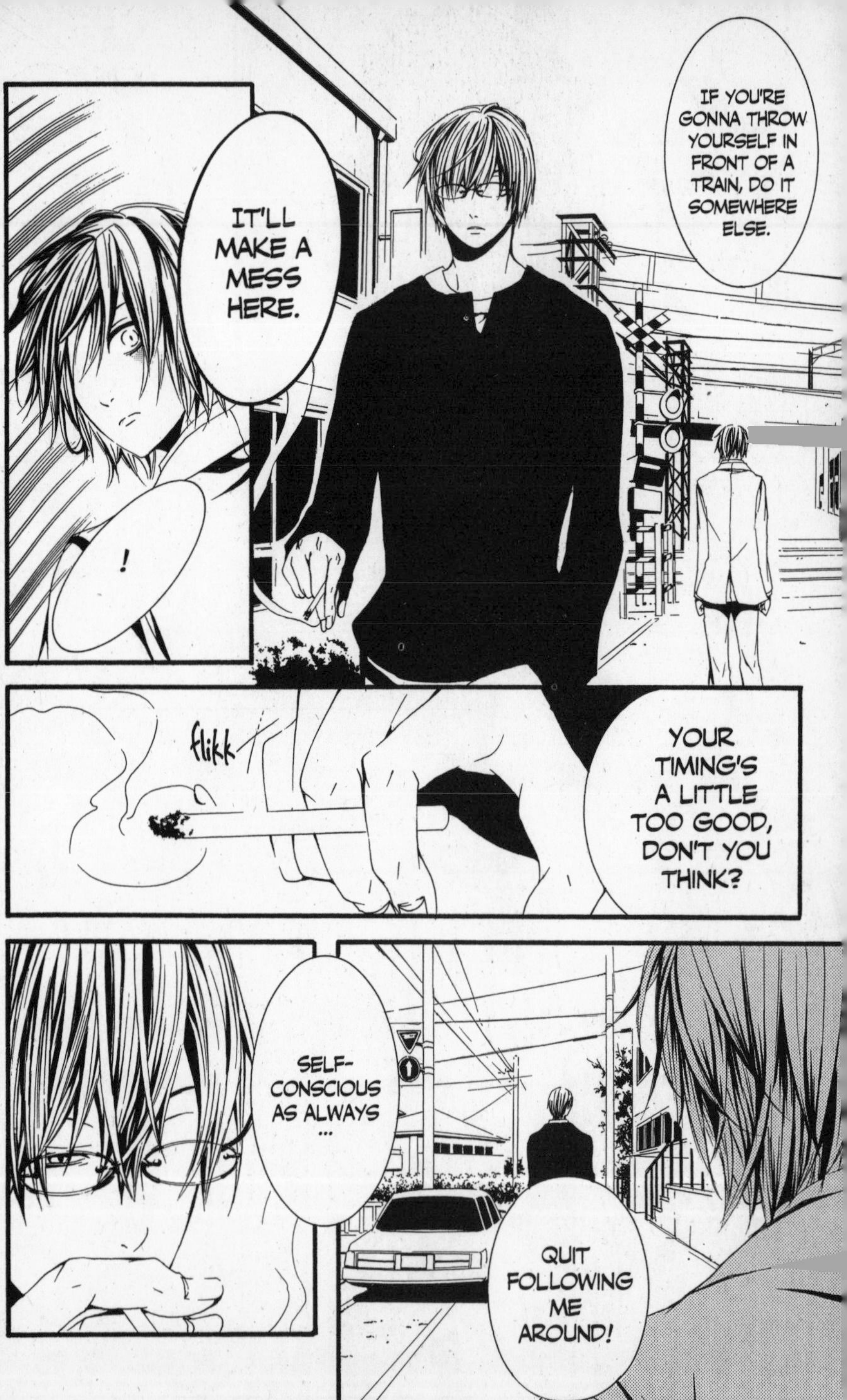
IF YOU'RE GONNA THROW YOURSELF IN FRONT OF A TRAIN, DO IT SOMEWHERE ELSE.
IT'LL MAKE A MESS HERE.
!
YOUR TIMING'S A LITTLE TOO GOOD, DON'T YOU THINK?
flikk
QUIT FOLLOWING ME AROUND!
SELF-CONSCIOUS AS ALWAYS...

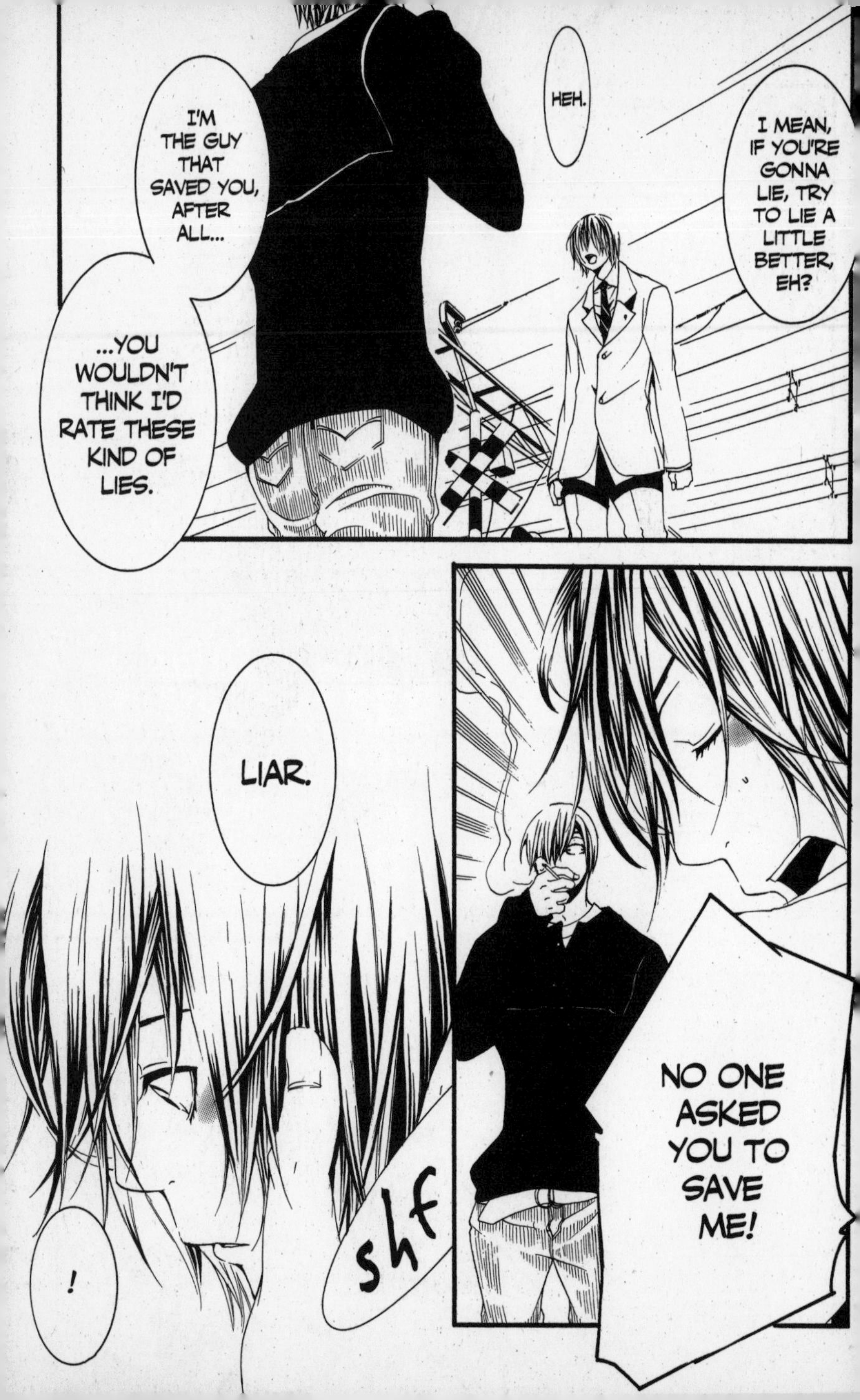
I MEAN, IF YOU'RE GONNA LIE, TRY TO LIE A LITTLE BETTER, EH?
HEH.
I'M THE GUY THAT SAVED YOU, AFTER ALL...
...YOU WOULDN'T THINK I'D RATE THESE KIND OF LIES.
NO ONE ASKED YOU TO SAVE ME!
LIAR.
shf
!

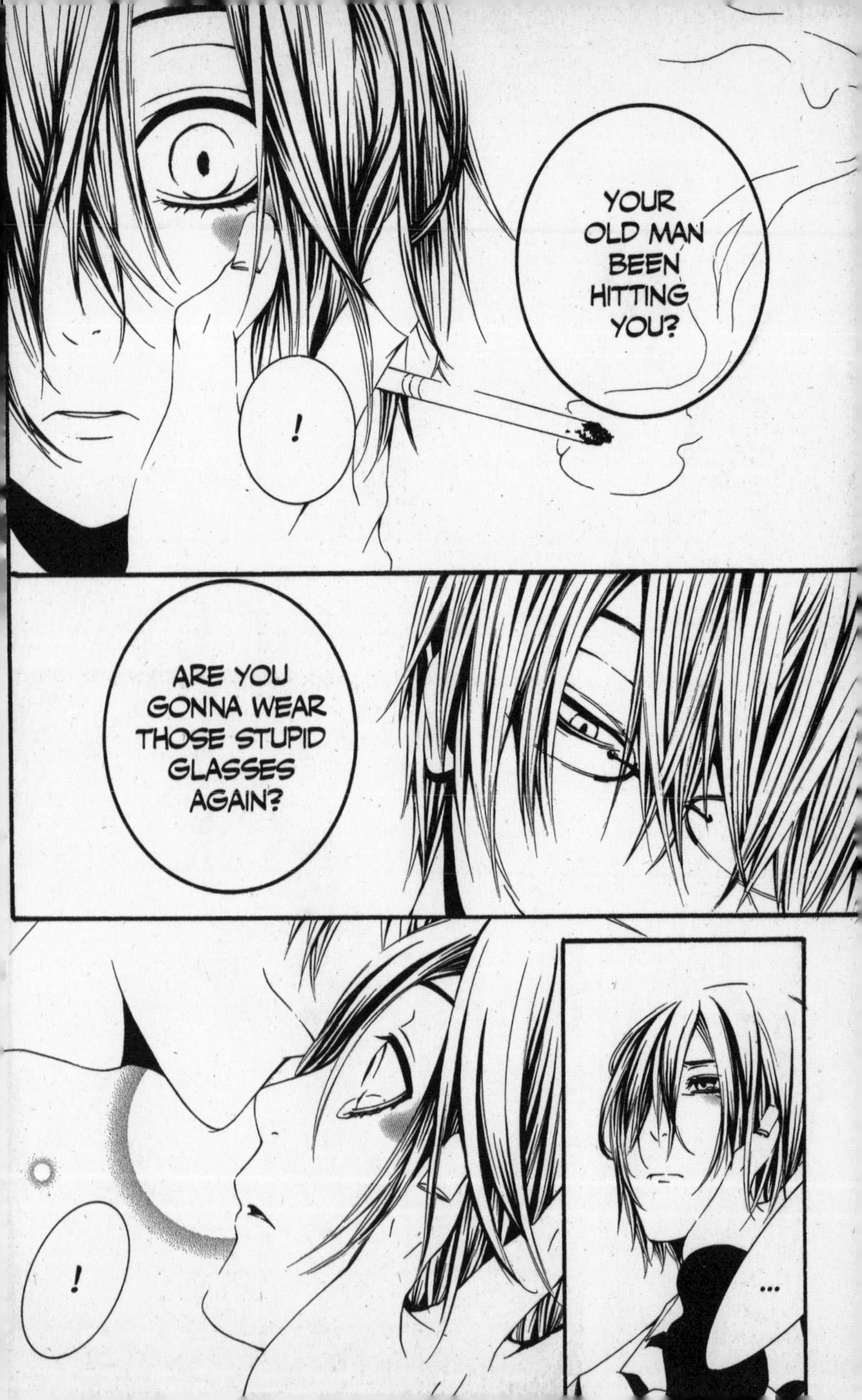
YOUR OLD MAN BEEN HITTING YOU?
!
ARE YOU GONNA WEAR THOSE STUPID GLASSES AGAIN?
...
!

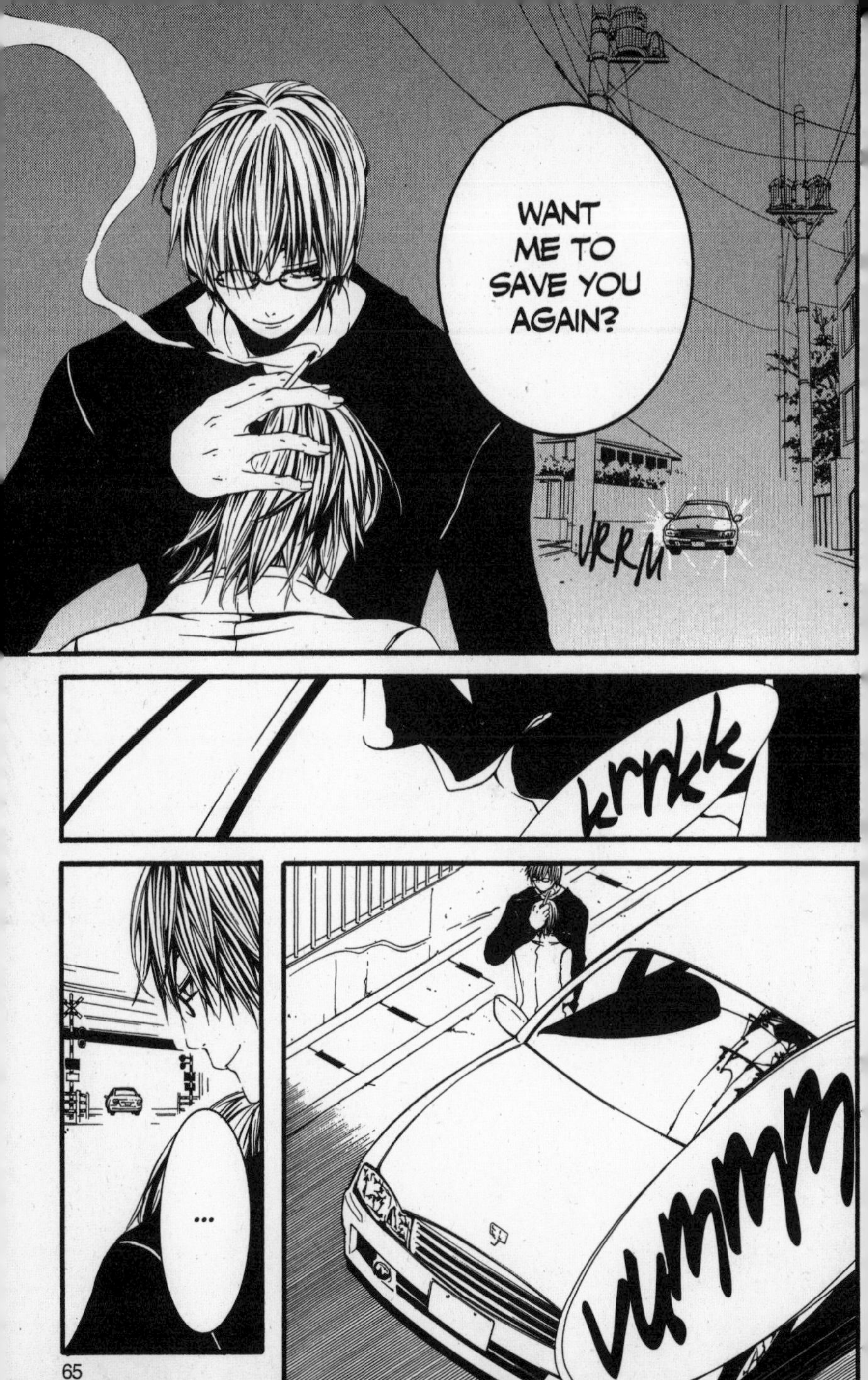
WANT ME TO SAVE YOU AGAIN?
VRRM
krrkk
vummm
...

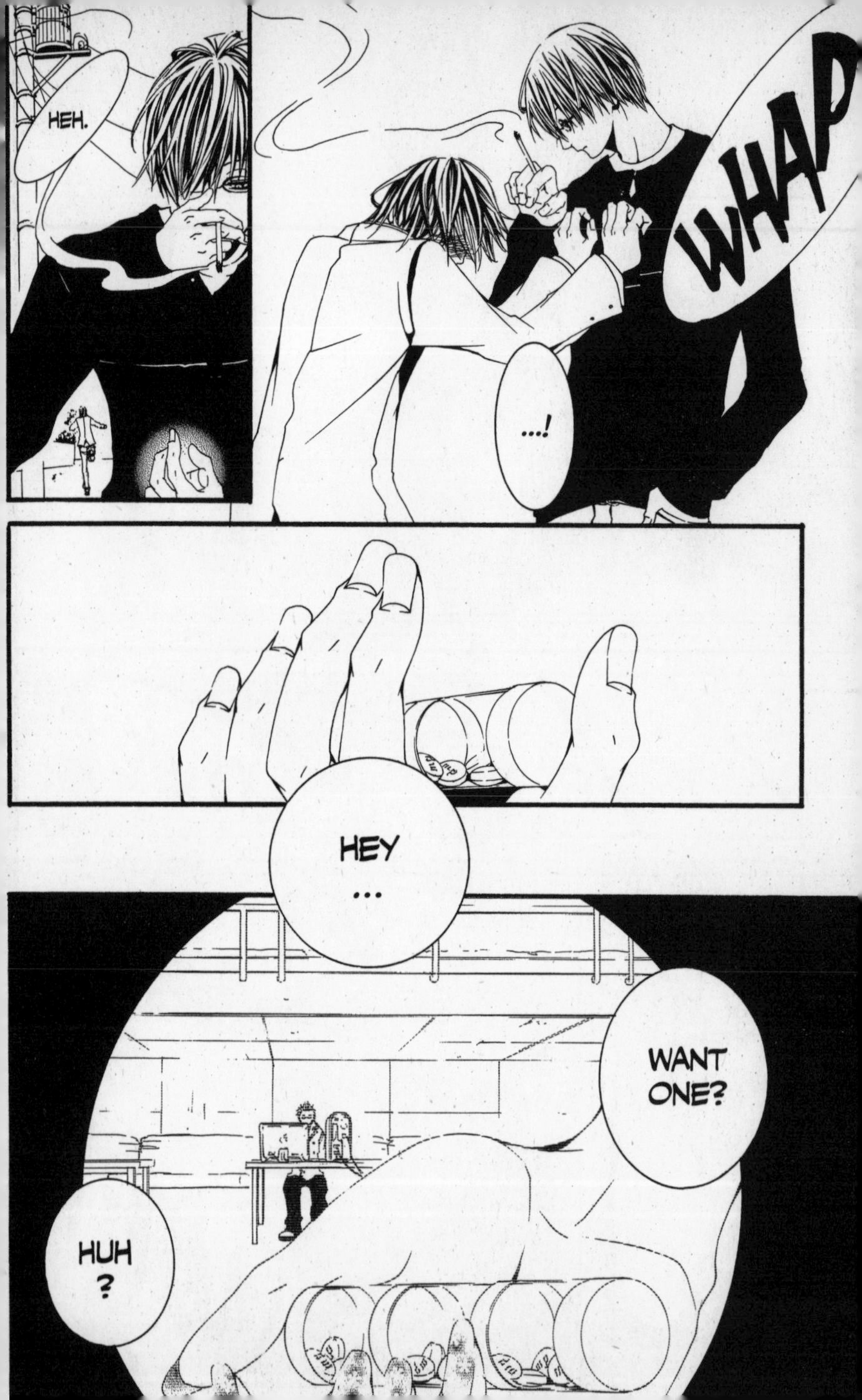
WHAP
...!
HEH.
HEY ...
WANT ONE?
HUH?

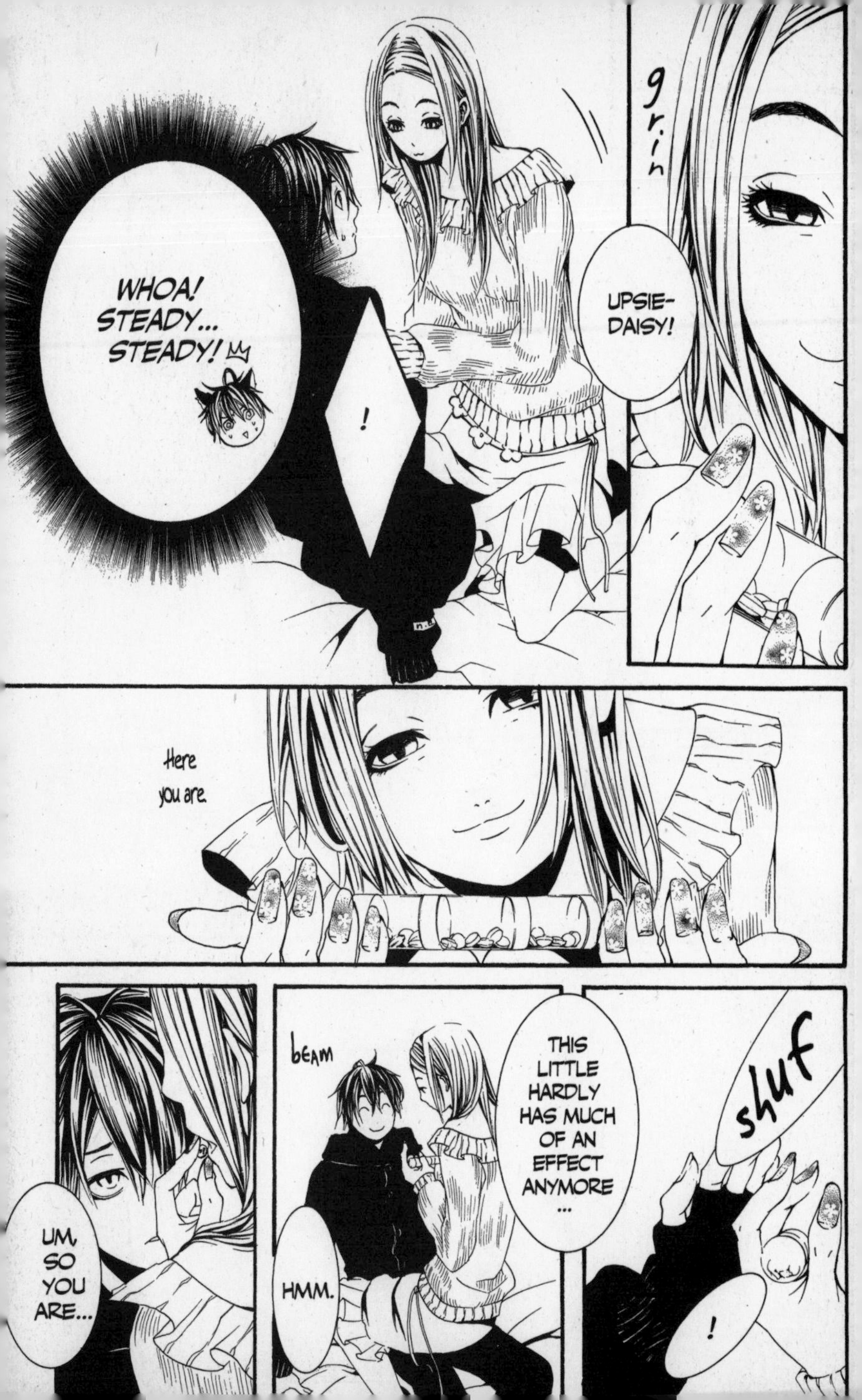
grin
UPSIE-DAISY!
!
WHOA! STEADY... STEADY!
Here you are.
shuf
!
THIS LITTLE HARDLY HAS MUCH OF AN EFFECT ANYMORE...
beam
HMM.
UM, SO YOU ARE...

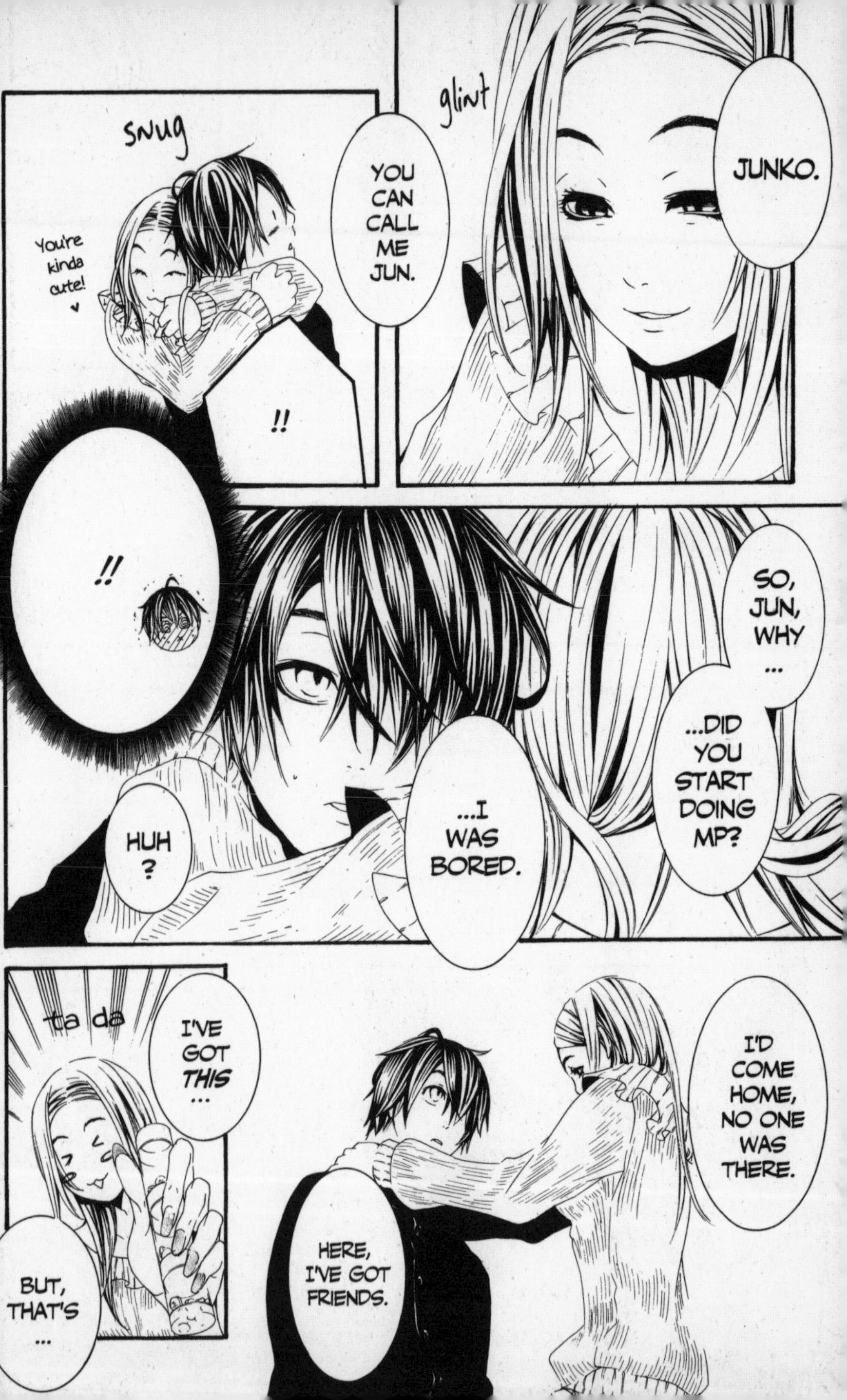

glint
JUNKO.
YOU CAN CALL ME JUN.
snug
You're kinda cute! ♥
!!
SO, JUN, WHY...
...DID YOU START DOING MP?
...I WAS BORED.
HUH?
!!
I'D COME HOME, NO ONE WAS THERE.
HERE, I'VE GOT FRIENDS.
ta da
I'VE GOT *THIS*...
BUT, THAT'S...

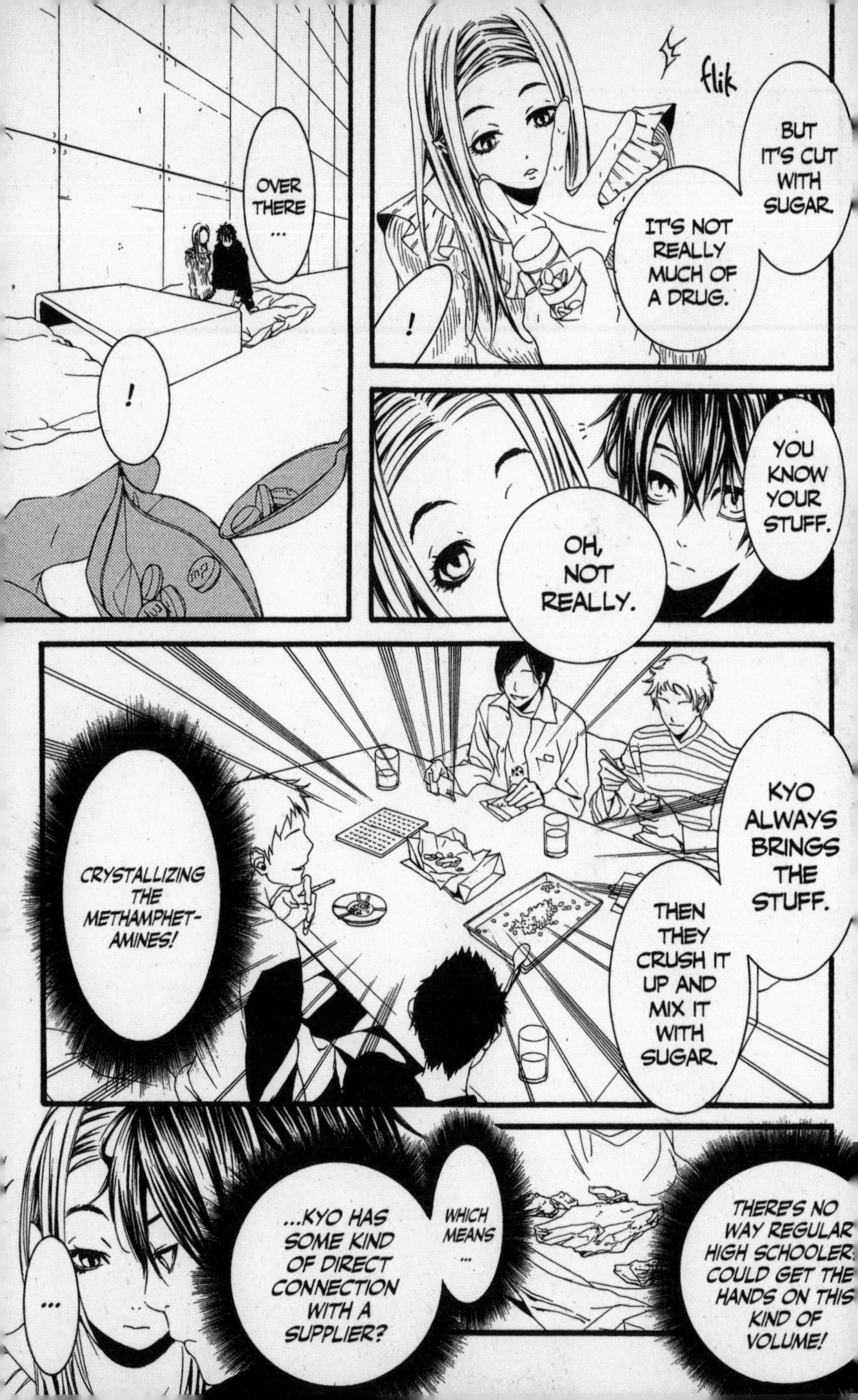
flik
BUT IT'S CUT WITH SUGAR.
IT'S NOT REALLY MUCH OF A DRUG.
!
YOU KNOW YOUR STUFF.
OH, NOT REALLY.
OVER THERE ...
!
KYO ALWAYS BRINGS THE STUFF.
THEN THEY CRUSH IT UP AND MIX IT WITH SUGAR.
CRYSTALLIZING THE METHAMPHET-AMINES!
THERE'S NO WAY REGULAR HIGH SCHOOLER COULD GET THE HANDS ON THIS KIND OF VOLUME!
WHICH MEANS ...
...KYO HAS SOME KIND OF DIRECT CONNECTION WITH A SUPPLIER?
...

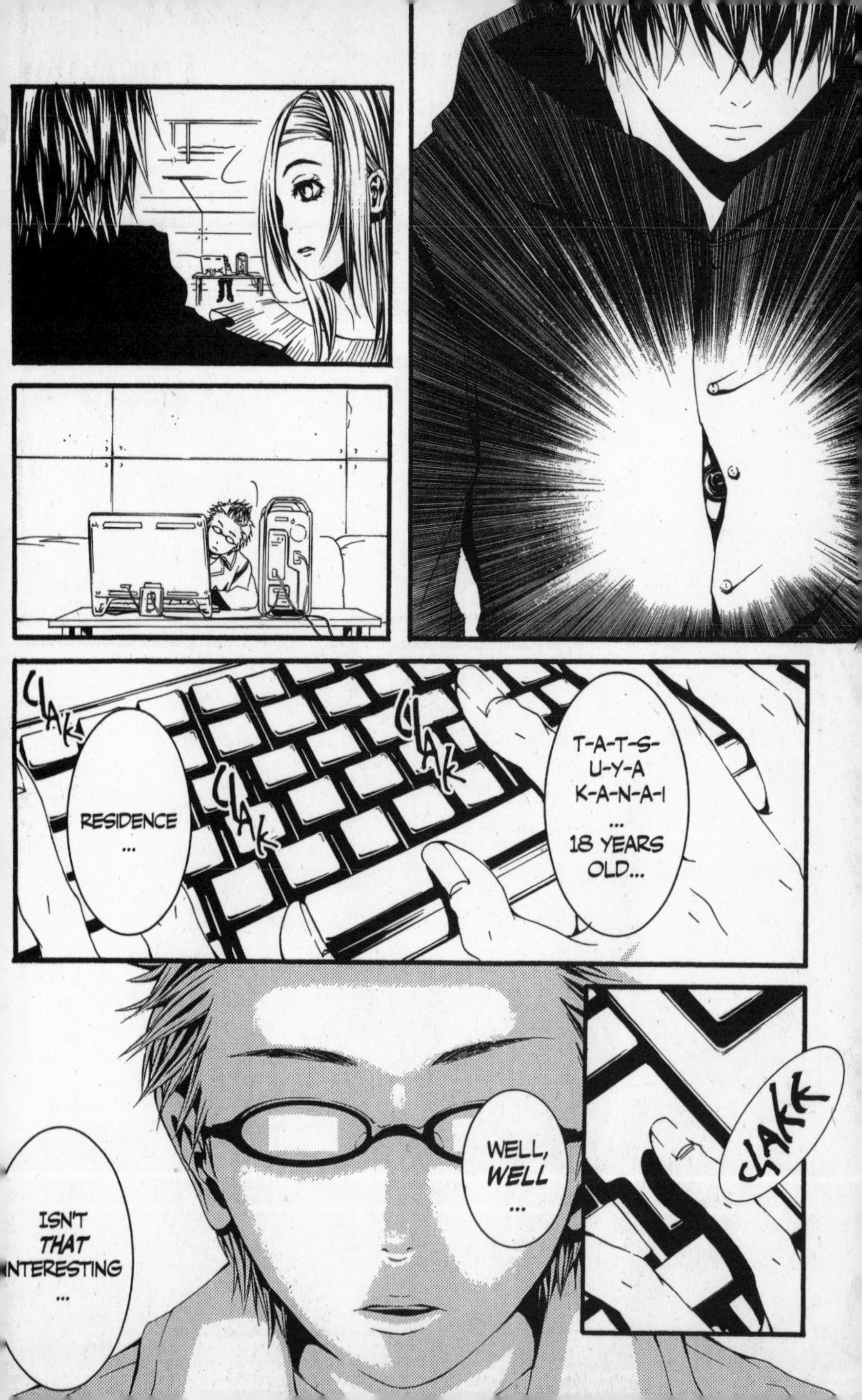
T-A-T-S-U-Y-A K-A-N-A-I ... 18 YEARS OLD...
CLAK
CLAK
CLAK
RESIDENCE ...
CLAKK
WELL, *WELL* ...
ISN'T *THAT* INTERESTING ...

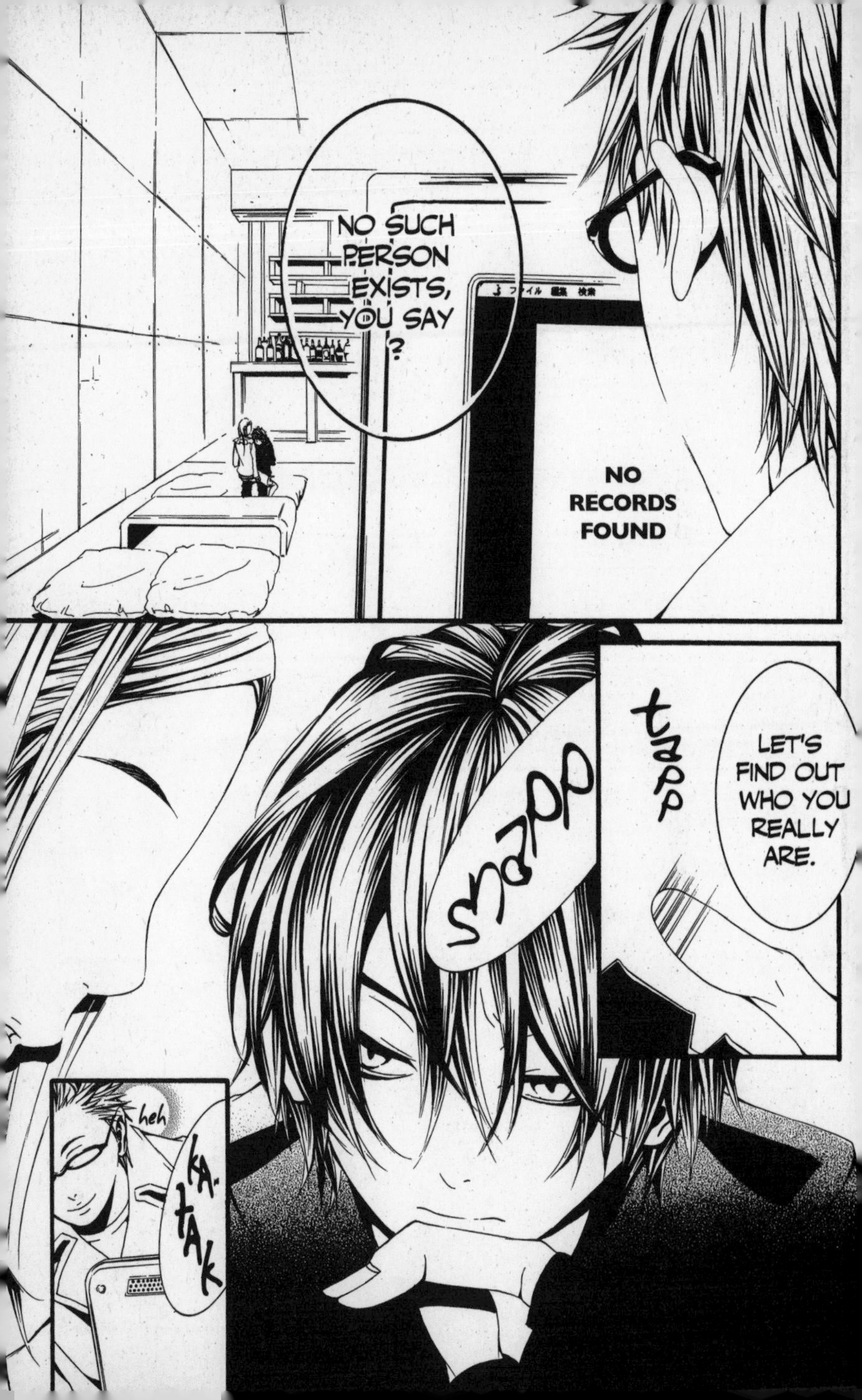
NO SUCH PERSON EXISTS, YOU SAY?
NO RECORDS FOUND
LET'S FIND OUT WHO YOU REALLY ARE.
tapp
snapp
heh
KA-TAK

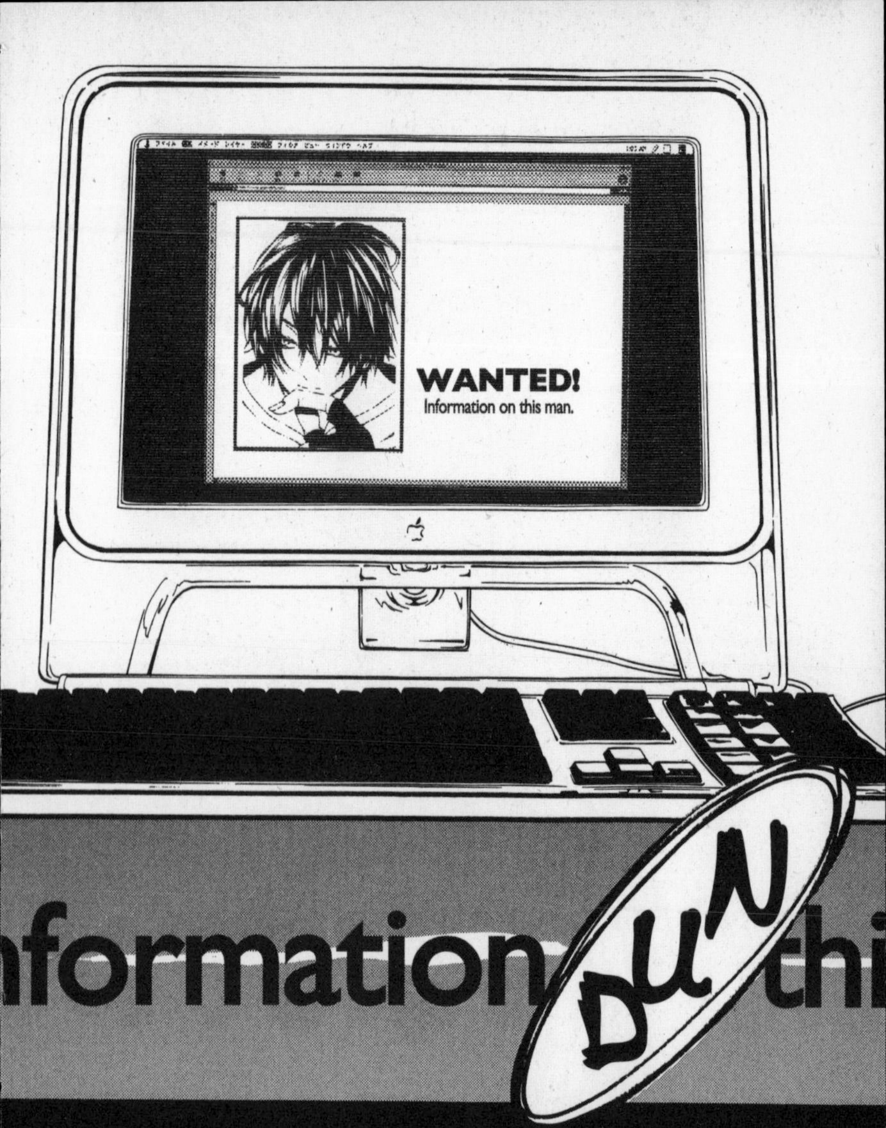
WANTED!
Information on this man.
nformation DUN thi

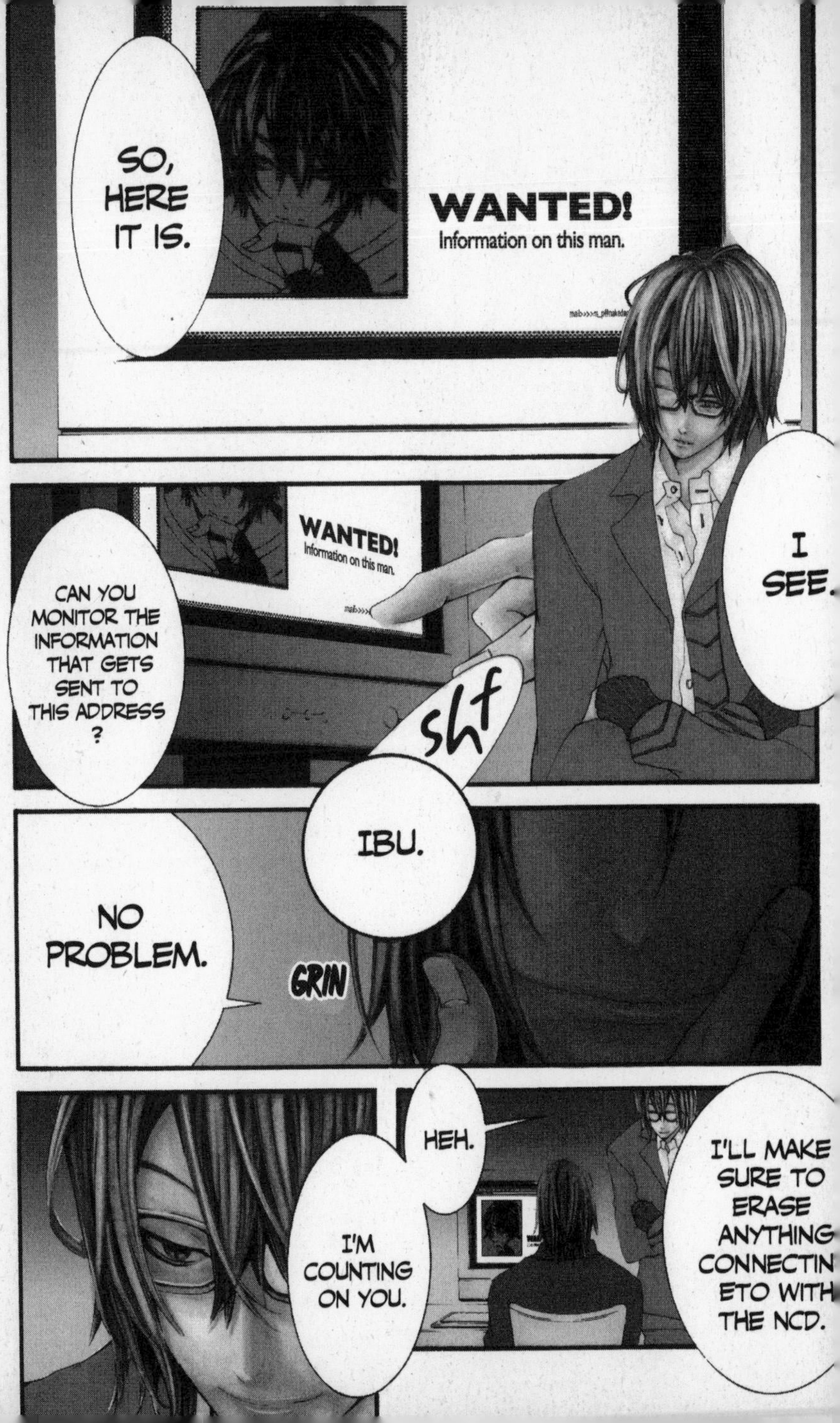
SO, HERE IT IS.
WANTED!
Information on this man.
I SEE.
WANTED!
Information on this man.
CAN YOU MONITOR THE INFORMATION THAT GETS SENT TO THIS ADDRESS ?
shf
IBU.
NO PROBLEM.
GRIN
I'LL MAKE SURE TO ERASE ANYTHING CONNECTIN ETO WITH THE NCD.
HEH.
I'M COUNTING ON YOU.

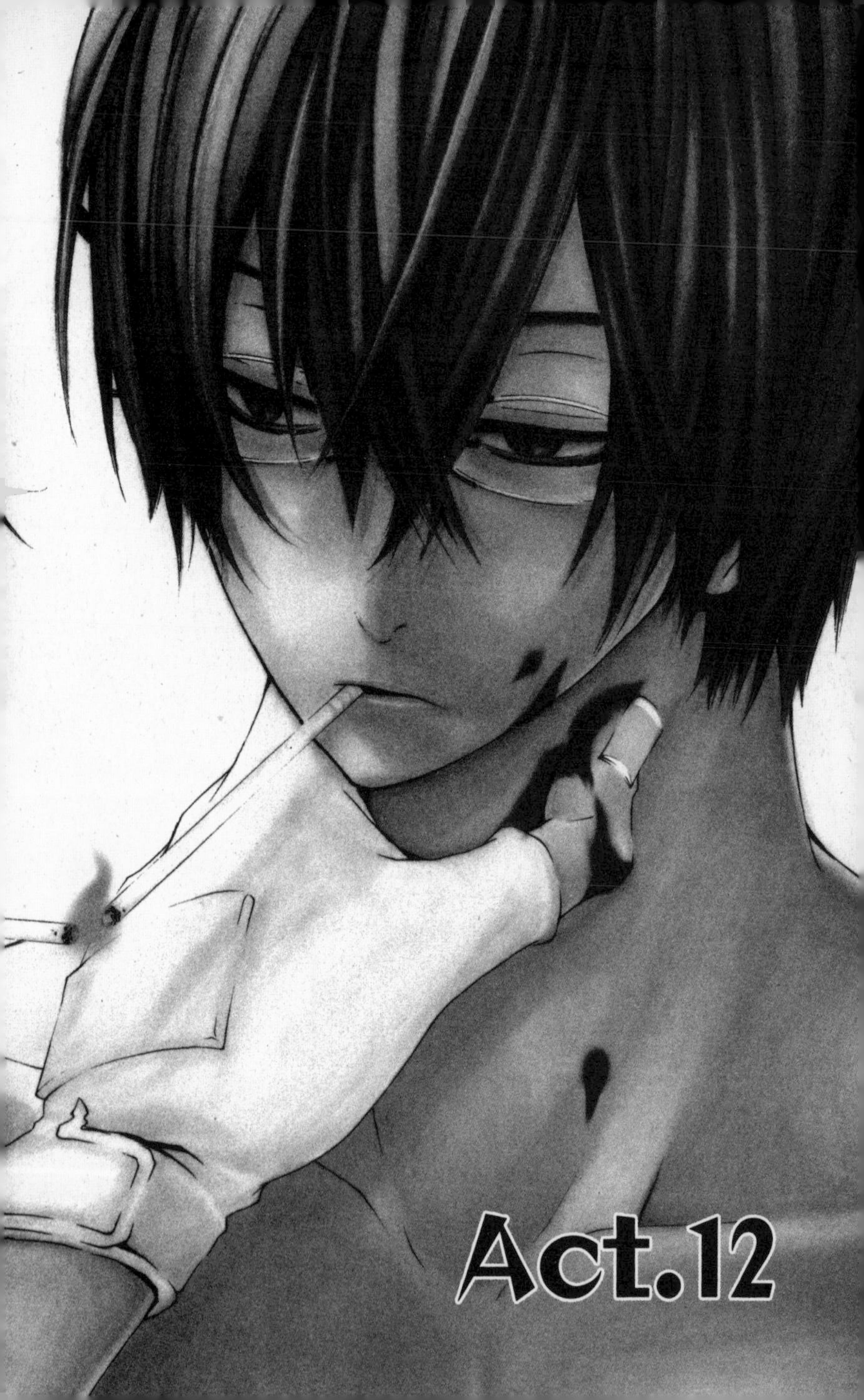
Act.12

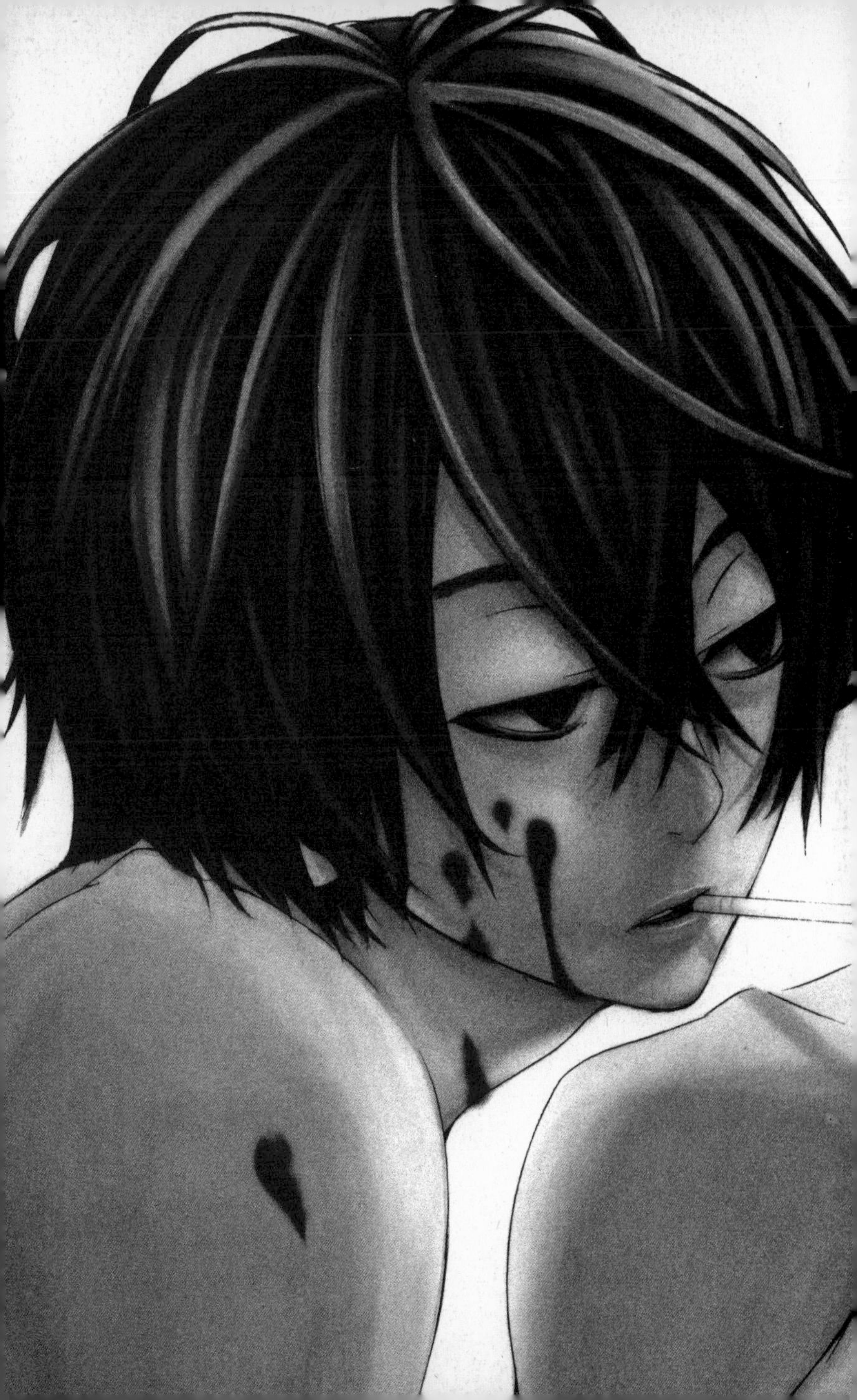

[switch]
スイッチ

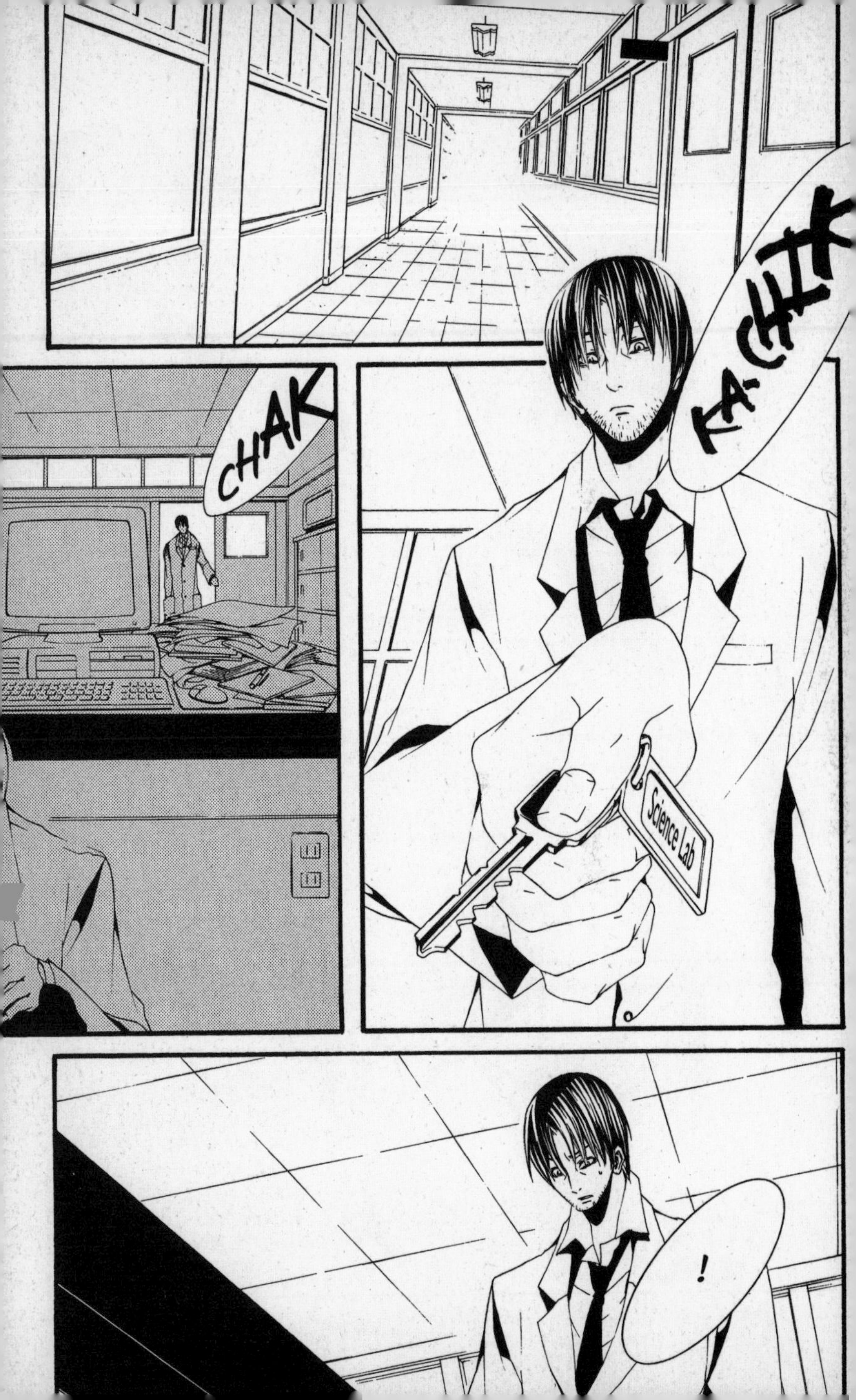
KA-CHIK
Science Lab
CHAK
!

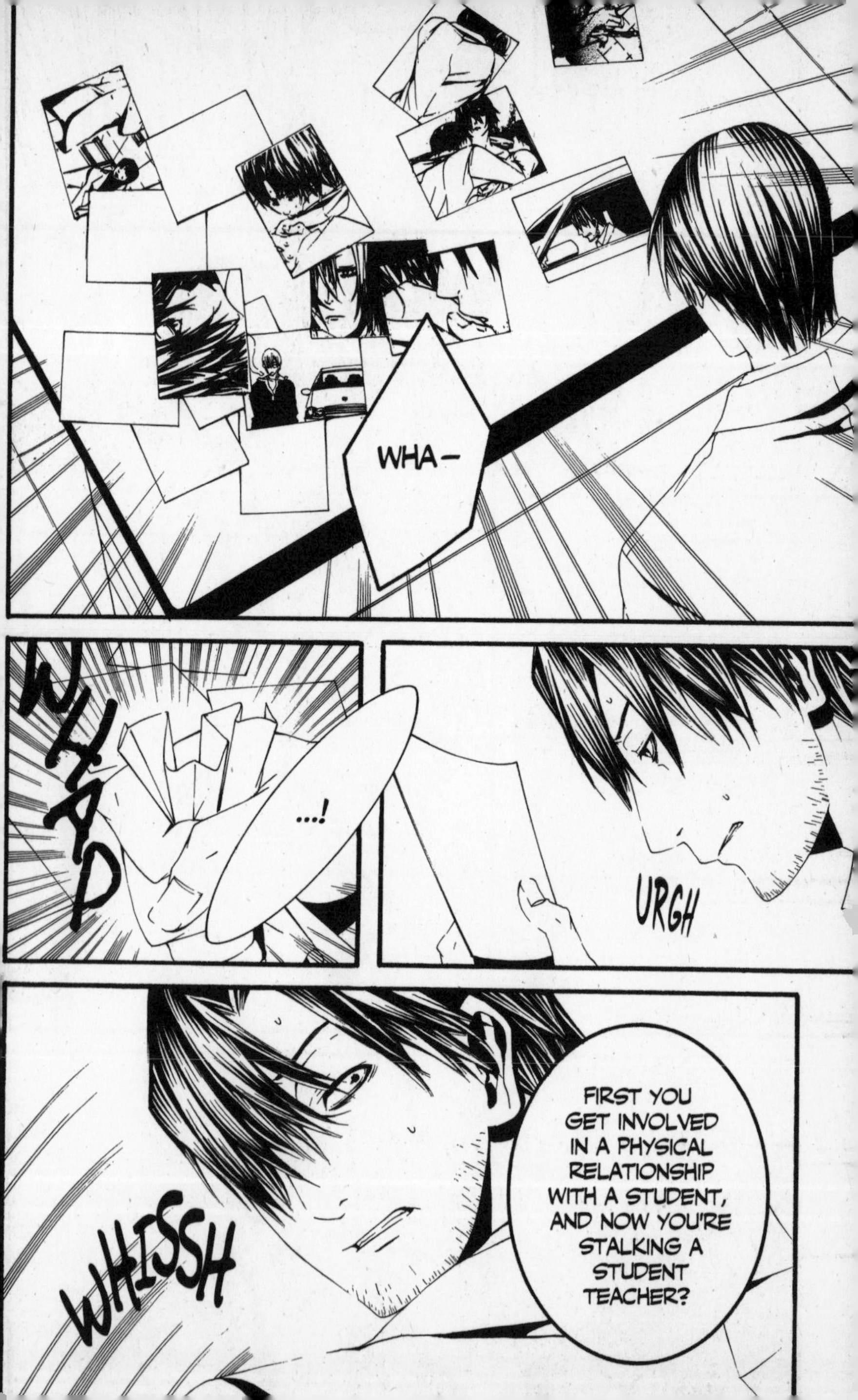
WHA-
URGH
WHAP
...!
FIRST YOU GET INVOLVED IN A PHYSICAL RELATIONSHIP WITH A STUDENT, AND NOW YOU'RE STALKING A STUDENT TEACHER?
WHISSH

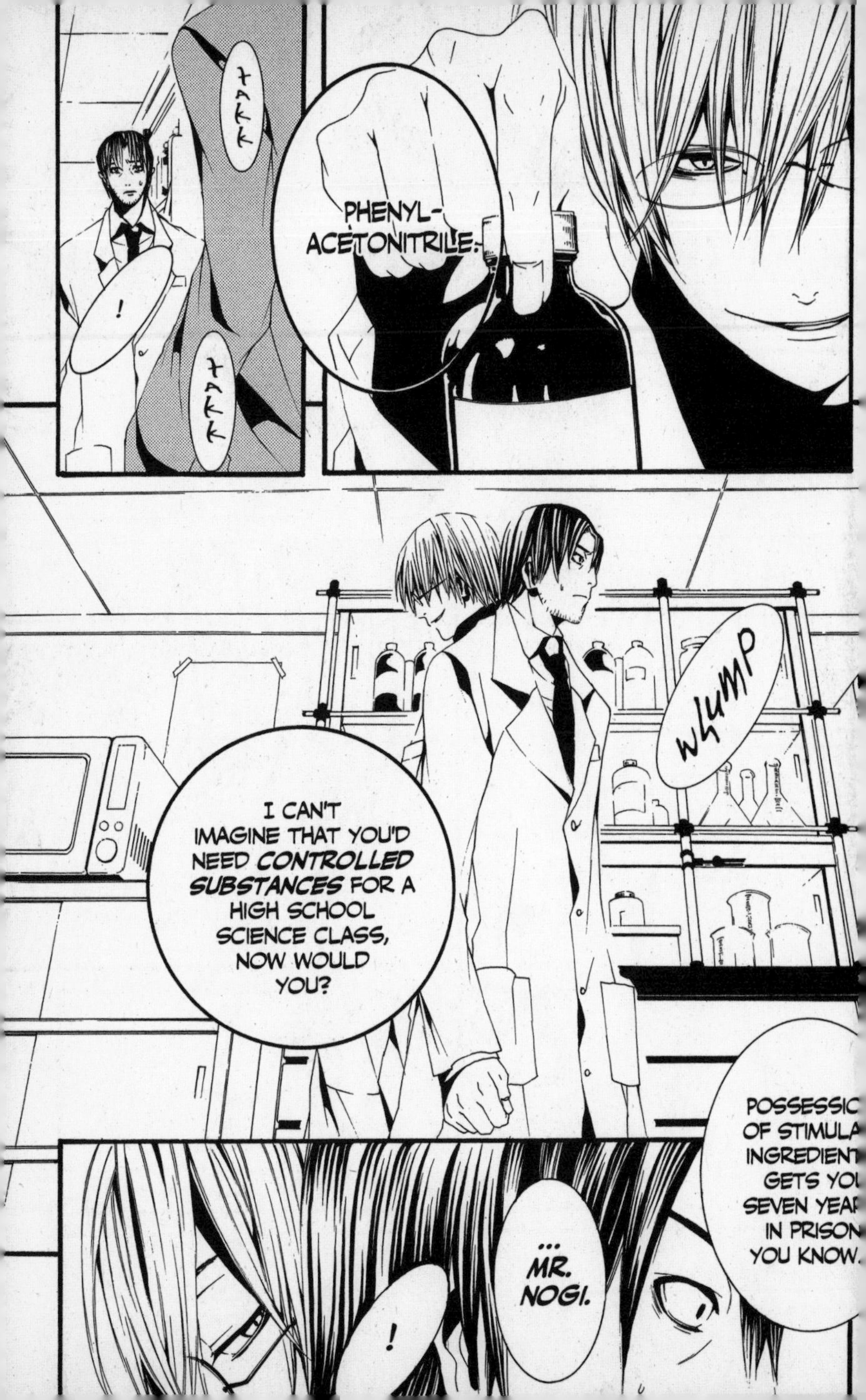
PHENYL-ACETONITRILE.
TAKK
!
TAKK
WHUMP
I CAN'T IMAGINE THAT YOU'D NEED *CONTROLLED SUBSTANCES* FOR A HIGH SCHOOL SCIENCE CLASS, NOW WOULD YOU?
POSSESSIC OF STIMULA INGREDIENT GETS YOU SEVEN YEAR IN PRISON YOU KNOW.
...MR. NOGI.
!

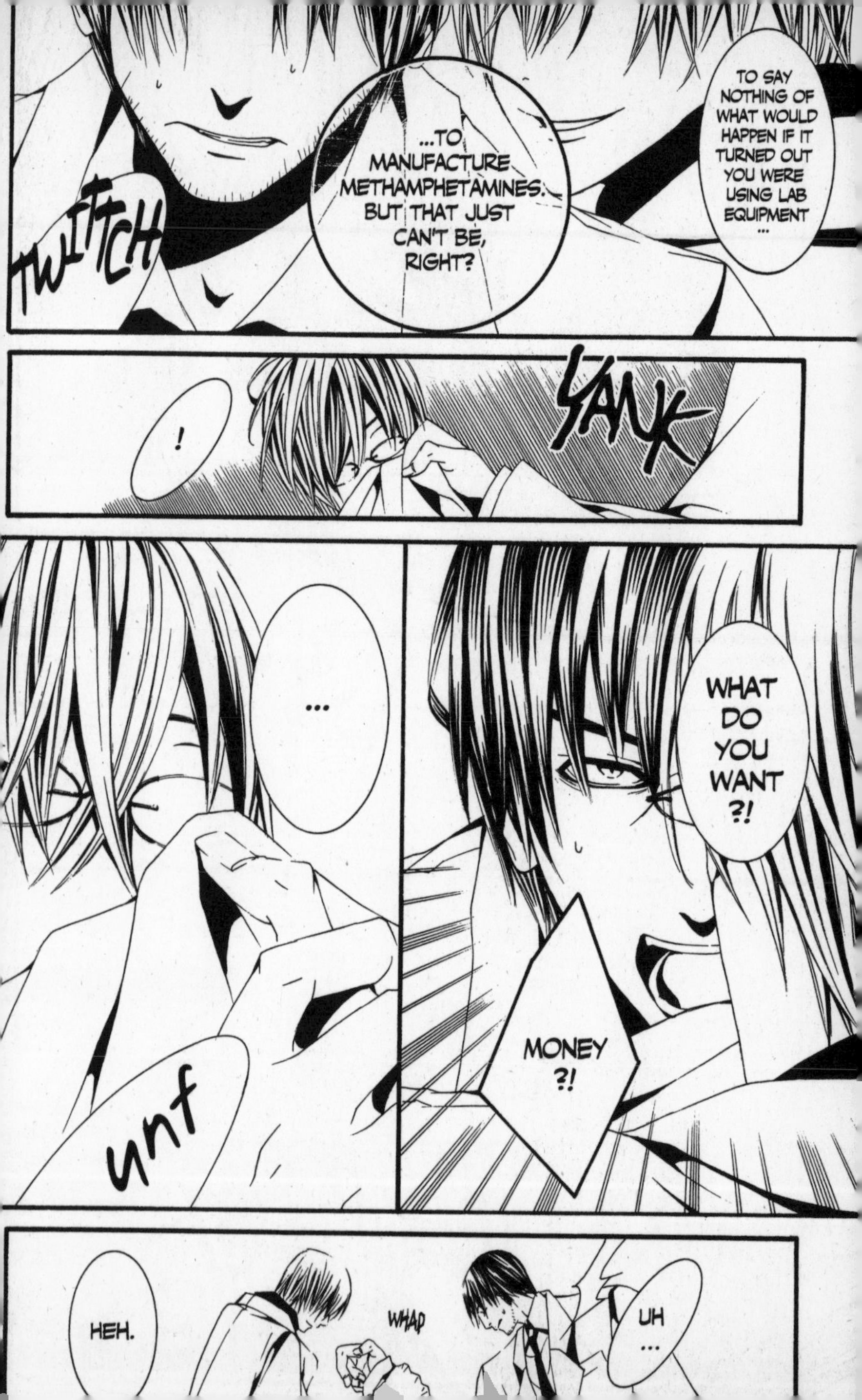

TO SAY NOTHING OF WHAT WOULD HAPPEN IF IT TURNED OUT YOU WERE USING LAB EQUIPMENT ...
...TO MANUFACTURE METHAMPHETAMINES. BUT THAT JUST CAN'T BE, RIGHT?
TWITCH
YANK
!
WHAT DO YOU WANT ?!
MONEY ?!
...
unf
UH ...
WHAP
HEH.

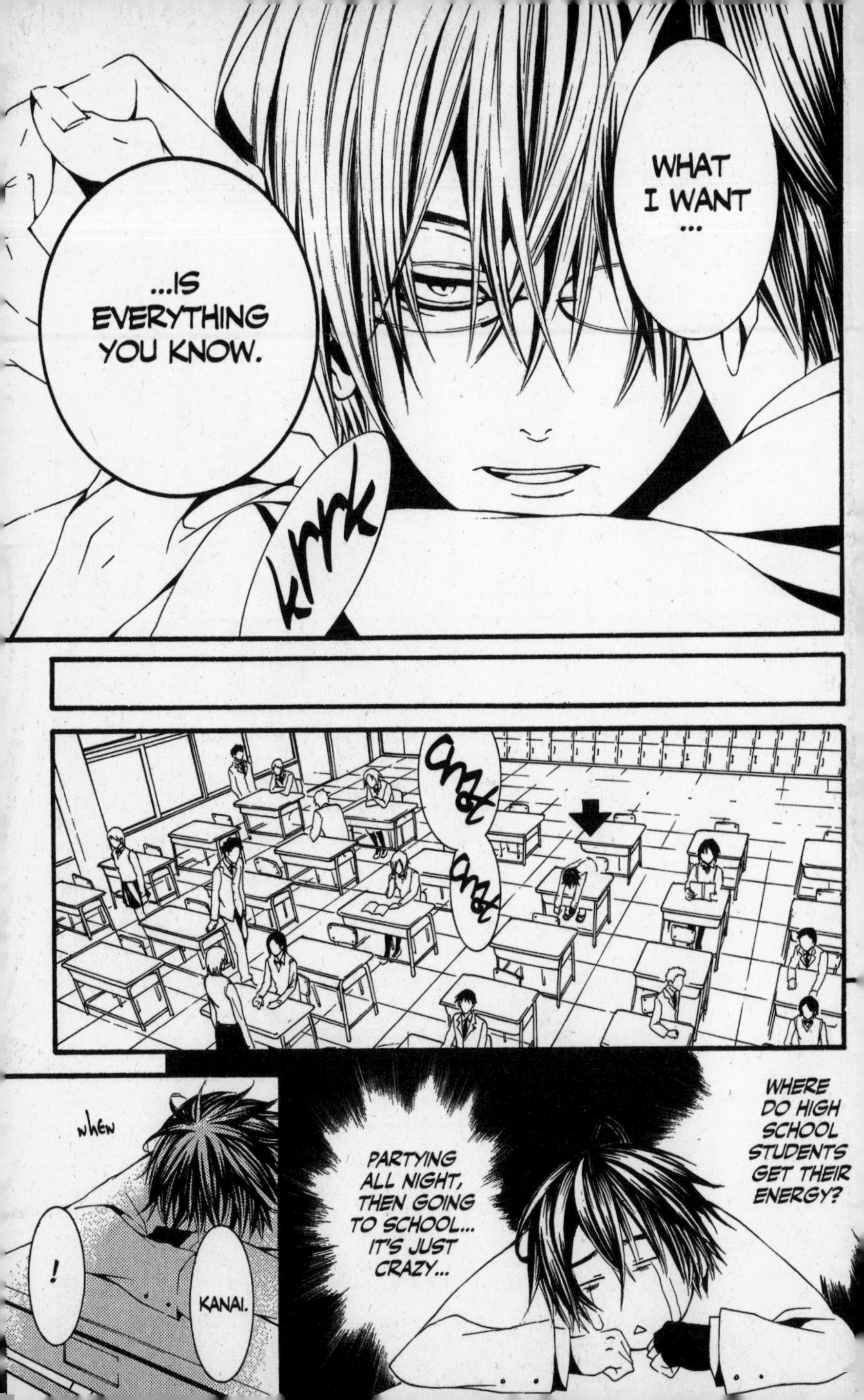
WHAT I WANT ...
...IS EVERYTHING YOU KNOW.
krrk
WHERE DO HIGH SCHOOL STUDENTS GET THEIR ENERGY?
PARTYING ALL NIGHT, THEN GOING TO SCHOOL... IT'S JUST CRAZY...
whew
KANAI.
!

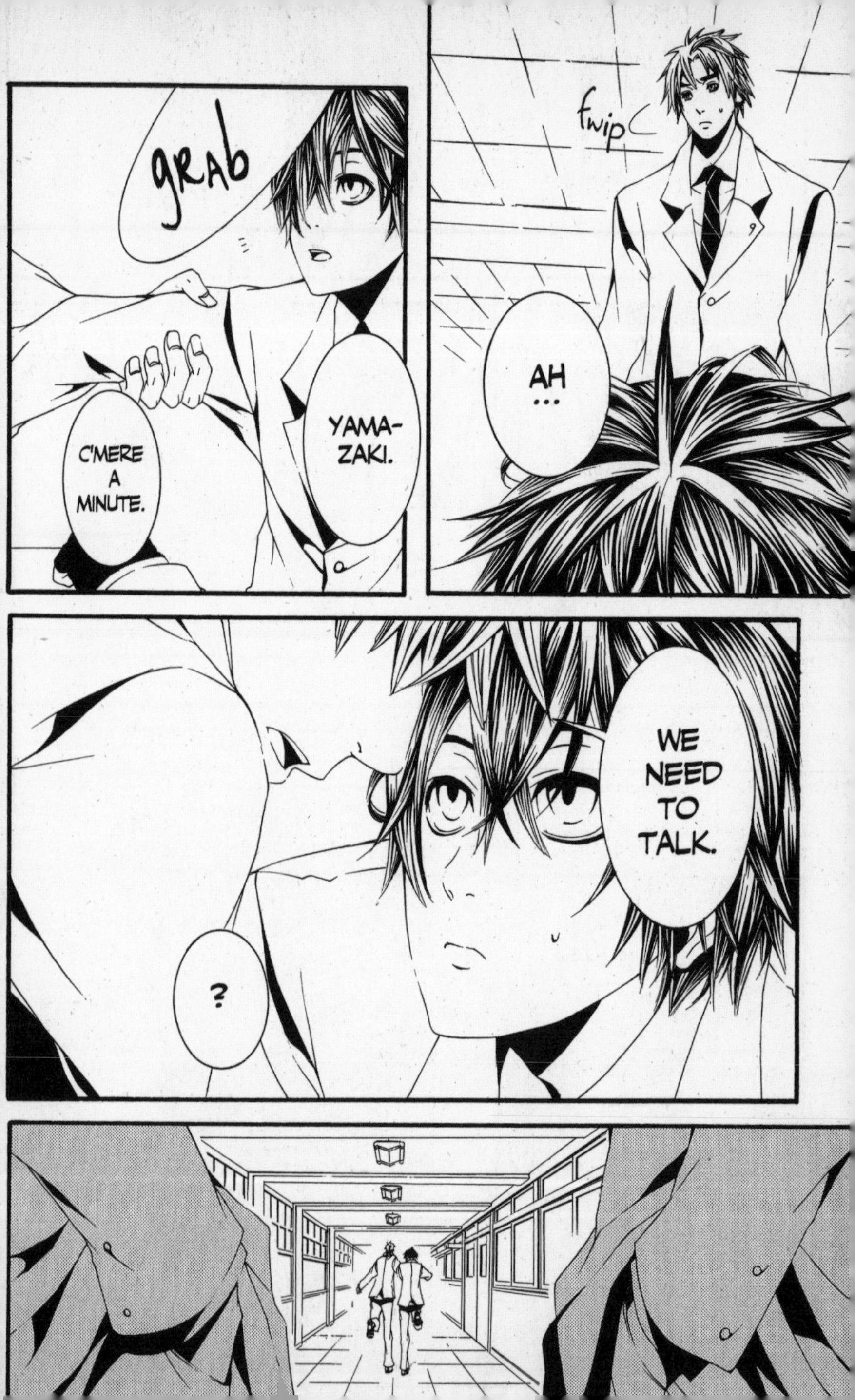
fwip
AH ...
grab
YAMA-ZAKI.
C'MERE A MINUTE.
WE NEED TO TALK.
?

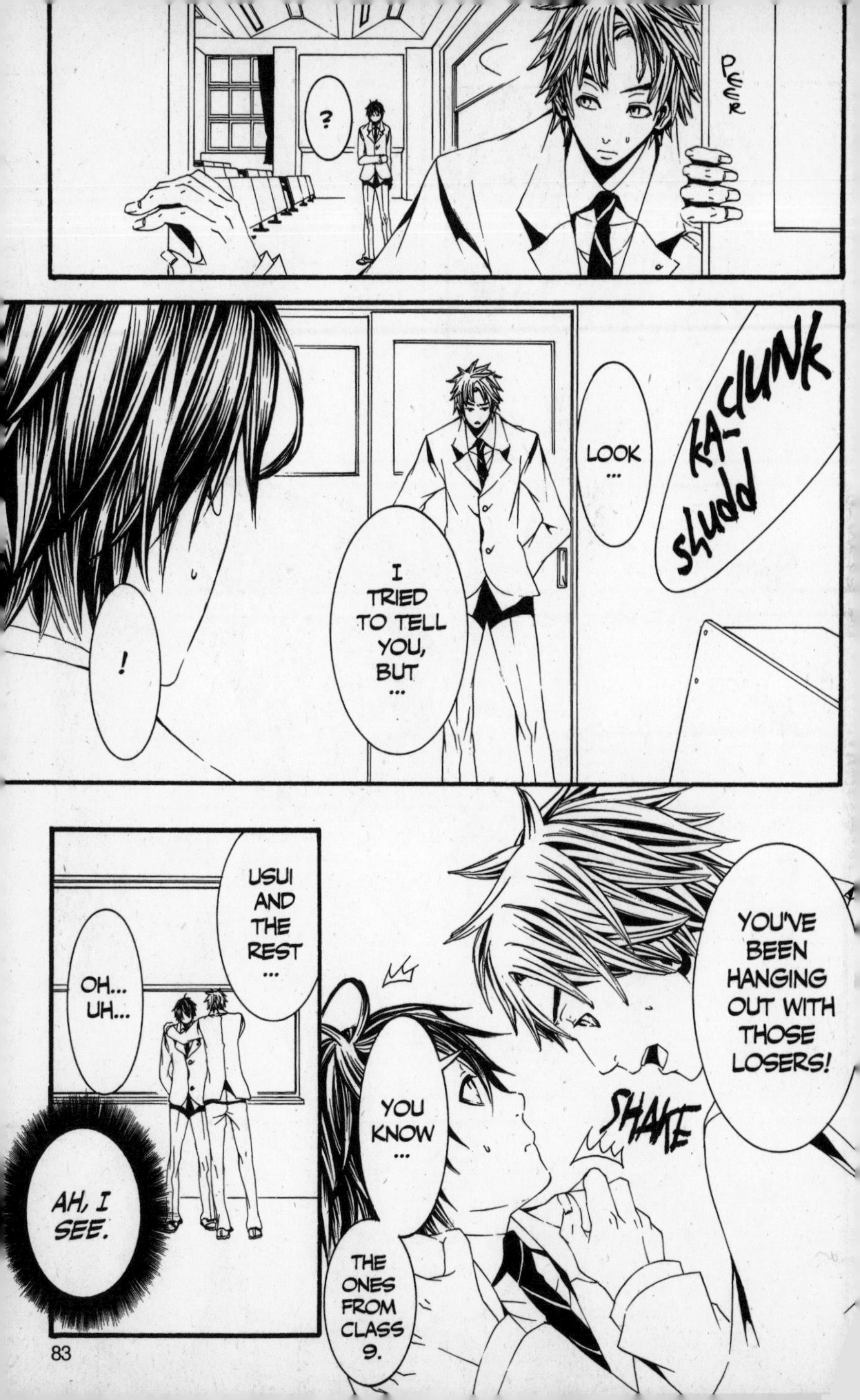
PEER
?
KA-CLUNK
SHUDD
LOOK...
I TRIED TO TELL YOU, BUT...
!
YOU'VE BEEN HANGING OUT WITH THOSE LOSERS!
SHAKE
YOU KNOW...
THE ONES FROM CLASS 9.
USUI AND THE REST...
OH... UH...
AH, I SEE.

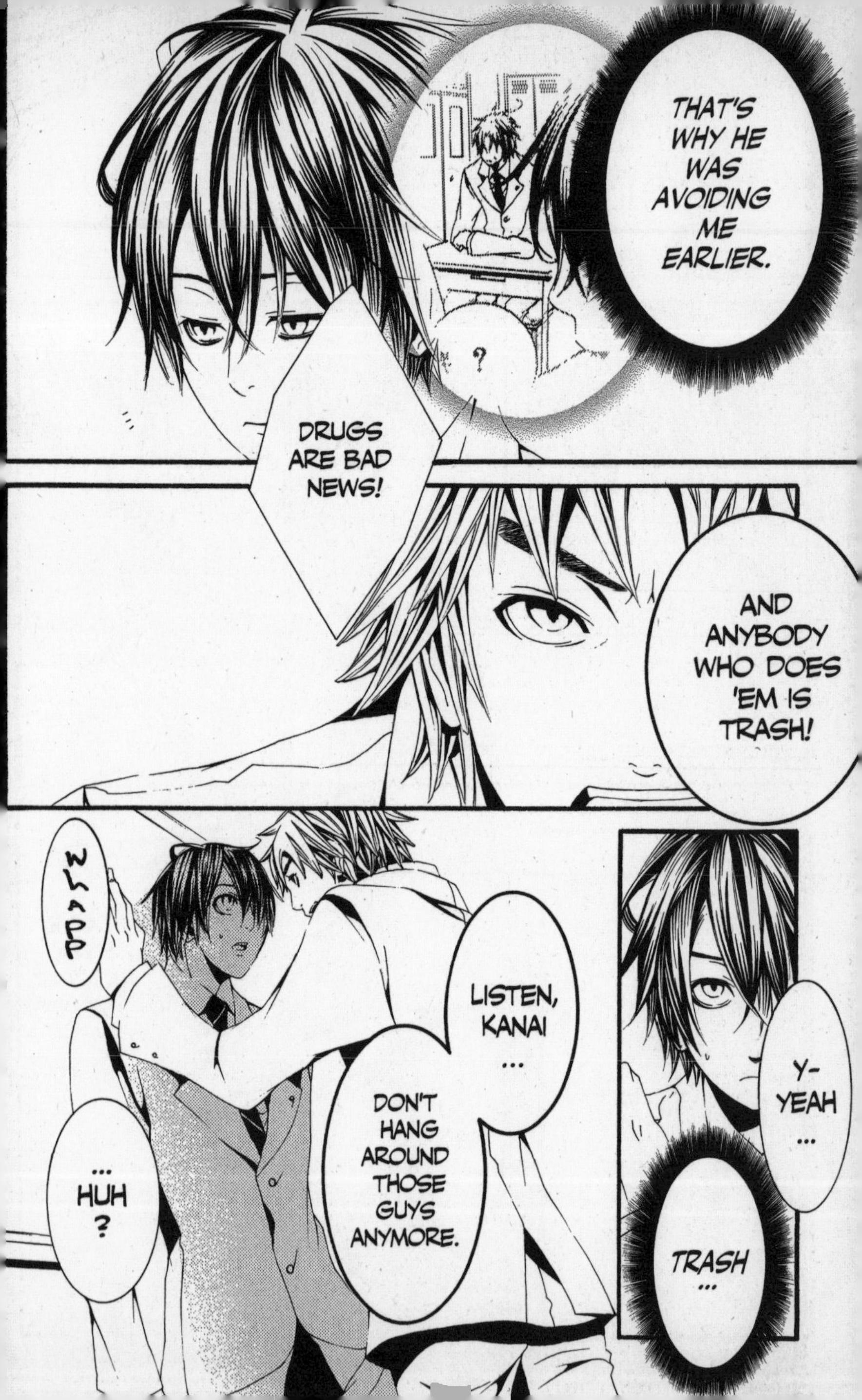
THAT'S WHY HE WAS AVOIDING ME EARLIER.
?
DRUGS ARE BAD NEWS!
AND ANYBODY WHO DOES 'EM IS TRASH!
Y-YEAH ...
TRASH ...
LISTEN, KANAI ...
DON'T HANG AROUND THOSE GUYS ANYMORE.
... HUH ?
WHAPP

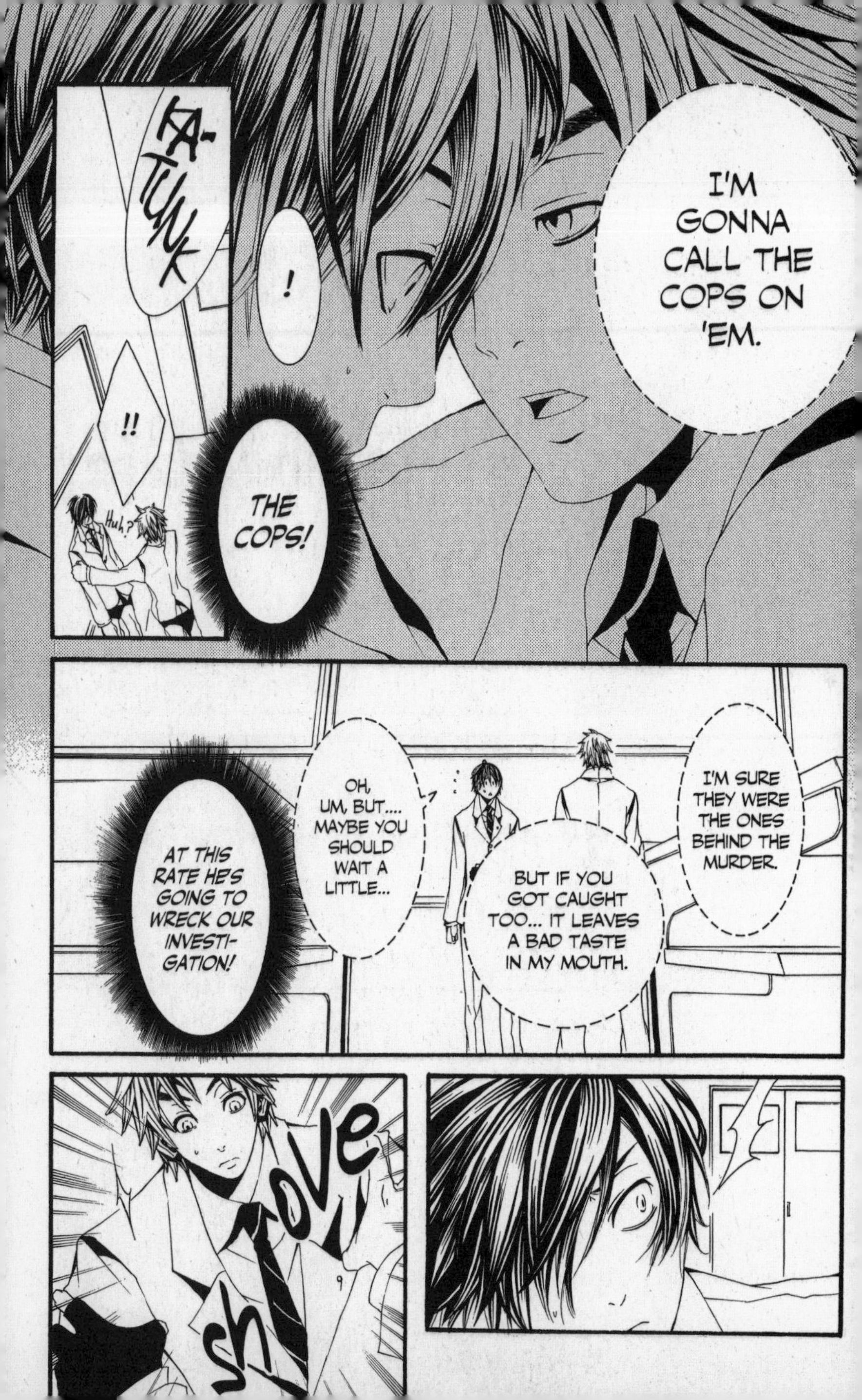
I'M GONNA CALL THE COPS ON 'EM.
!
THE COPS!
KA-TUNK
!!
Huh?
I'M SURE THEY WERE THE ONES BEHIND THE MURDER.
BUT IF YOU GOT CAUGHT TOO... IT LEAVES A BAD TASTE IN MY MOUTH.
OH, UM, BUT.... MAYBE YOU SHOULD WAIT A LITTLE...
AT THIS RATE HE'S GOING TO WRECK OUR INVESTIGATION!
shove

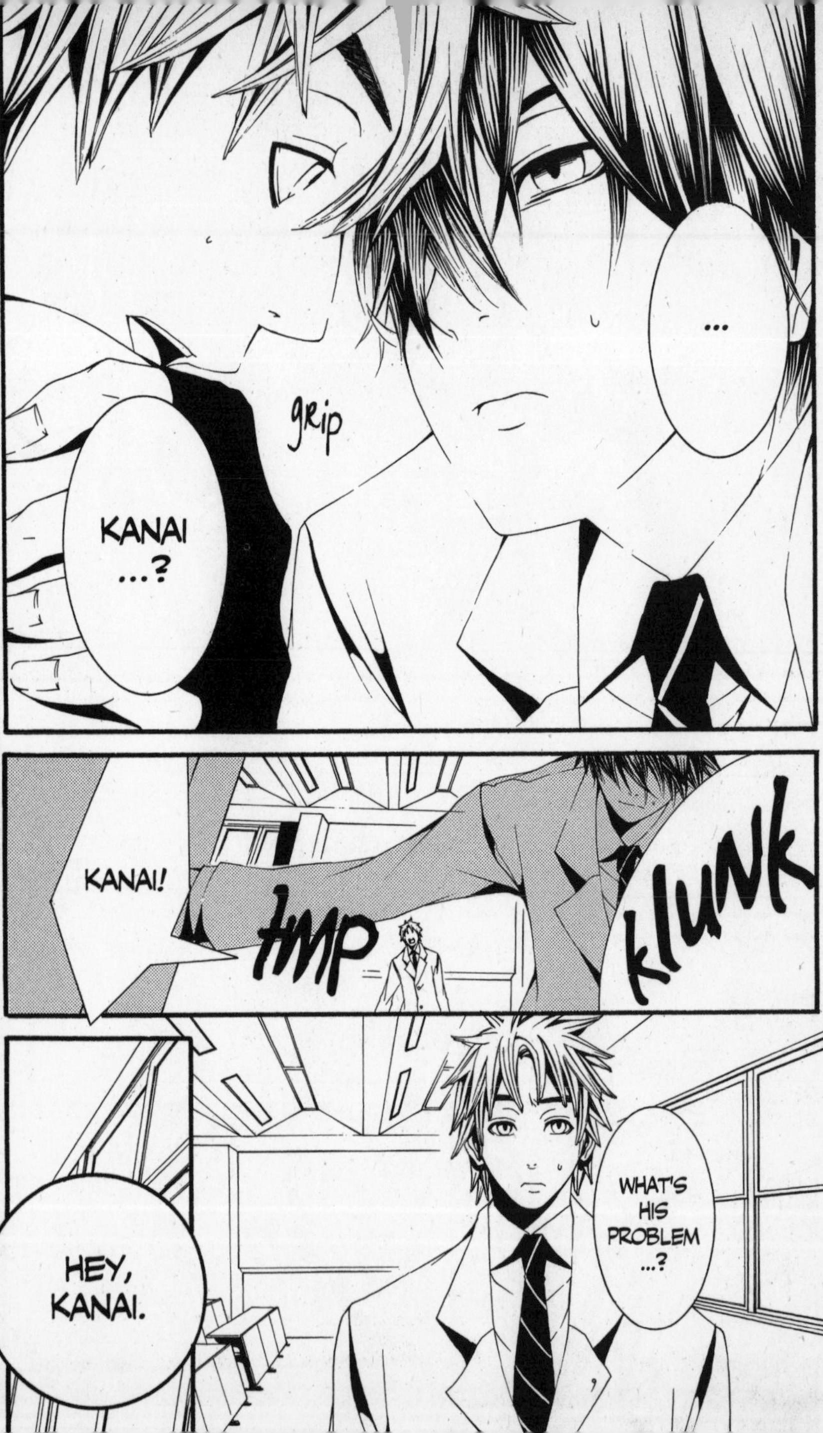
...
grip
KANAI ...?
klunk
tmp
KANAI!
WHAT'S HIS PROBLEM ...?
HEY, KANAI.

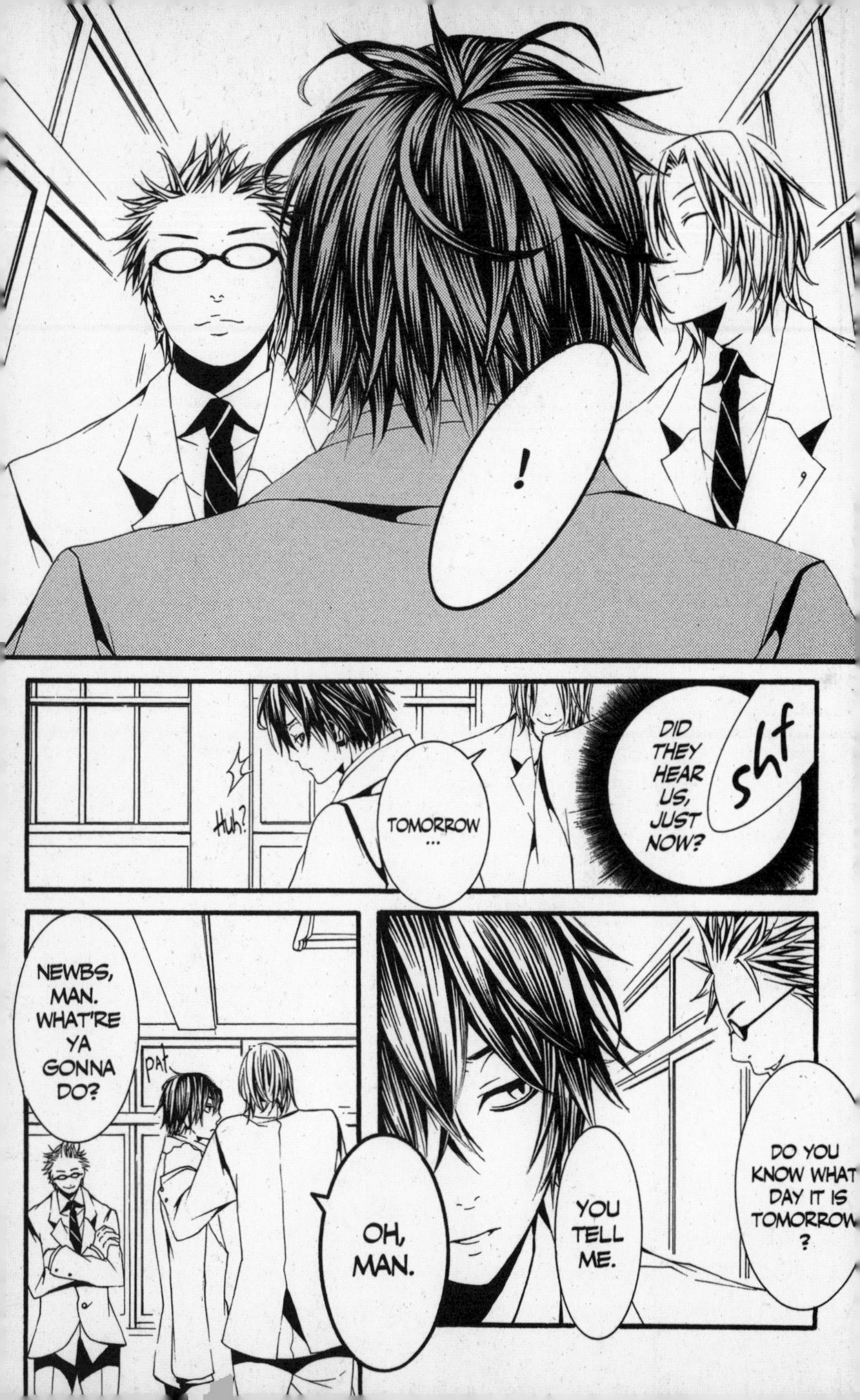
!
shf
DID THEY HEAR US, JUST NOW?
TOMORROW...
Huh?
DO YOU KNOW WHAT DAY IT IS TOMORROW?
YOU TELL ME.
OH, MAN.
NEWBS, MAN. WHAT'RE YA GONNA DO?
pat

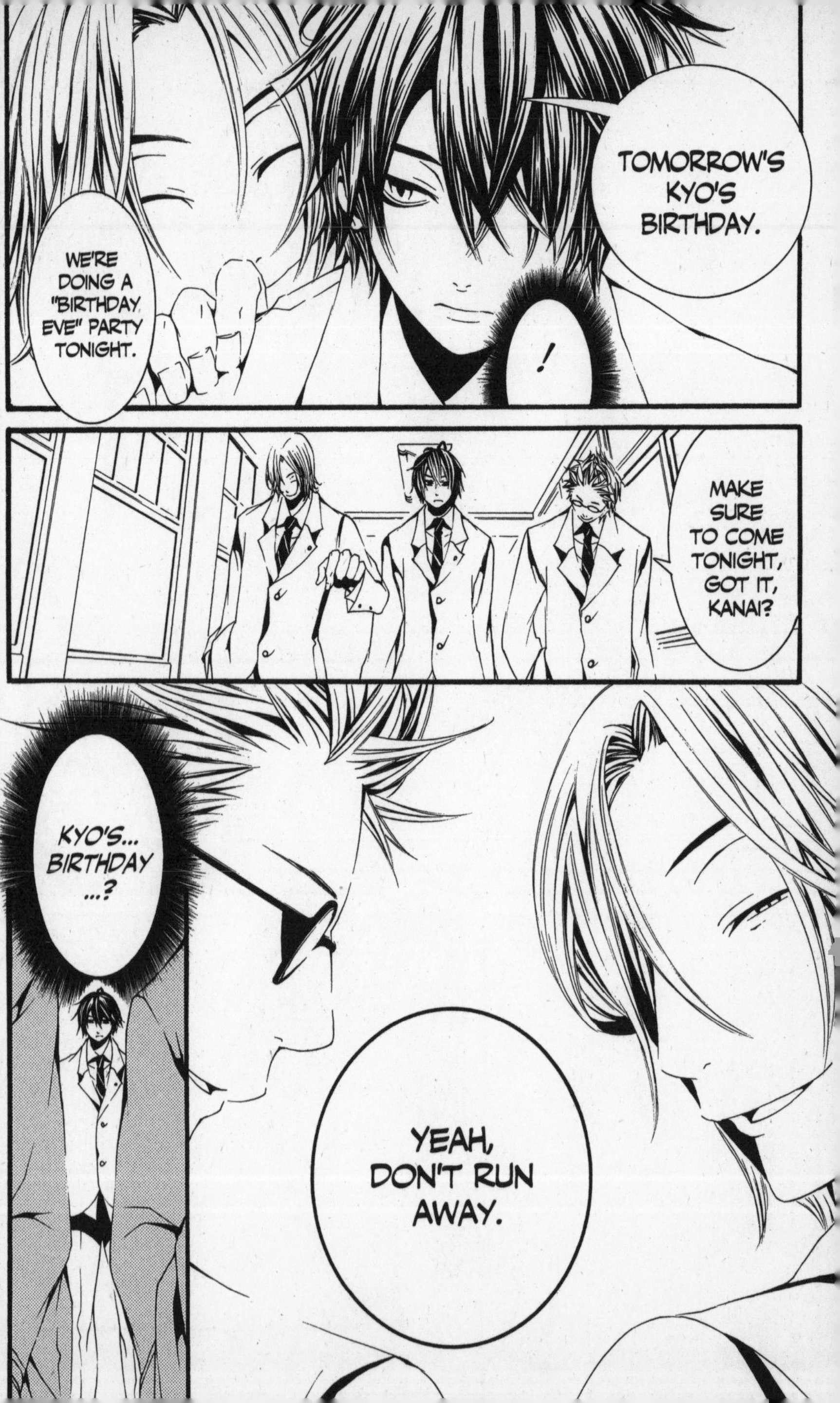
TOMORROW'S KYO'S BIRTHDAY.
WE'RE DOING A "BIRTHDAY EVE" PARTY TONIGHT.
!
MAKE SURE TO COME TONIGHT, GOT IT, KANAI?
YEAH, DON'T RUN AWAY.
KYO'S... BIRTHDAY ...?

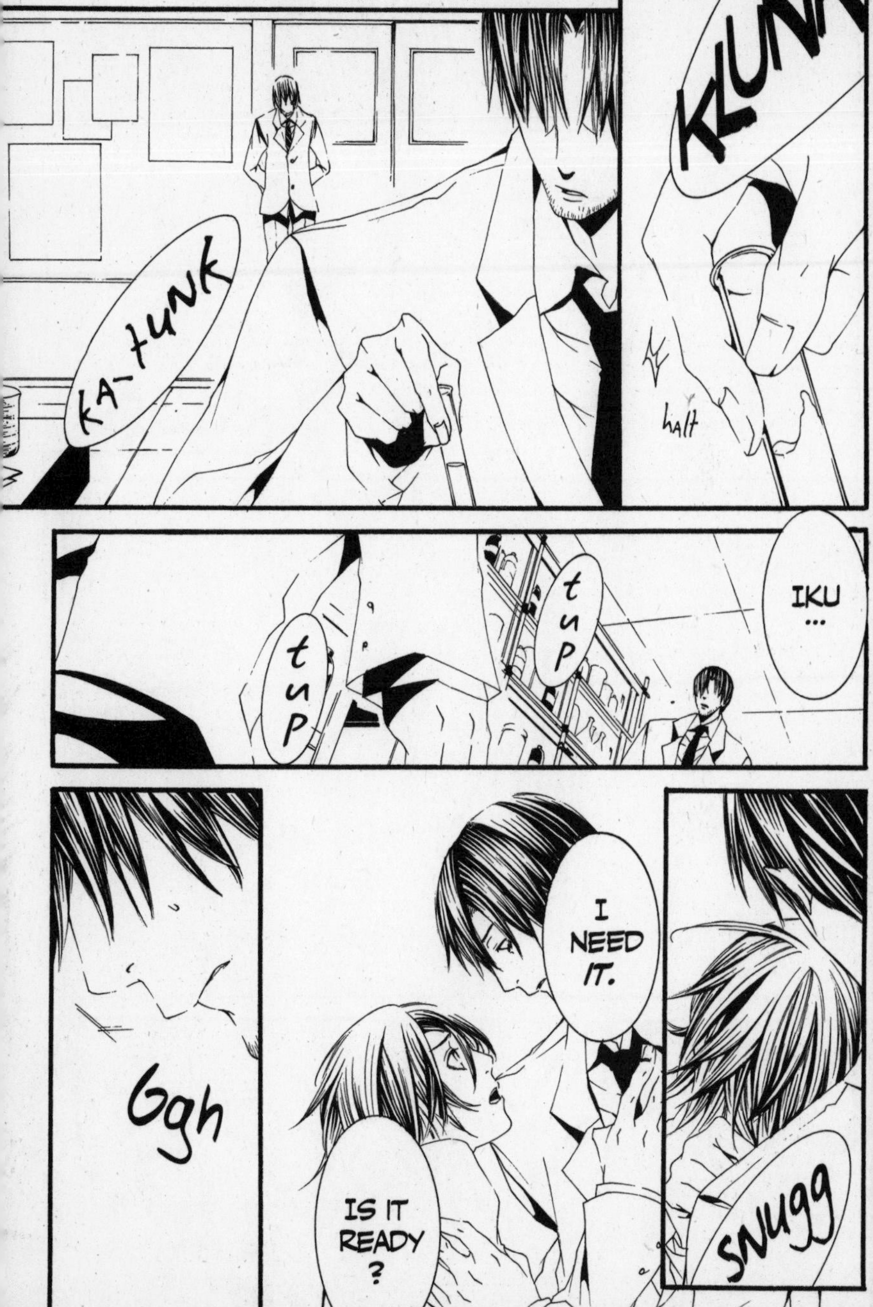
KLUNK
halt
KA-TUNK
IKU ...
tup
tup
SNUGG
I NEED IT.
IS IT READY ?
Ggh

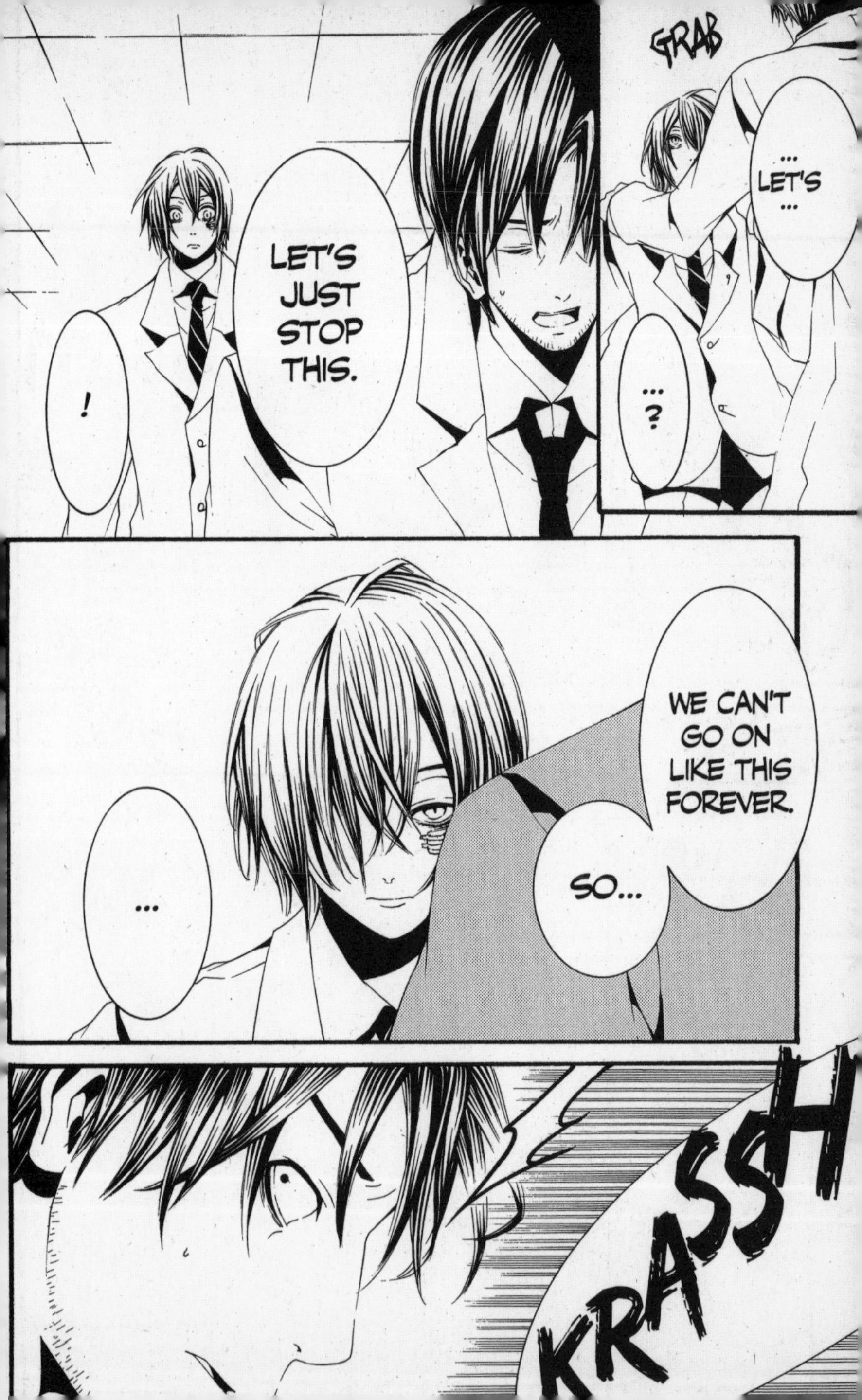
GRAB
... LET'S ...
... ?
LET'S JUST STOP THIS.
!
WE CAN'T GO ON LIKE THIS FOREVER.
SO...
...
KRASSH

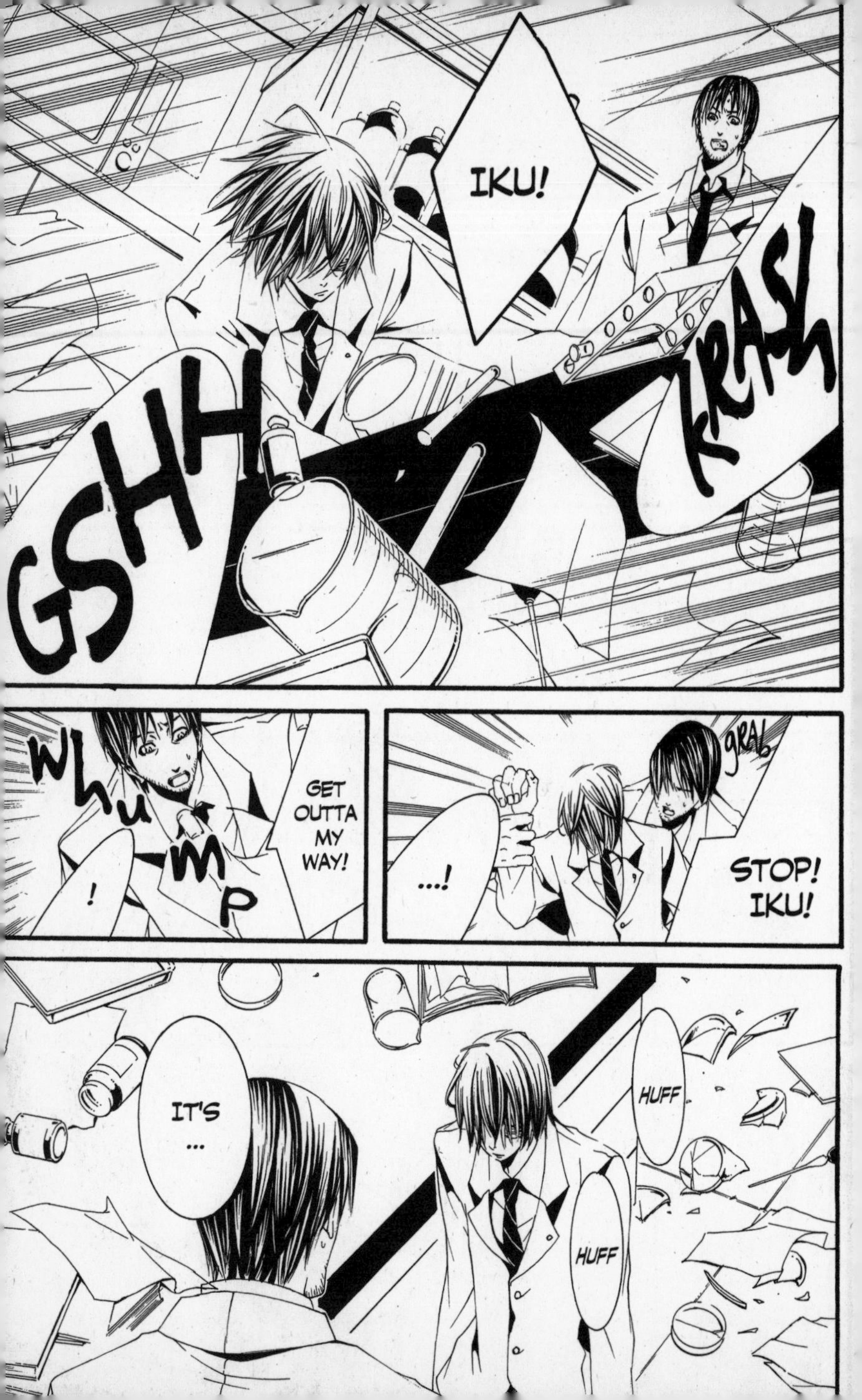
IKU!
KRASH
GSHH
GRAB
STOP! IKU!
...!
GET OUTTA MY WAY!
WHUMP
!
HUFF
HUFF
IT'S ...

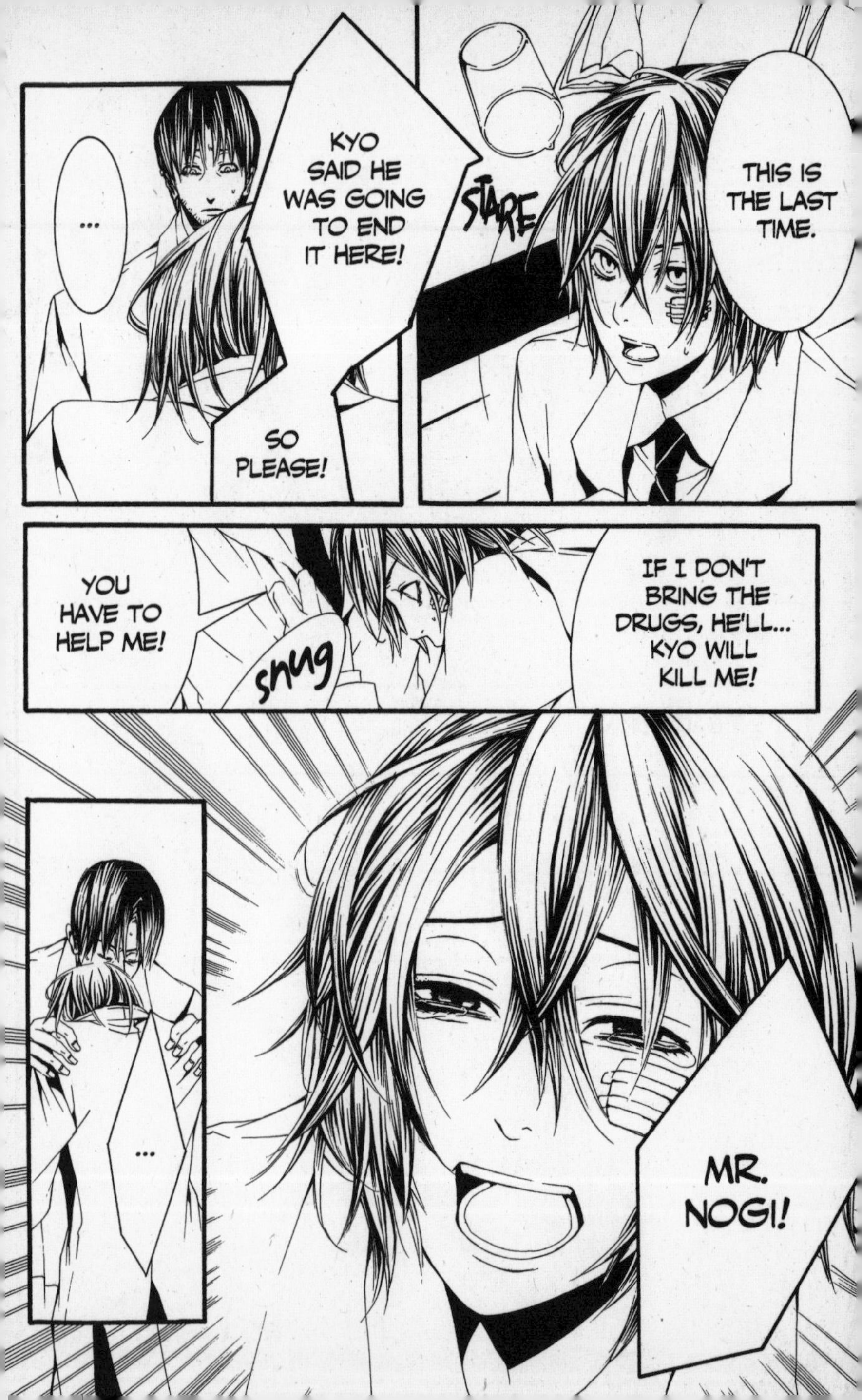
THIS IS THE LAST TIME.
STARE
KYO SAID HE WAS GOING TO END IT HERE!
SO PLEASE!
...
IF I DON'T BRING THE DRUGS, HE'LL... KYO WILL KILL ME!
snug
YOU HAVE TO HELP ME!
MR. NOGI!
...

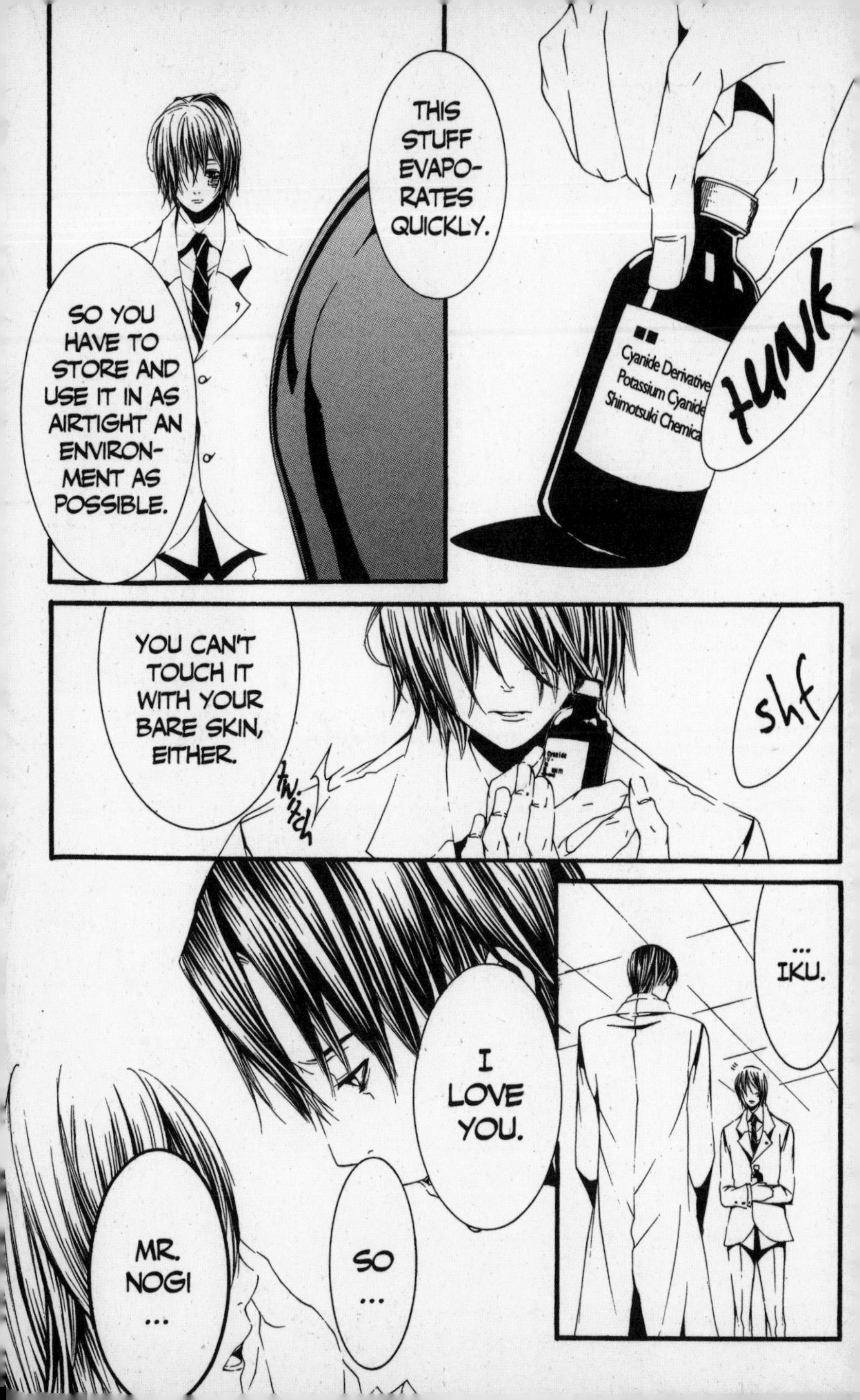
TUNK
Cyanide Derivative
Potassium Cyanide
Shimotsuki Chemica
THIS STUFF EVAPO-RATES QUICKLY.
SO YOU HAVE TO STORE AND USE IT IN AS AIRTIGHT AN ENVIRON-MENT AS POSSIBLE.
shf
YOU CAN'T TOUCH IT WITH YOUR BARE SKIN, EITHER.
twitch
... IKU.
I LOVE YOU.
SO ...
MR. NOGI ...

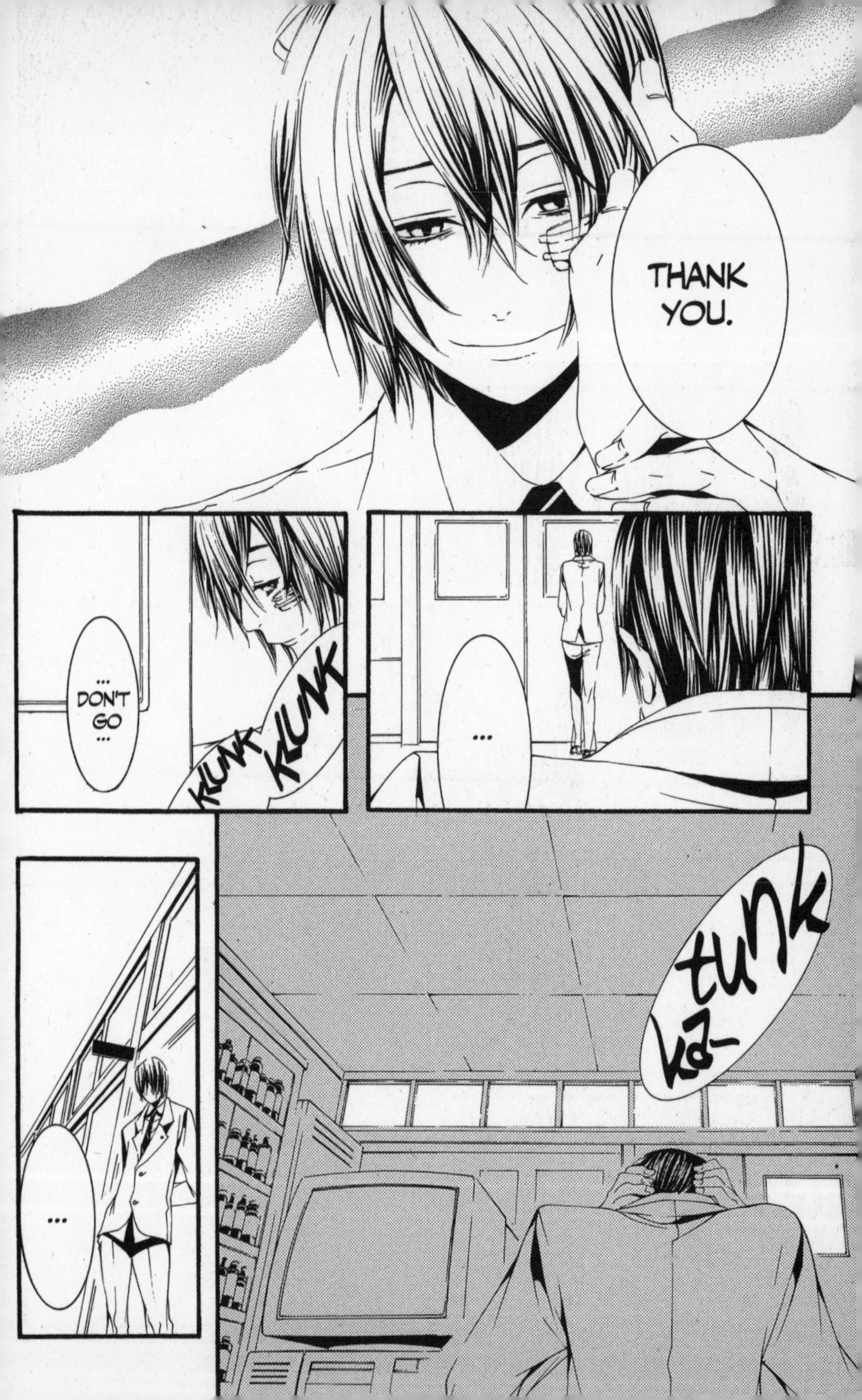
THANK YOU.
...
KLUNK KLUNK
... DON'T GO ...
ka-tunk
...

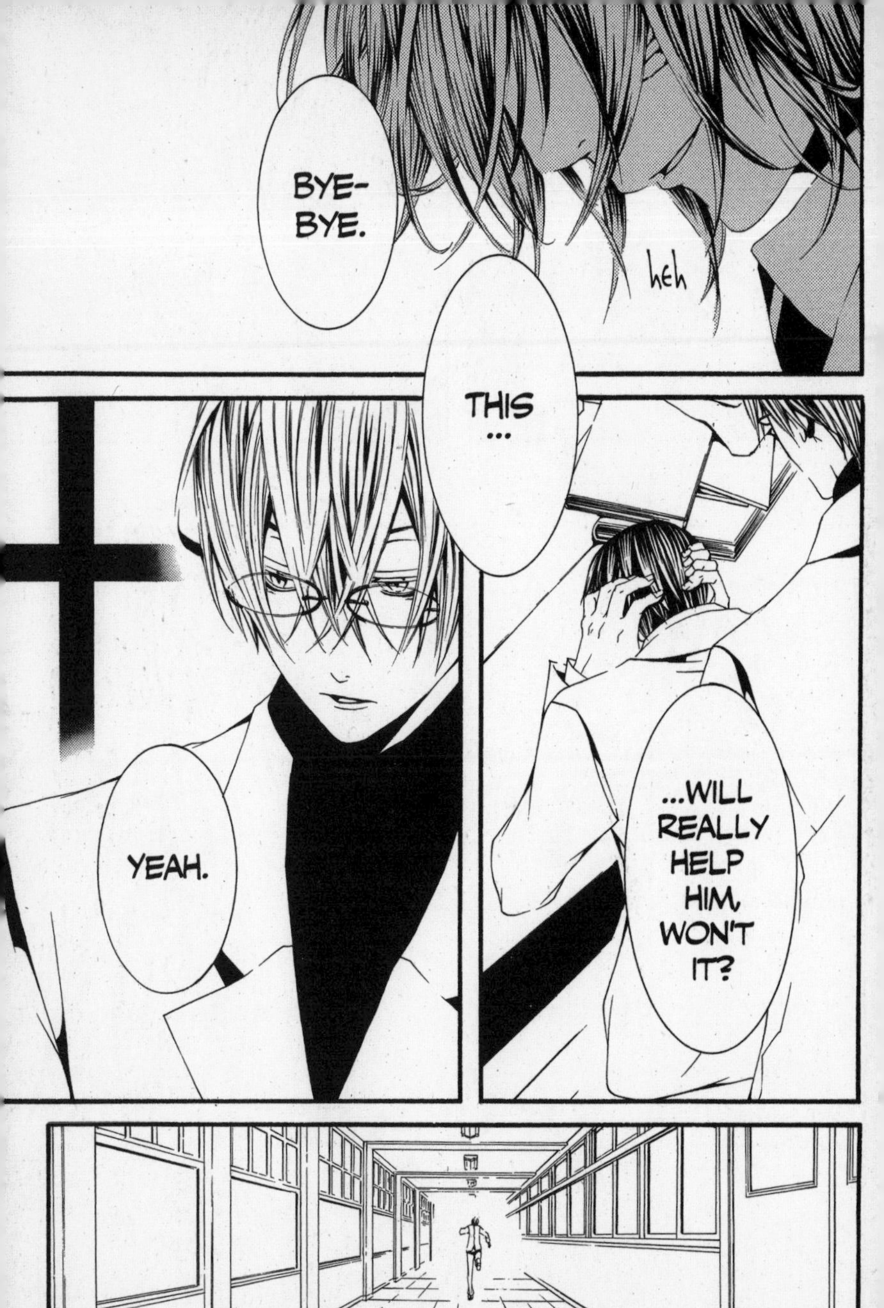
BYE-BYE.
heh
THIS ...
...WILL REALLY HELP HIM, WON'T IT?
YEAH.

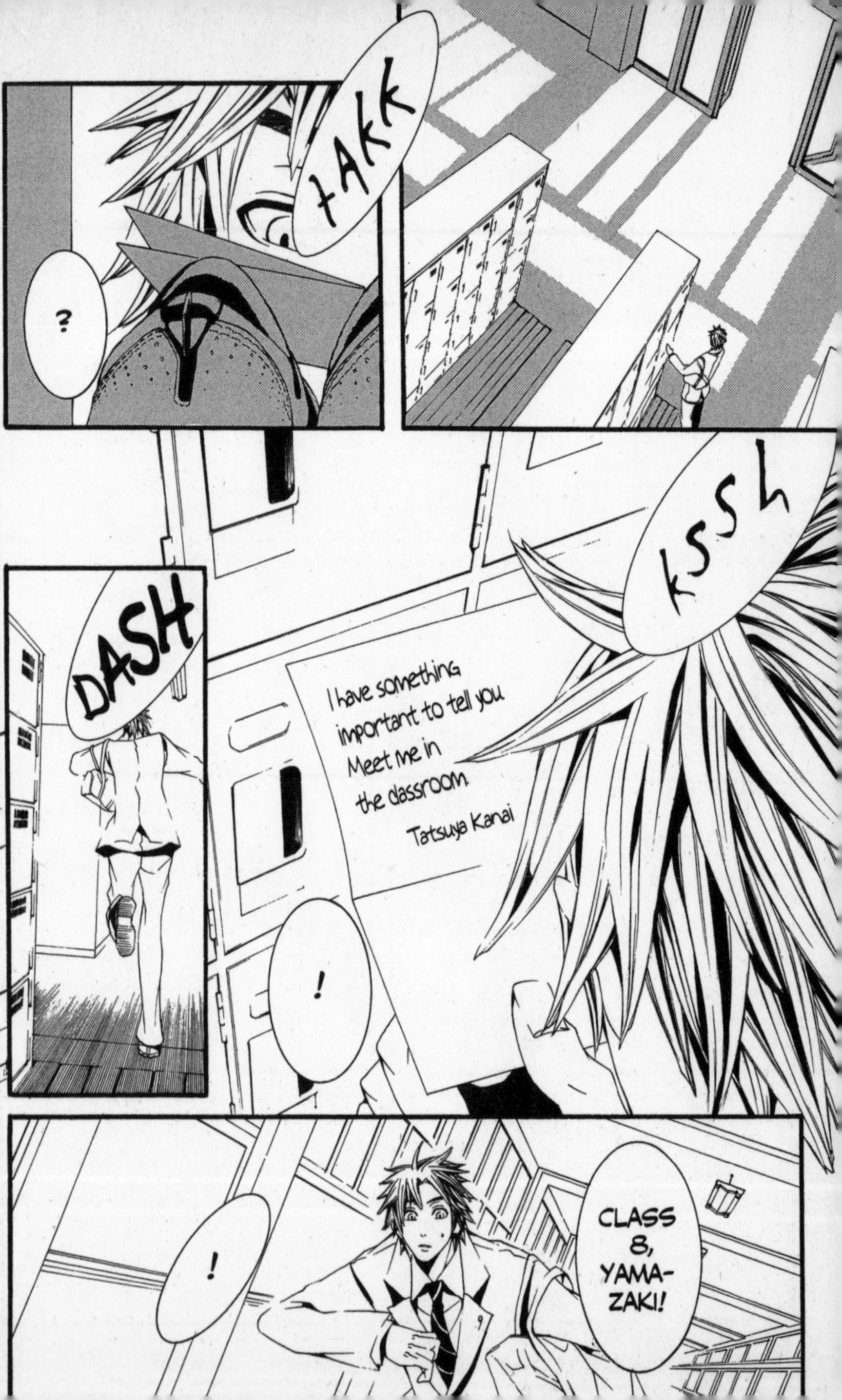
takk
?
kssh
I have something
important to tell you
Meet me in
the classroom
Tatsuya Kanai
!
DASH
CLASS 8, YAMA-ZAKI!
!

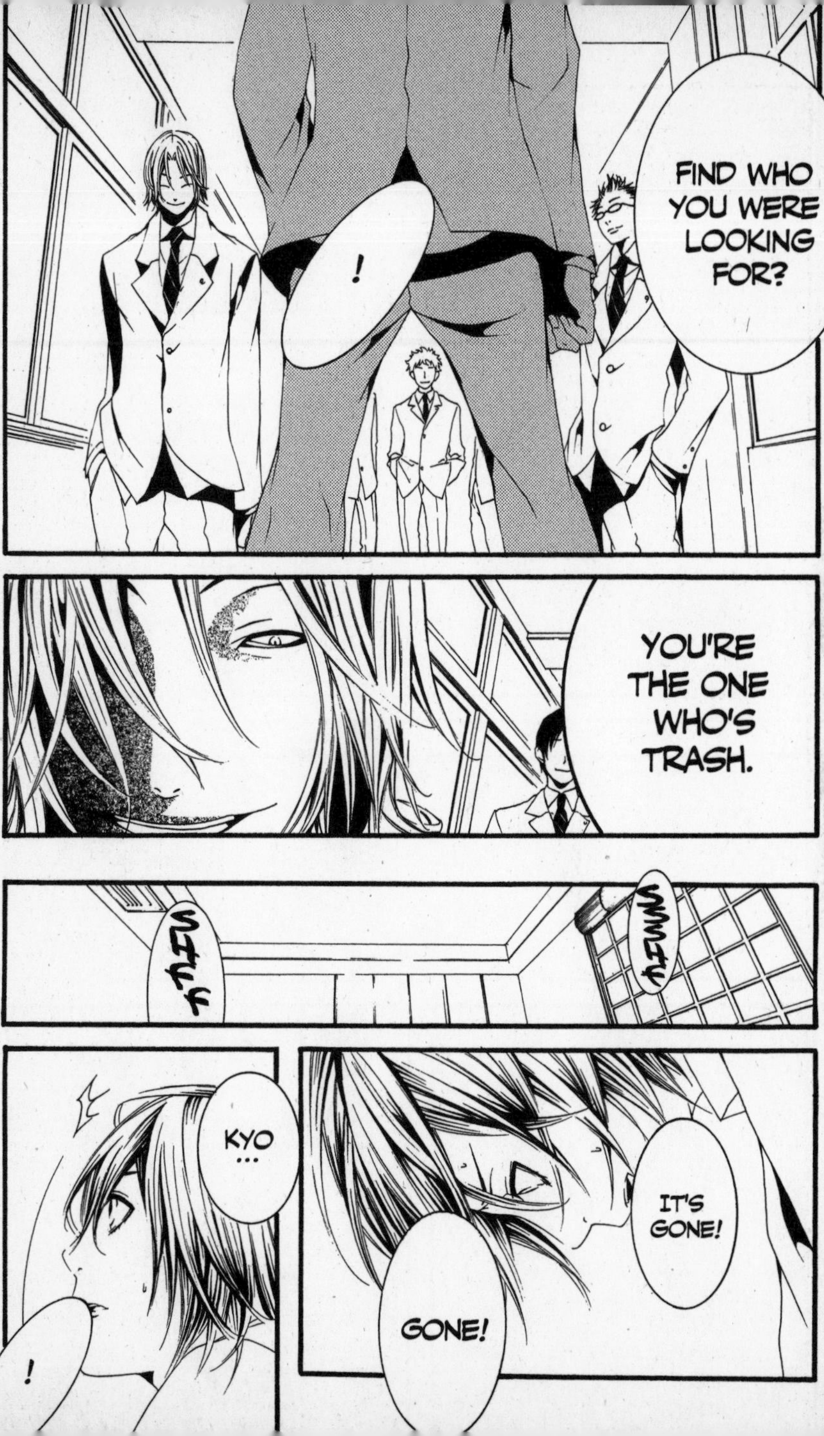
FIND WHO YOU WERE LOOKING FOR?
!
YOU'RE THE ONE WHO'S TRASH.
SNIFF
SNIFF
IT'S GONE!
GONE!
KYO...
!

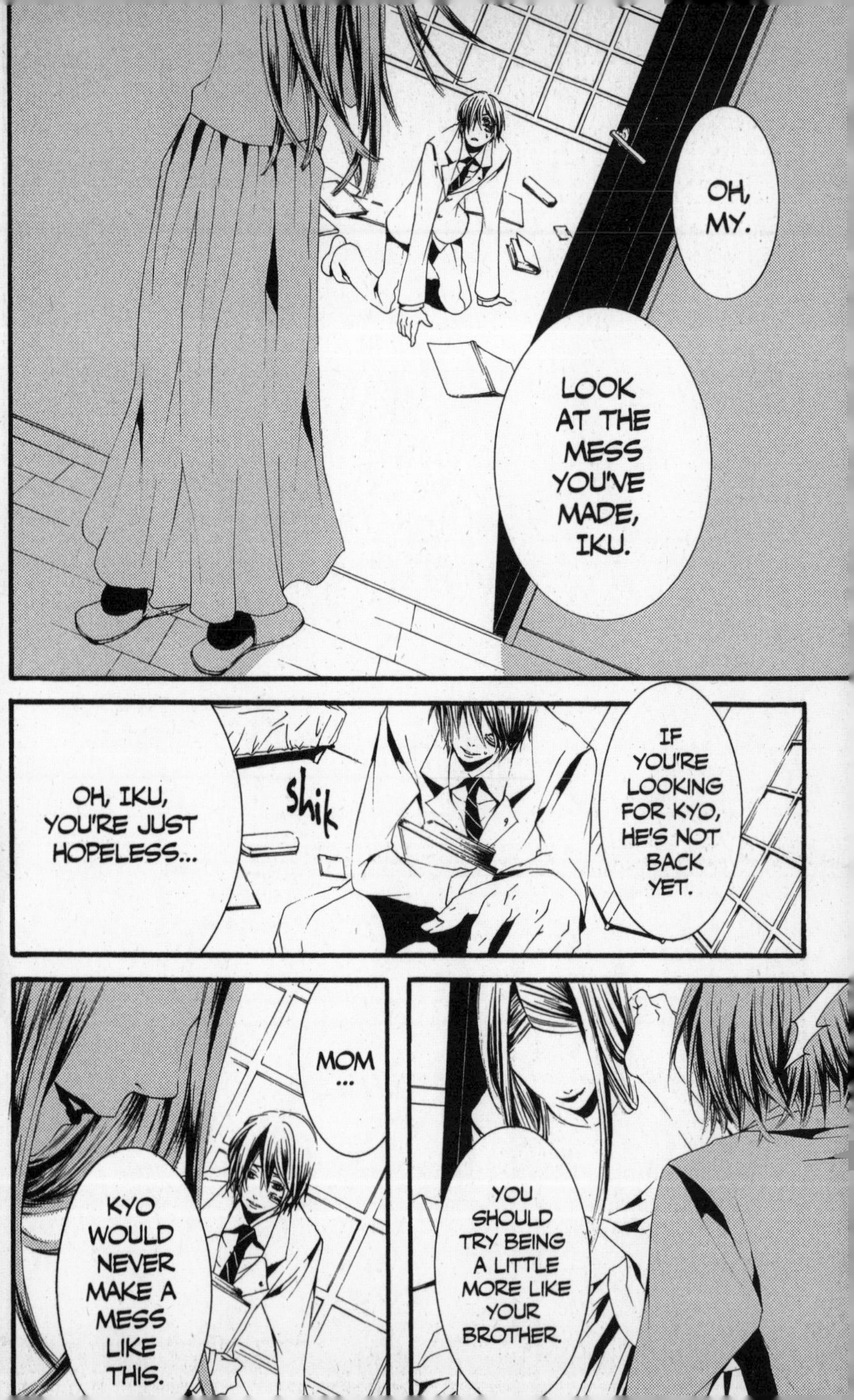
OH, MY.
LOOK AT THE MESS YOU'VE MADE, IKU.
IF YOU'RE LOOKING FOR KYO, HE'S NOT BACK YET.
shik
OH, IKU, YOU'RE JUST HOPELESS...
YOU SHOULD TRY BEING A LITTLE MORE LIKE YOUR BROTHER.
MOM...
KYO WOULD NEVER MAKE A MESS LIKE THIS.

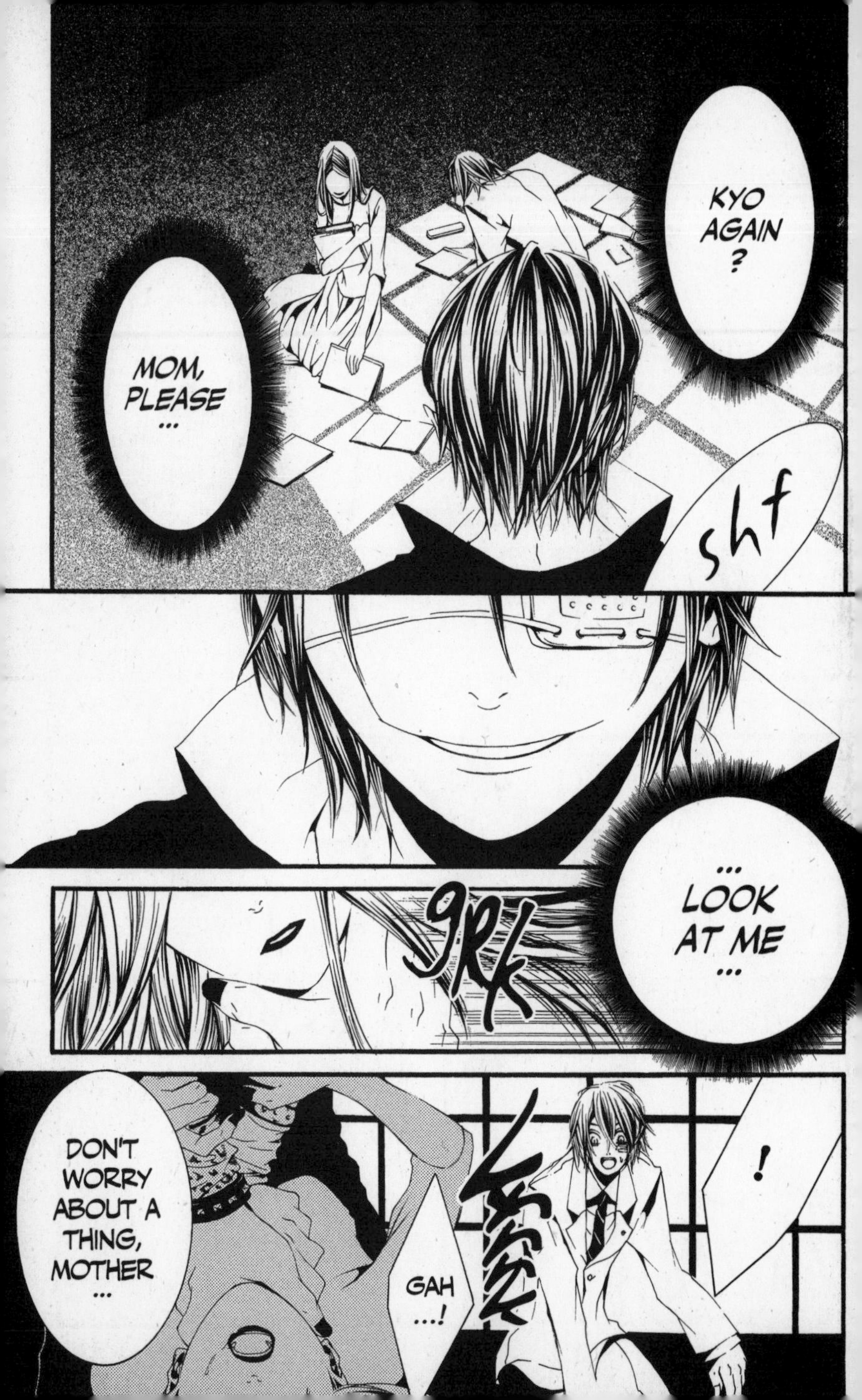
KYO AGAIN ?
MOM, PLEASE ...
shf
... LOOK AT ME ...
grk
!
GAH ...!
DON'T WORRY ABOUT A THING, MOTHER ...

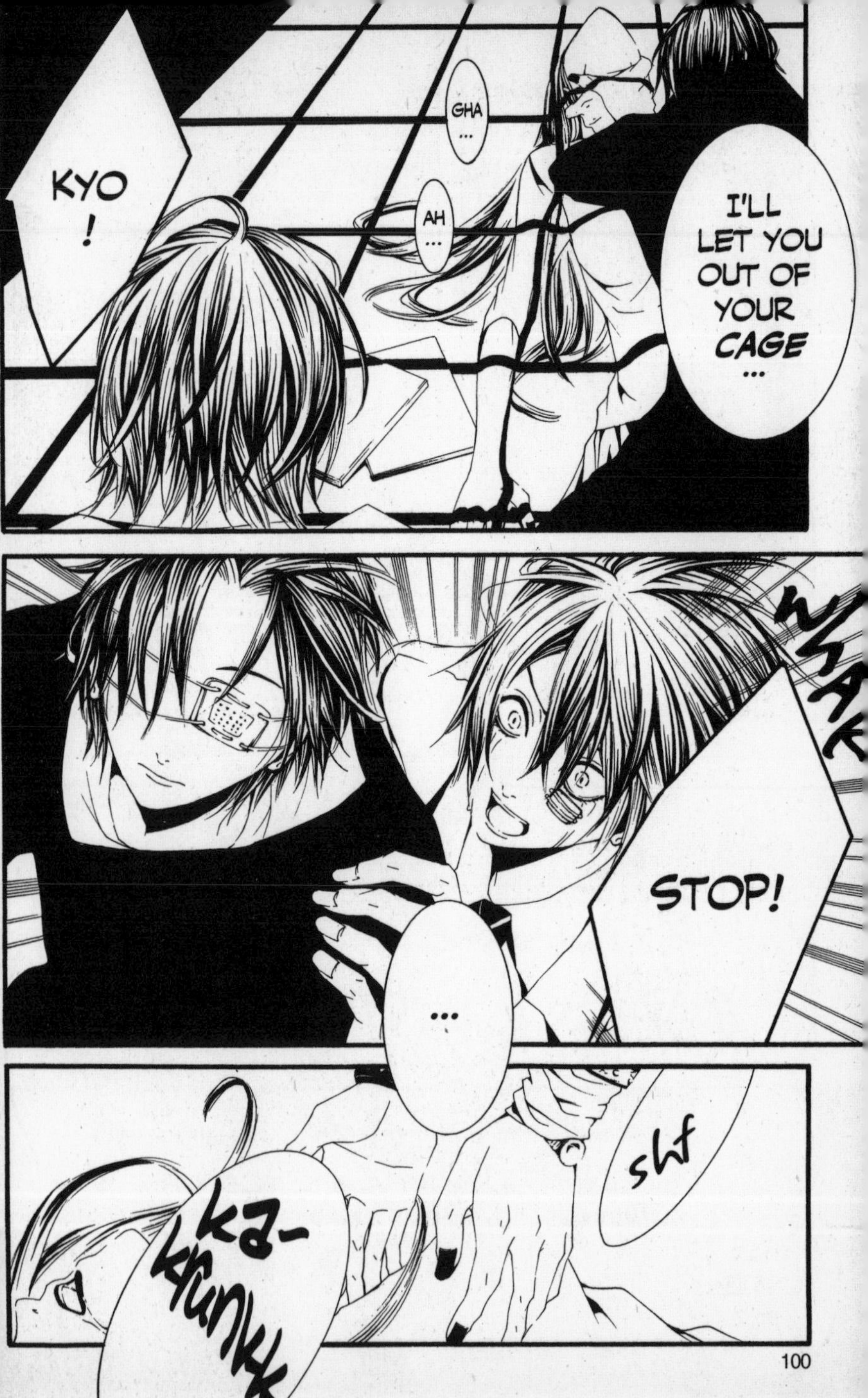
I'LL LET YOU OUT OF YOUR CAGE ...
GHA ...
AH ...
KYO !
WHAK
STOP!
...
shf
ka-krunkk

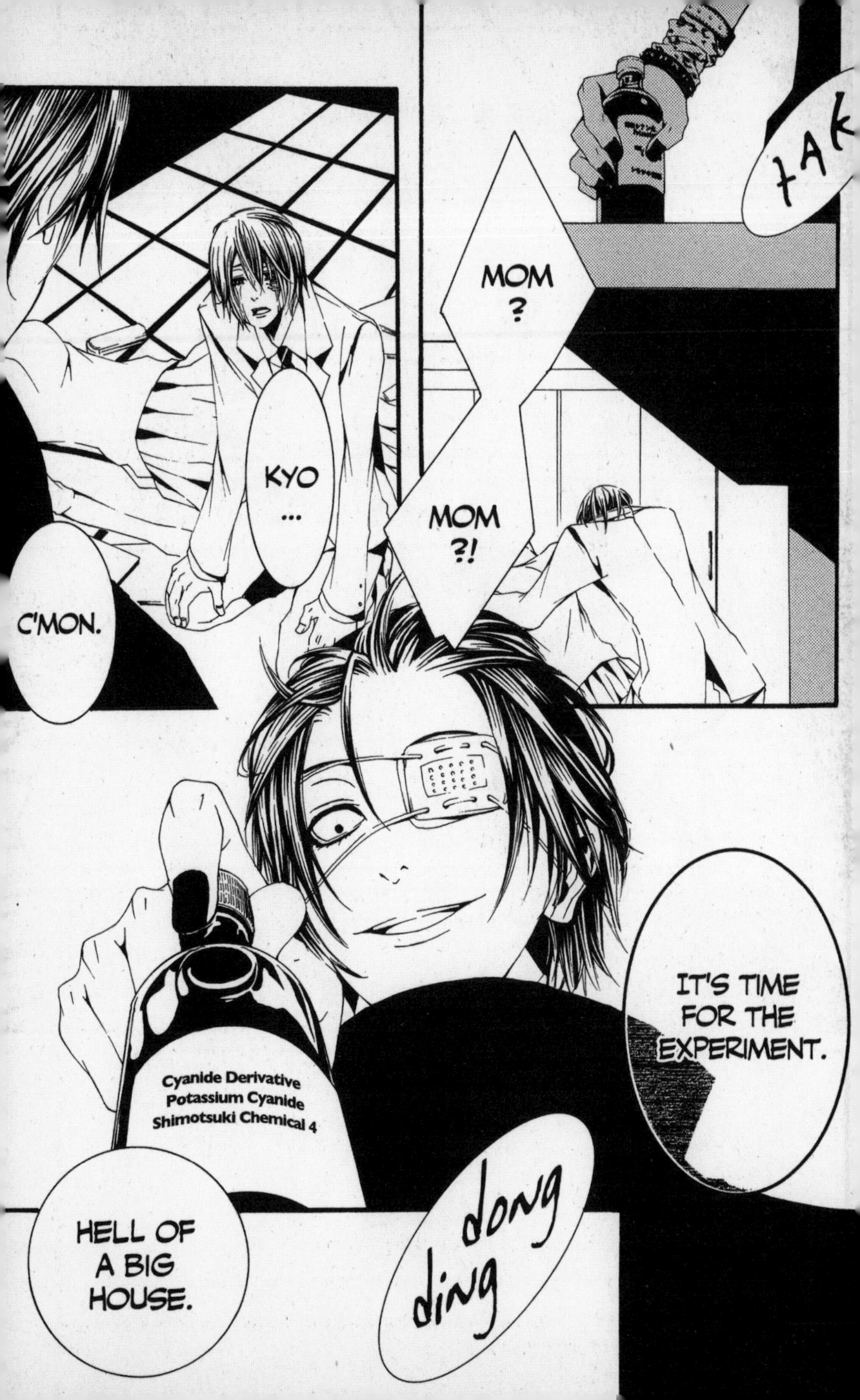
TAK
MOM ?
MOM ?!
KYO ...
C'MON.
IT'S TIME FOR THE EXPERIMENT.
Cyanide Derivative
Potassium Cyanide
Shimotsuki Chemical 4
ding dong
HELL OF A BIG HOUSE.

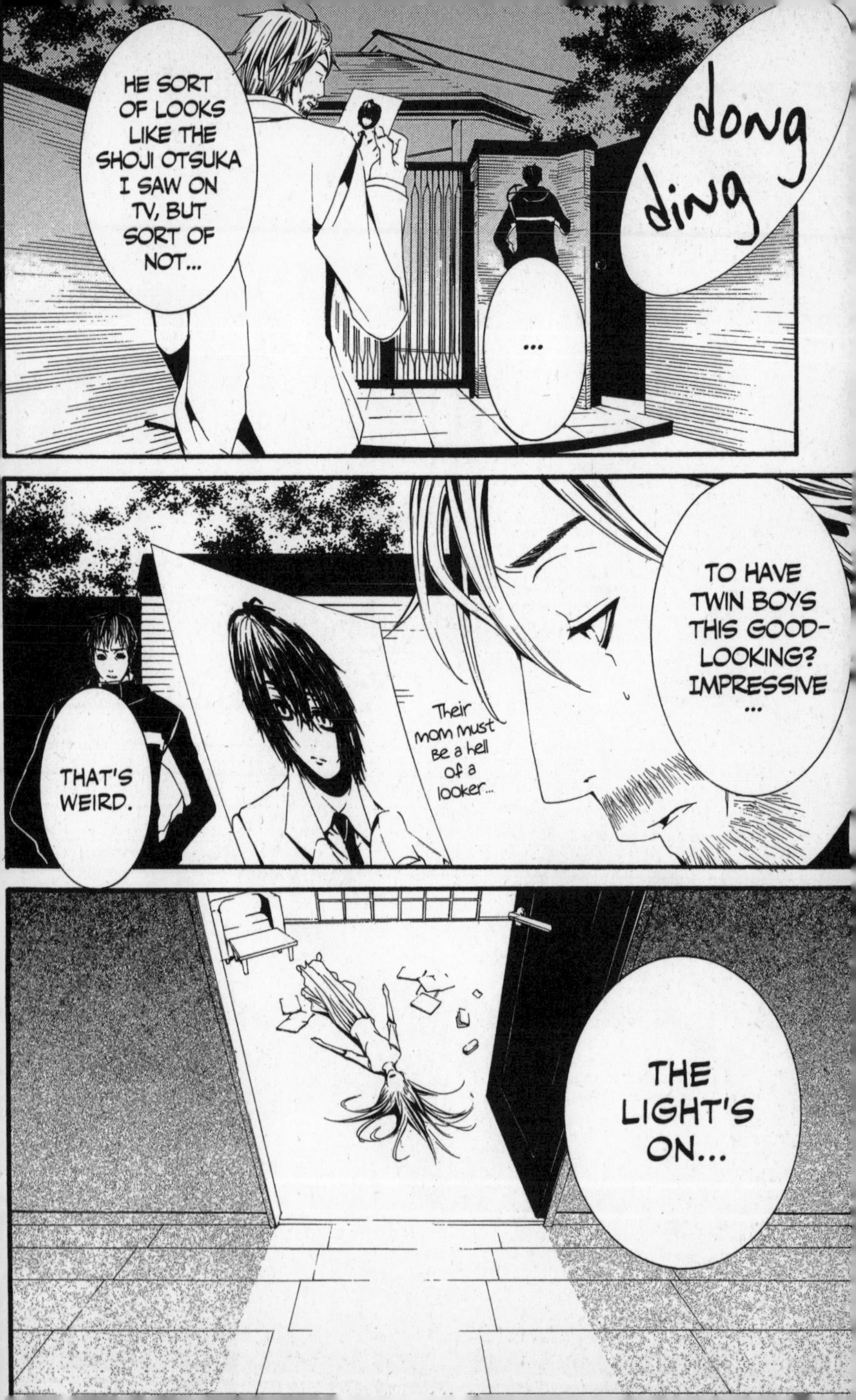
dong ding
...
HE SORT OF LOOKS LIKE THE SHOJI OTSUKA I SAW ON TV, BUT SORT OF NOT...
TO HAVE TWIN BOYS THIS GOOD-LOOKING? IMPRESSIVE ...
Their mom must be a hell of a looker...
THAT'S WEIRD.
THE LIGHT'S ON...

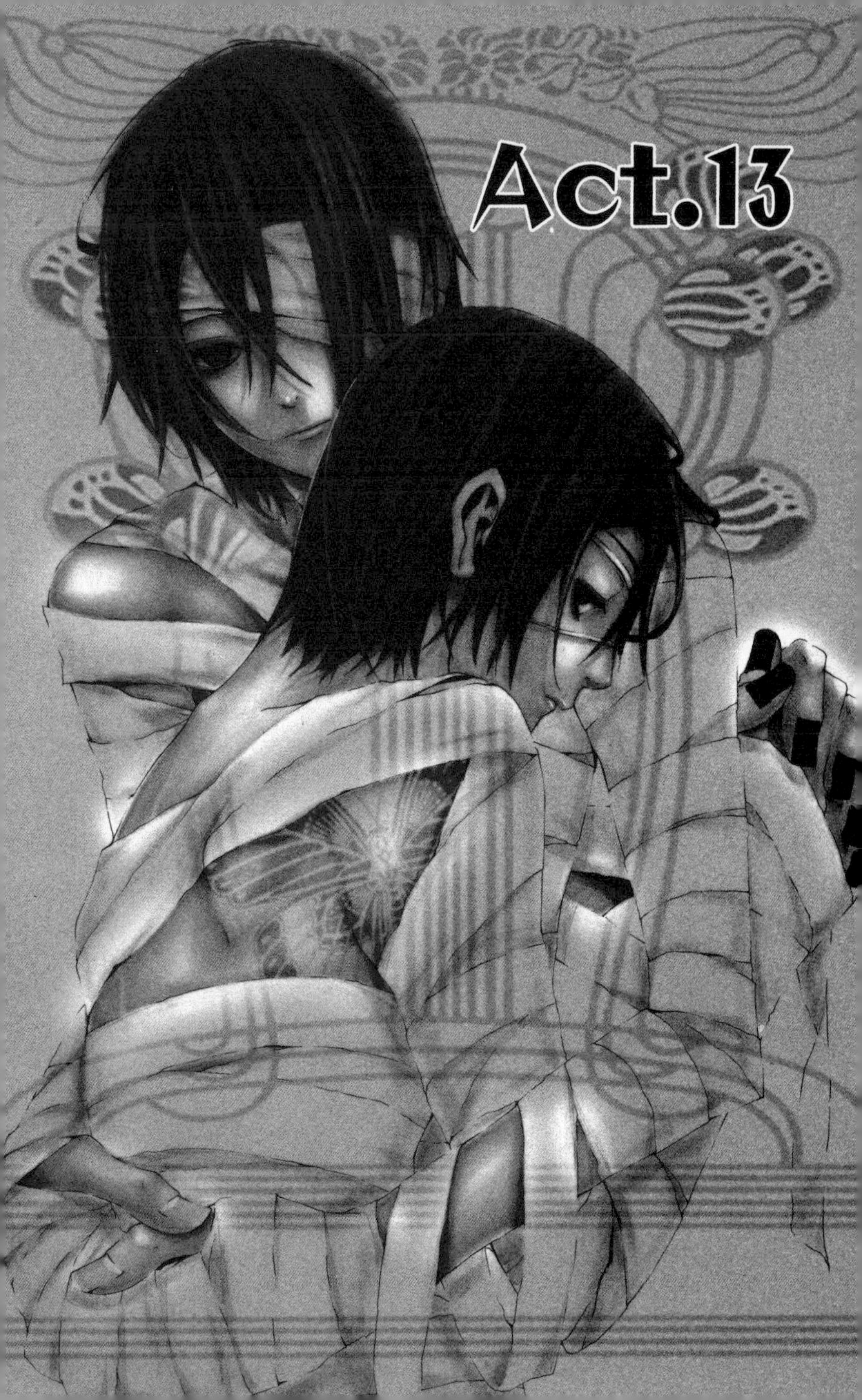
Act.13

[switch]
スイッチ

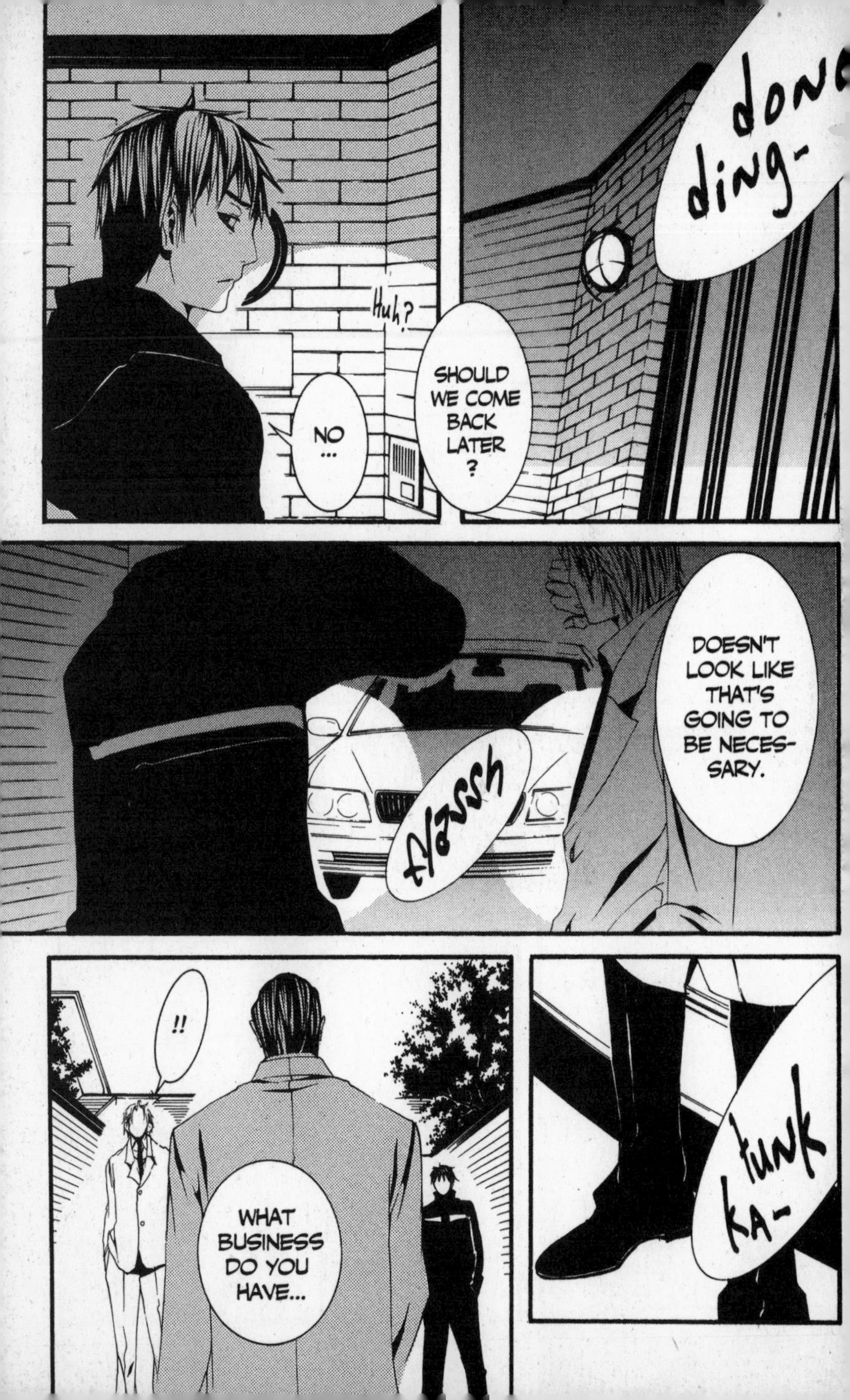
ding-dong
Huh?
SHOULD WE COME BACK LATER?
NO ...
DOESN'T LOOK LIKE THAT'S GOING TO BE NECES-SARY.
flasssh
ka-tunk
!!
WHAT BUSINESS DO YOU HAVE...

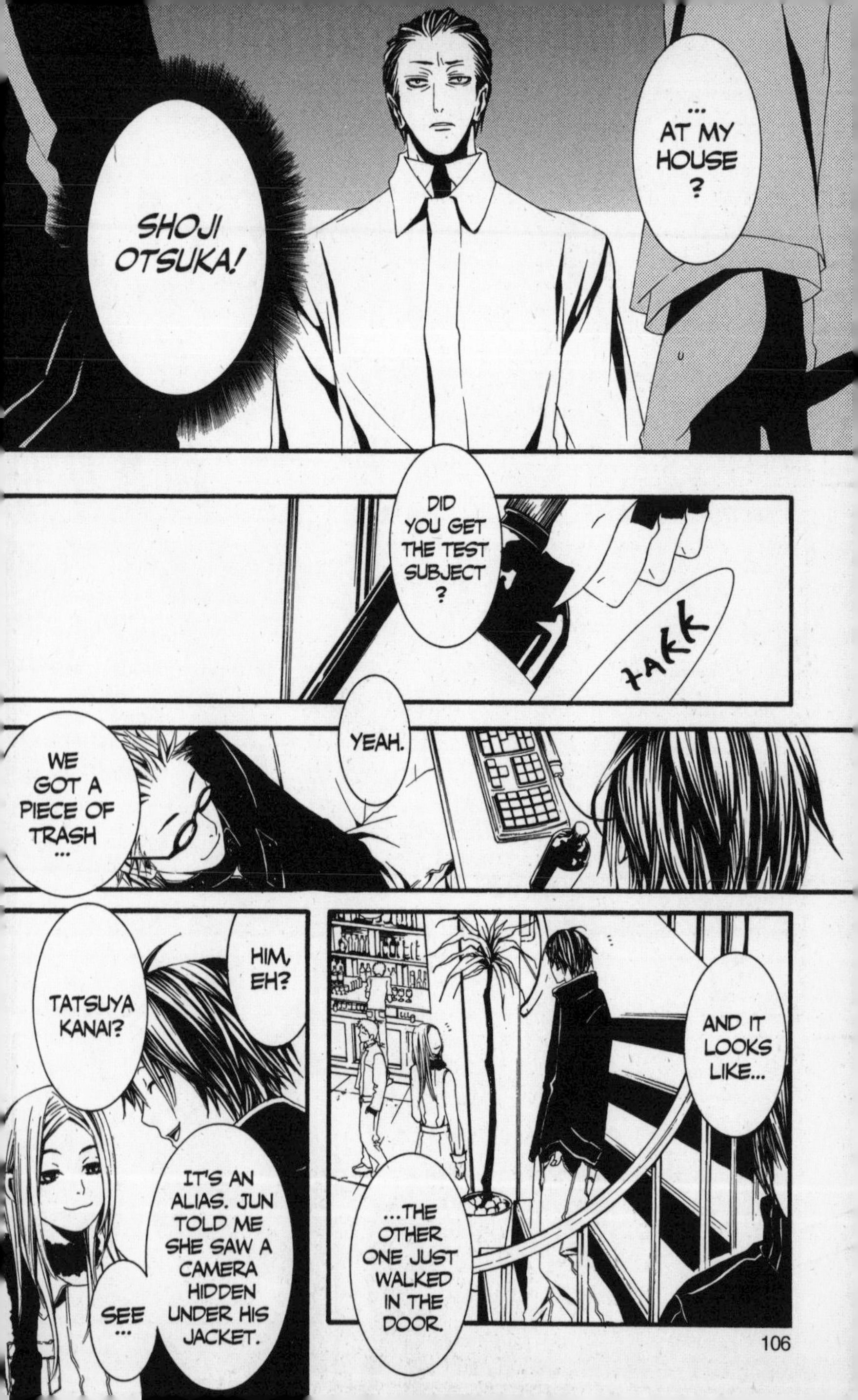
... AT MY HOUSE ?
SHOJI OTSUKA!
DID YOU GET THE TEST SUBJECT ?
TAKK
YEAH.
WE GOT A PIECE OF TRASH ...
AND IT LOOKS LIKE...
...THE OTHER ONE JUST WALKED IN THE DOOR.
HIM, EH?
TATSUYA KANAI?
IT'S AN ALIAS. JUN TOLD ME SHE SAW A CAMERA HIDDEN UNDER HIS JACKET.
SEE ...

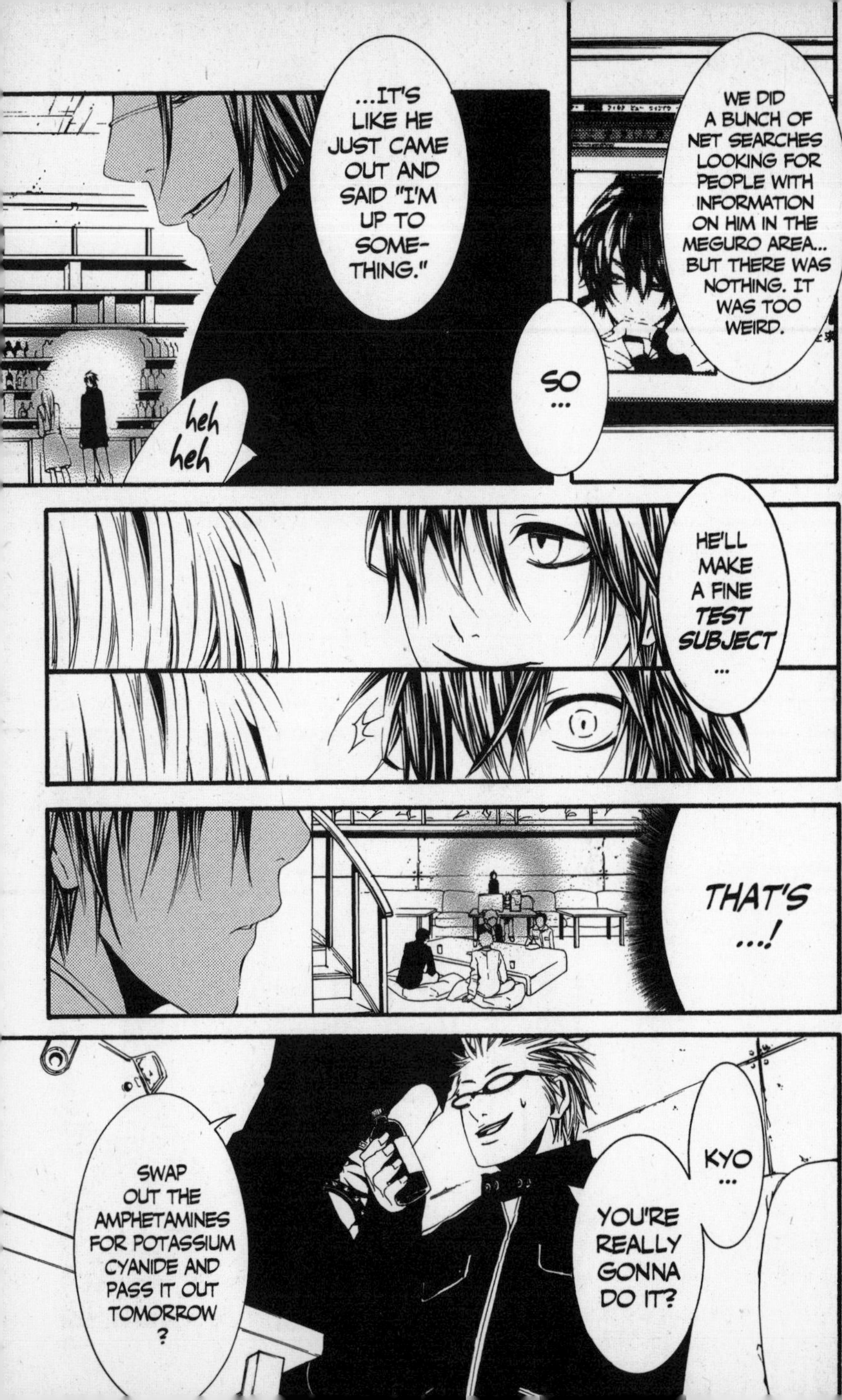
WE DID A BUNCH OF NET SEARCHES LOOKING FOR PEOPLE WITH INFORMATION ON HIM IN THE MEGURO AREA... BUT THERE WAS NOTHING. IT WAS TOO WEIRD.
SO ...
...IT'S LIKE HE JUST CAME OUT AND SAID "I'M UP TO SOME-THING."
heh heh
HE'LL MAKE A FINE TEST SUBJECT ...
THAT'S ...!
KYO ...
YOU'RE REALLY GONNA DO IT?
SWAP OUT THE AMPHETAMINES FOR POTASSIUM CYANIDE AND PASS IT OUT TOMORROW ?

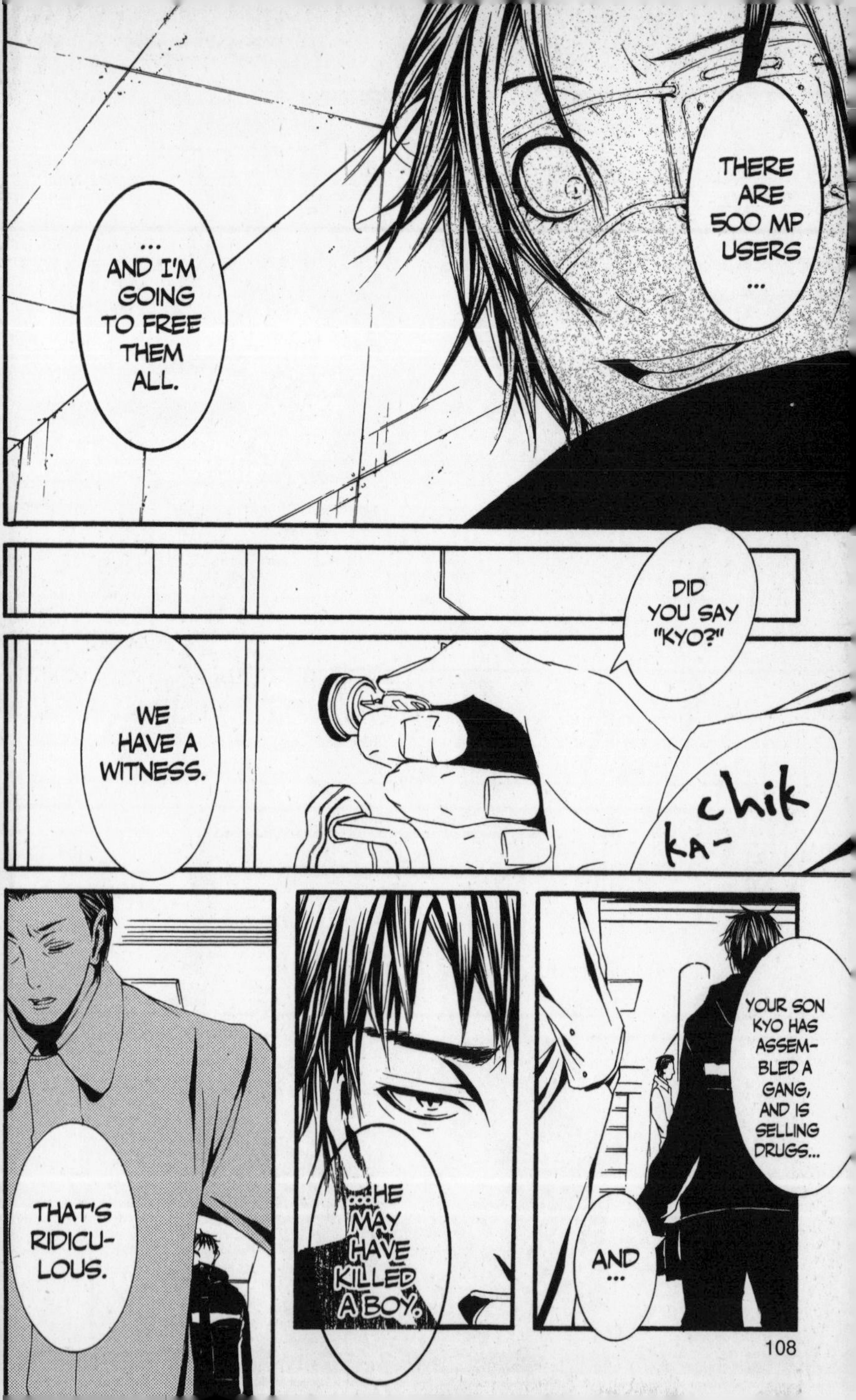
THERE ARE 500 MP USERS ...
... AND I'M GOING TO FREE THEM ALL.
DID YOU SAY "KYO?"
KA-CHIK
WE HAVE A WITNESS.
YOUR SON KYO HAS ASSEM-BLED A GANG, AND IS SELLING DRUGS...
AND ...
...HE MAY HAVE KILLED A BOY.
THAT'S RIDICU-LOUS.

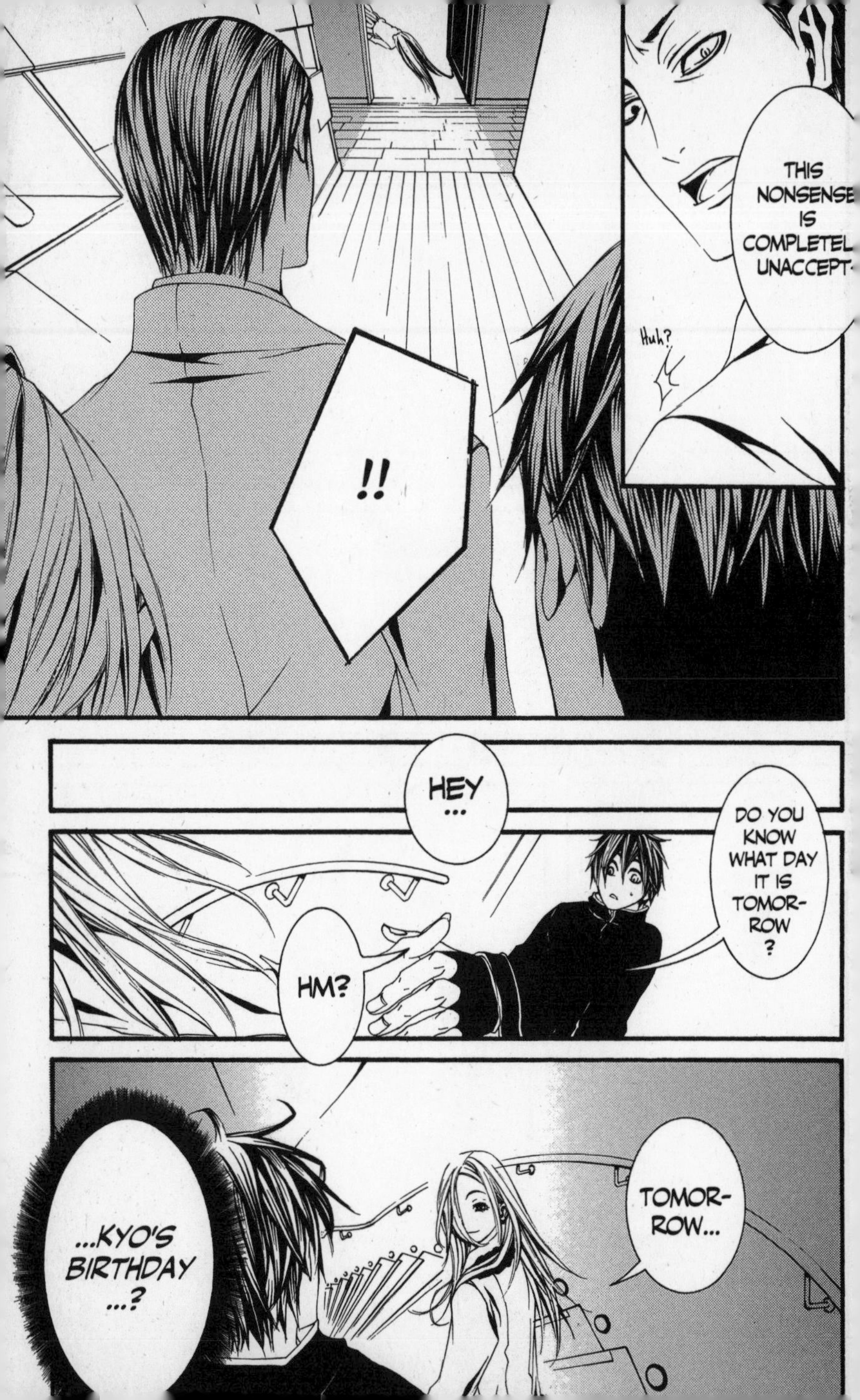
THIS NONSENSE IS COMPLETEL UNACCEPT-
Huh?
!!
HEY...
DO YOU KNOW WHAT DAY IT IS TOMOR-ROW?
HM?
TOMOR-ROW...
...KYO'S BIRTHDAY...?

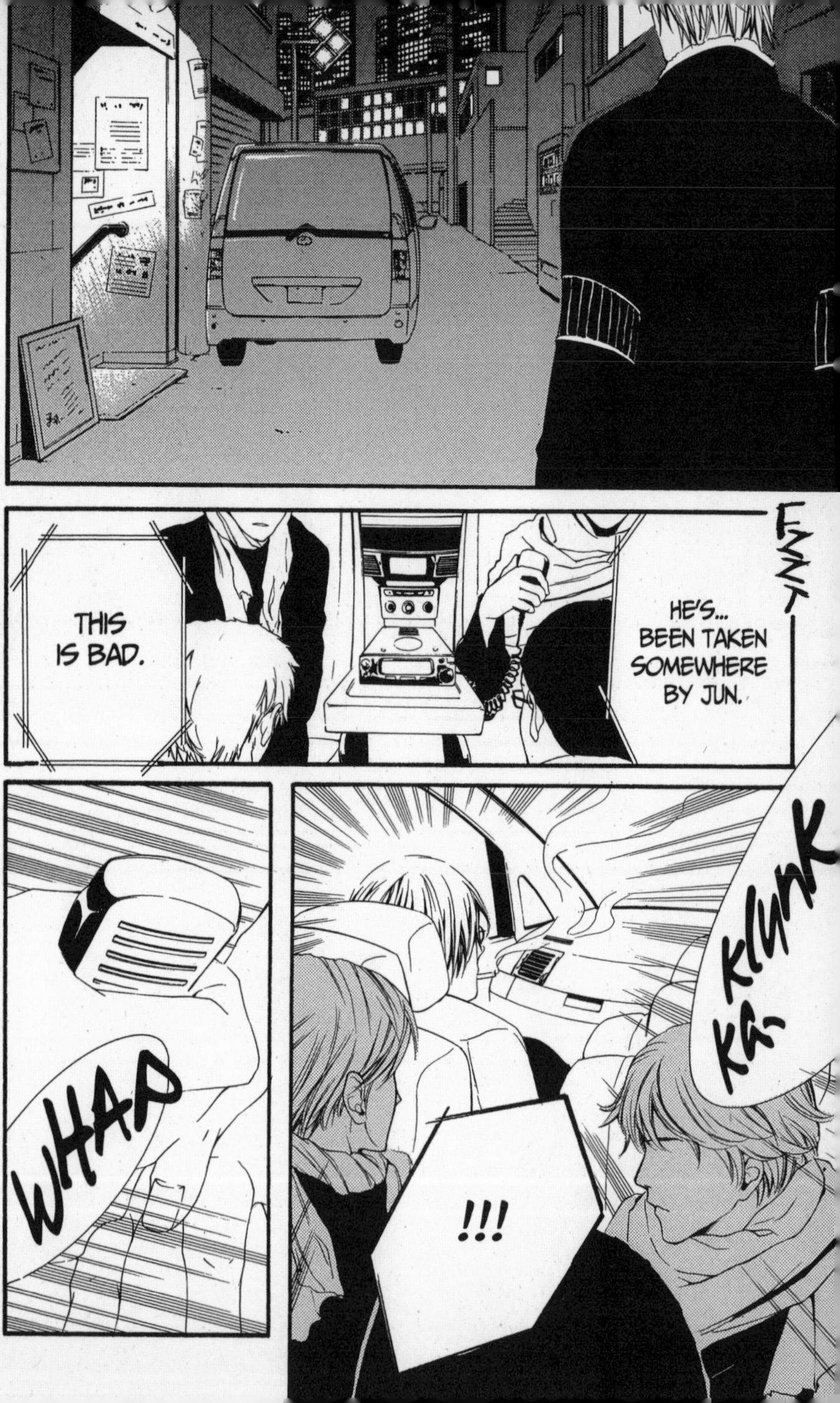
FZZT
HE'S... BEEN TAKEN SOMEWHERE BY JUN.
THIS IS BAD.
KA-KLUNK
!!!
WHAP

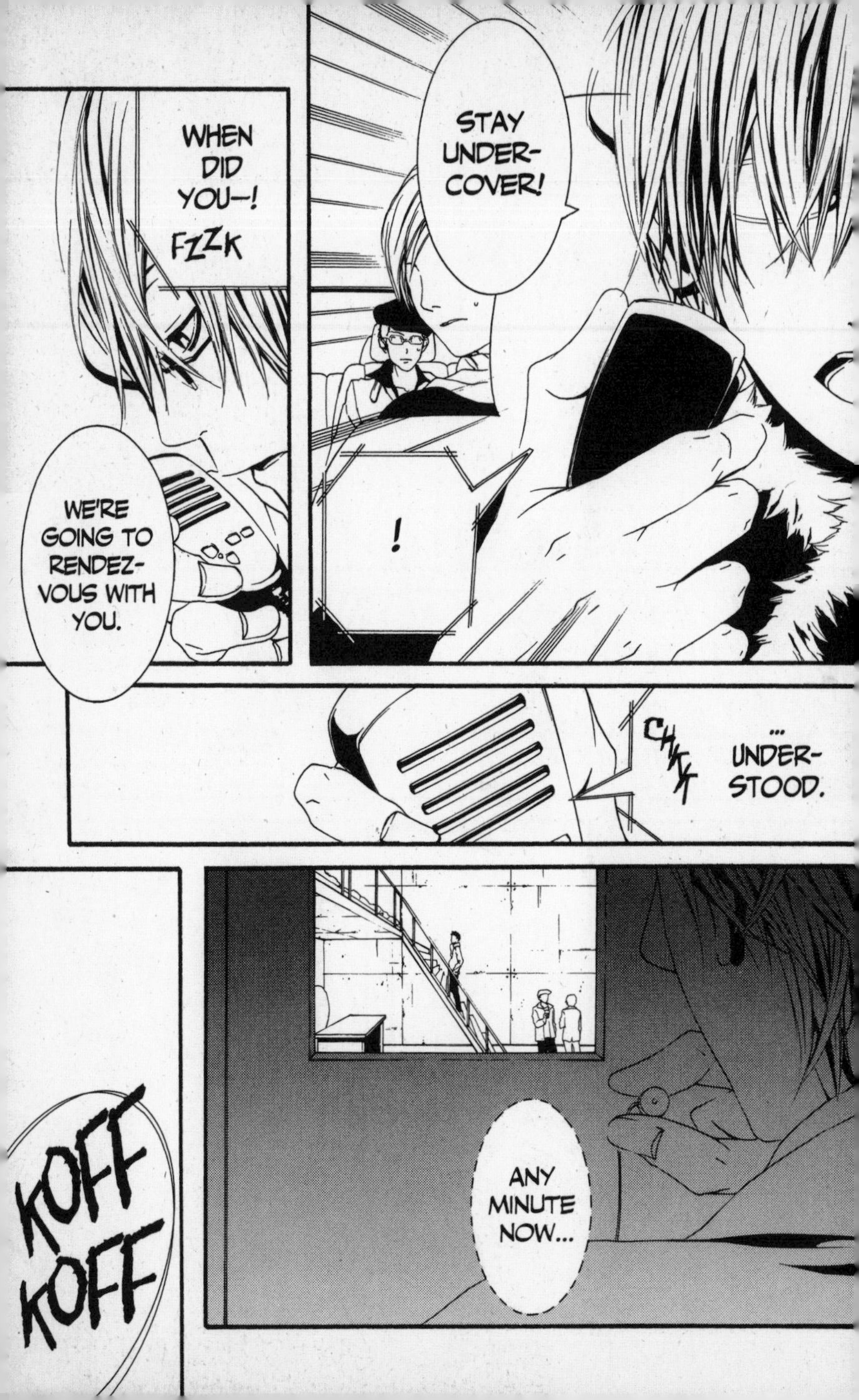
STAY UNDER-COVER!
!
WHEN DID YOU--!
FZZK
WE'RE GOING TO RENDEZ-VOUS WITH YOU.
CHKKK
... UNDER-STOOD.
ANY MINUTE NOW...
KOFF KOFF

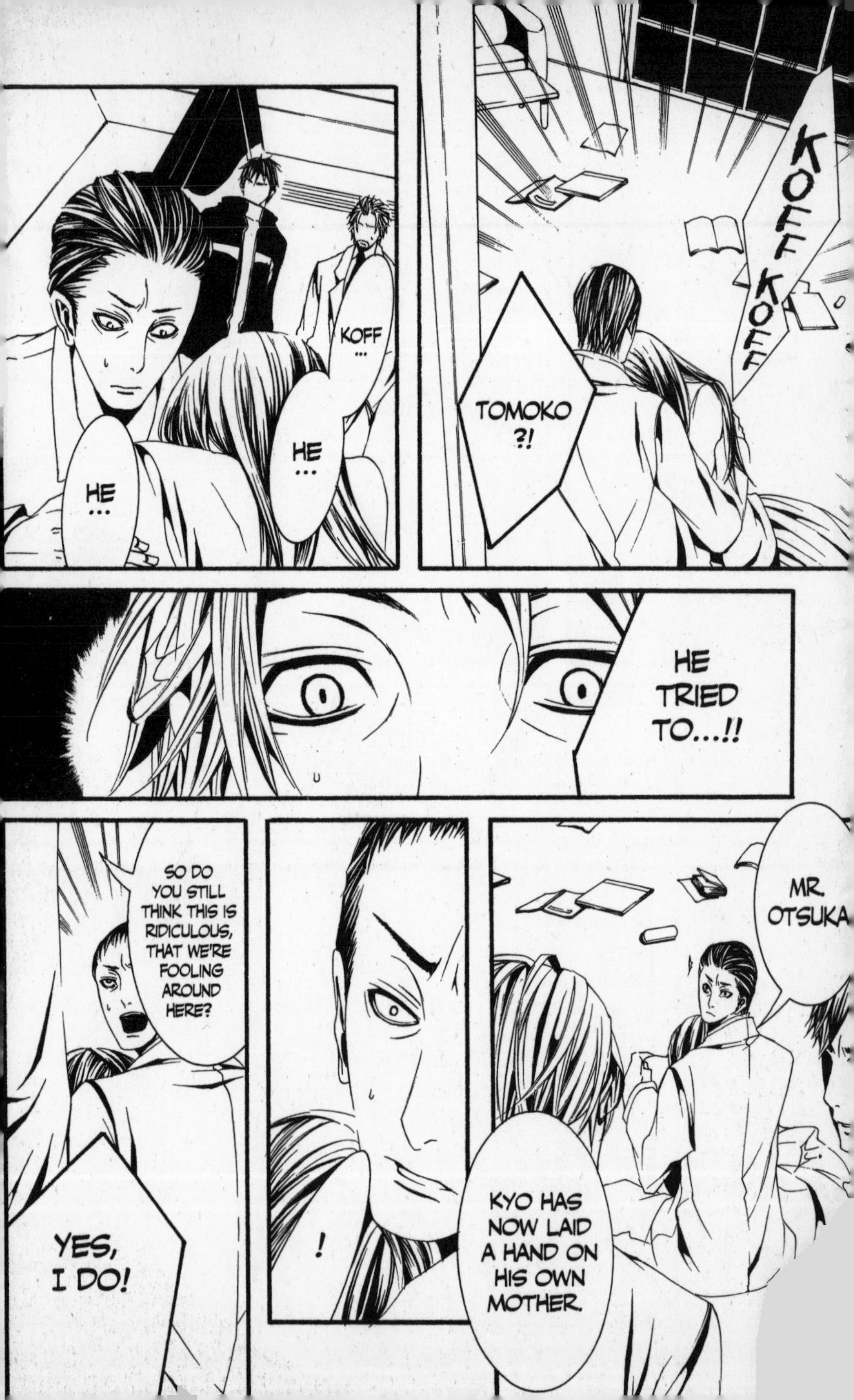
KOFF KOFF KOFF
TOMOKO?!
KOFF...
HE...
HE...
HE TRIED TO...!!
MR. OTSUKA
KYO HAS NOW LAID A HAND ON HIS OWN MOTHER.
!
SO DO YOU STILL THINK THIS IS RIDICULOUS, THAT WE'RE FOOLING AROUND HERE?
YES, I DO!

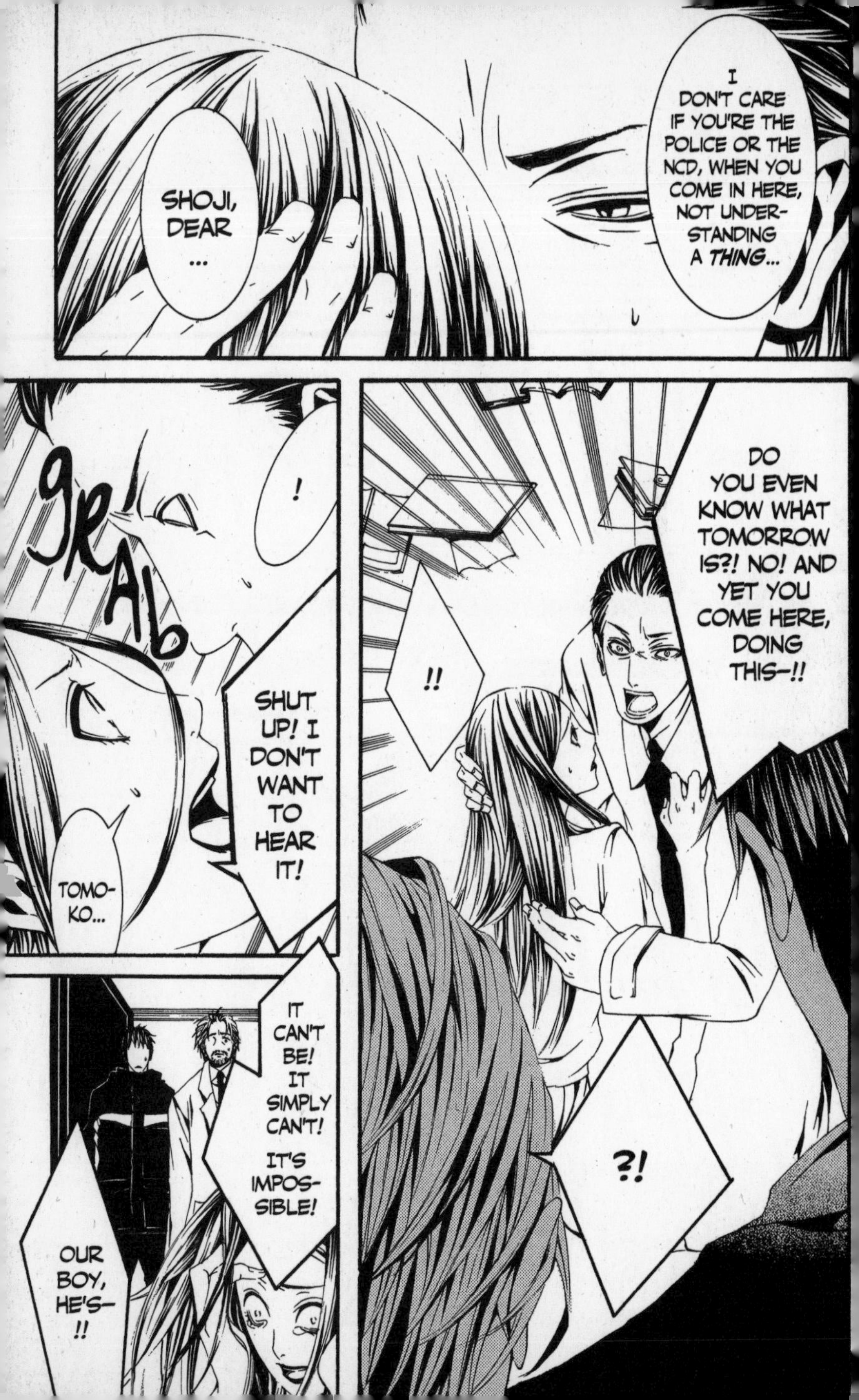
I DON'T CARE IF YOU'RE THE POLICE OR THE NCD, WHEN YOU COME IN HERE, NOT UNDER-STANDING A *THING*...
SHOJI, DEAR ...
DO YOU EVEN KNOW WHAT TOMORROW IS?! NO! AND YET YOU COME HERE, DOING THIS-!!
!!
?!
!
GRAB
SHUT UP! I DON'T WANT TO HEAR IT!
TOMO-KO...
IT CAN'T BE! IT SIMPLY CAN'T!
IT'S IMPOS-SIBLE!
OUR BOY, HE'S-!!

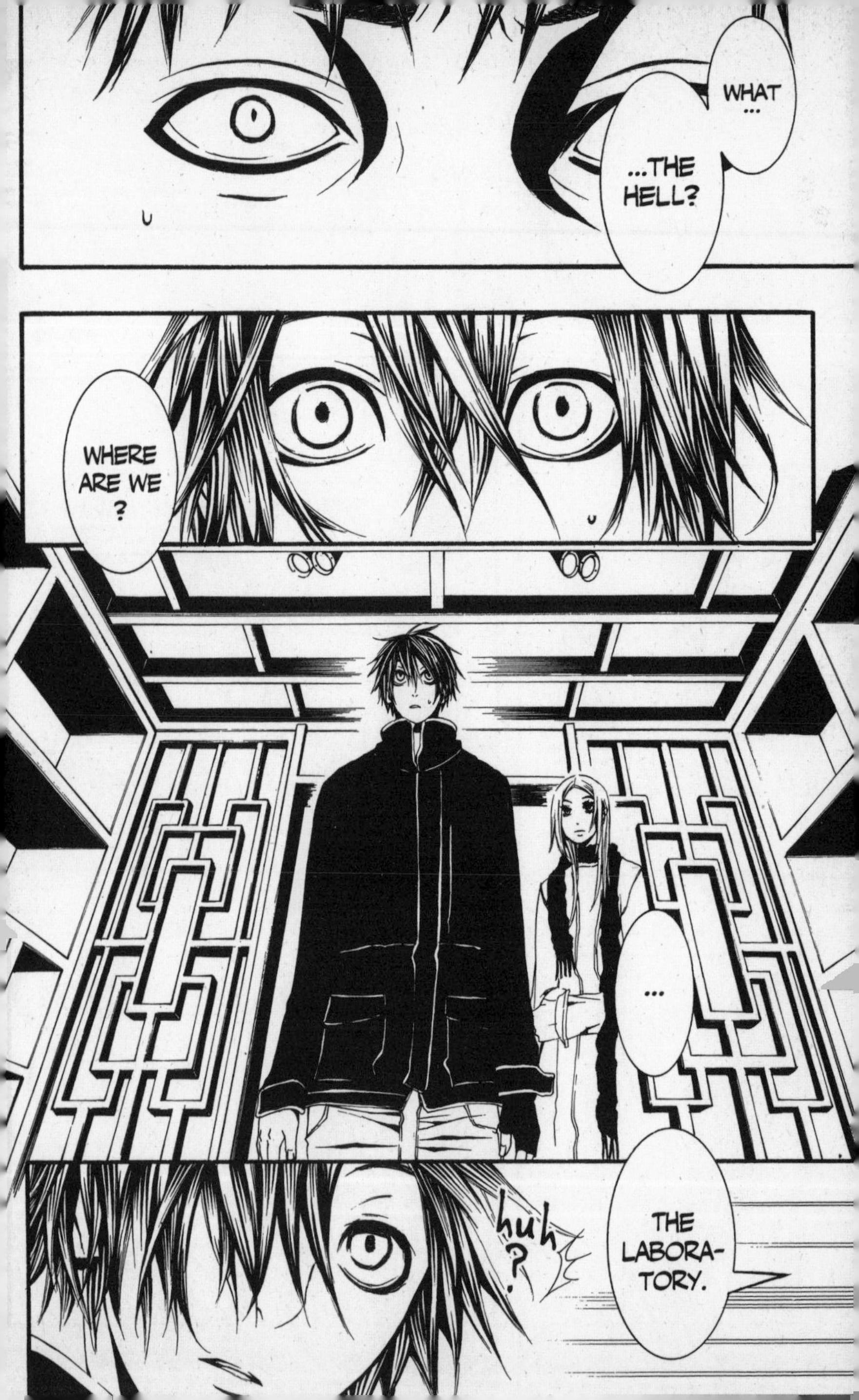
WHAT ...
...THE HELL?
WHERE ARE WE ?
...
THE LABORA-TORY.
huh ?

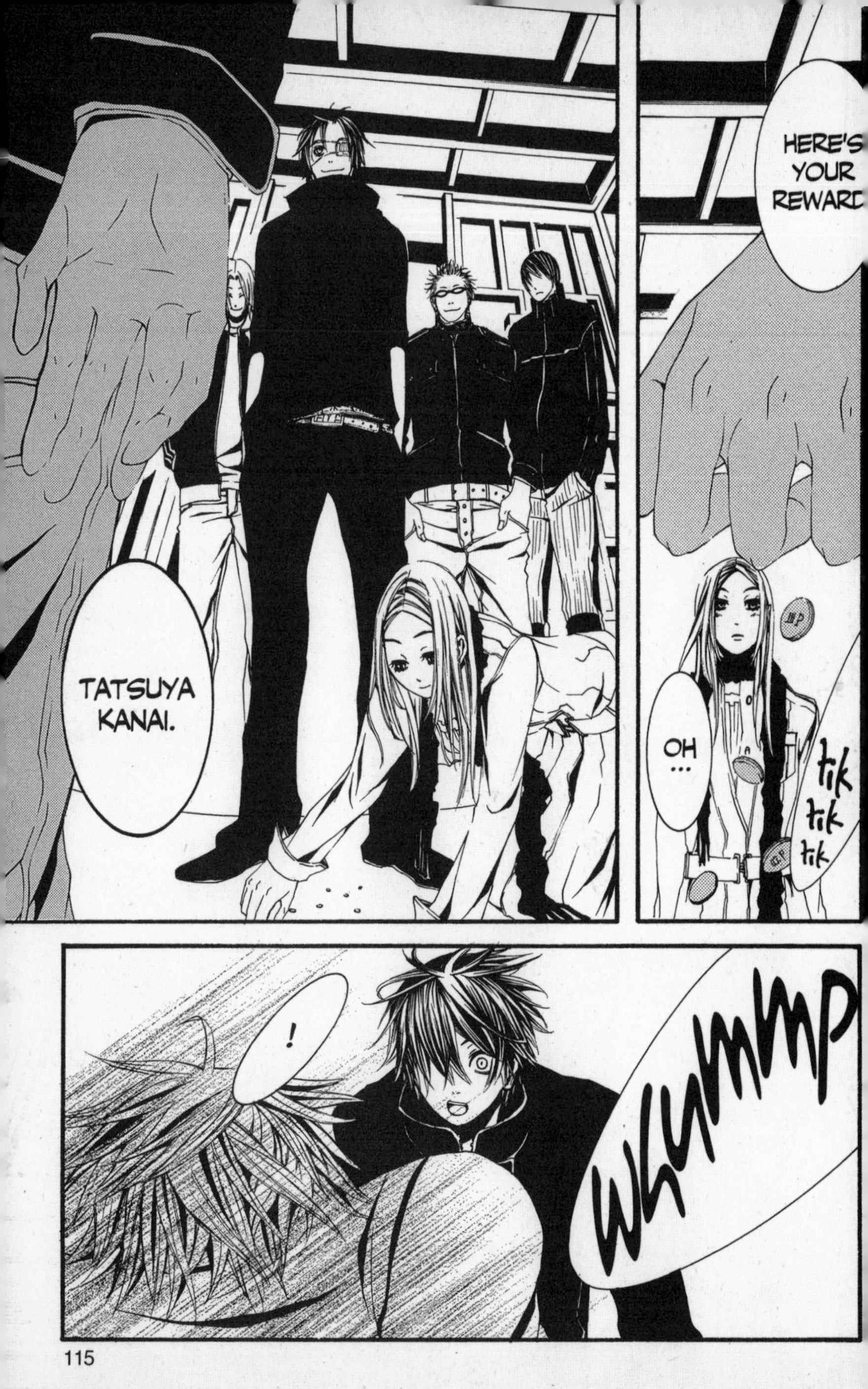
HERE'S YOUR REWARD
OH ...
tik tik tik
TATSUYA KANAI.
!
WHUMMP

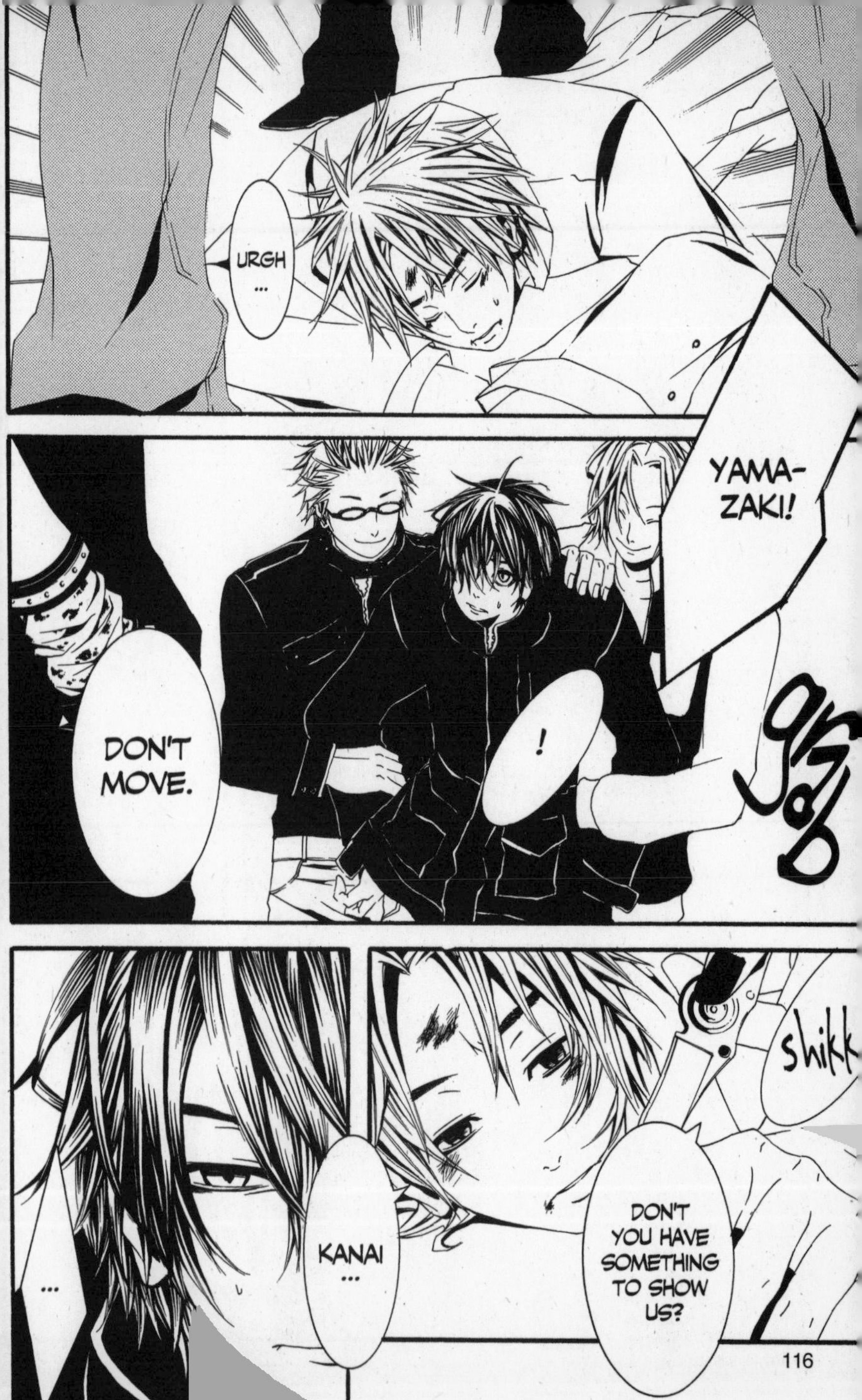
URGH ...
YAMA-ZAKI!
grab
!
DON'T MOVE.
shikk
DON'T YOU HAVE SOMETHING TO SHOW US?
KANAI ...
...

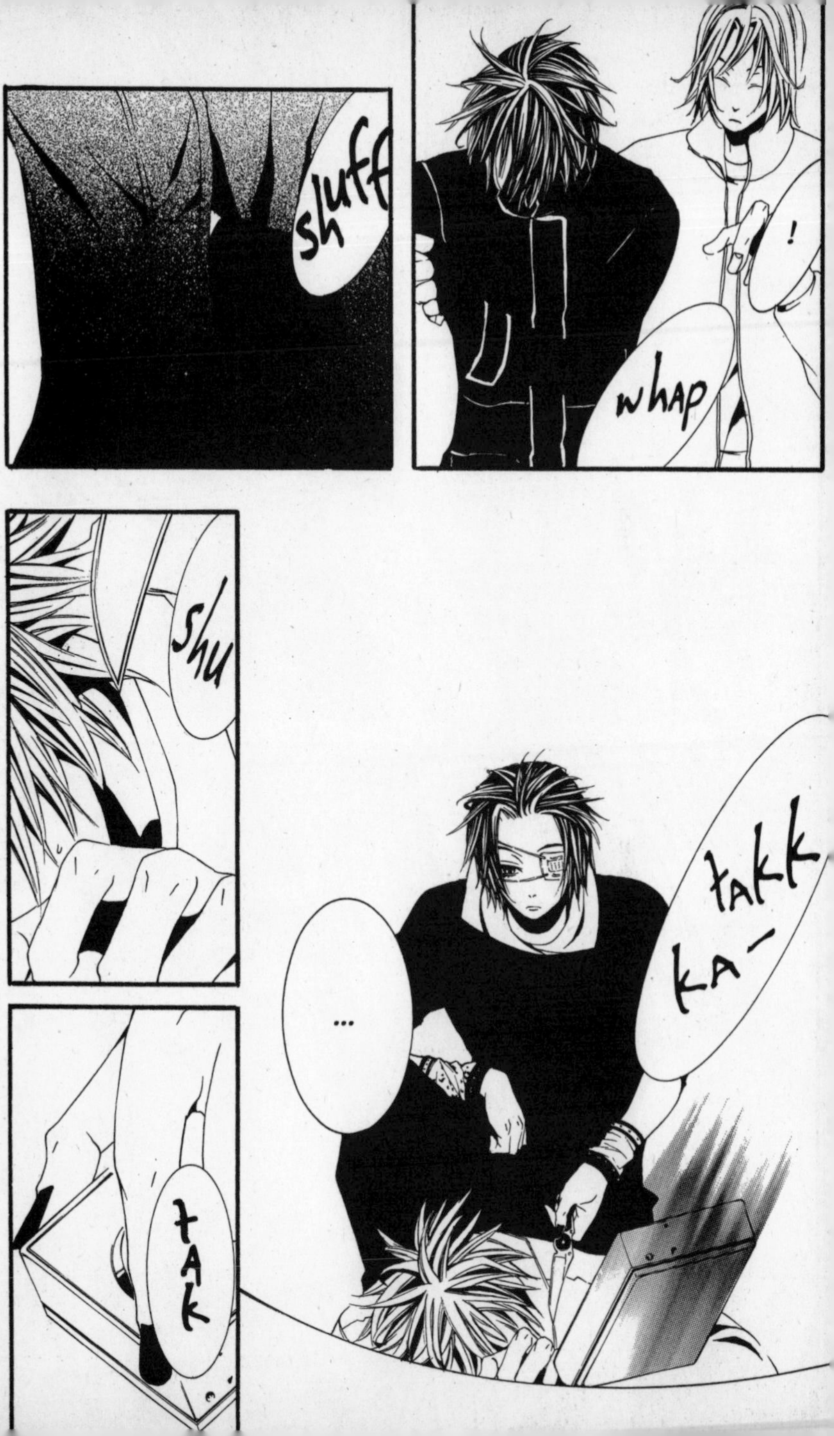
!
whap
shuff
takk ka-
...
shu
tak

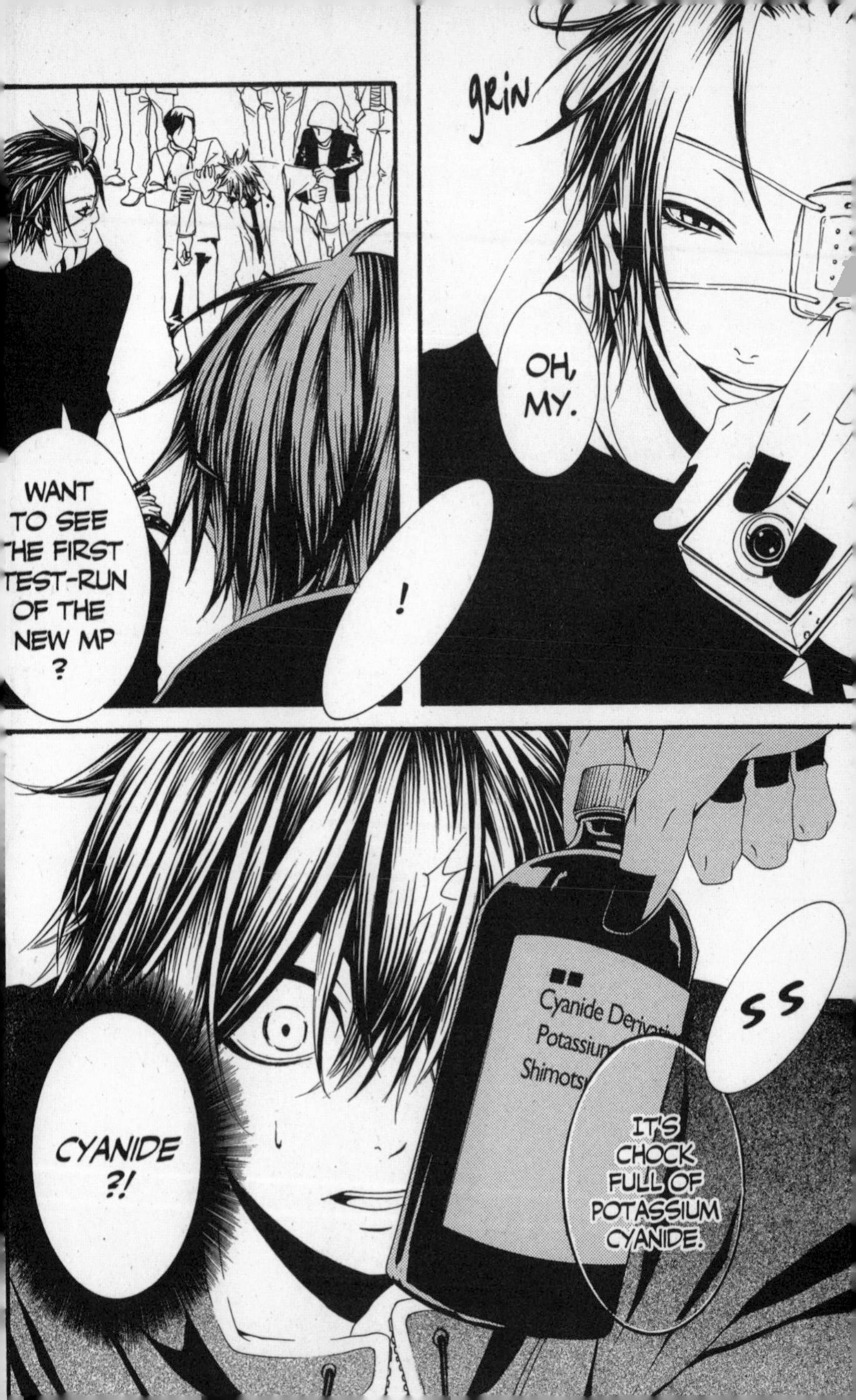
GRIN
OH, MY.
WANT TO SEE THE FIRST TEST-RUN OF THE NEW MP?
!
SS
IT'S CHOCK FULL OF POTASSIUM CYANIDE.
CYANIDE?!

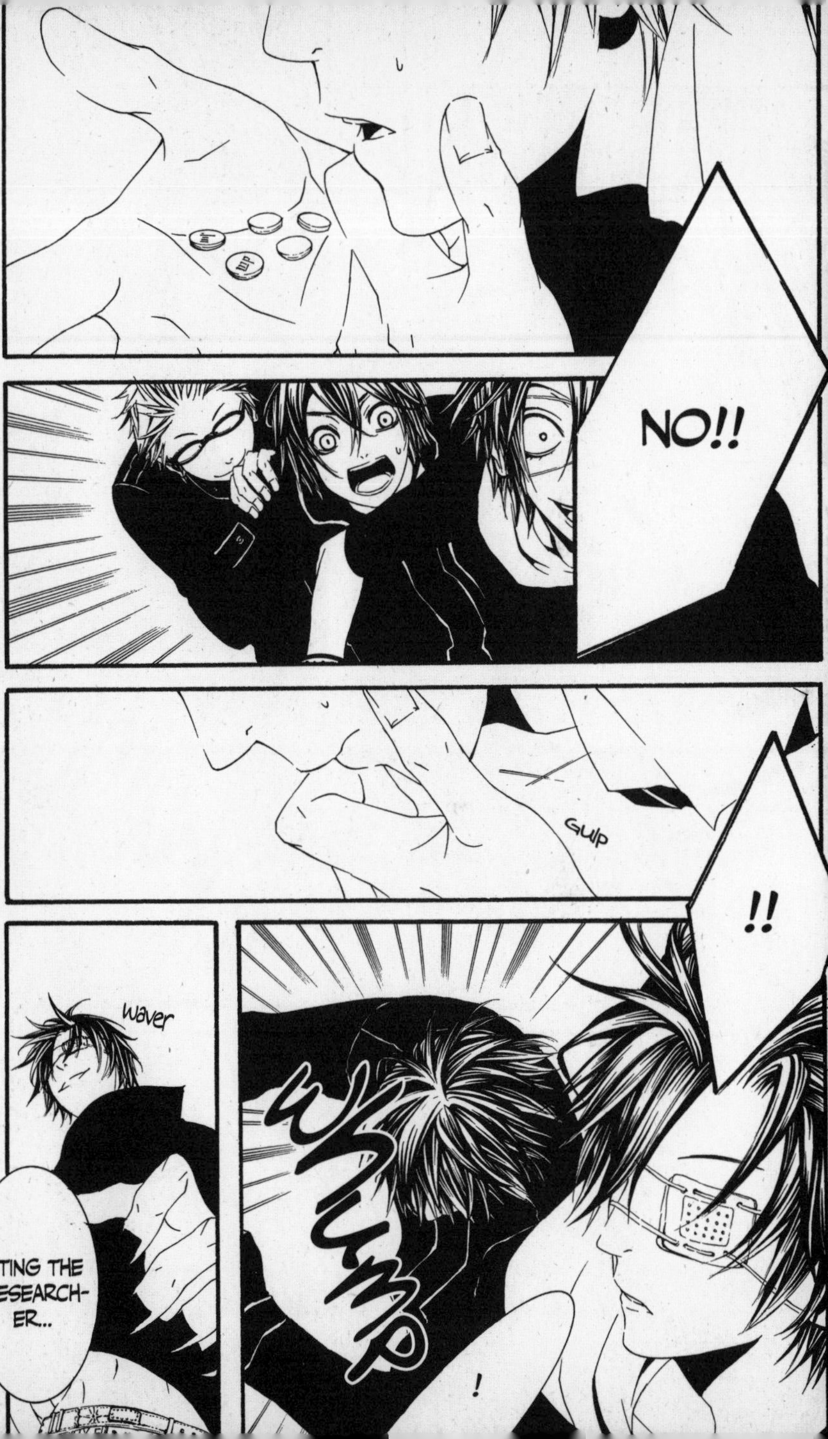
NO!!
Gulp
!!
WHUMP
!
waver
BITING THE RESEARCH-ER...

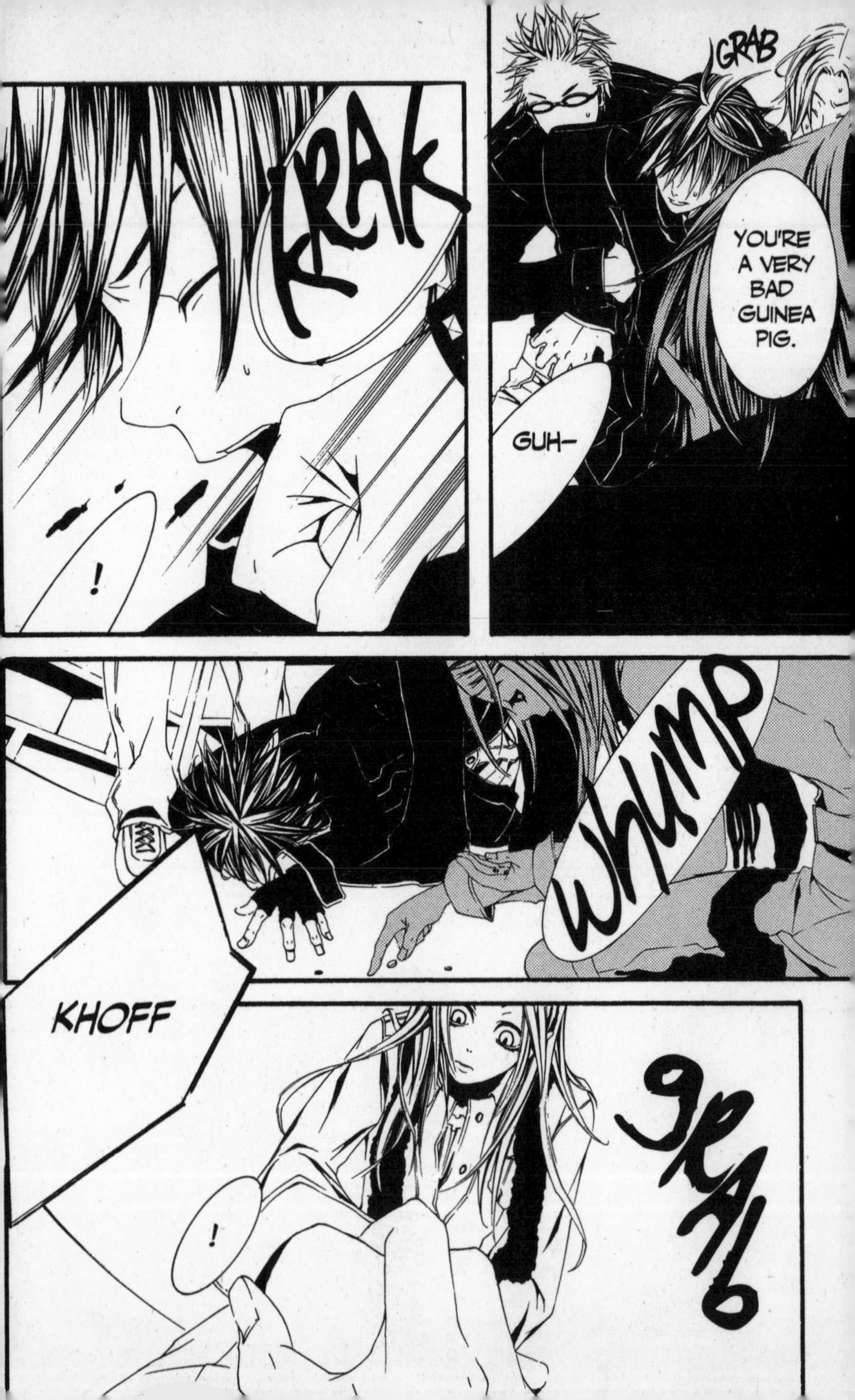
GRAB
YOU'RE A VERY BAD GUINEA PIG.
GUH-
KRAK
!
WHUMP
GRAB
KHOFF
!

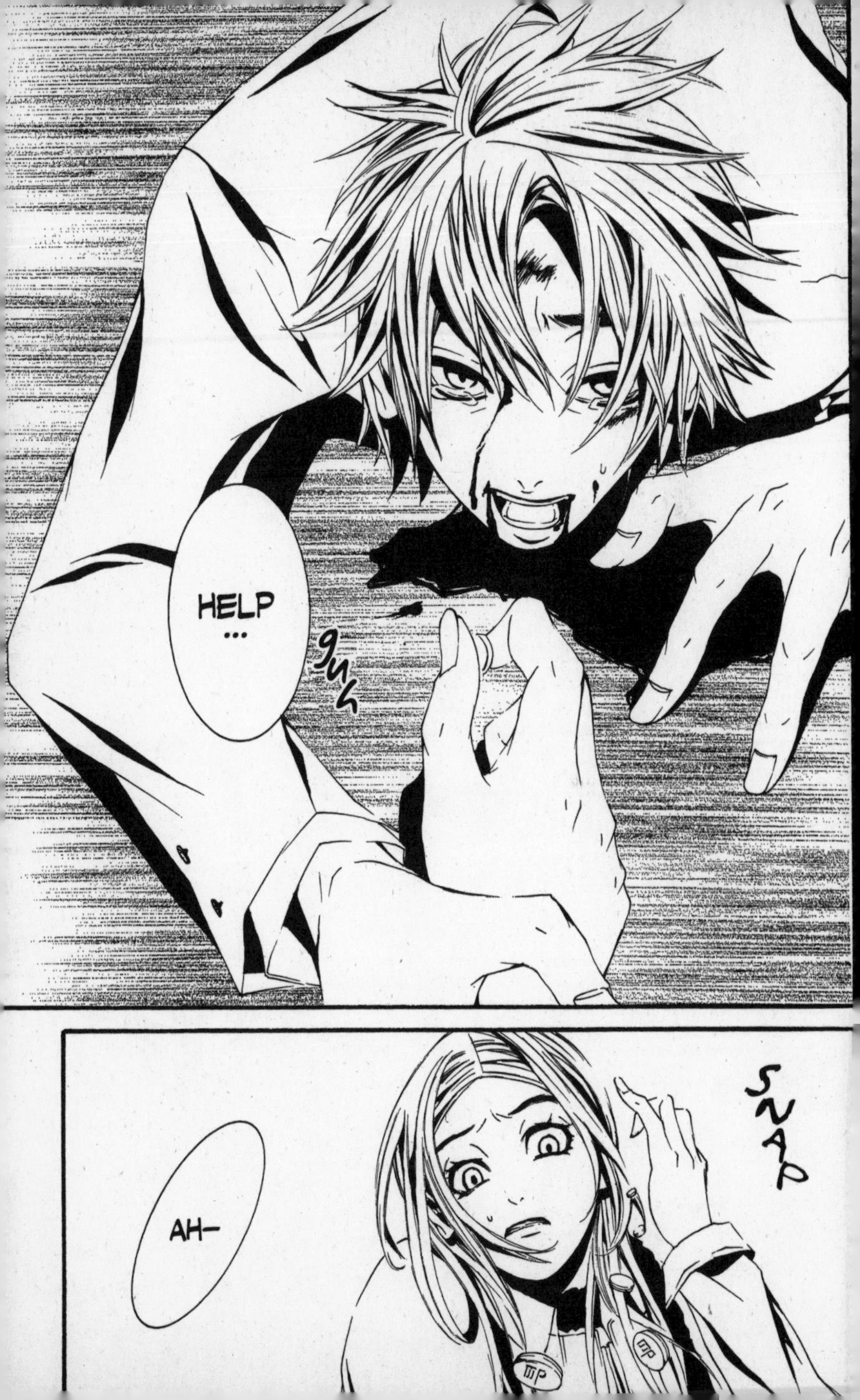
HELP ...
guh
SNAP
AH-

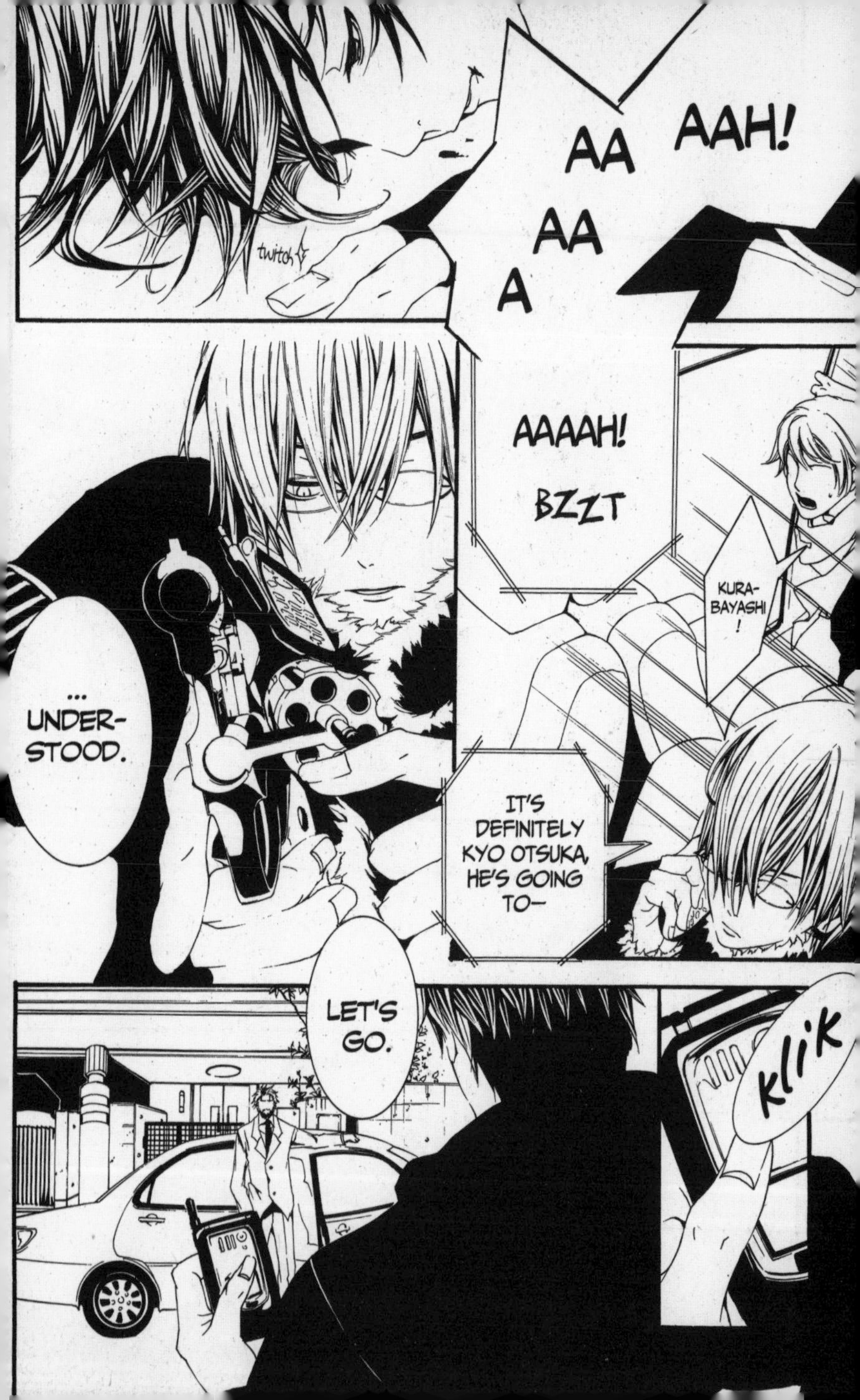

A AA AA AAH!
twitch
KURA-BAYASHI!
AAAAH!
BZZT
IT'S DEFINITELY KYO OTSUKA, HE'S GOING TO—
...UNDERSTOOD.
LET'S GO.
klik

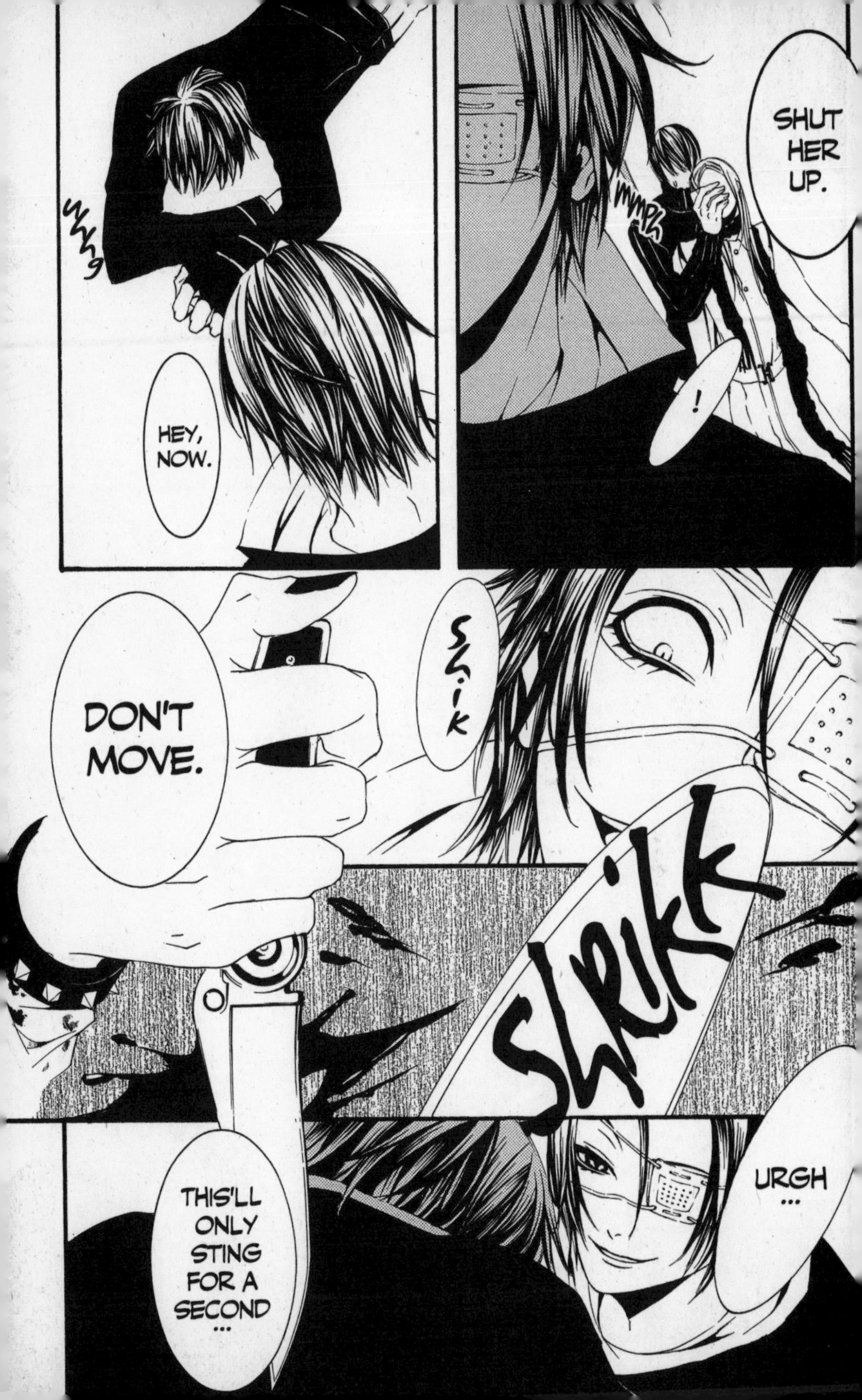
SHUT HER UP.
!
HEY, NOW.
SKRIK
DON'T MOVE.
SKRIK
URGH ...
THIS'LL ONLY STING FOR A SECOND ...

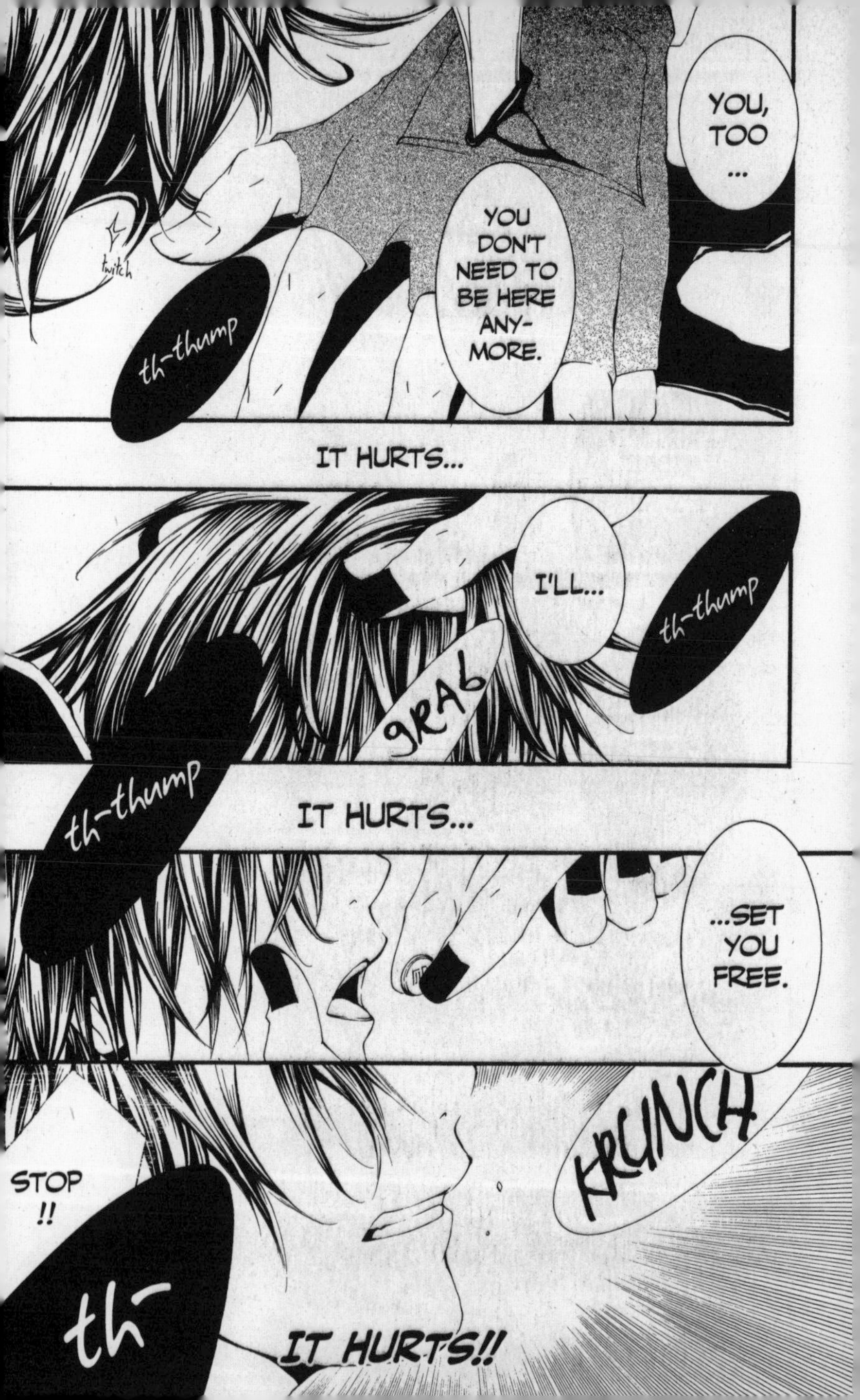
YOU, TOO ...
YOU DON'T NEED TO BE HERE ANY-MORE.
twitch
th-thump
IT HURTS...
th-thump
I'LL...
GRAB
th-thump
IT HURTS...
...SET YOU FREE.
KRUNCH
STOP !!
th-
IT HURTS!!

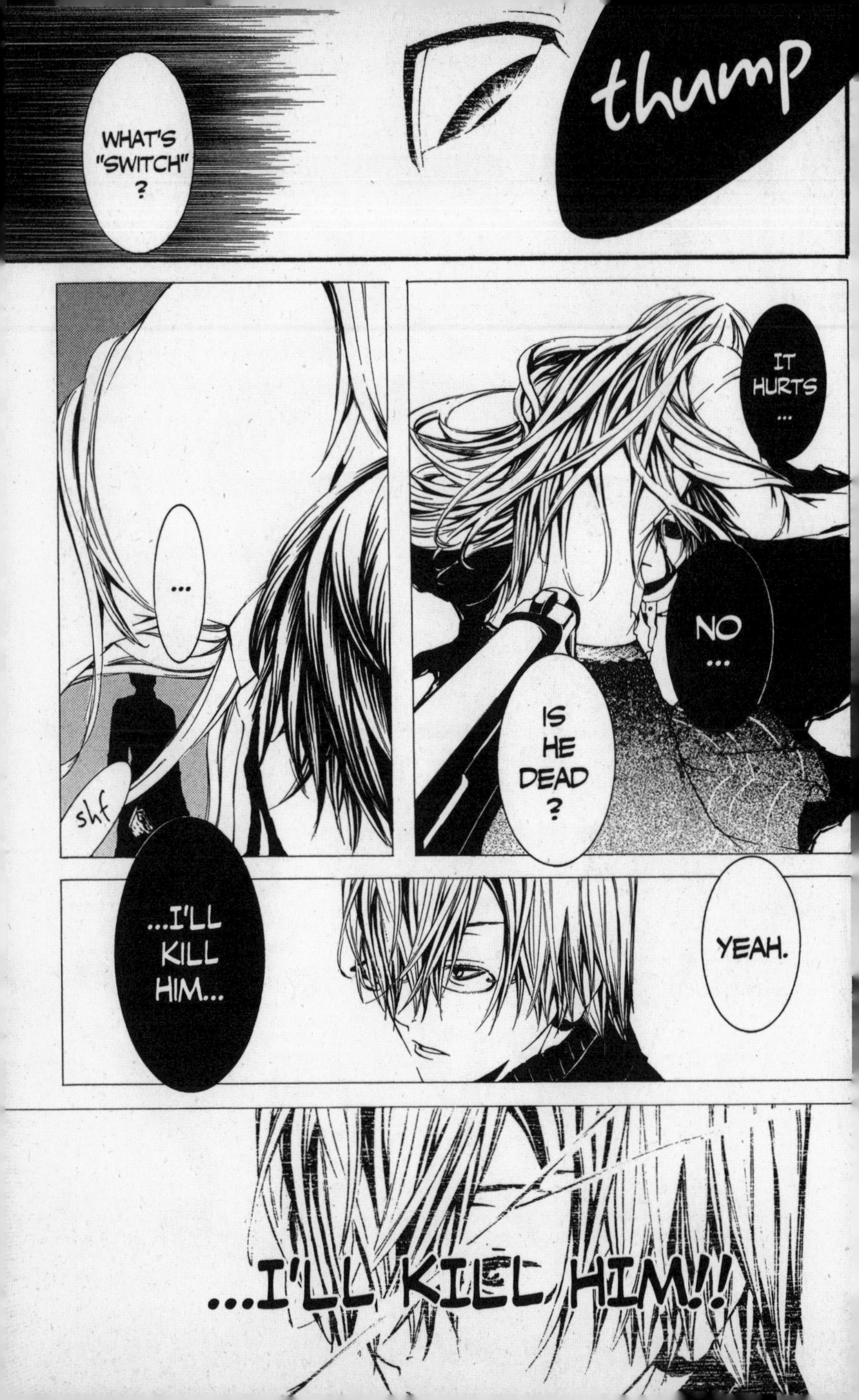
thump
WHAT'S "SWITCH" ?
IT HURTS ...
NO ...
IS HE DEAD ?
...
shf
YEAH.
...I'LL KILL HIM...
...I'LL KILL HIM!!

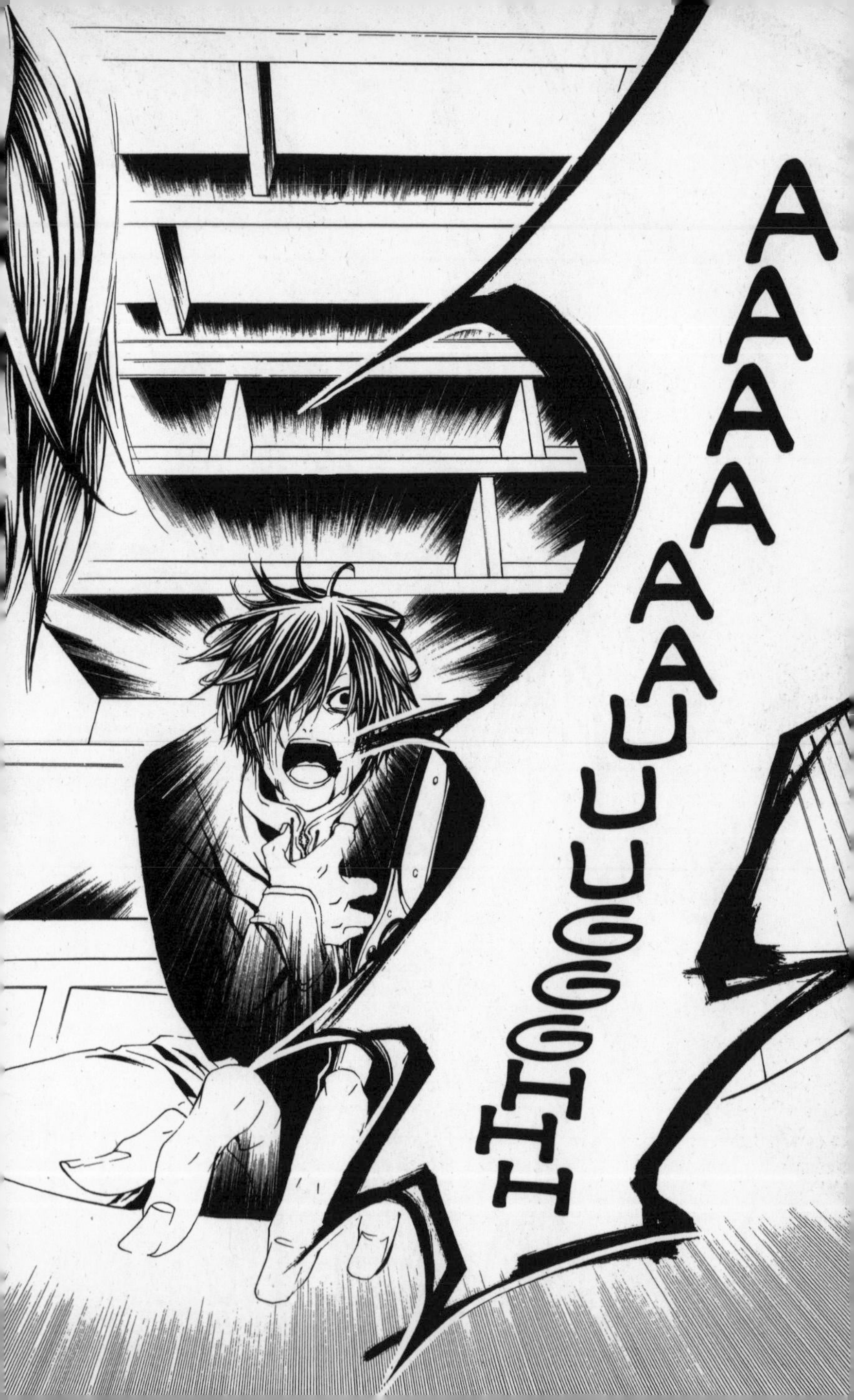
AAAAAAUUUGGGHHH

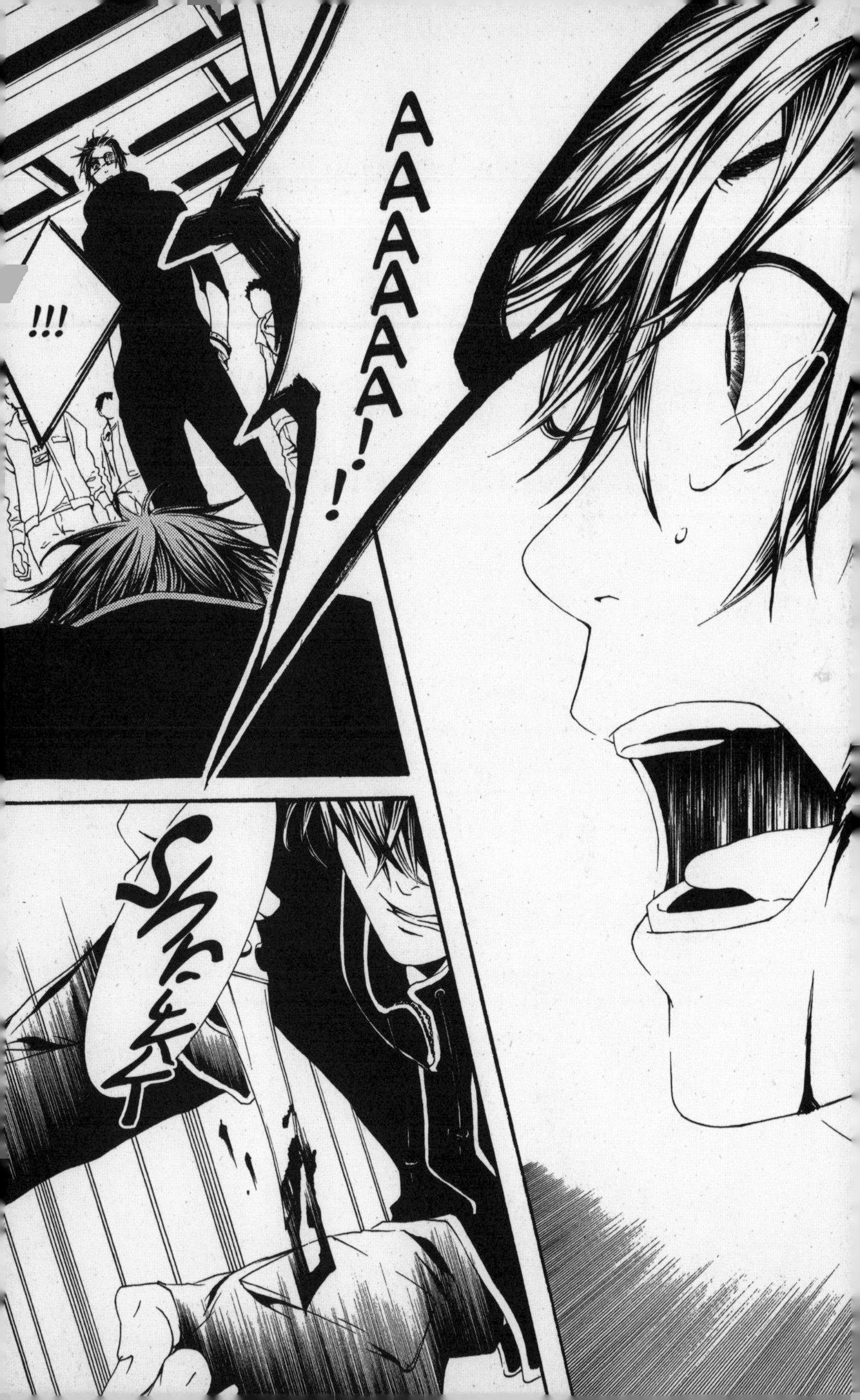
AAAAAA!!
!!!

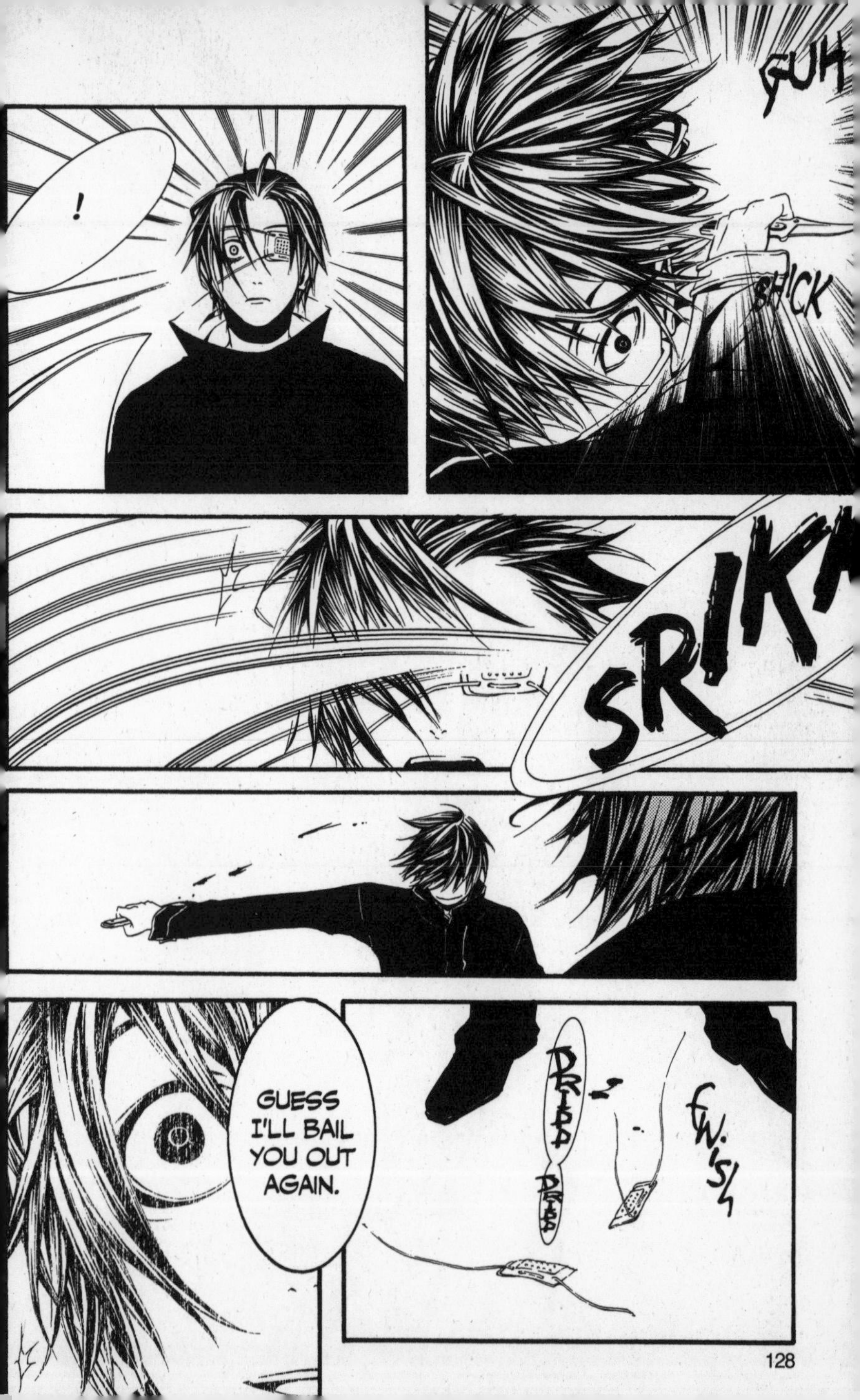
GUH
SHICK
!
SRIK
DRIPP
DRIPP
FWISH
GUESS I'LL BAIL YOU OUT AGAIN.

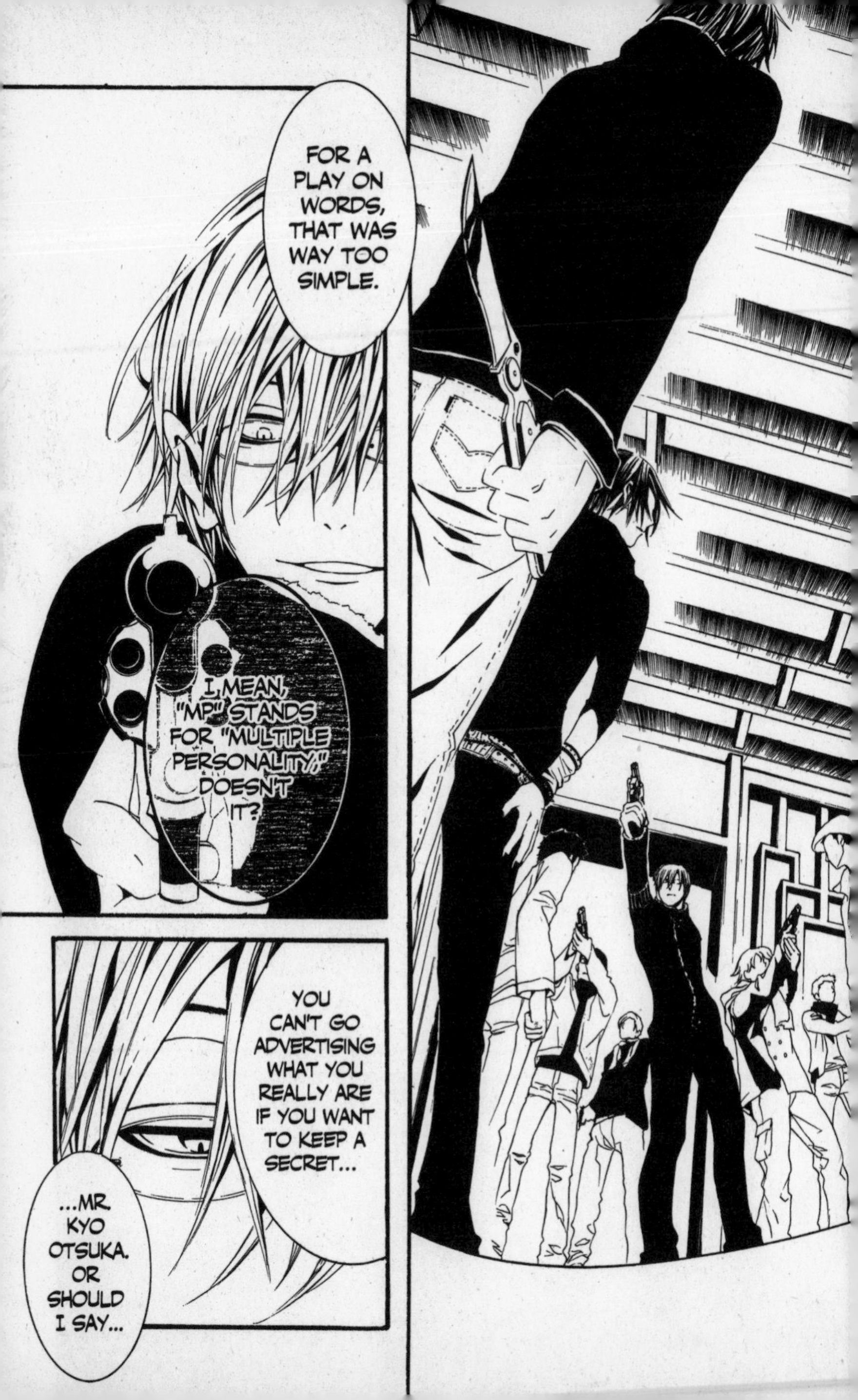
FOR A PLAY ON WORDS, THAT WAS WAY TOO SIMPLE.
I MEAN, "MP" STANDS FOR "MULTIPLE PERSONALITY," DOESN'T IT?
YOU CAN'T GO ADVERTISING WHAT YOU REALLY ARE IF YOU WANT TO KEEP A SECRET...
...MR. KYO OTSUKA. OR SHOULD I SAY...

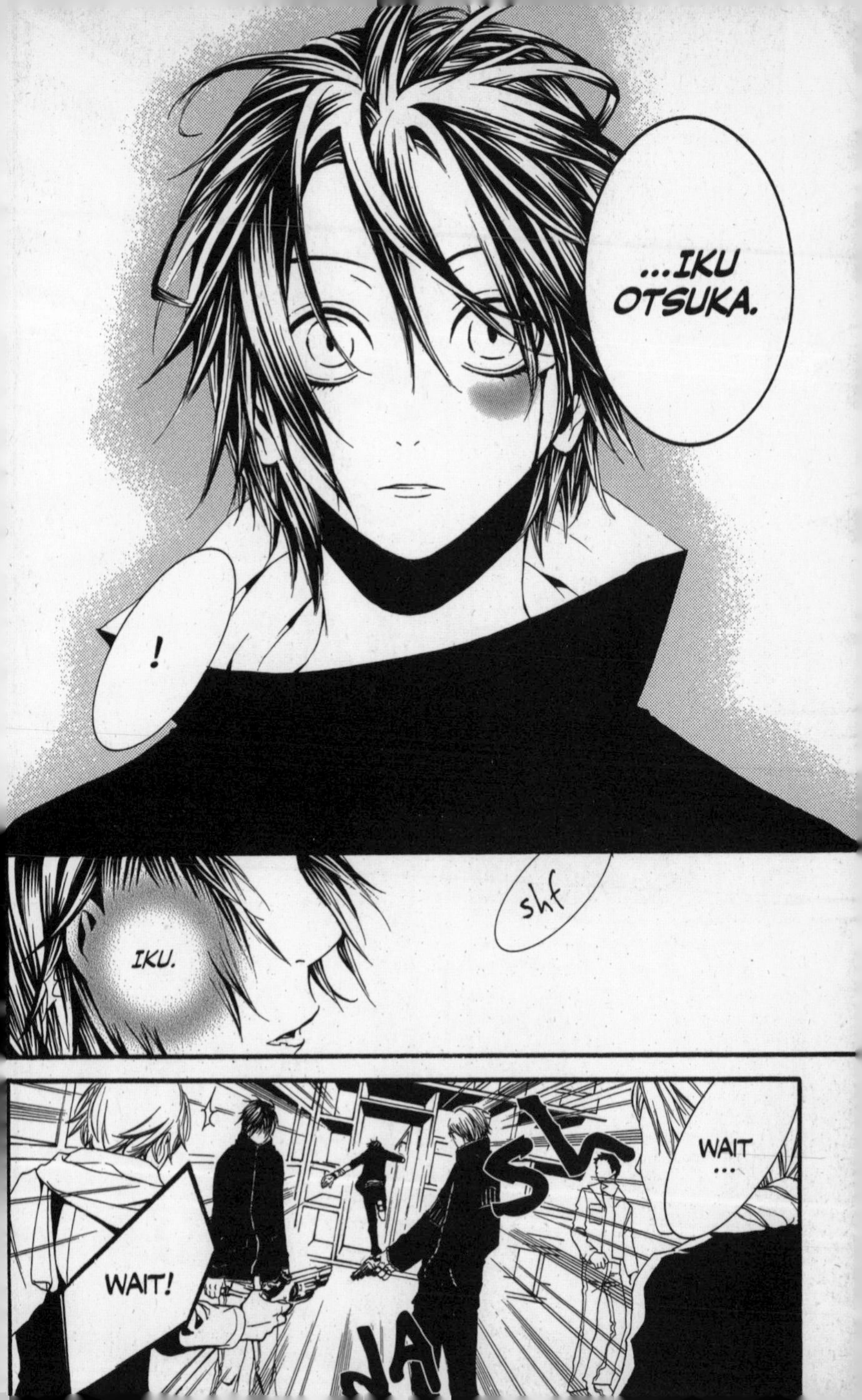
...IKU OTSUKA.
!
shf
IKU.
WAIT ...
WAIT!

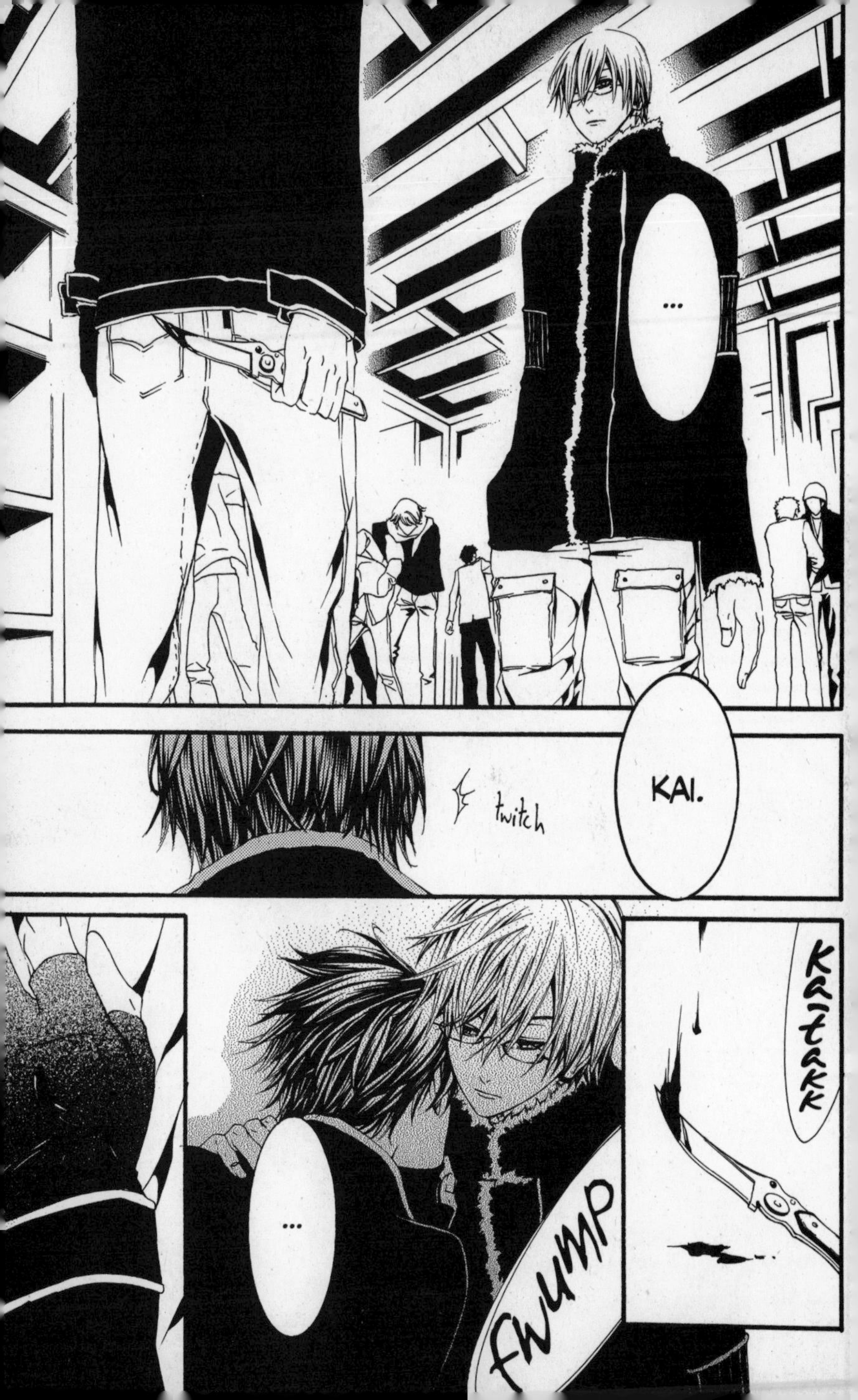
...
KAI.
twitch
KATAKK
FWUMP
...

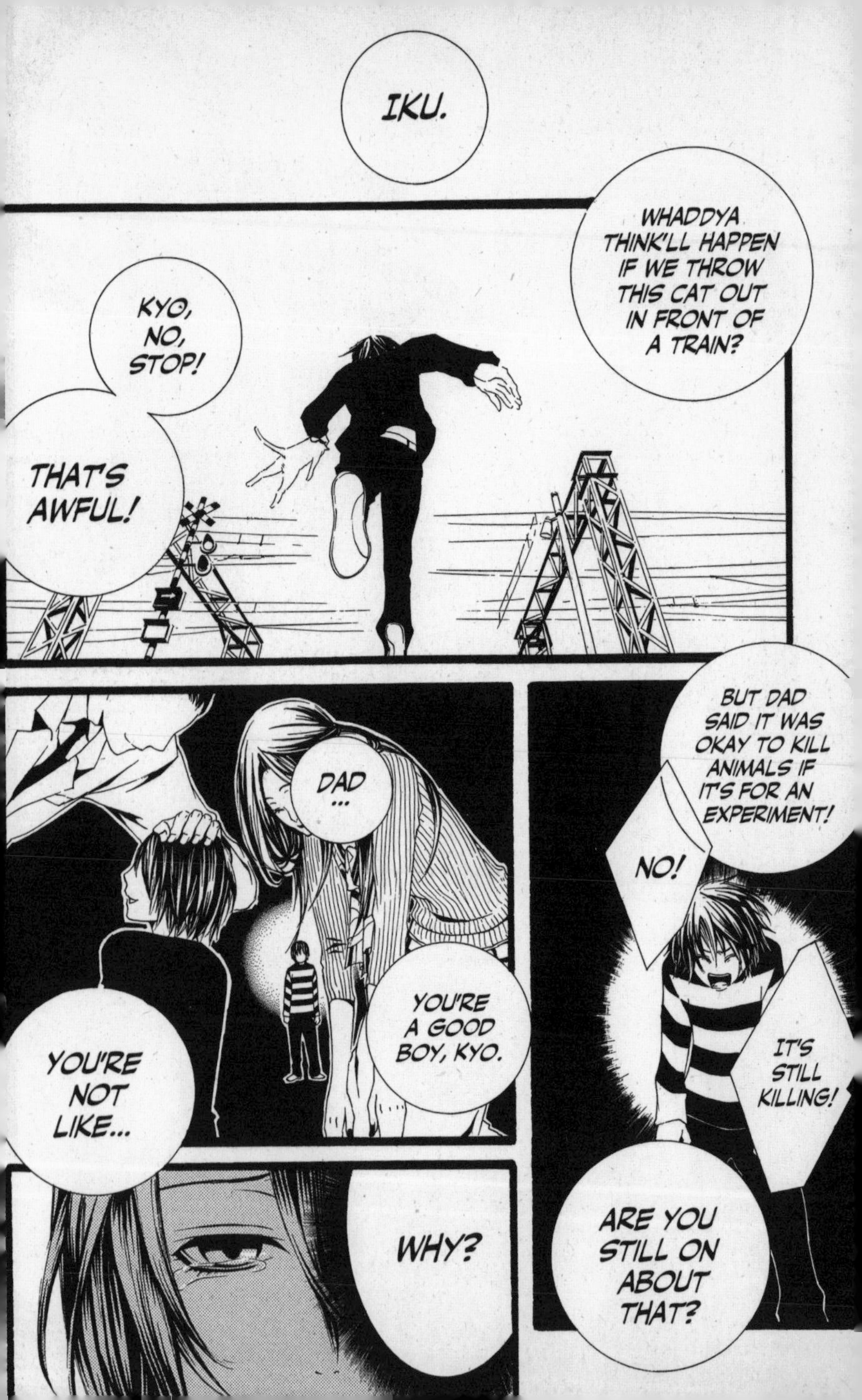
IKU.
WHADDYA THINK'LL HAPPEN IF WE THROW THIS CAT OUT IN FRONT OF A TRAIN?
KYO, NO, STOP!
THAT'S AWFUL!
BUT DAD SAID IT WAS OKAY TO KILL ANIMALS IF IT'S FOR AN EXPERIMENT!
NO!
IT'S STILL KILLING!
ARE YOU STILL ON ABOUT THAT?
DAD...
YOU'RE A GOOD BOY, KYO.
YOU'RE NOT LIKE...
WHY?

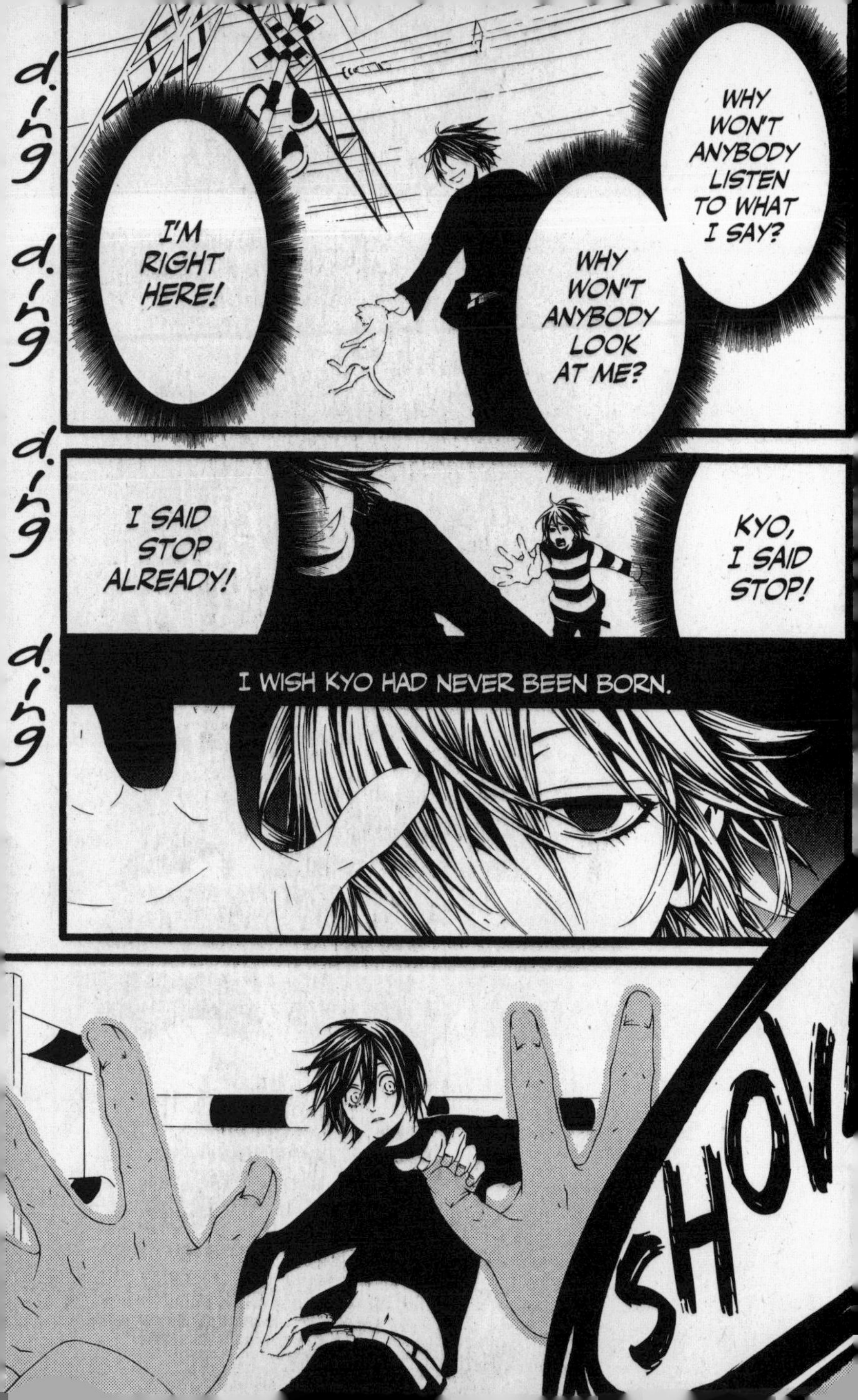
WHY WON'T ANYBODY LISTEN TO WHAT I SAY?
WHY WON'T ANYBODY LOOK AT ME?
I'M RIGHT HERE!
ding ding ding ding
KYO, I SAID STOP!
I SAID STOP ALREADY!
I WISH KYO HAD NEVER BEEN BORN.
SHOV

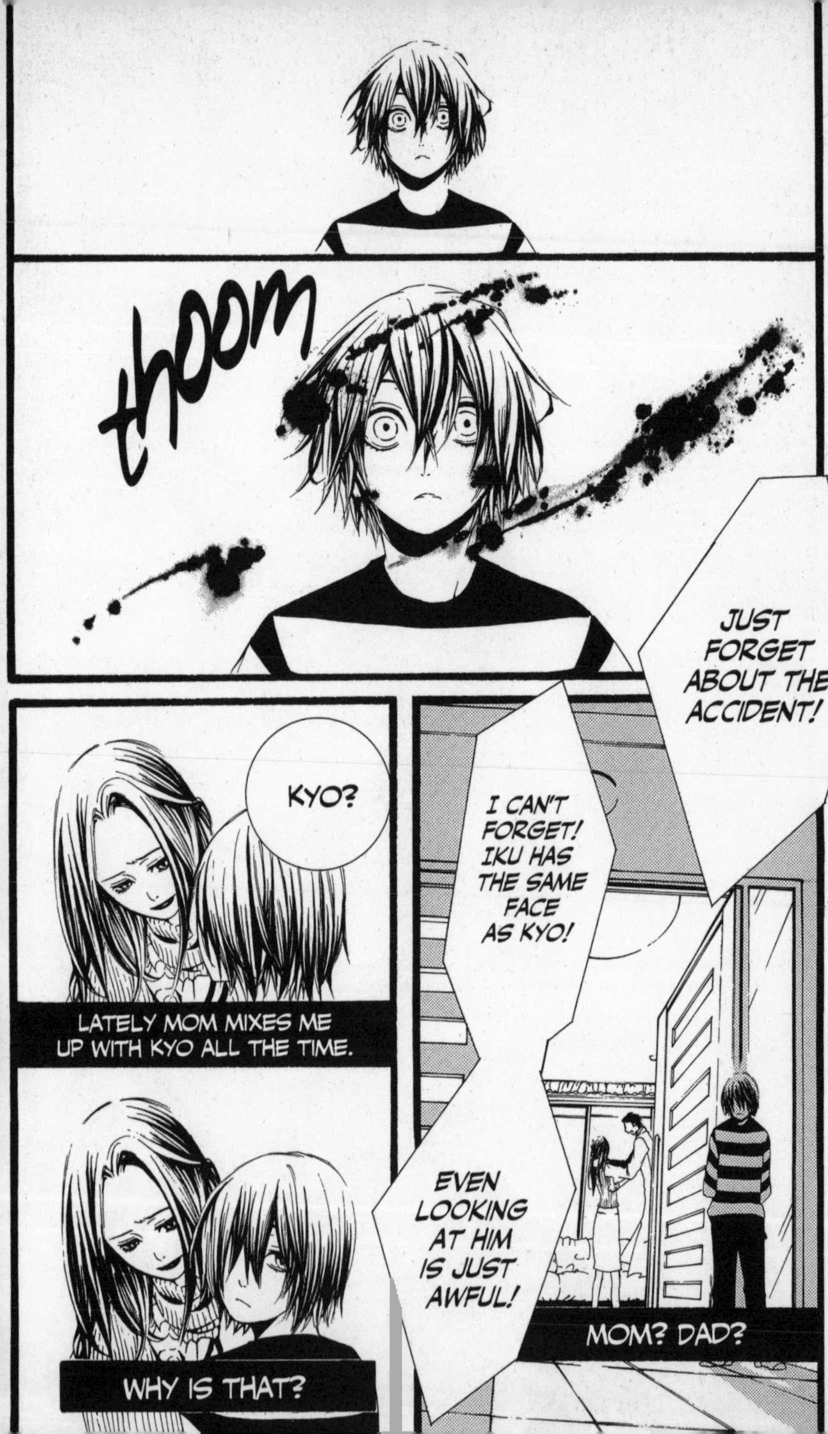
thoom
JUST FORGET ABOUT THE ACCIDENT!
I CAN'T FORGET! IKU HAS THE SAME FACE AS KYO!
EVEN LOOKING AT HIM IS JUST AWFUL!
MOM? DAD?
KYO?
LATELY MOM MIXES ME UP WITH KYO ALL THE TIME.
WHY IS THAT?

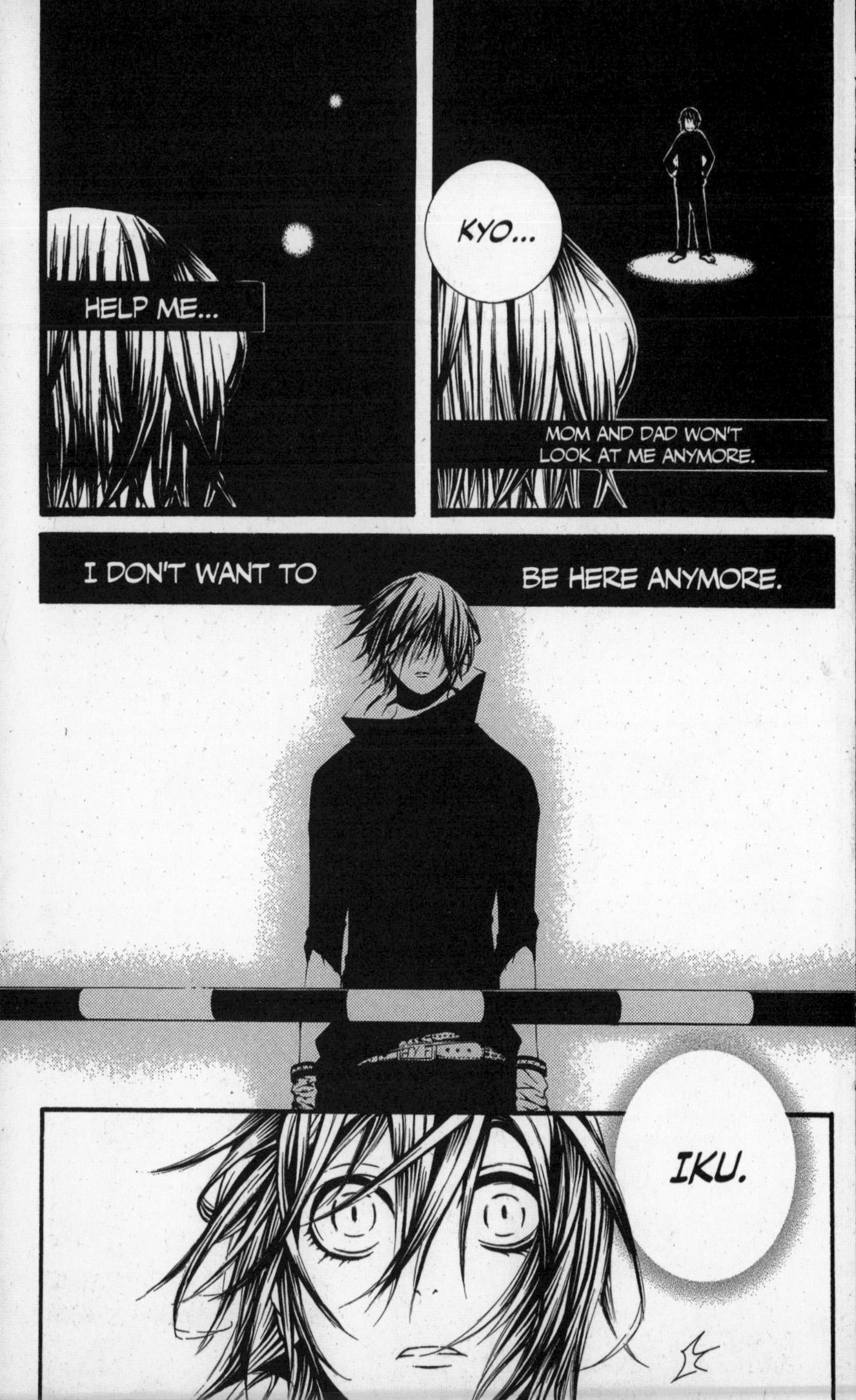
KYO...
MOM AND DAD WON'T LOOK AT ME ANYMORE.
HELP ME...
I DON'T WANT TO BE HERE ANYMORE.
IKU.

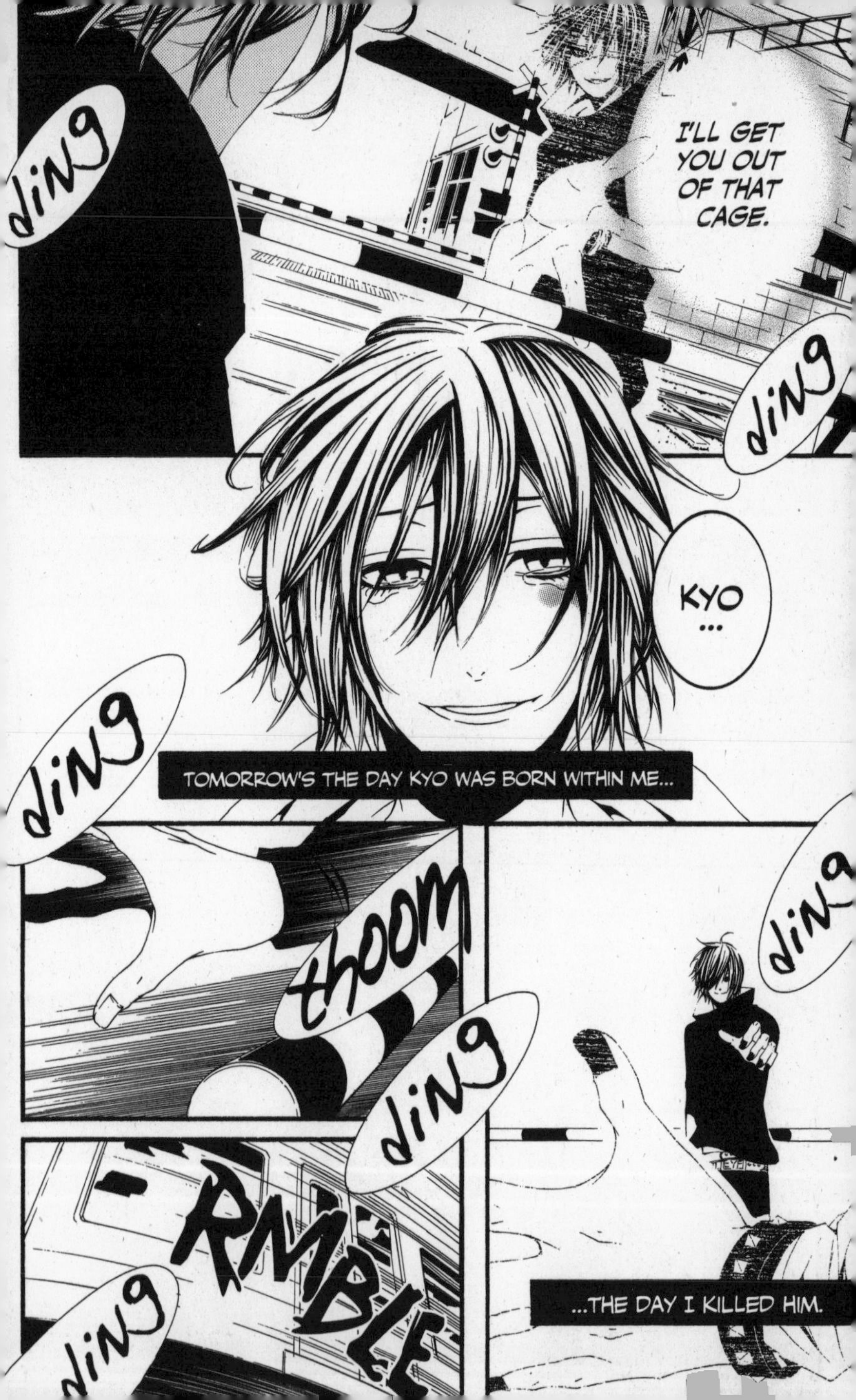
I'LL GET YOU OUT OF THAT CAGE.
ding
ding
KYO ...
ding
TOMORROW'S THE DAY KYO WAS BORN WITHIN ME...
ding
...THE DAY I KILLED HIM.
thoom
ding
RMBLE
ding

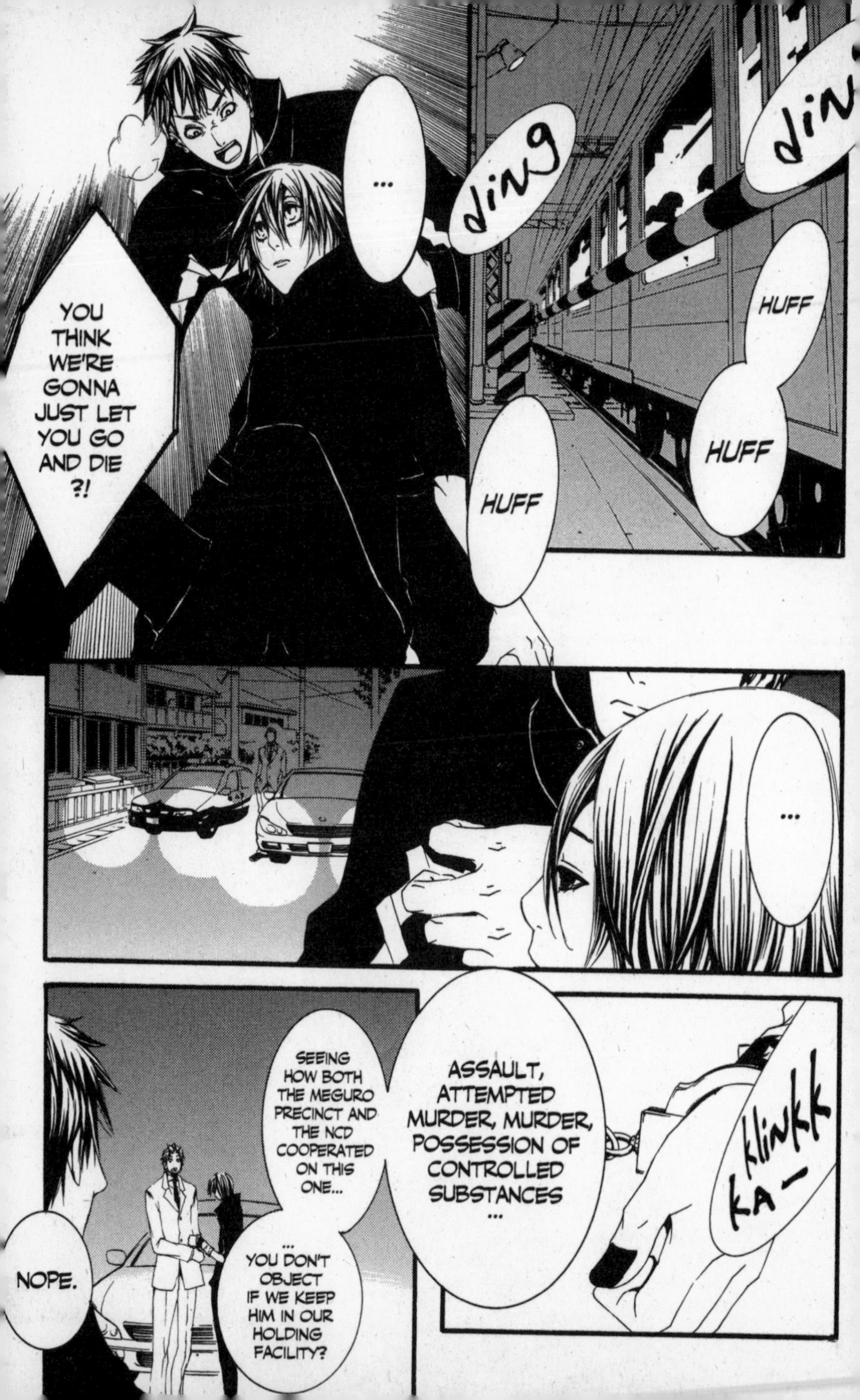
ding
ding
HUFF
HUFF
HUFF
...
YOU THINK WE'RE GONNA JUST LET YOU GO AND DIE ?!
...
ka— klinkk
ASSAULT, ATTEMPTED MURDER, MURDER, POSSESSION OF CONTROLLED SUBSTANCES ...
SEEING HOW BOTH THE MEGURO PRECINCT AND THE NCD COOPERATED ON THIS ONE...
... YOU DON'T OBJECT IF WE KEEP HIM IN OUR HOLDING FACILITY?
NOPE.

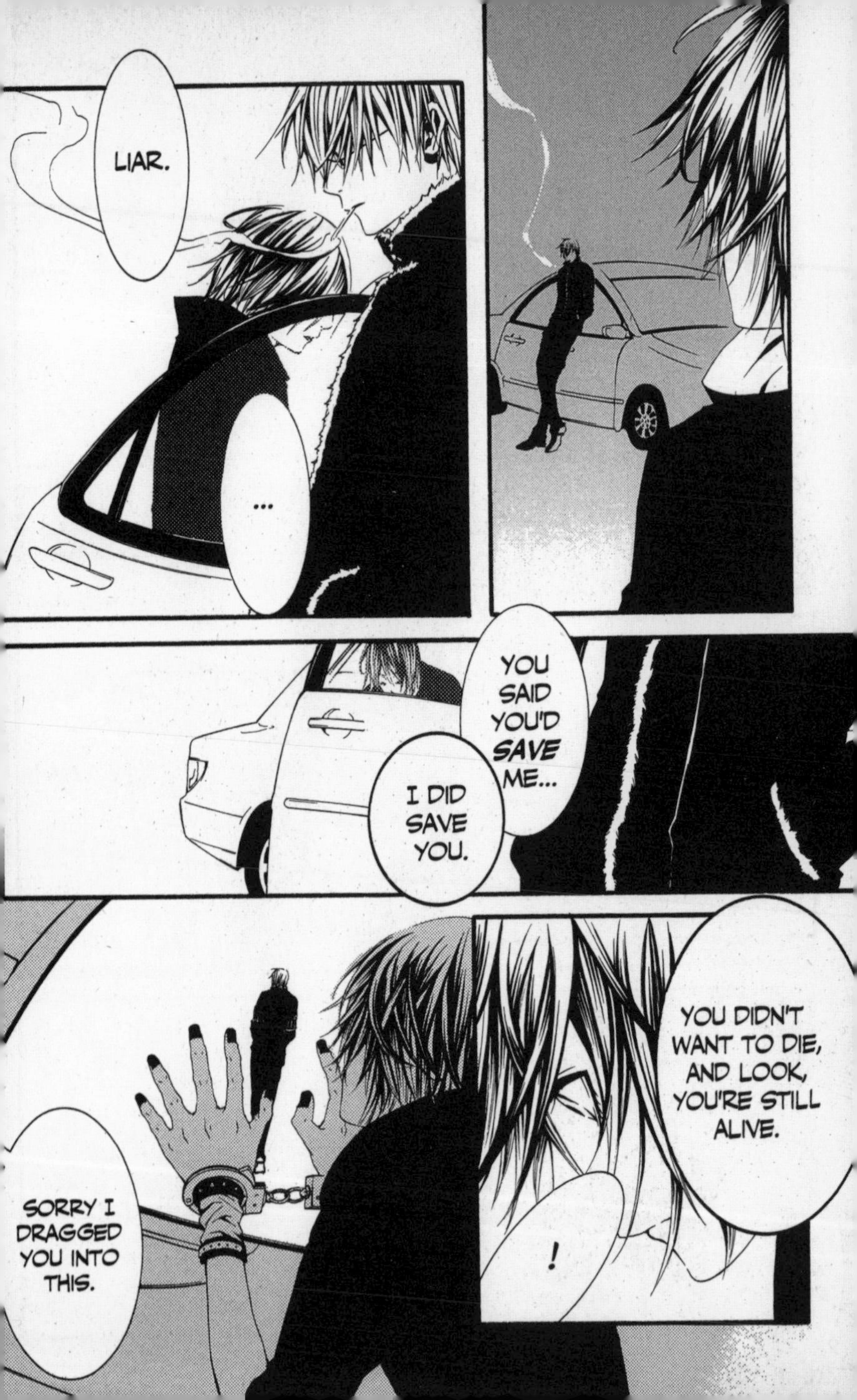
LIAR.
...
YOU SAID YOU'D SAVE ME...
I DID SAVE YOU.
YOU DIDN'T WANT TO DIE, AND LOOK, YOU'RE STILL ALIVE.
!
SORRY I DRAGGED YOU INTO THIS.

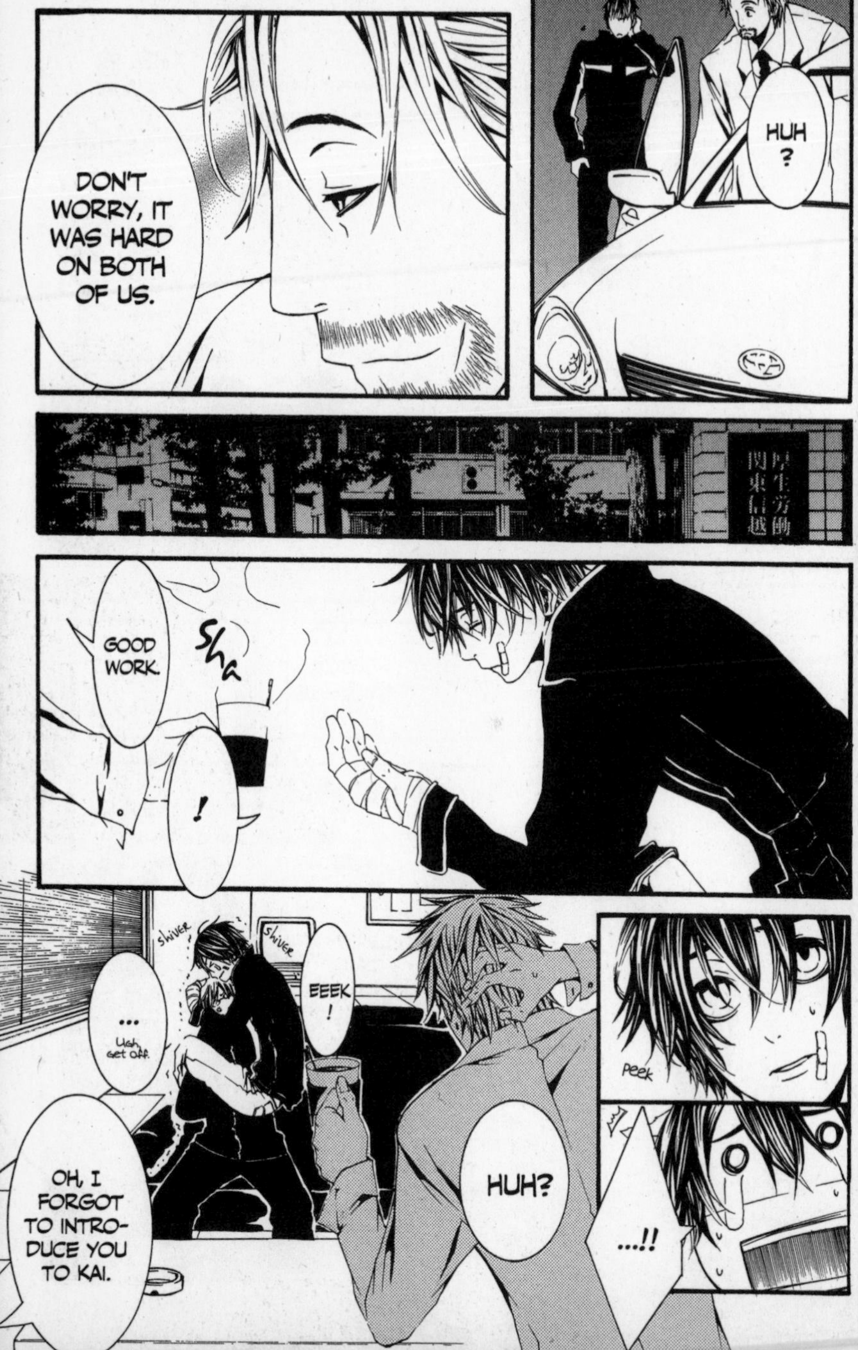
HUH ?
DON'T WORRY, IT WAS HARD ON BOTH OF US.
厚生労働
関東信越
GOOD WORK.
Sha
!
peek
...!!
EEEK !
shiver
shiver
...
Ugh, Get off.
HUH?
OH, I FORGOT TO INTRO-DUCE YOU TO KAI.

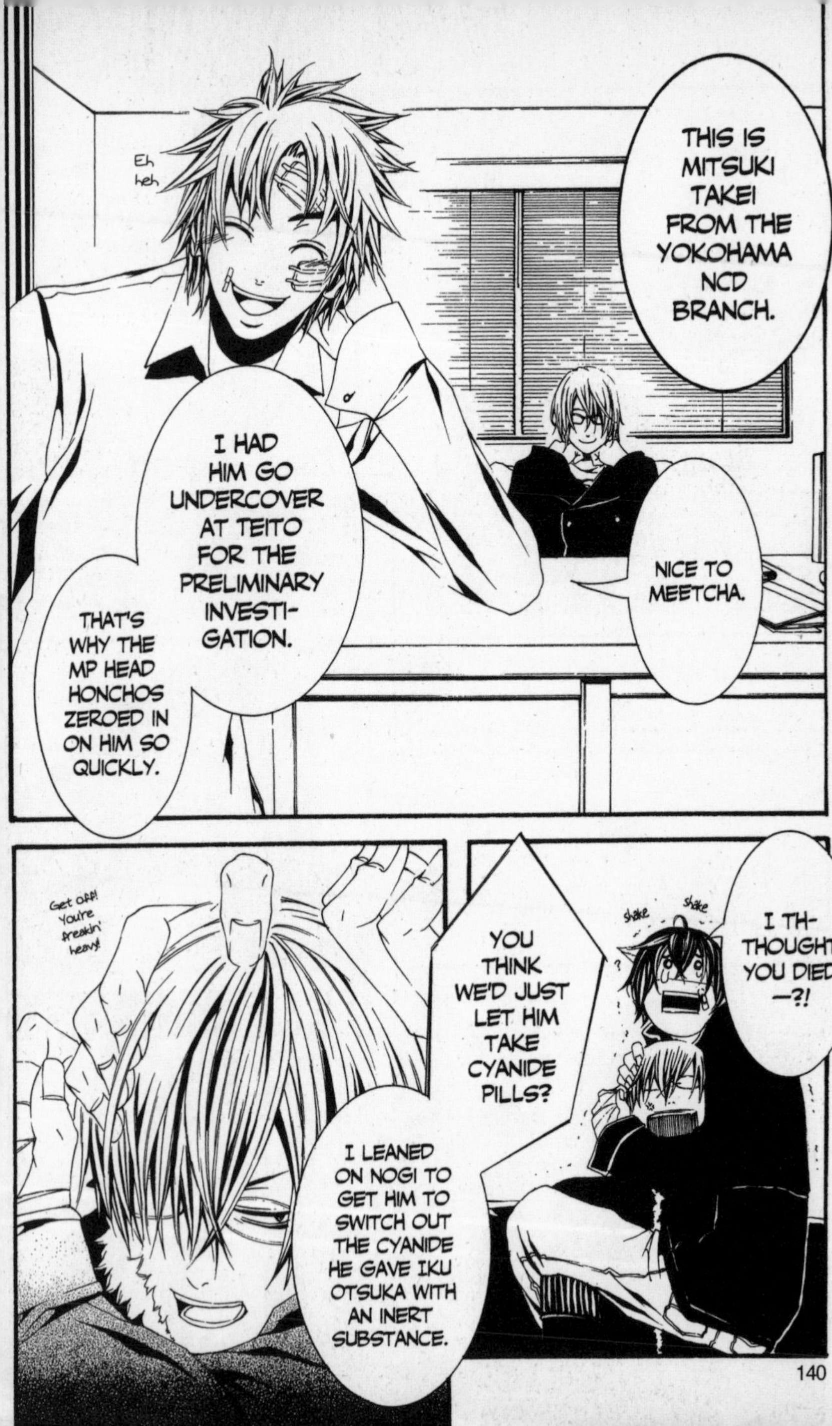
THIS IS MITSUKI TAKEI FROM THE YOKOHAMA NCD BRANCH.
NICE TO MEETCHA.
Eh heh
I HAD HIM GO UNDERCOVER AT TEITO FOR THE PRELIMINARY INVESTI-GATION.
THAT'S WHY THE MP HEAD HONCHOS ZEROED IN ON HIM SO QUICKLY.
I TH-THOUGHT YOU DIED—?!
Shake
Shake
YOU THINK WE'D JUST LET HIM TAKE CYANIDE PILLS?
I LEANED ON NOGI TO GET HIM TO SWITCH OUT THE CYANIDE HE GAVE IKU OTSUKA WITH AN INERT SUBSTANCE.
Get off! You're freakin' heavy!

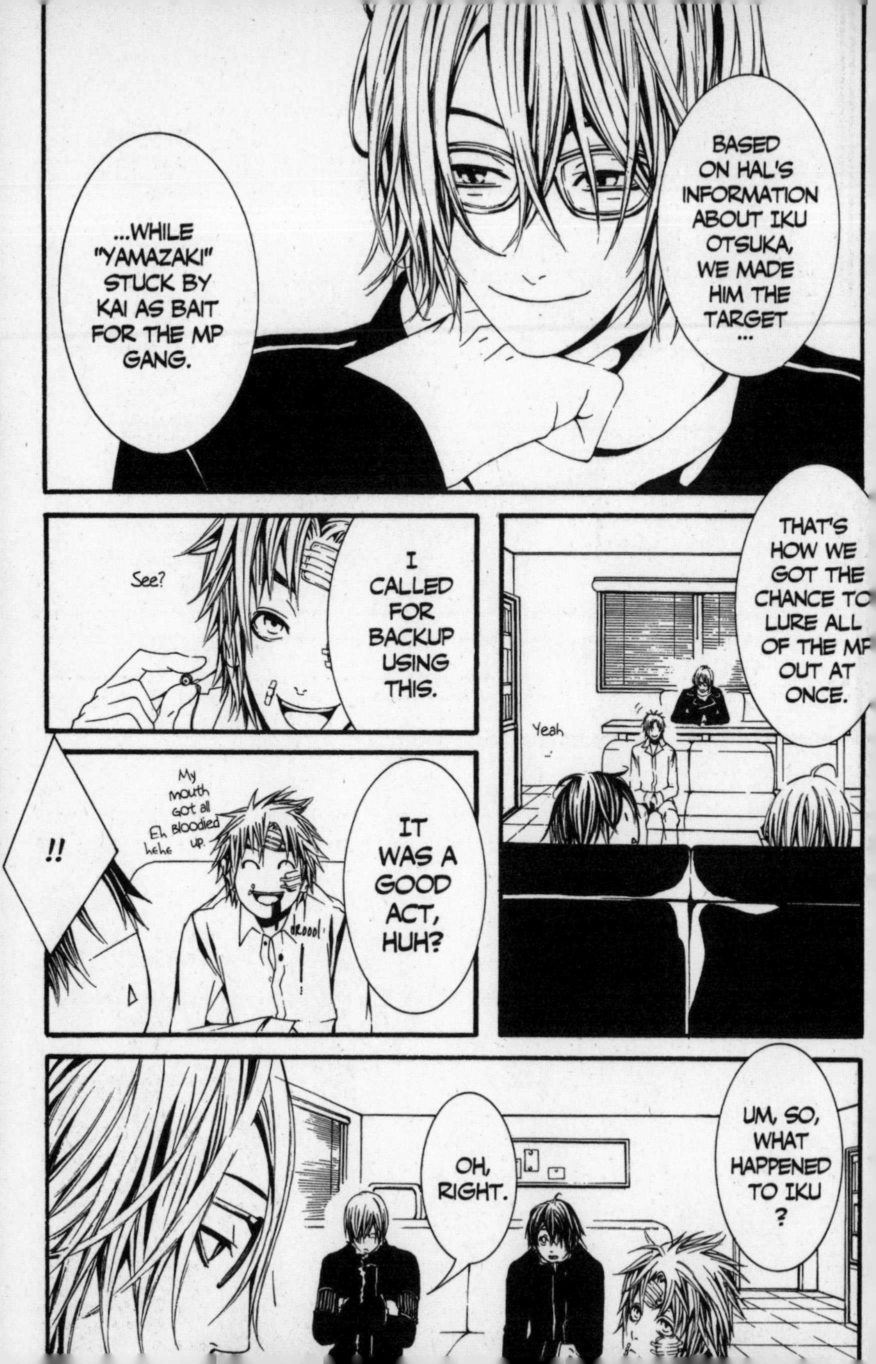
BASED ON HAL'S INFORMATION ABOUT IKU OTSUKA, WE MADE HIM THE TARGET...
...WHILE "YAMAZAKI" STUCK BY KAI AS BAIT FOR THE MP GANG.
THAT'S HOW WE GOT THE CHANCE TO LURE ALL OF THE MP OUT AT ONCE.
Yeah
I CALLED FOR BACKUP USING THIS.
See?
IT WAS A GOOD ACT, HUH?
My mouth got all bloodied up.
Eh hehe
drool
!!
UM, SO, WHAT HAPPENED TO IKU?
OH, RIGHT.

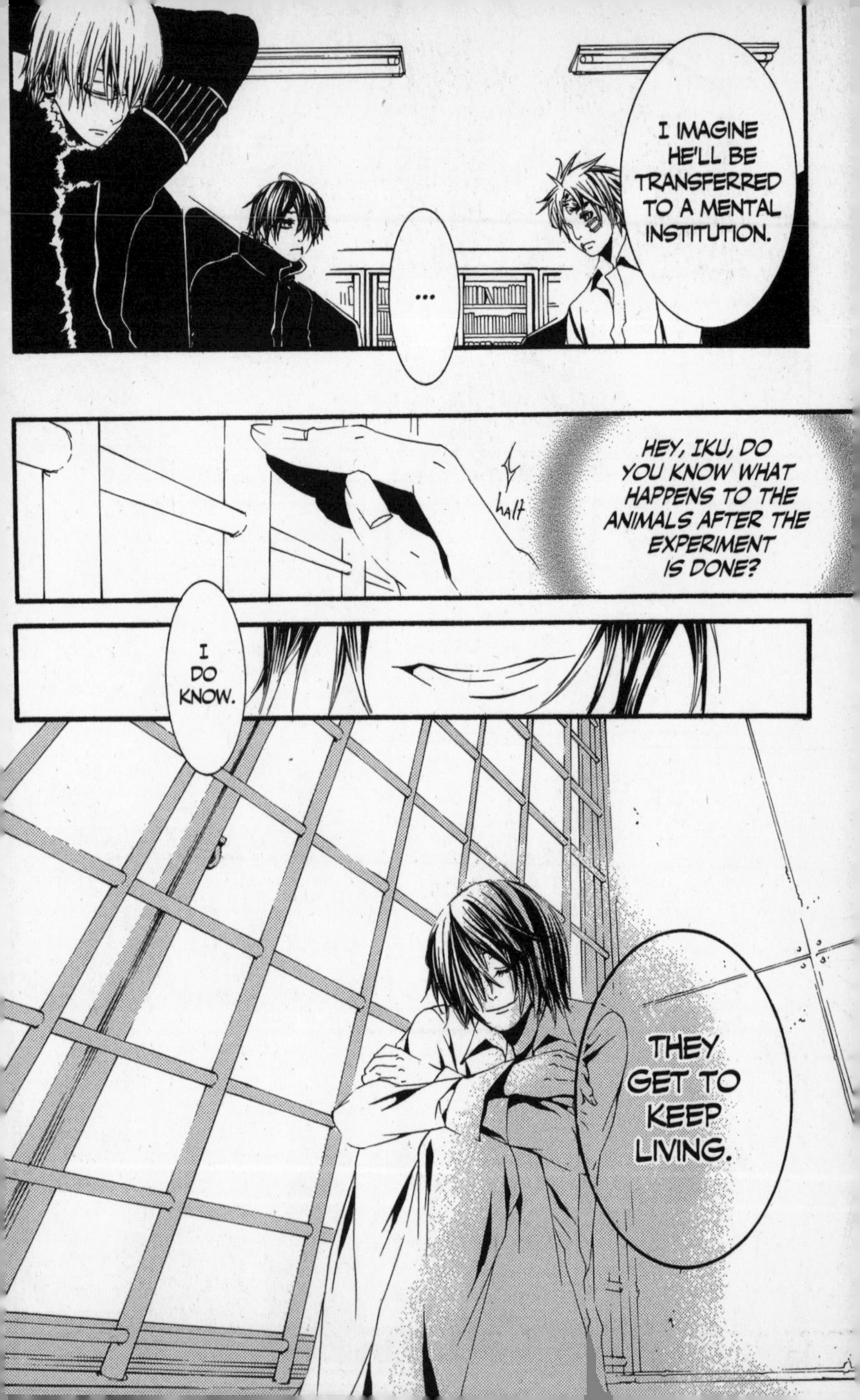
I IMAGINE HE'LL BE TRANSFERRED TO A MENTAL INSTITUTION.
...
HEY, IKU, DO YOU KNOW WHAT HAPPENS TO THE ANIMALS AFTER THE EXPERIMENT IS DONE?
halt
I DO KNOW.
THEY GET TO KEEP LIVING.

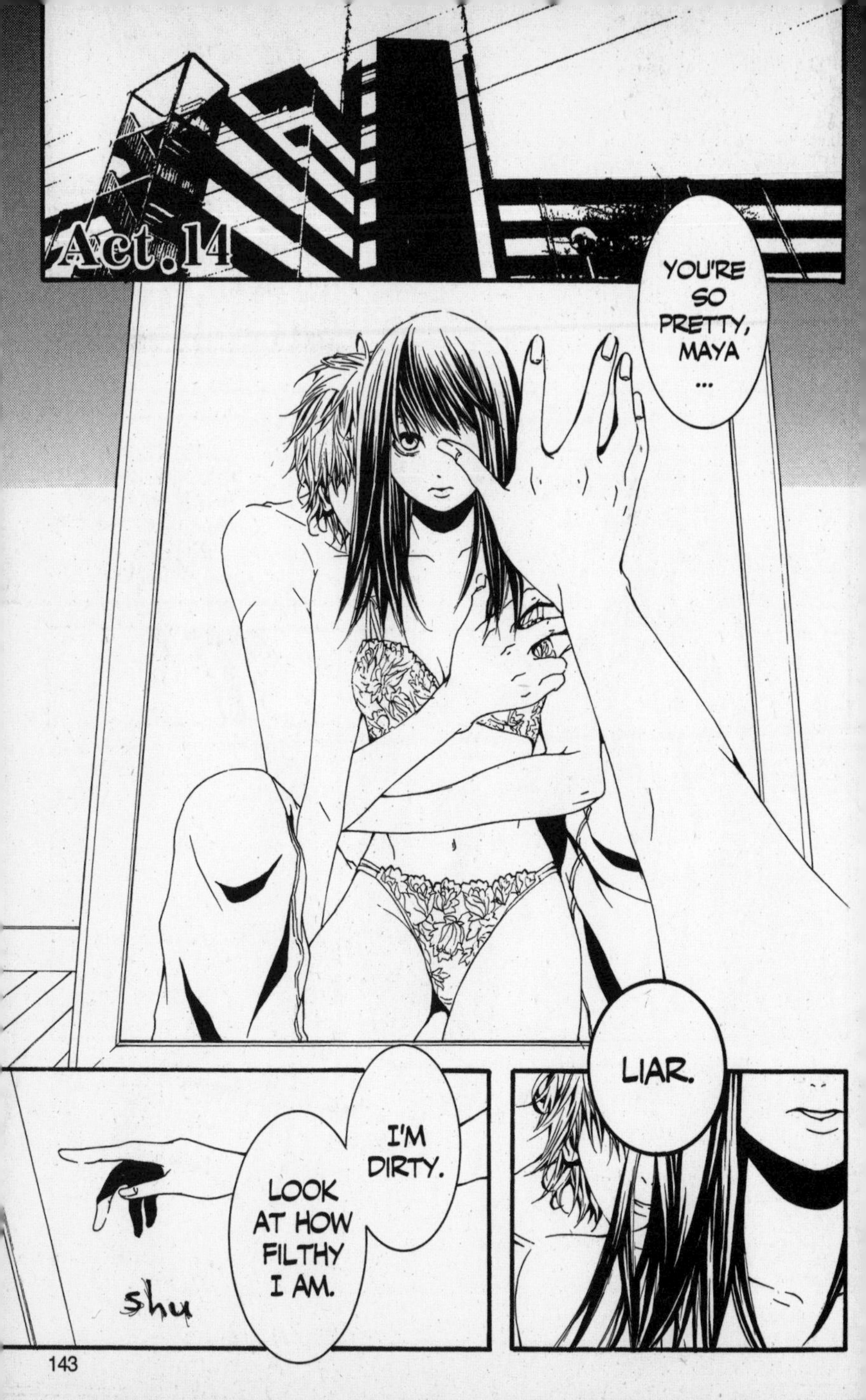
Act. 14
YOU'RE SO PRETTY, MAYA ...
LIAR.
I'M DIRTY.
LOOK AT HOW FILTHY I AM.
shu

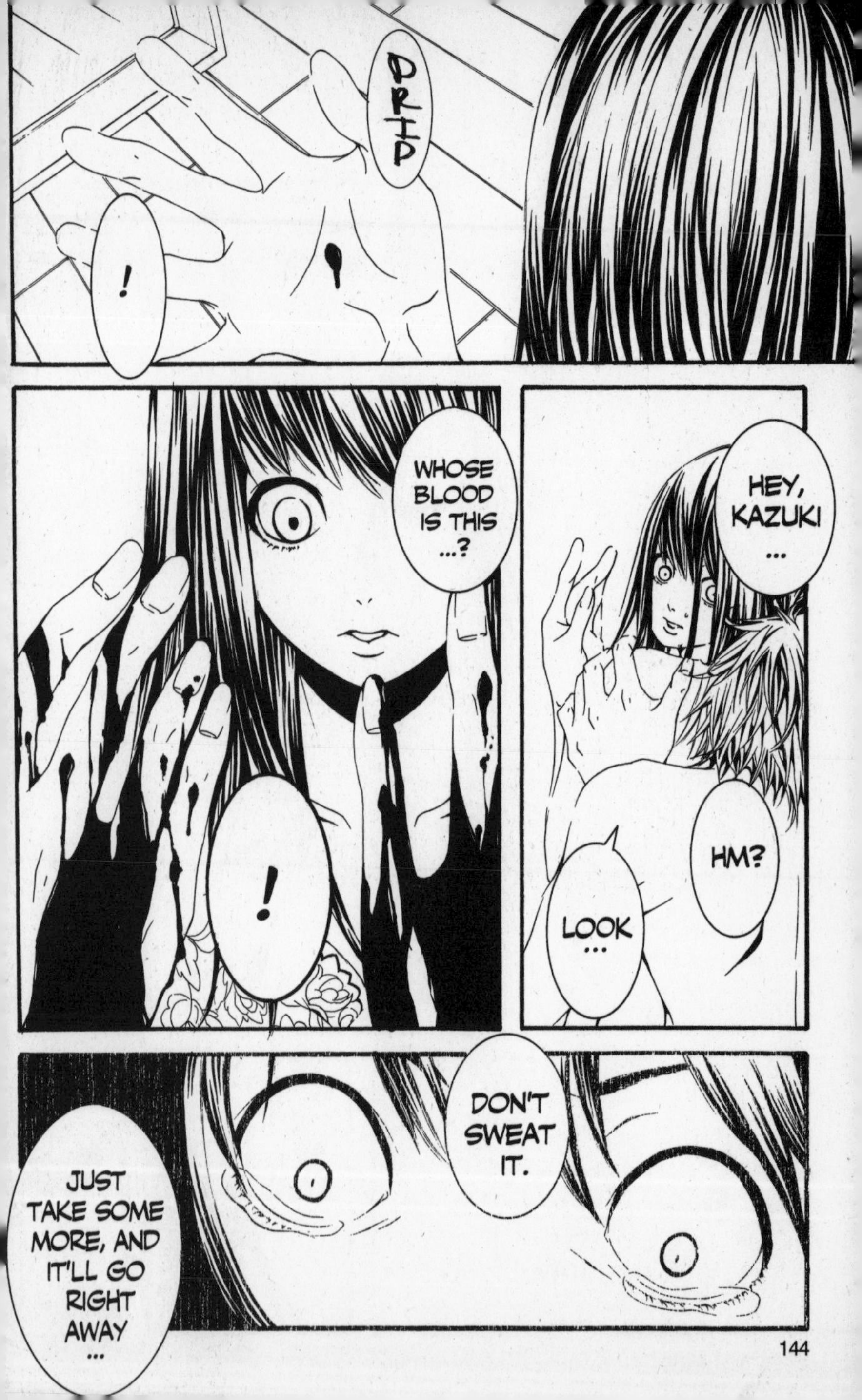
DRIP
!
HEY, KAZUKI ...
HM?
LOOK ...
WHOSE BLOOD IS THIS ...?
!
DON'T SWEAT IT.
JUST TAKE SOME MORE, AND IT'LL GO RIGHT AWAY ...

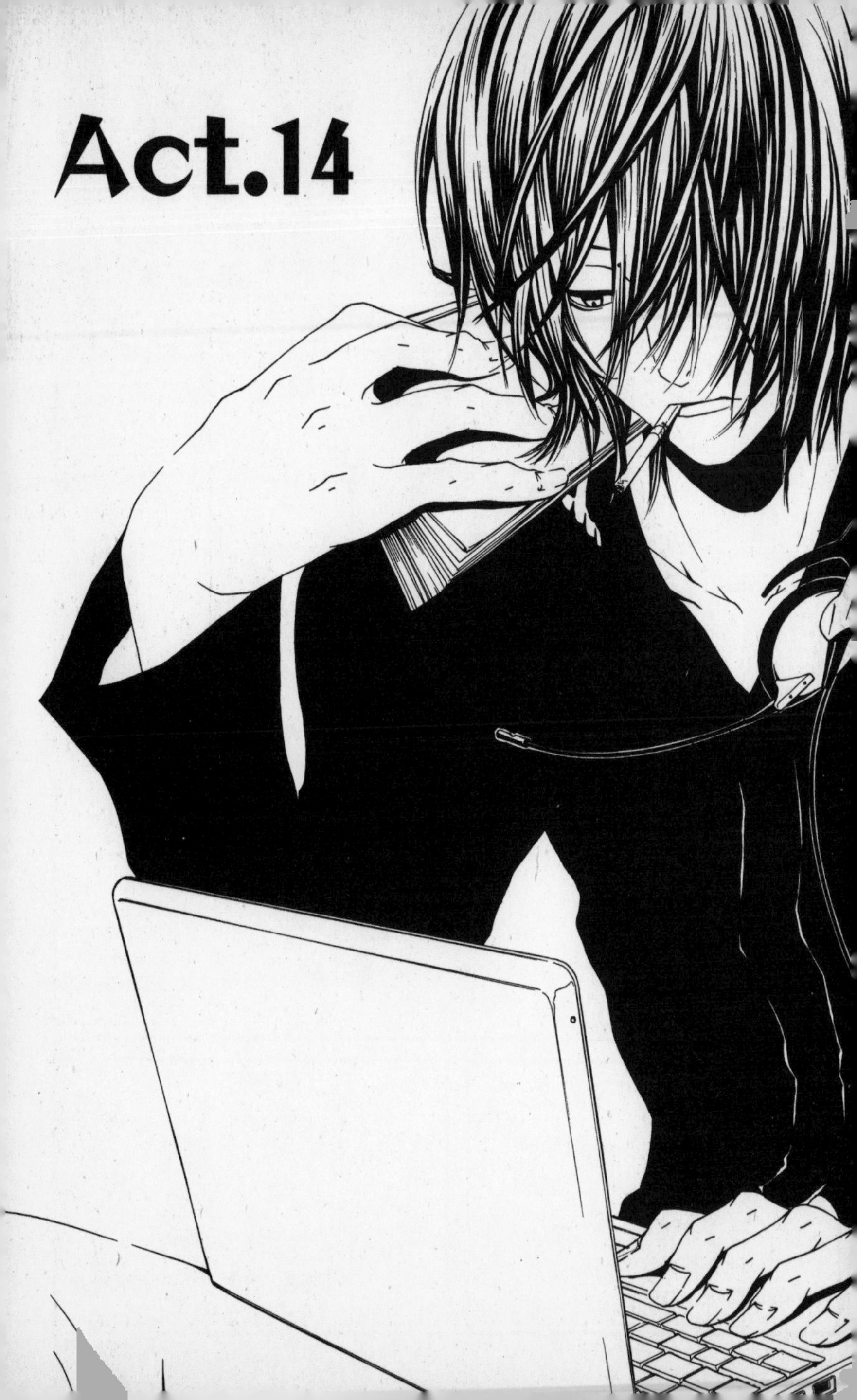
Act.14

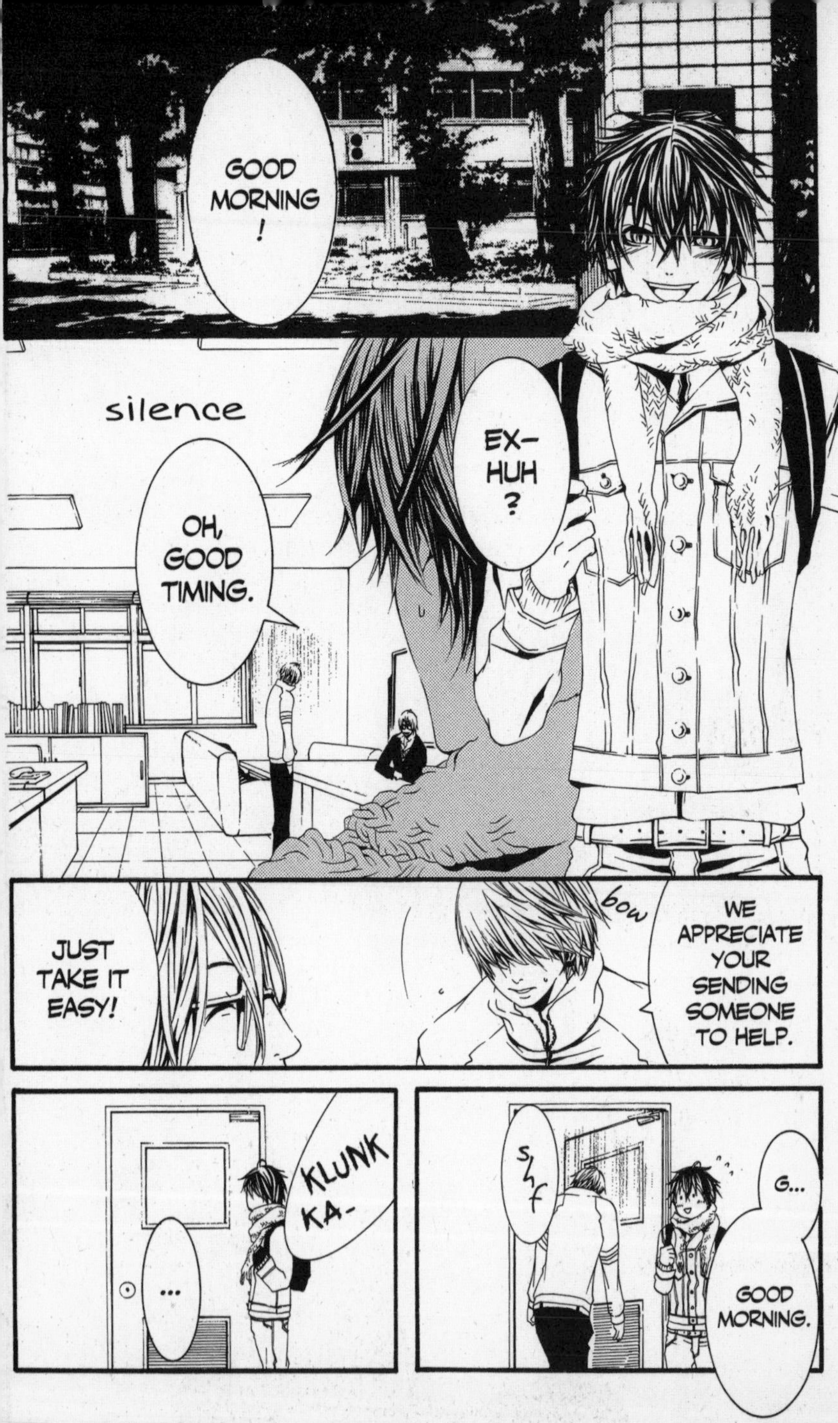
GOOD MORNING!
EX-HUH?
silence
OH, GOOD TIMING.
WE APPRECIATE YOUR SENDING SOMEONE TO HELP.
bow
JUST TAKE IT EASY!
G...
GOOD MORNING.
shf
KLUNK KA-
...

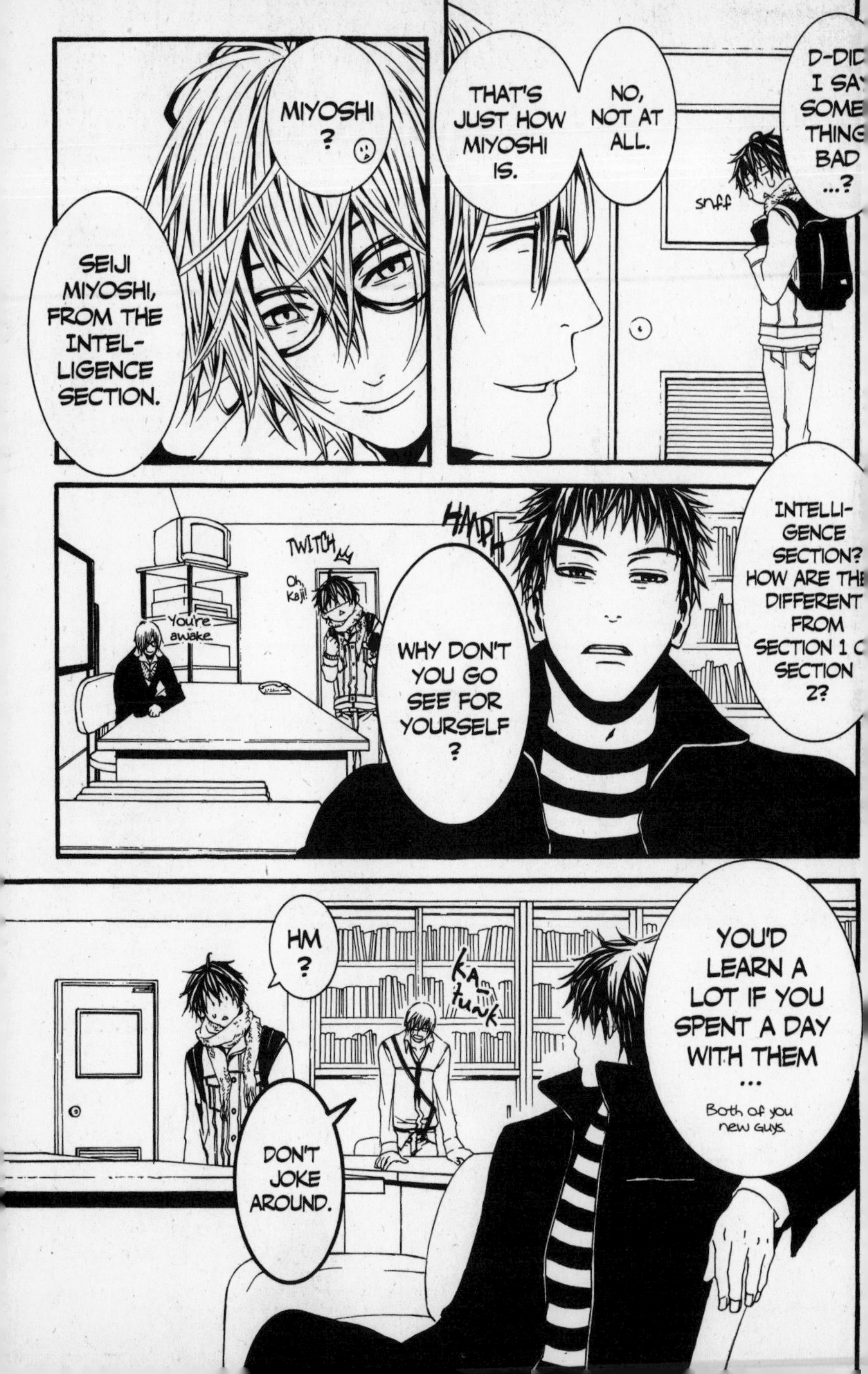
D-DID I SAY SOMETHING BAD ...?
snff
NO, NOT AT ALL.
THAT'S JUST HOW MIYOSHI IS.
MIYOSHI ?
SEIJI MIYOSHI, FROM THE INTEL-LIGENCE SECTION.
INTELLI-GENCE SECTION? HOW ARE THE DIFFERENT FROM SECTION 1 C SECTION 2?
HMPH
WHY DON'T YOU GO SEE FOR YOURSELF ?
TWITCH
Oh, Kaji!
You're awake.
YOU'D LEARN A LOT IF YOU SPENT A DAY WITH THEM ...
Both of you new guys.
KA-TUNK
HM ?
DON'T JOKE AROUND.

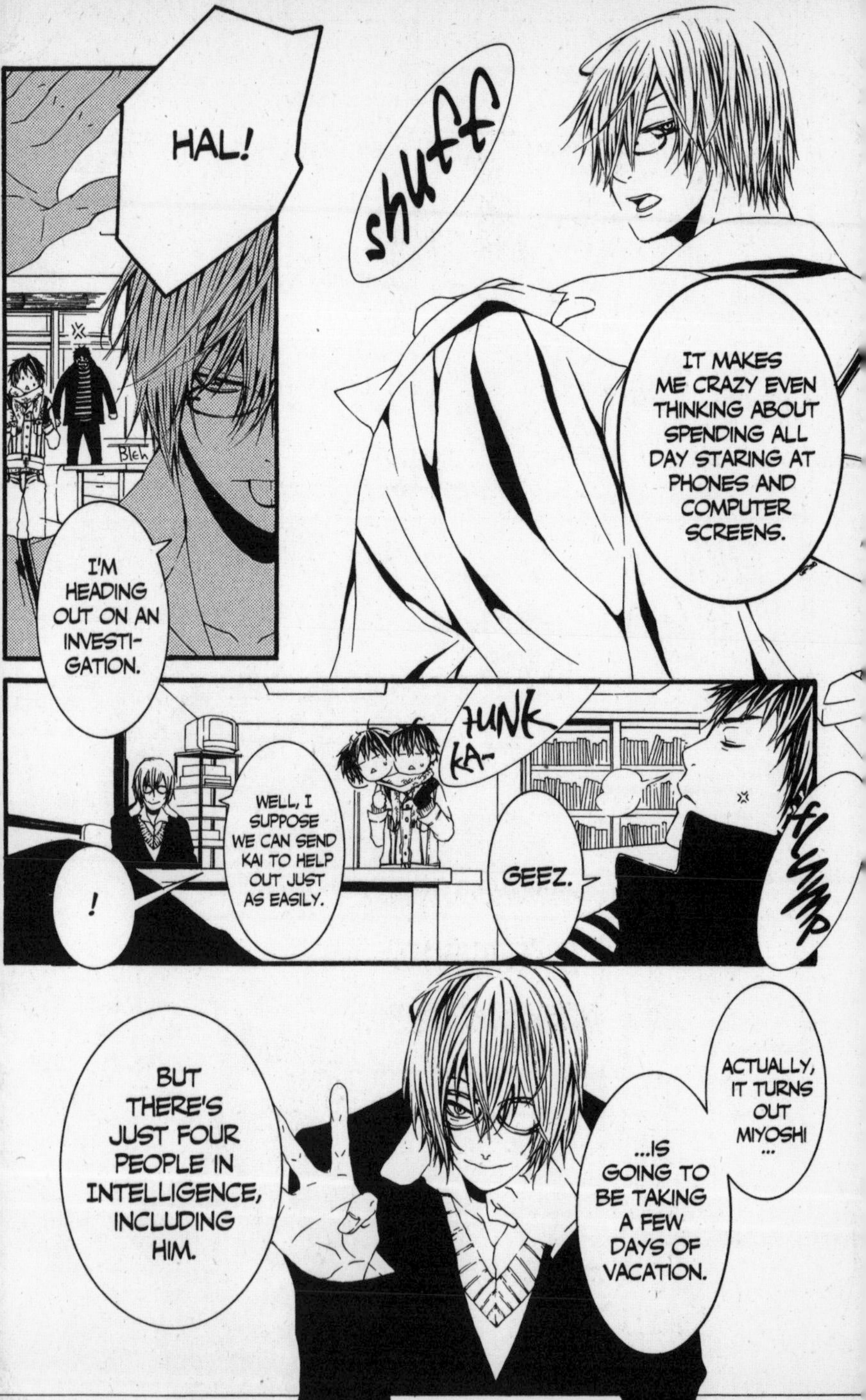
shuff
IT MAKES ME CRAZY EVEN THINKING ABOUT SPENDING ALL DAY STARING AT PHONES AND COMPUTER SCREENS.
HAL!
Bleh
I'M HEADING OUT ON AN INVESTIGATION.
FLUMP
GEEZ.
KA-THUNK
WELL, I SUPPOSE WE CAN SEND KAI TO HELP OUT JUST AS EASILY.
!
ACTUALLY, IT TURNS OUT MIYOSHI ...
...IS GOING TO BE TAKING A FEW DAYS OF VACATION.
BUT THERE'S JUST FOUR PEOPLE IN INTELLIGENCE, INCLUDING HIM.

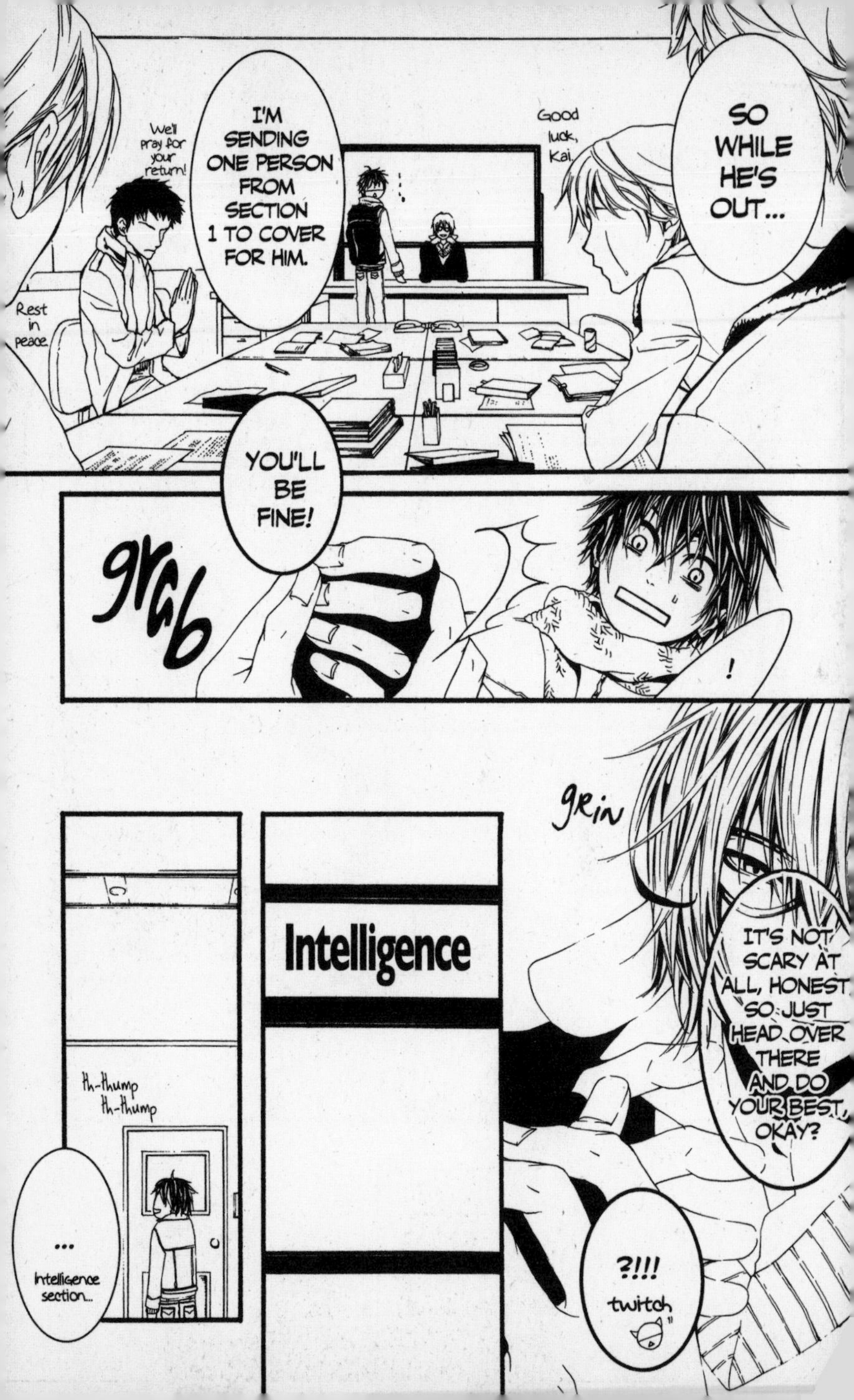
SO WHILE HE'S OUT...
Good luck, Kai.
I'M SENDING ONE PERSON FROM SECTION 1 TO COVER FOR HIM.
We'll pray for your return!
Rest in peace.
YOU'LL BE FINE!
!
grab
grin
IT'S NOT SCARY AT ALL, HONEST. SO JUST HEAD OVER THERE AND DO YOUR BEST, OKAY?
?!!!
twitch
Intelligence
th-thump th-thump
...
Intelligence section...

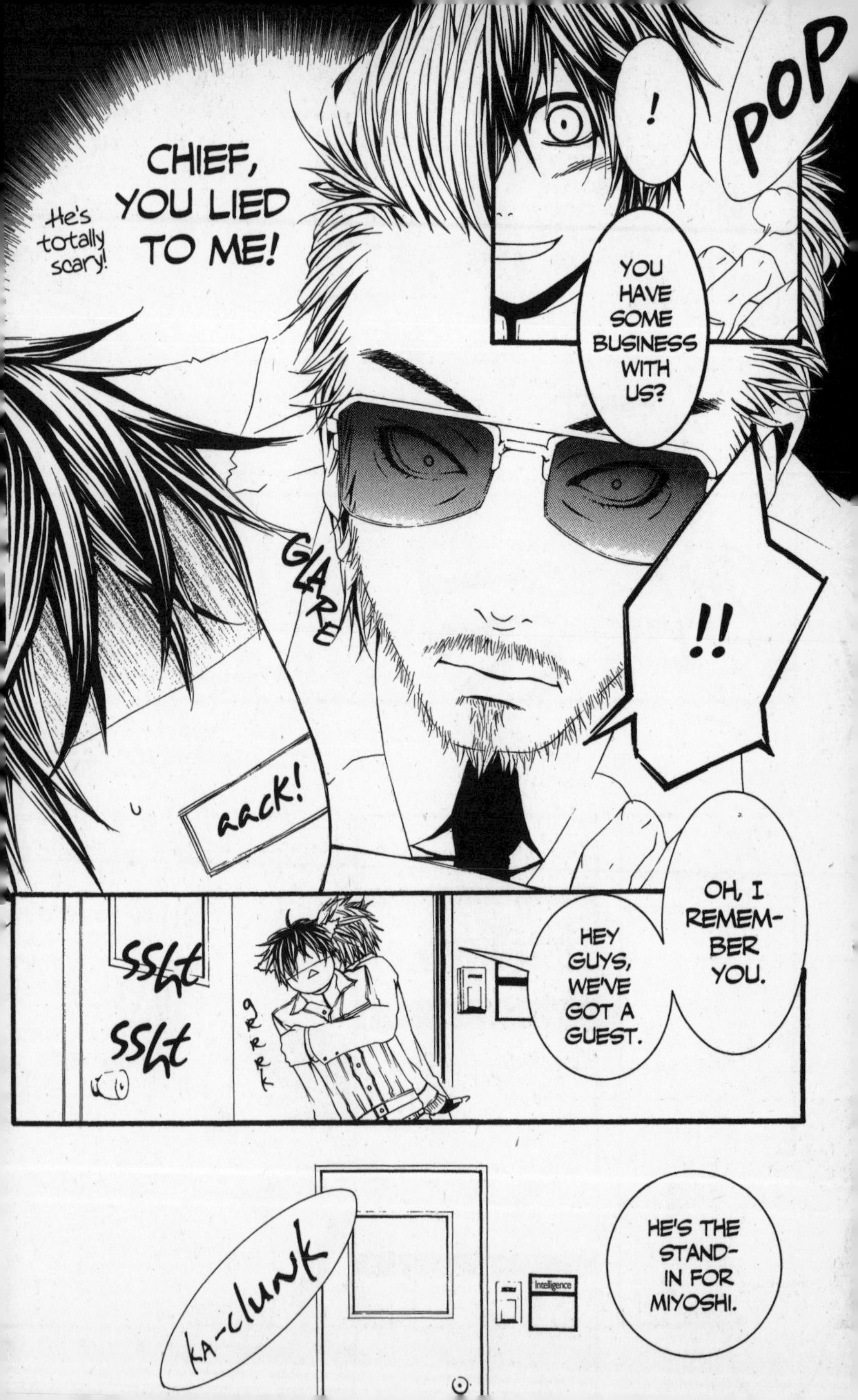
POP
!
YOU HAVE SOME BUSINESS WITH US?
CHIEF, YOU LIED TO ME!
He's totally scary!
!!
GLARE
aack!
OH, I REMEM-BER YOU.
HEY GUYS, WE'VE GOT A GUEST.
grrrk
sslt
sslt
HE'S THE STAND-IN FOR MIYOSHI.
Intelligence
ka-clunk

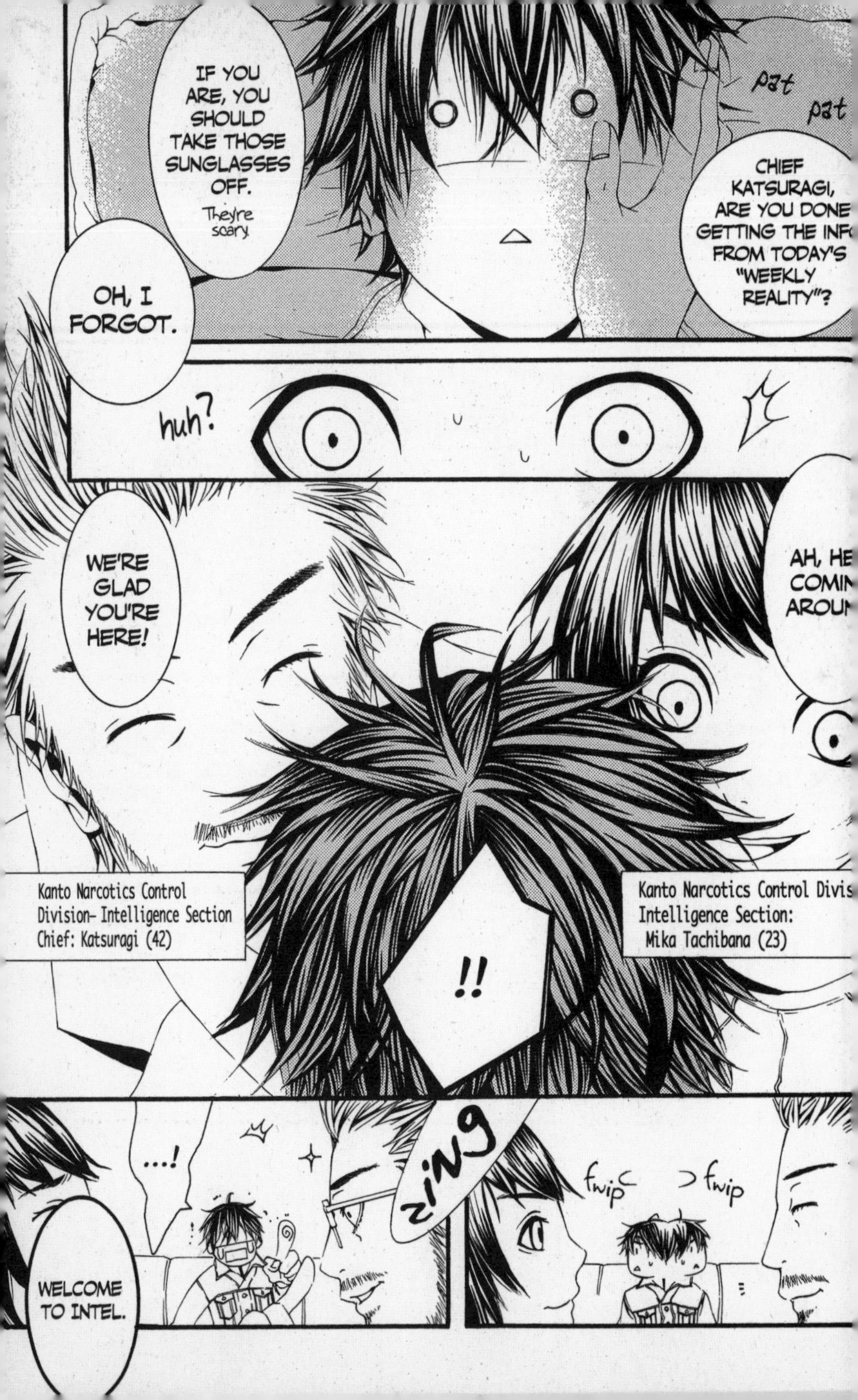
pat
pat
CHIEF KATSURAGI, ARE YOU DONE GETTING THE INF FROM TODAY'S "WEEKLY REALITY"?
IF YOU ARE, YOU SHOULD TAKE THOSE SUNGLASSES OFF.
They're scary.
OH, I FORGOT.
huh?
AH, HE COMIN AROUN
Kanto Narcotics Control Divis Intelligence Section: Mika Tachibana (23)
!!
WE'RE GLAD YOU'RE HERE!
Kanto Narcotics Control Division- Intelligence Section Chief: Katsuragi (42)
fwip
fwip
zing
...!
WELCOME TO INTEL.

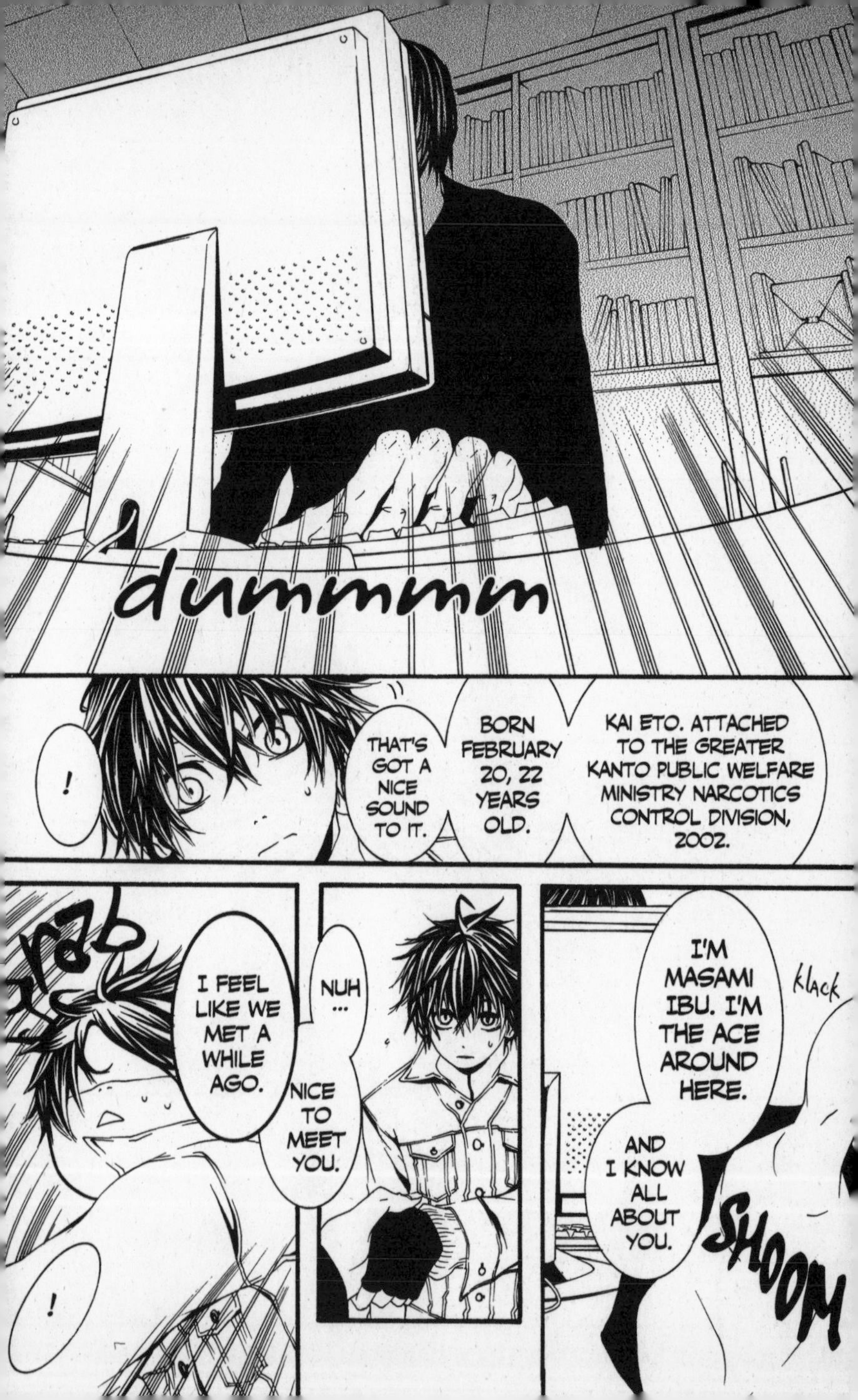
dummmmm
KAI ETO. ATTACHED TO THE GREATER KANTO PUBLIC WELFARE MINISTRY NARCOTICS CONTROL DIVISION, 2002.
BORN FEBRUARY 20, 22 YEARS OLD.
THAT'S GOT A NICE SOUND TO IT.
!
klack
I'M MASAMI IBU. I'M THE ACE AROUND HERE.
AND I KNOW ALL ABOUT YOU.
SHOOM
NUH ...
NICE TO MEET YOU.
grab
I FEEL LIKE WE MET A WHILE AGO.
!

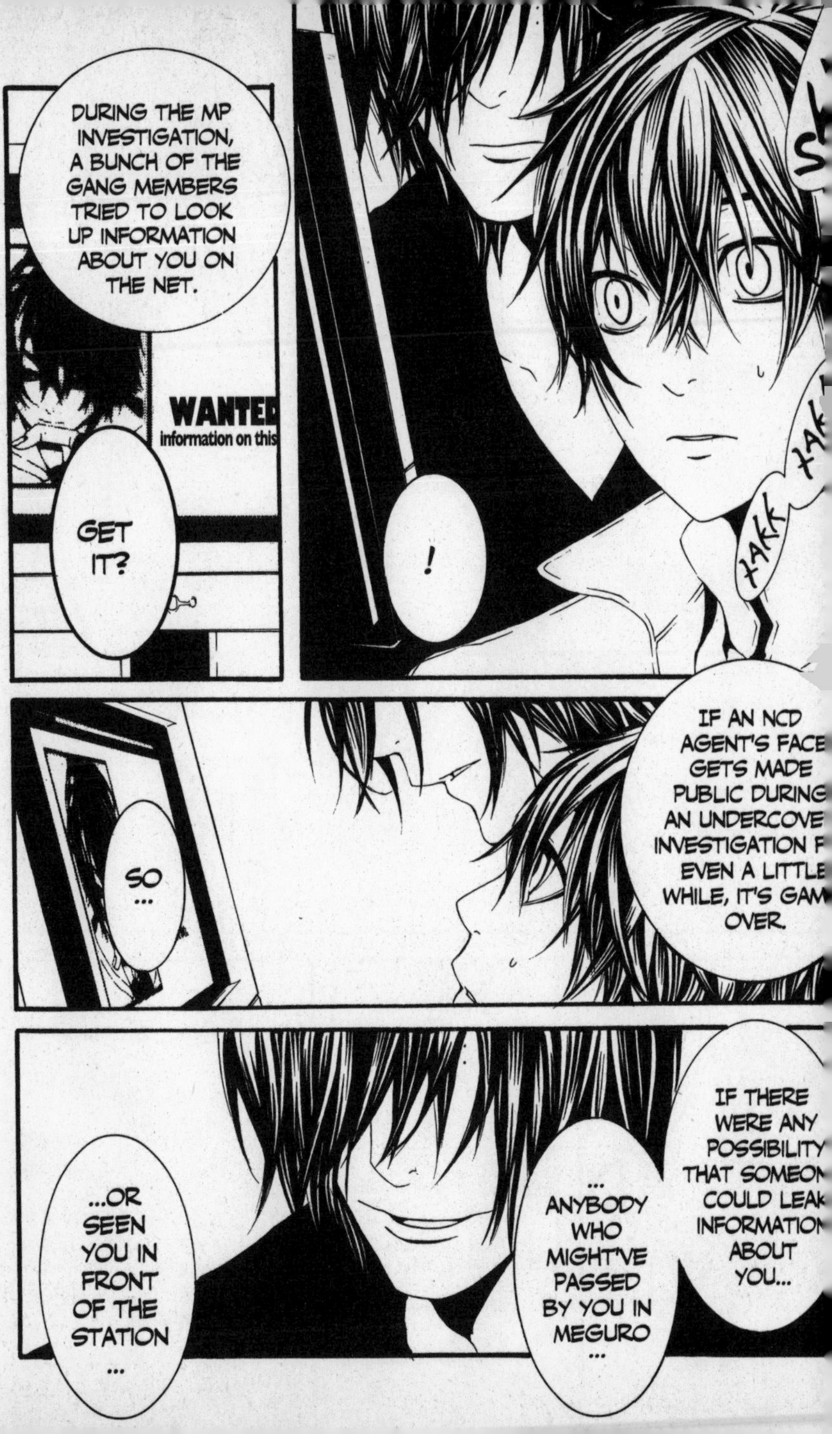
TAKK
!
DURING THE MP INVESTIGATION, A BUNCH OF THE GANG MEMBERS TRIED TO LOOK UP INFORMATION ABOUT YOU ON THE NET.
WANTED
information on this
GET IT?
IF AN NCD AGENT'S FACE GETS MADE PUBLIC DURING AN UNDERCOVE INVESTIGATION F EVEN A LITTLE WHILE, IT'S GAM OVER.
SO ...
IF THERE WERE ANY POSSIBILITY THAT SOMEON COULD LEAK INFORMATION ABOUT YOU...
... ANYBODY WHO MIGHT'VE PASSED BY YOU IN MEGURO ...
...OR SEEN YOU IN FRONT OF THE STATION ...

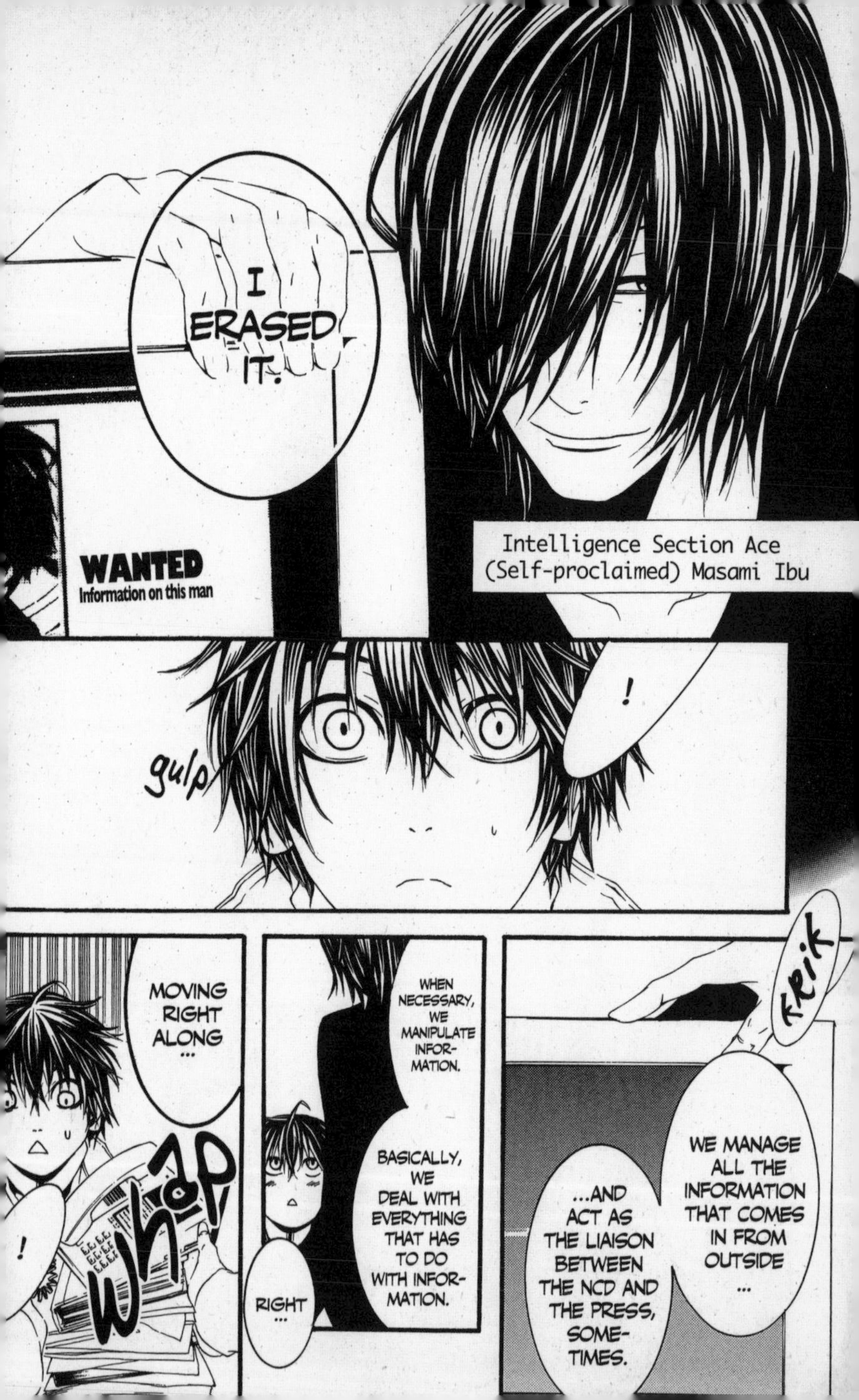
I ERASED IT.
Intelligence Section Ace (Self-proclaimed) Masami Ibu
WANTED
Information on this man
!
gulp
KRIK
WE MANAGE ALL THE INFORMATION THAT COMES IN FROM OUTSIDE ...
...AND ACT AS THE LIAISON BETWEEN THE NCD AND THE PRESS, SOMETIMES.
WHEN NECESSARY, WE MANIPULATE INFORMATION.
BASICALLY, WE DEAL WITH EVERYTHING THAT HAS TO DO WITH INFORMATION.
RIGHT ...
MOVING RIGHT ALONG ...
WHAP
!

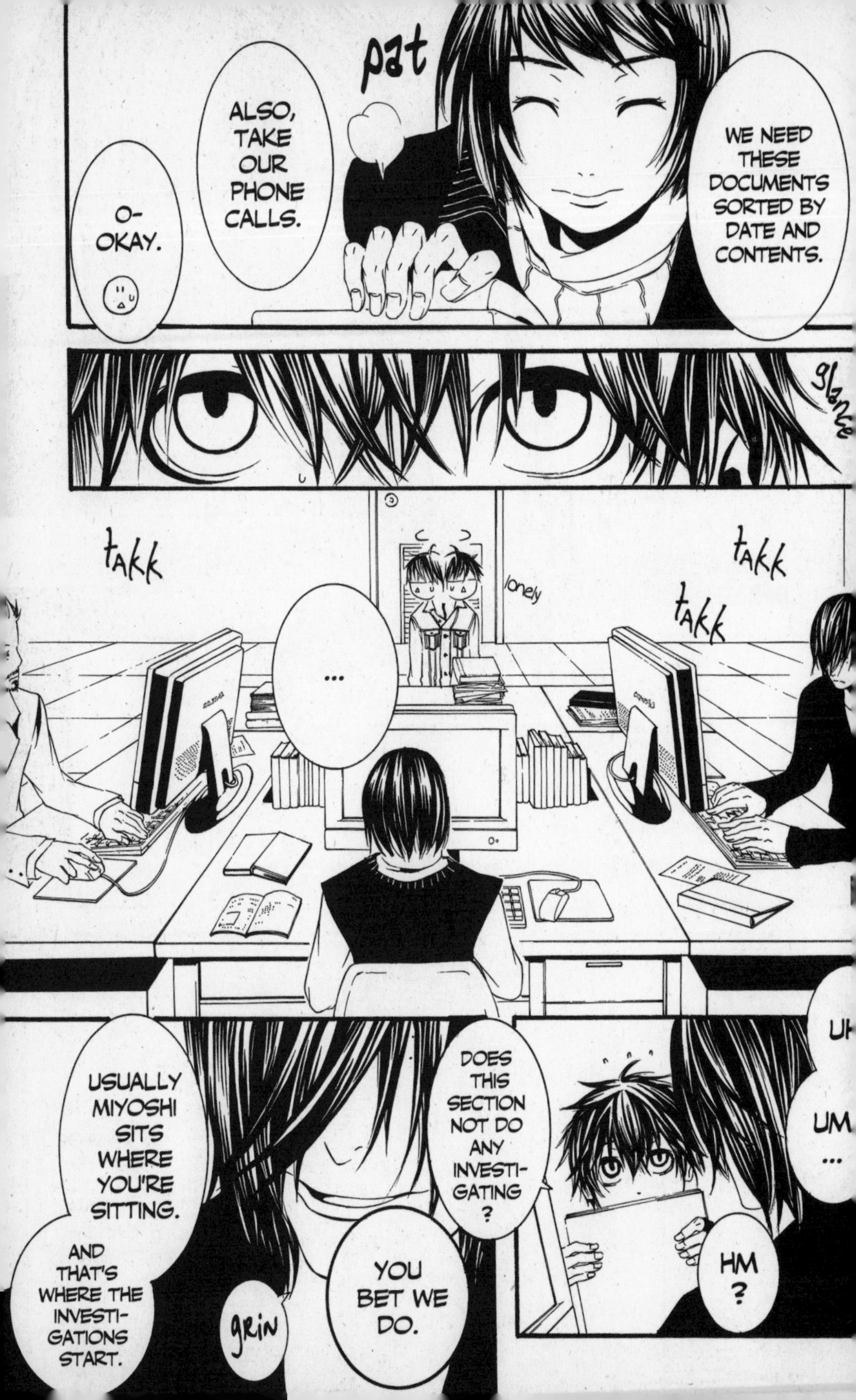
WE NEED THESE DOCUMENTS SORTED BY DATE AND CONTENTS.
pat
ALSO, TAKE OUR PHONE CALLS.
O-OKAY.
glance
takk
takk
lonely
...
takk
UH UM ...
DOES THIS SECTION NOT DO ANY INVESTIGATING ?
HM ?
YOU BET WE DO.
grin
USUALLY MIYOSHI SITS WHERE YOU'RE SITTING.
AND THAT'S WHERE THE INVESTIGATIONS START.

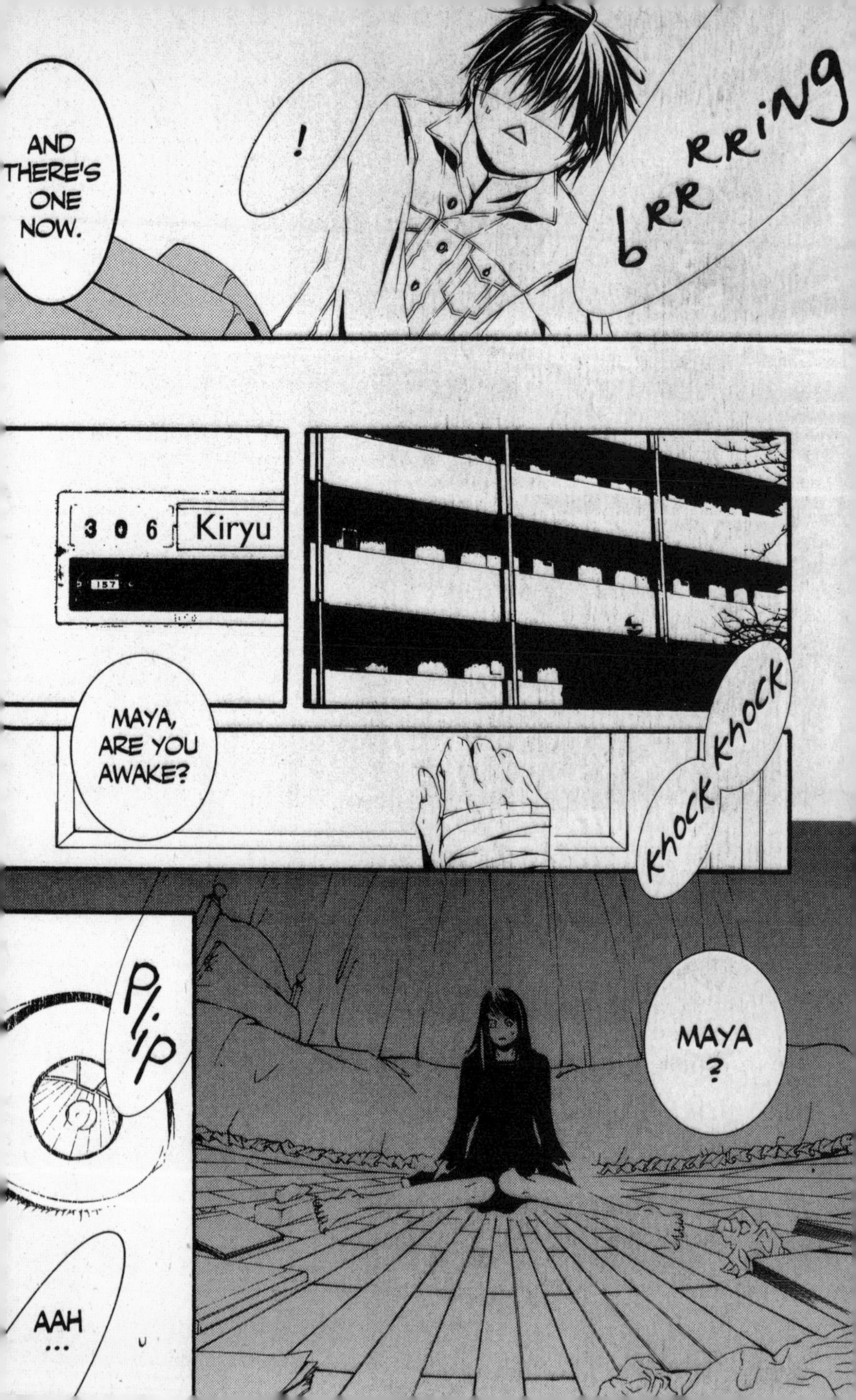
bRRRRING
!
AND THERE'S ONE NOW.
306 Kiryu
knock knock
MAYA, ARE YOU AWAKE?
MAYA ?
Plip
AAH ...

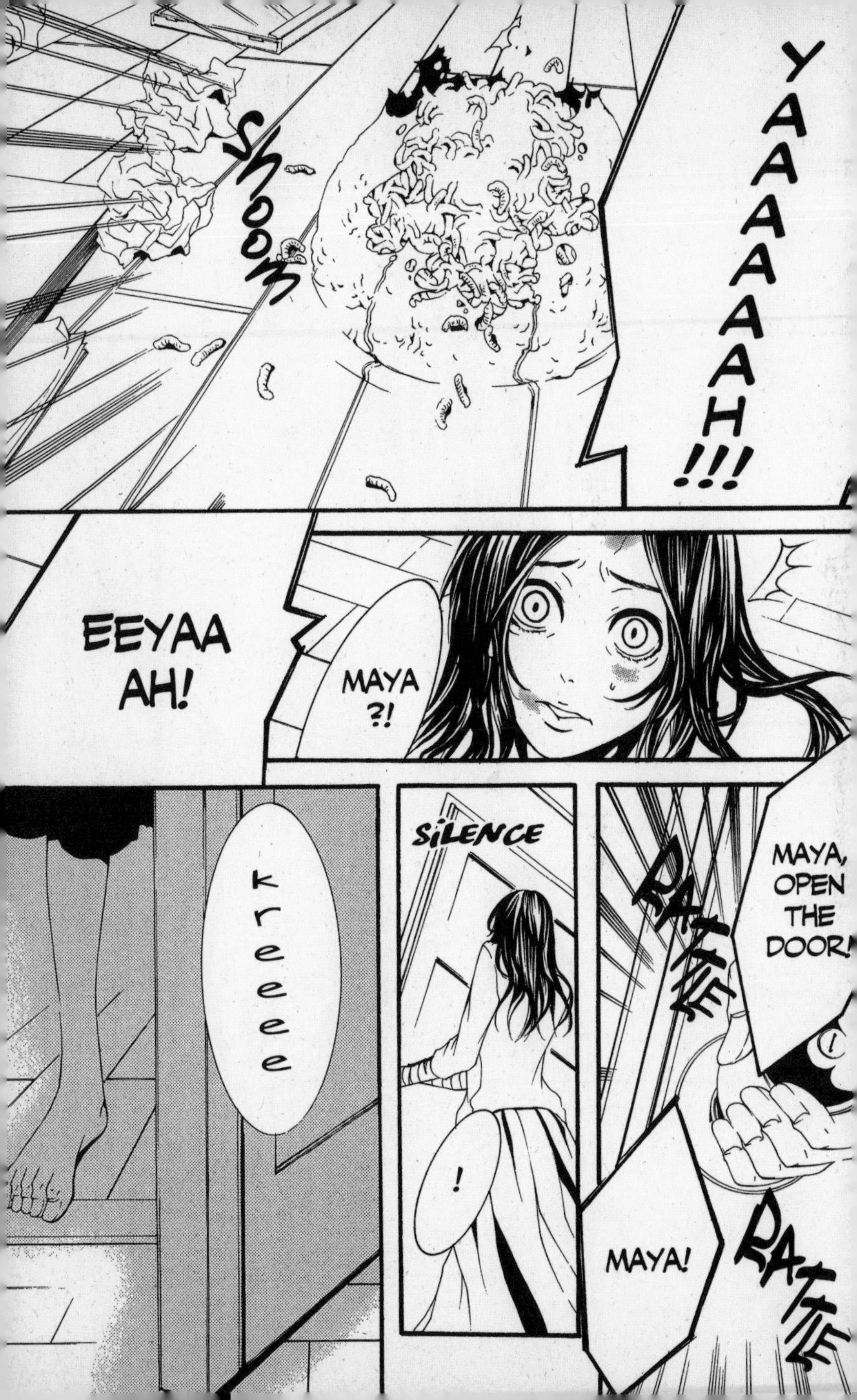
YAAAAAAH!!!
SHOOM
MAYA ?!
EEYAA AH!
MAYA, OPEN THE DOOR!
RATTLE
RATTLE
MAYA!
SILENCE
!
kreeee

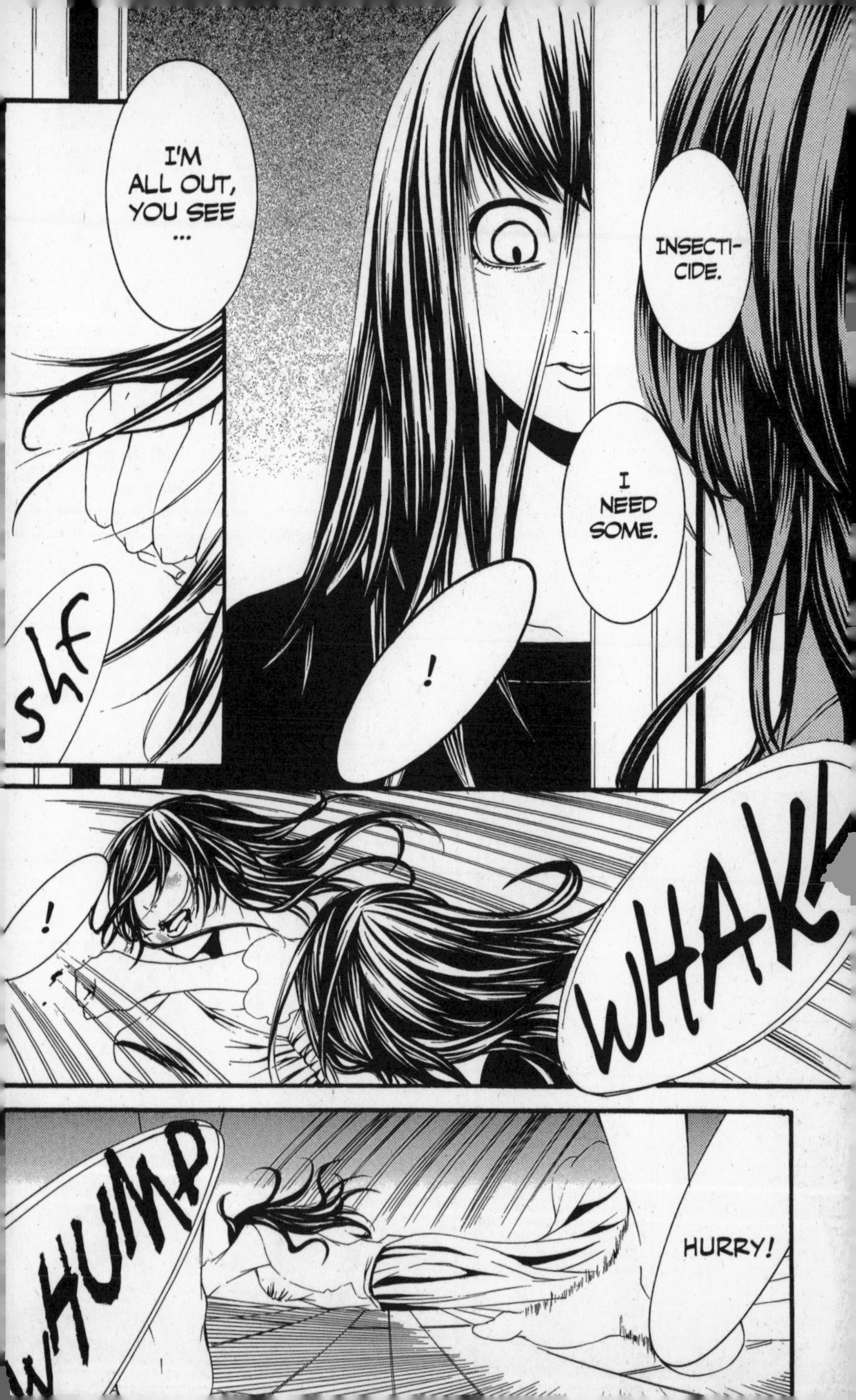
INSECTI-CIDE.
I NEED SOME.
!
I'M ALL OUT, YOU SEE ...
shf
WHAK
!
HURRY!
WHUMP

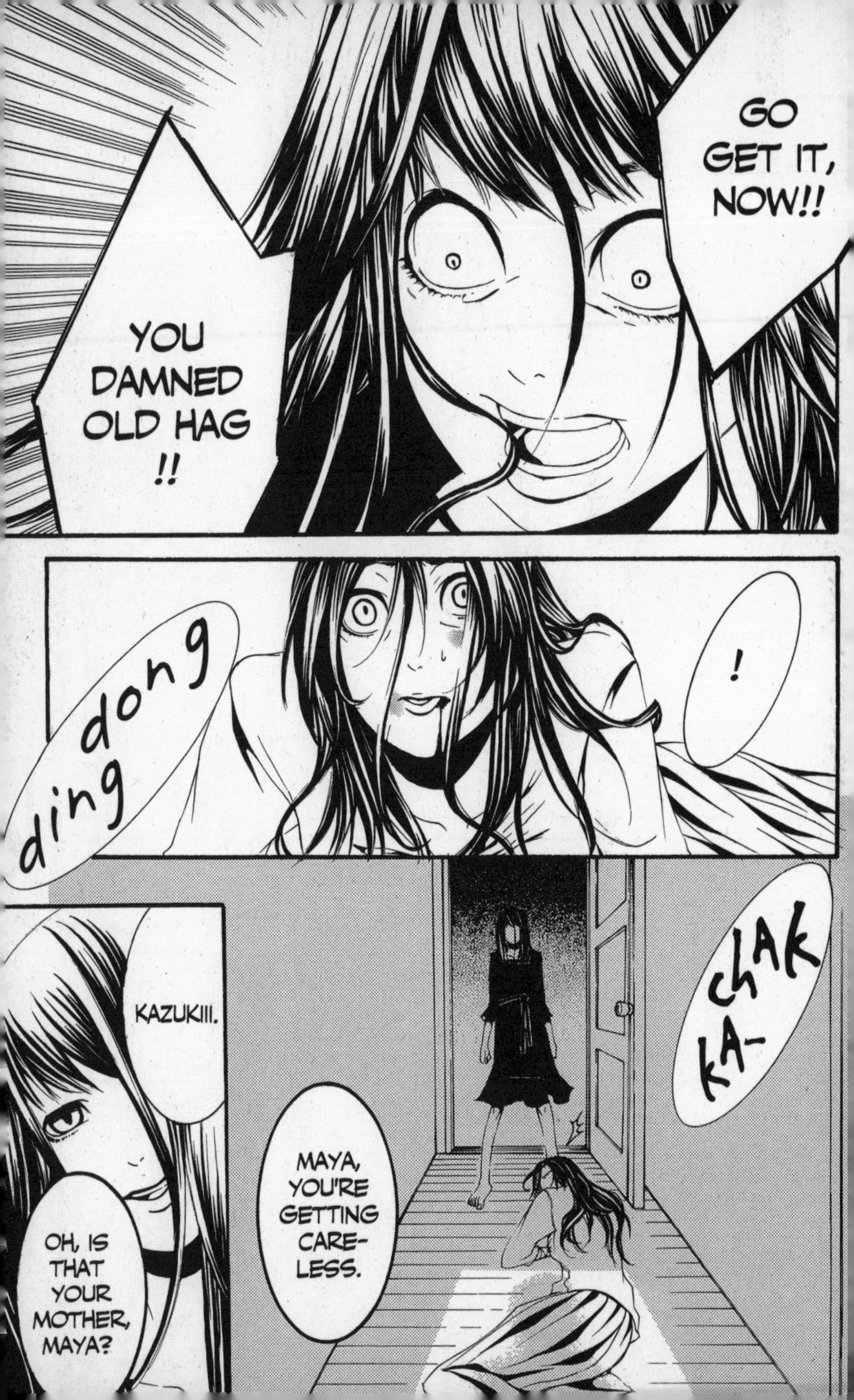
GO GET IT, NOW!!
YOU DAMNED OLD HAG !!
!
ding dong
KA-CHAK
MAYA, YOU'RE GETTING CARE-LESS.
KAZUKIII.
OH, IS THAT YOUR MOTHER, MAYA?

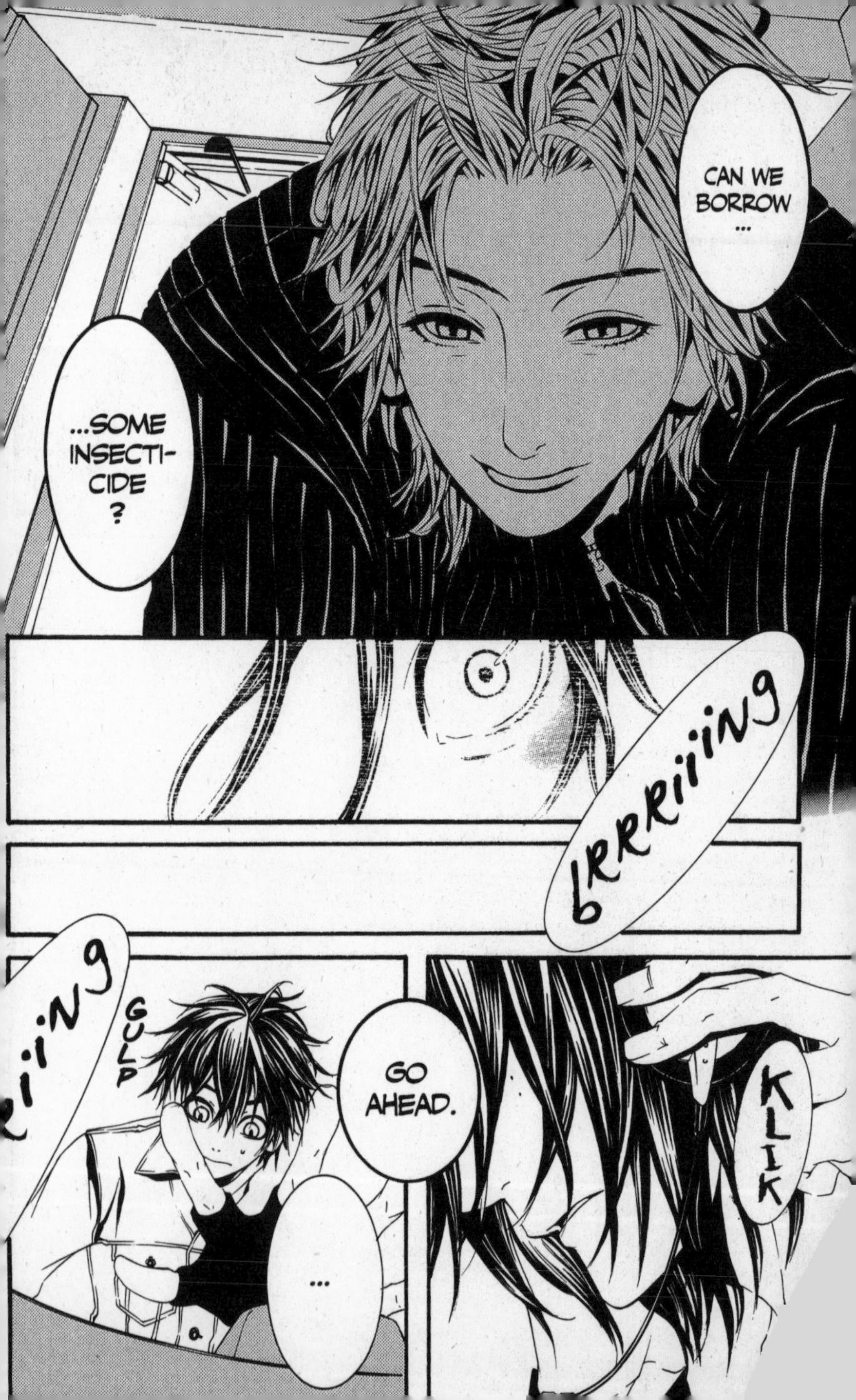
CAN WE BORROW ...
...SOME INSECTI- CIDE ?
bRRRiiing
KLIK
GO AHEAD.
riiing
GULP
...

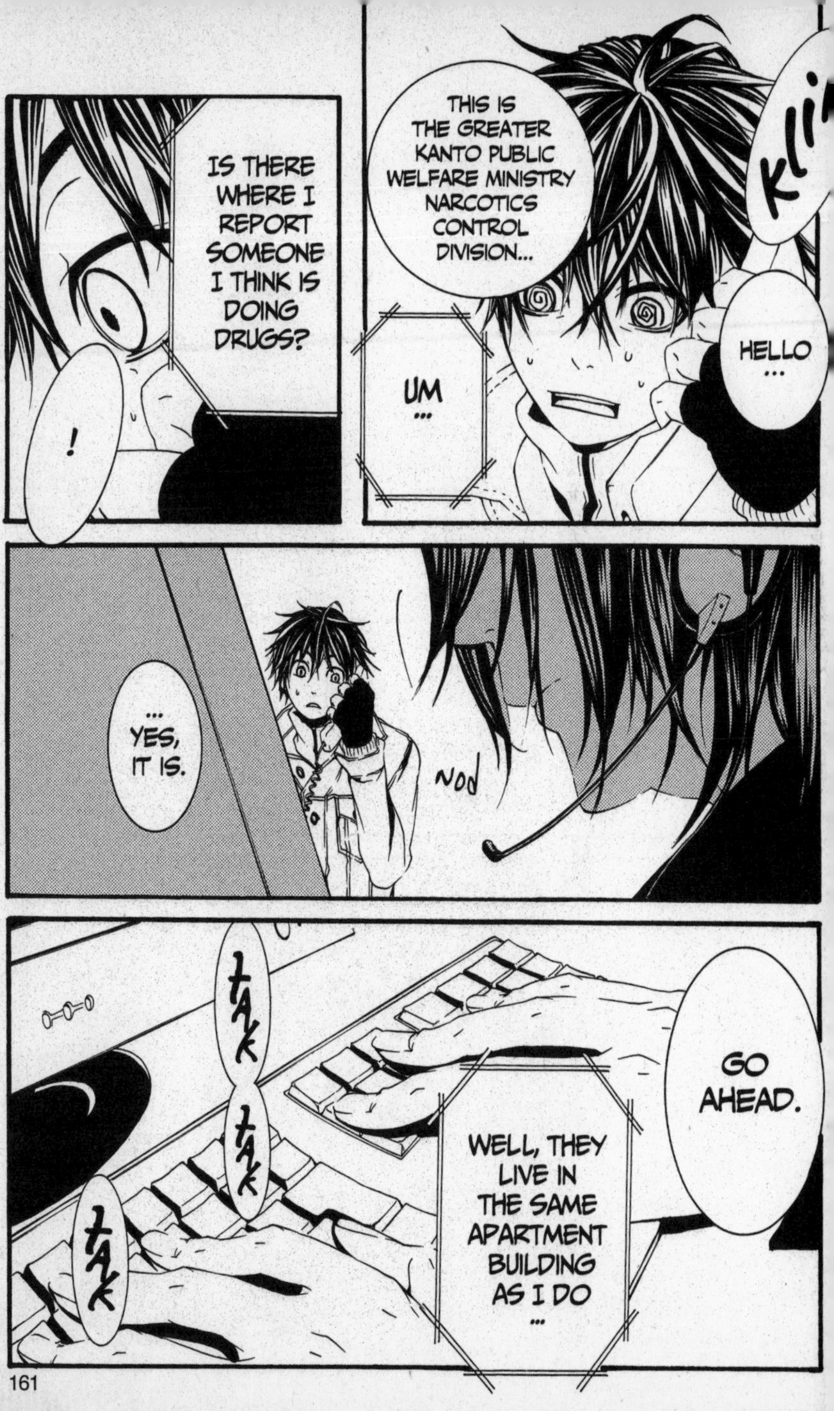
HELLO ...
THIS IS THE GREATER KANTO PUBLIC WELFARE MINISTRY NARCOTICS CONTROL DIVISION...
UM ...
IS THERE WHERE I REPORT SOMEONE I THINK IS DOING DRUGS?
!
NOD
... YES, IT IS.
GO AHEAD.
TAK
TAK
TAK
WELL, THEY LIVE IN THE SAME APARTMENT BUILDING AS I DO ...

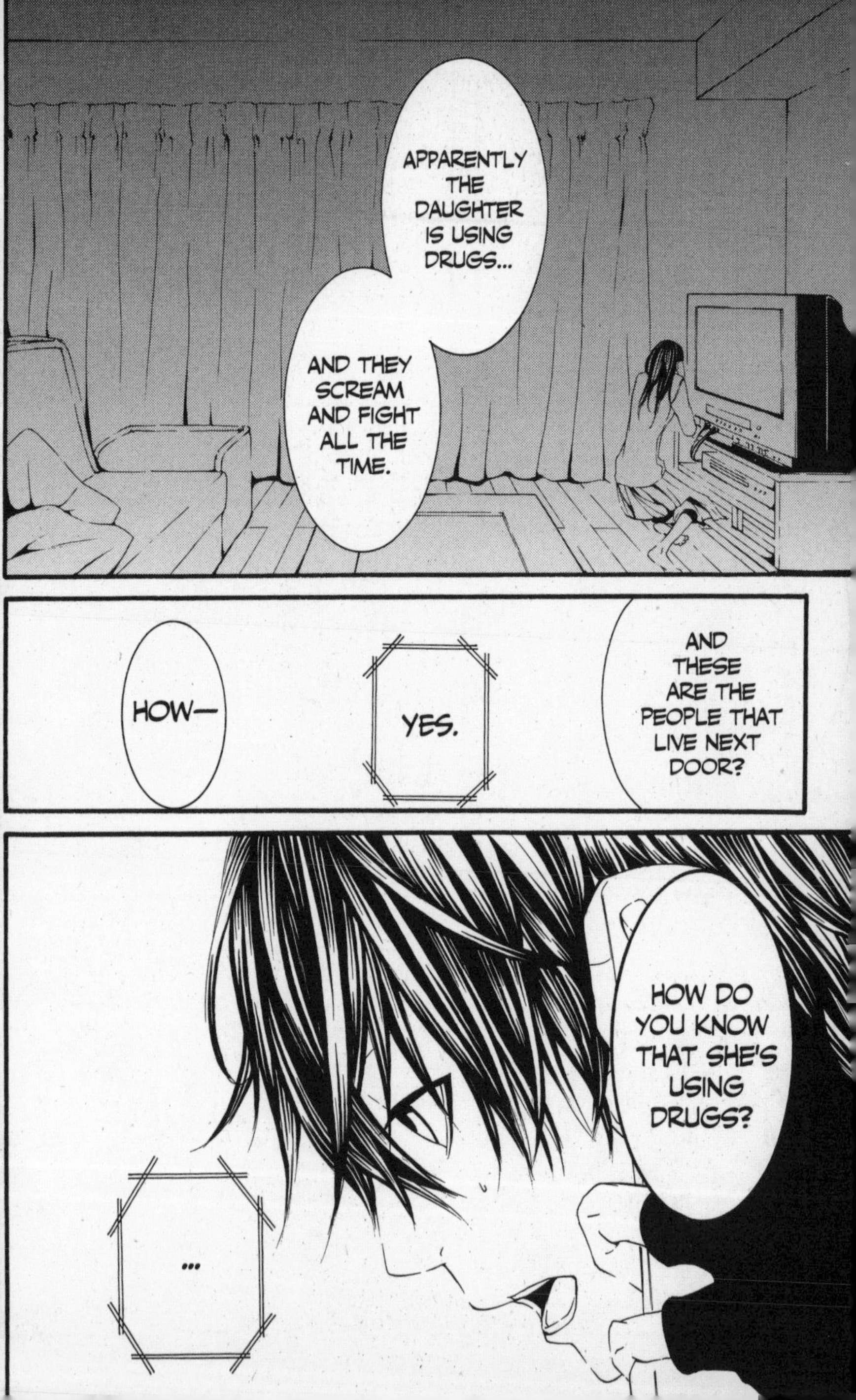
APPARENTLY THE DAUGHTER IS USING DRUGS...
AND THEY SCREAM AND FIGHT ALL THE TIME.
AND THESE ARE THE PEOPLE THAT LIVE NEXT DOOR?
YES.
HOW—
HOW DO YOU KNOW THAT SHE'S USING DRUGS?
...

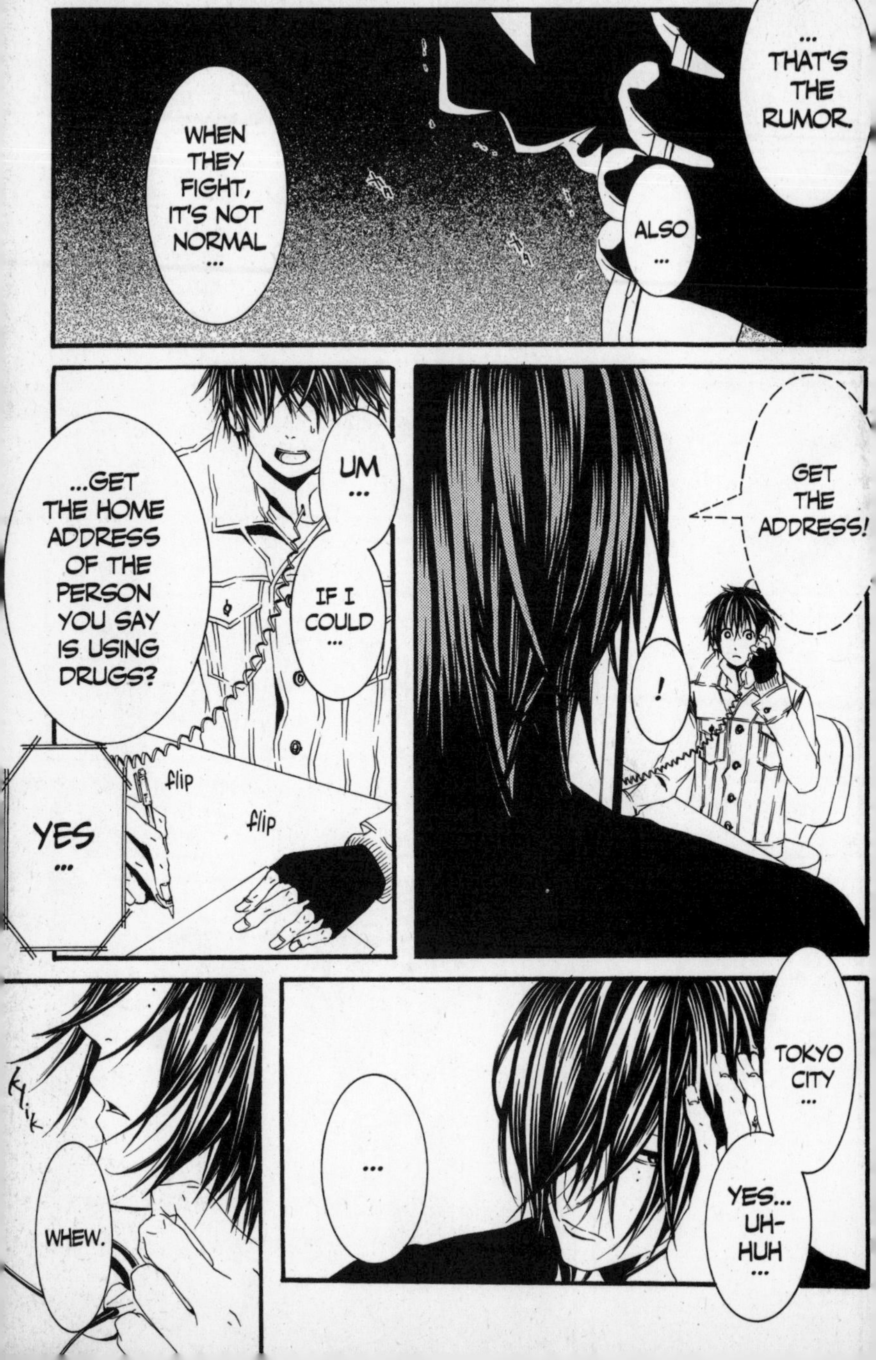
...THAT'S THE RUMOR.
ALSO...
WHEN THEY FIGHT, IT'S NOT NORMAL...
GET THE ADDRESS!
!
UM...
IF I COULD...
...GET THE HOME ADDRESS OF THE PERSON YOU SAY IS USING DRUGS?
flip
flip
YES...
TOKYO CITY...
YES... UH-HUH...
...
klik
WHEW.

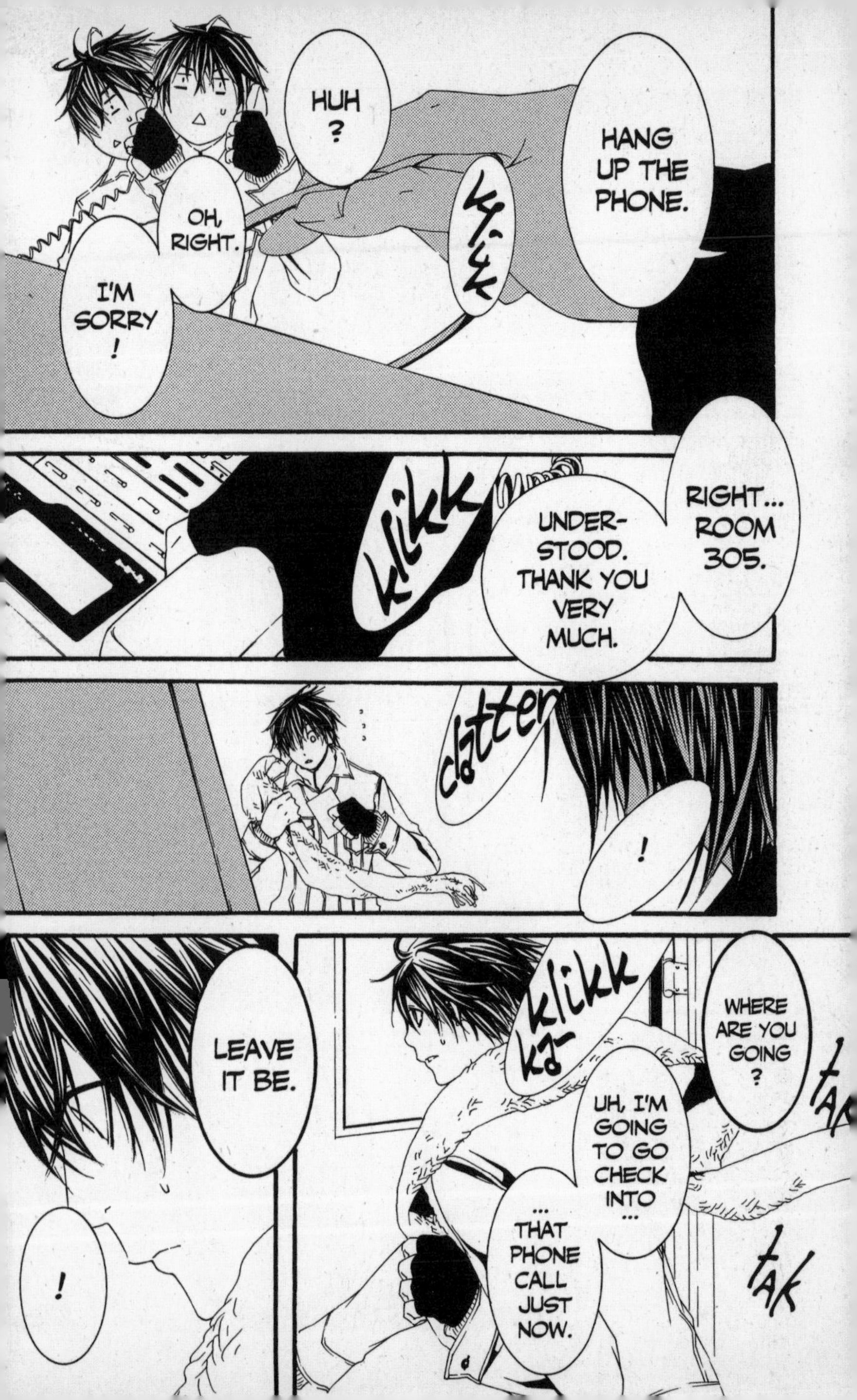
HANG UP THE PHONE.
klikk
HUH?
OH, RIGHT.
I'M SORRY!
RIGHT... ROOM 305.
UNDER-STOOD. THANK YOU VERY MUCH.
klikk
clatter
!
tak
WHERE ARE YOU GOING?
klikk
UH, I'M GOING TO GO CHECK INTO...
...THAT PHONE CALL JUST NOW.
tak
LEAVE IT BE.
!

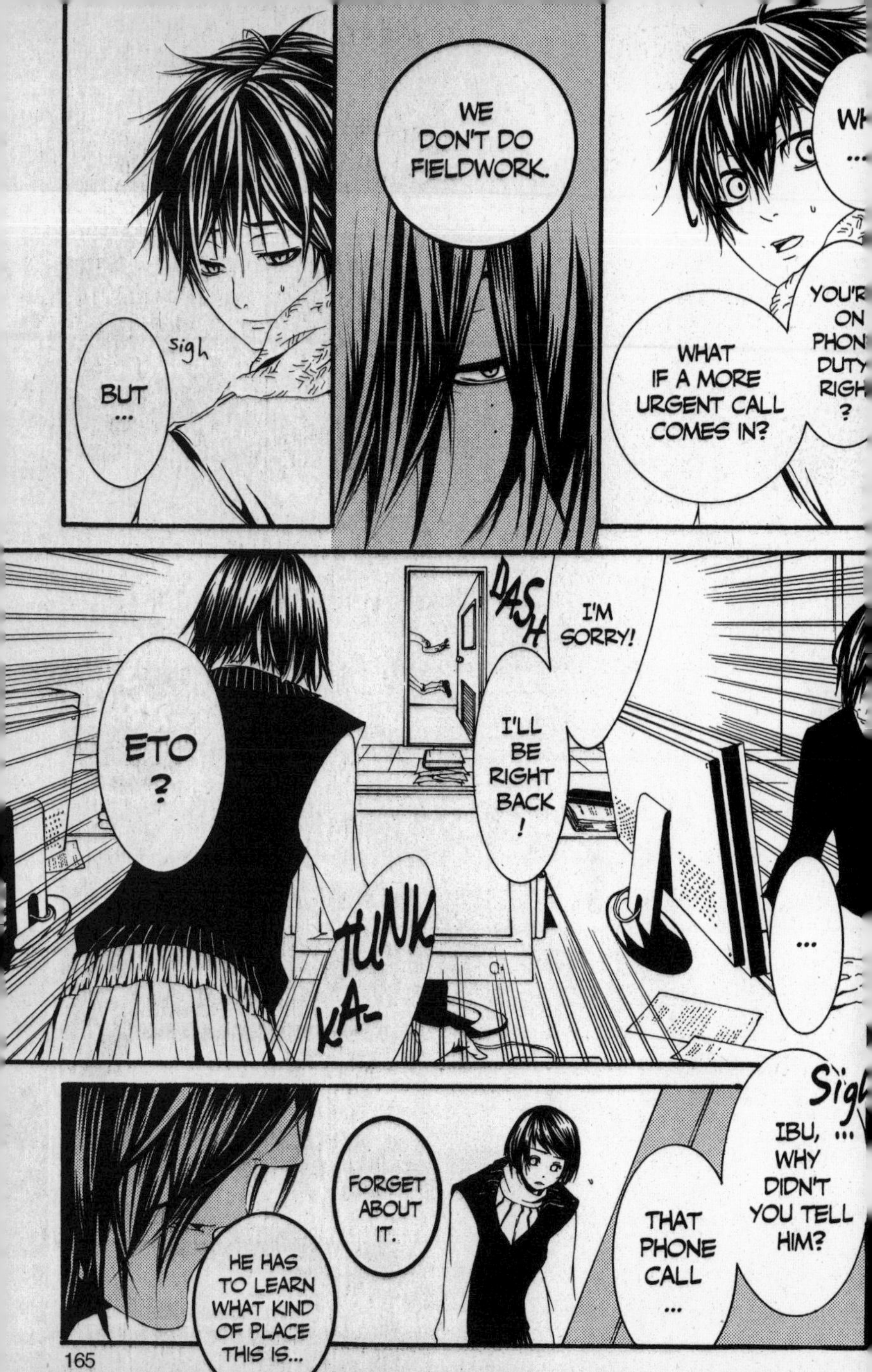
WH ...
YOU'R ON PHON DUTY RIGH ?
WHAT IF A MORE URGENT CALL COMES IN?
WE DON'T DO FIELDWORK.
sigh
BUT ...
I'M SORRY!
DASH
I'LL BE RIGHT BACK!
ETO?
...
KA-TUNK
Sigh
IBU, ... WHY DIDN'T YOU TELL HIM?
THAT PHONE CALL ...
FORGET ABOUT IT.
HE HAS TO LEARN WHAT KIND OF PLACE THIS IS...

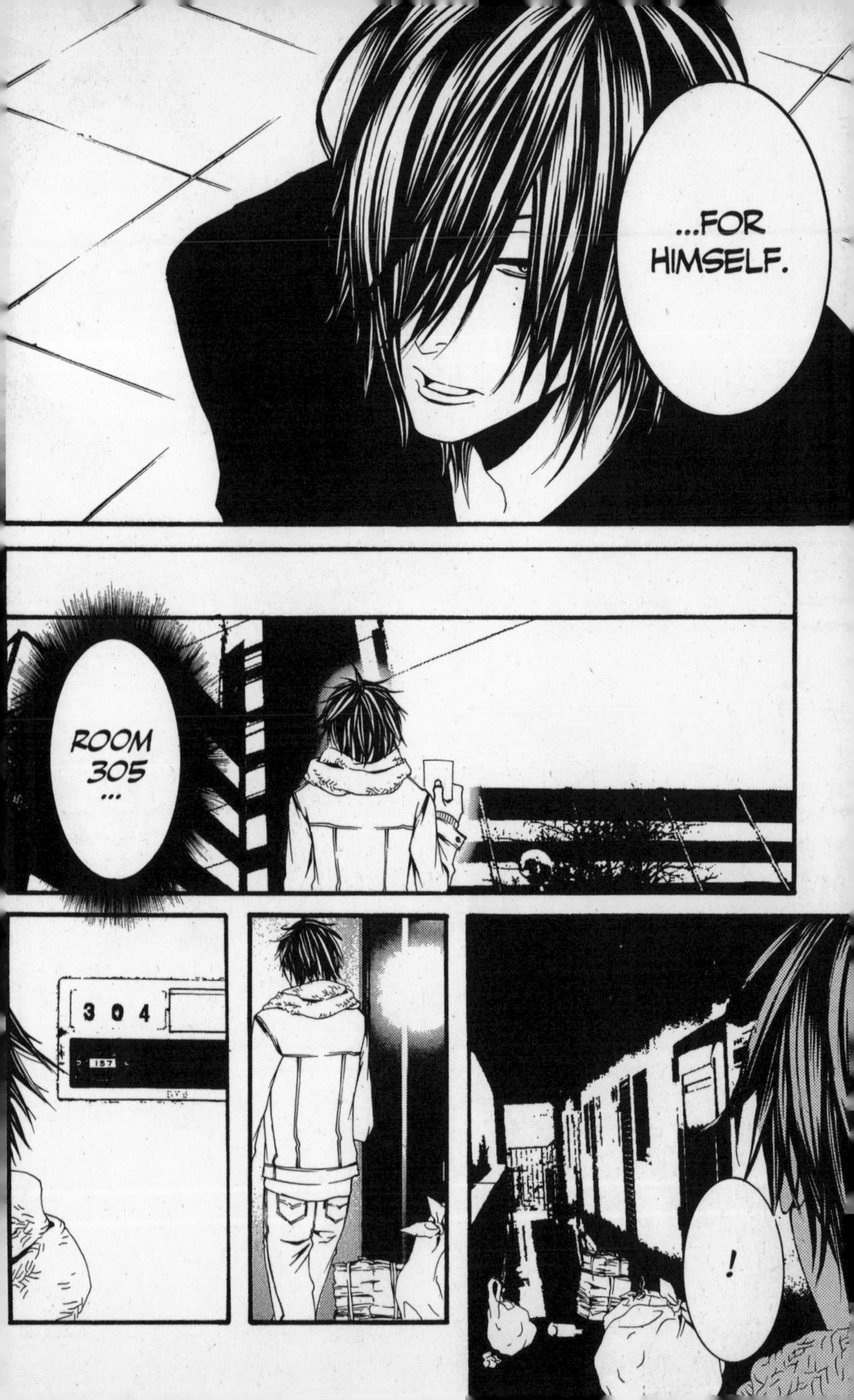
...FOR HIMSELF.
ROOM 305 ...
!
304

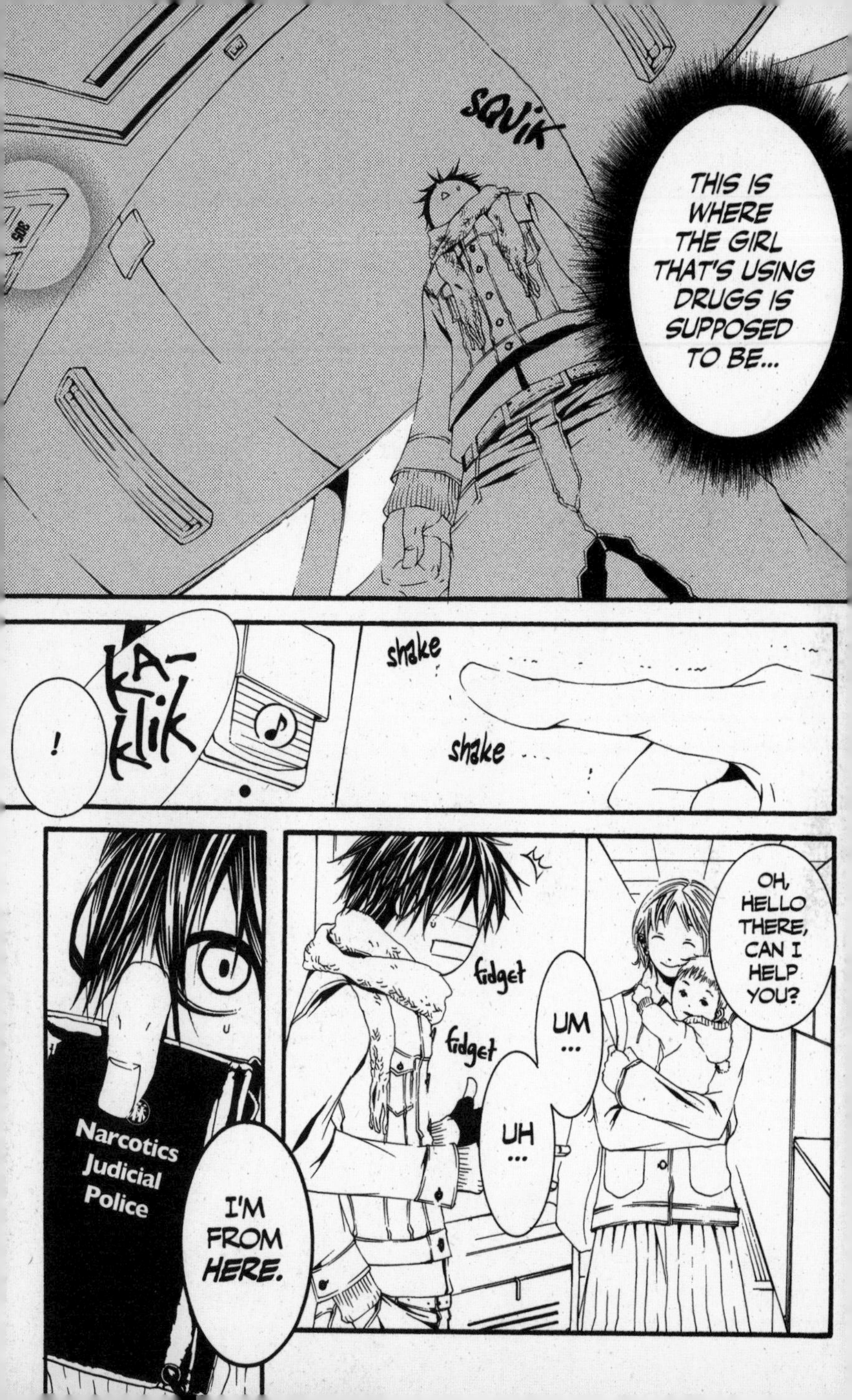
SQUIK
THIS IS WHERE THE GIRL THAT'S USING DRUGS IS SUPPOSED TO BE...
shake
shake
KA-KLIK
!
OH, HELLO THERE, CAN I HELP YOU?
fidget
fidget
UM...
UH...
Narcotics Judicial Police
I'M FROM HERE.

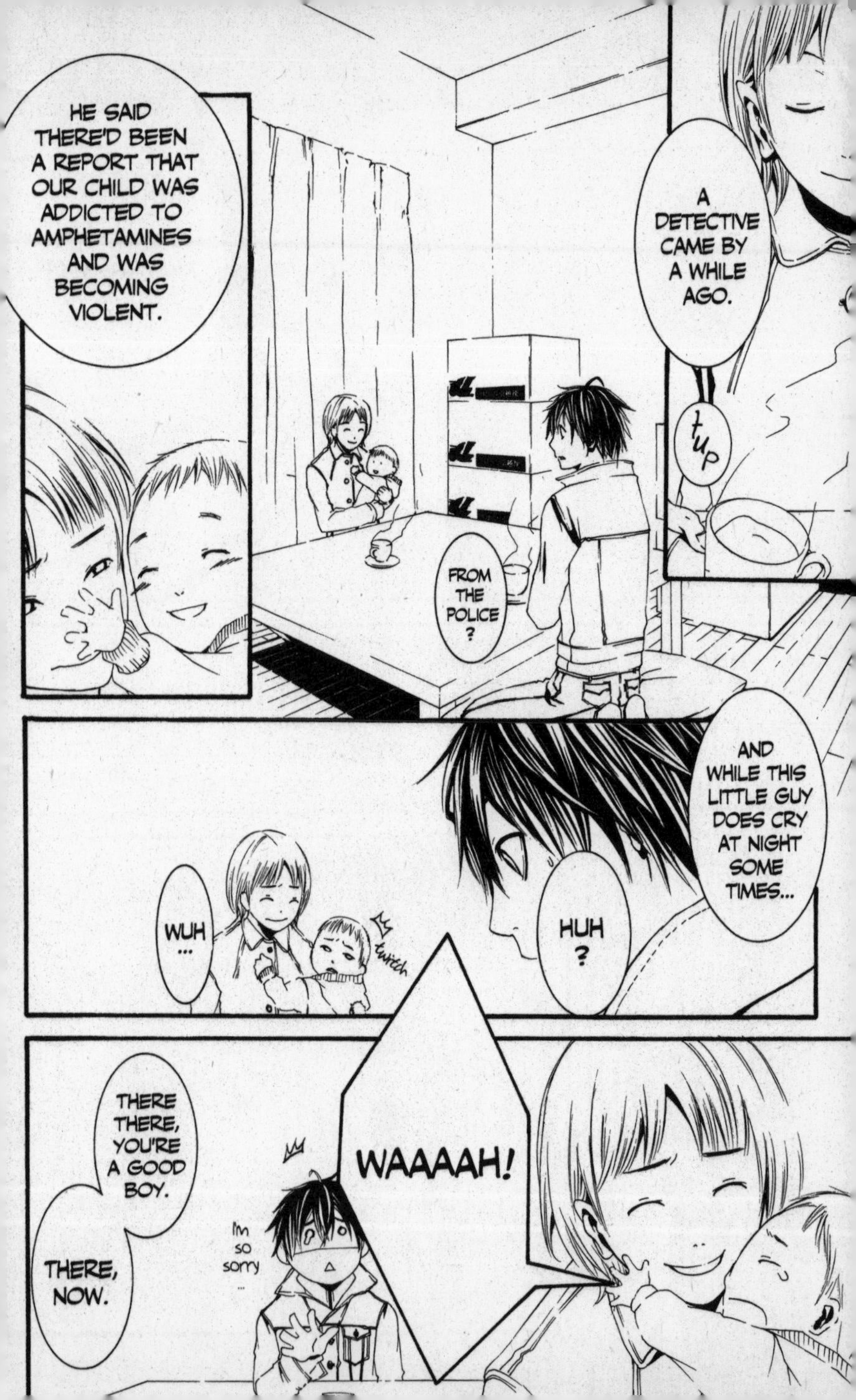
A DETECTIVE CAME BY A WHILE AGO.
tup
FROM THE POLICE?
HE SAID THERE'D BEEN A REPORT THAT OUR CHILD WAS ADDICTED TO AMPHETAMINES AND WAS BECOMING VIOLENT.
AND WHILE THIS LITTLE GUY DOES CRY AT NIGHT SOME TIMES...
HUH?
twitch
WUH...
WAAAAH!
THERE THERE, YOU'RE A GOOD BOY.
THERE, NOW.
I'm so sorry...

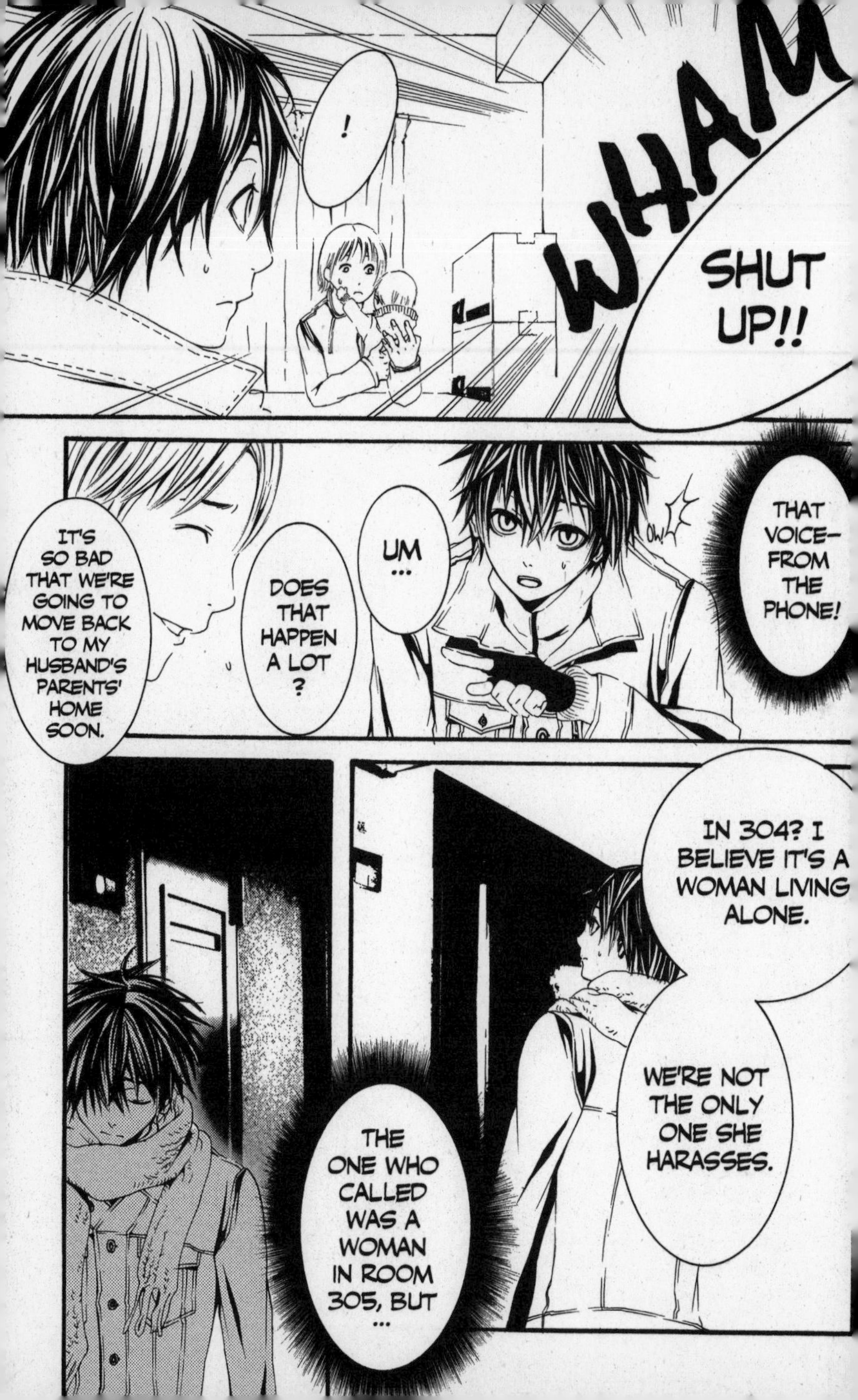
WHAM
SHUT UP!!
!
THAT VOICE—FROM THE PHONE!
OW!
UM...
DOES THAT HAPPEN A LOT?
IT'S SO BAD THAT WE'RE GOING TO MOVE BACK TO MY HUSBAND'S PARENTS' HOME SOON.
IN 304? I BELIEVE IT'S A WOMAN LIVING ALONE.
WE'RE NOT THE ONLY ONE SHE HARASSES.
THE ONE WHO CALLED WAS A WOMAN IN ROOM 305, BUT...

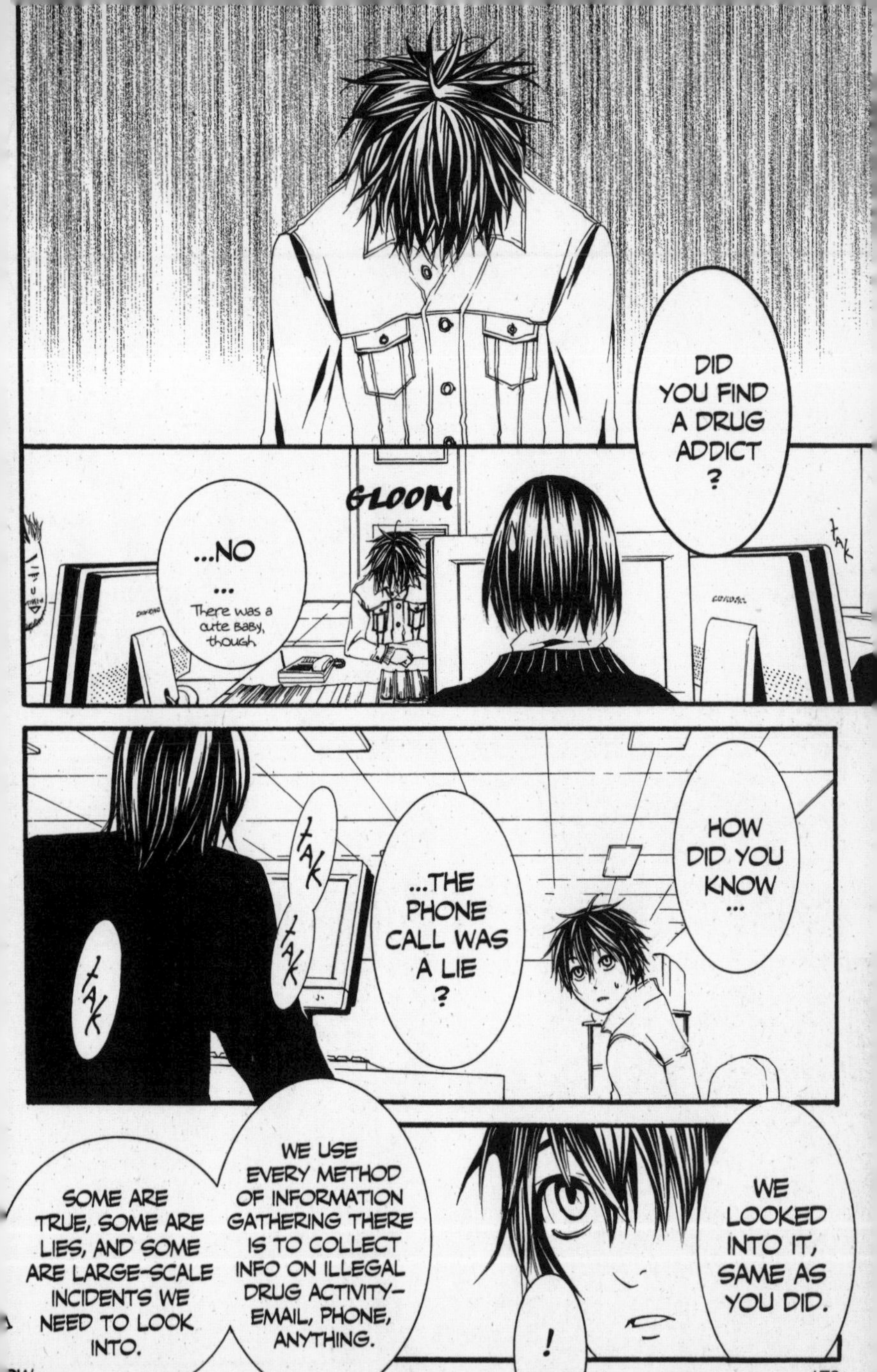
DID YOU FIND A DRUG ADDICT?
GLOOM
TAK
...NO ... There was a cute baby, though.
HOW DID YOU KNOW...
...THE PHONE CALL WAS A LIE?
TAK
TAK
TAK
WE LOOKED INTO IT, SAME AS YOU DID.
!
WE USE EVERY METHOD OF INFORMATION GATHERING THERE IS TO COLLECT INFO ON ILLEGAL DRUG ACTIVITY—EMAIL, PHONE, ANYTHING.
SOME ARE TRUE, SOME ARE LIES, AND SOME ARE LARGE-SCALE INCIDENTS WE NEED TO LOOK INTO.

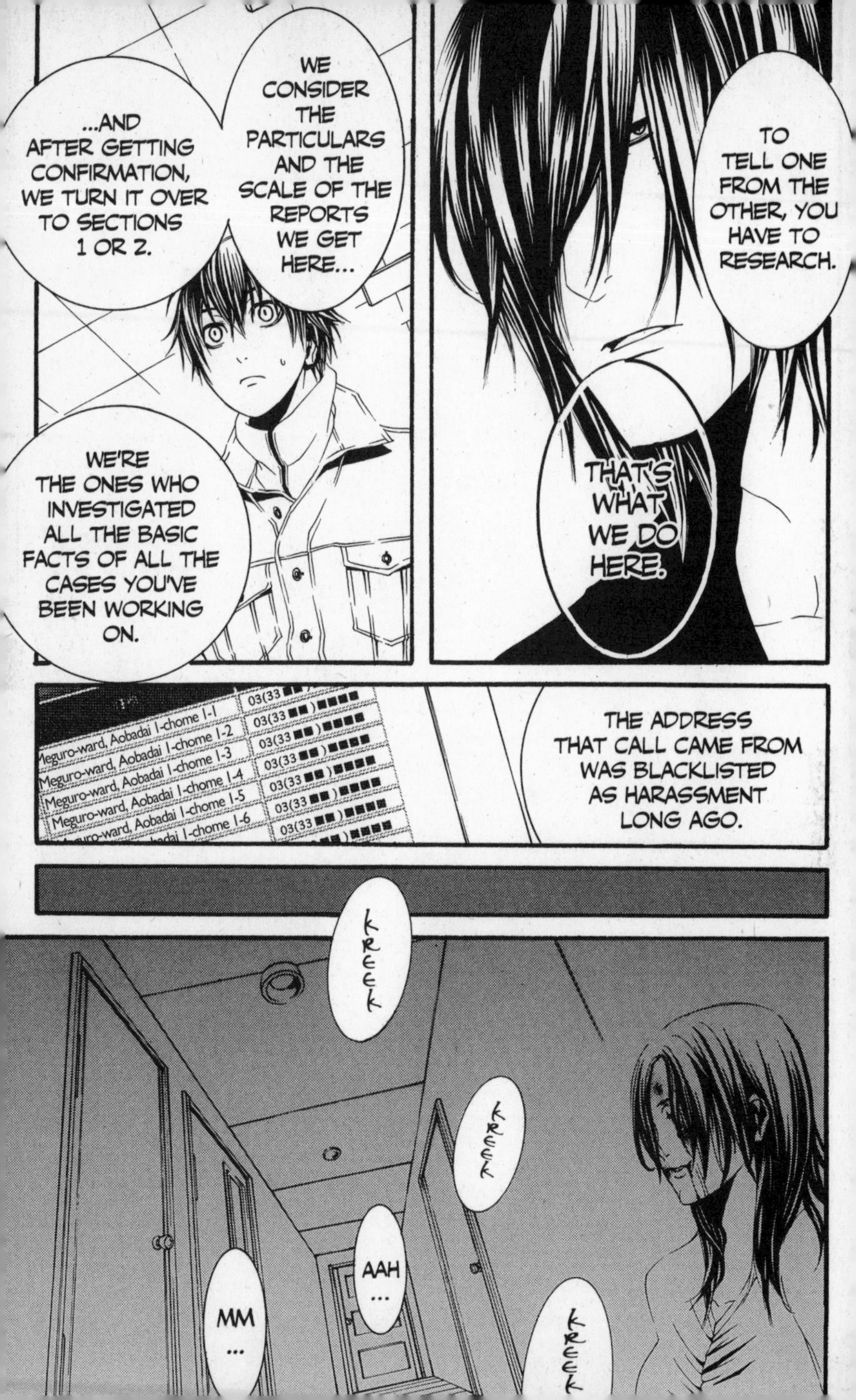
TO TELL ONE FROM THE OTHER, YOU HAVE TO RESEARCH.
THAT'S WHAT WE DO HERE.
WE CONSIDER THE PARTICULARS AND THE SCALE OF THE REPORTS WE GET HERE...
...AND AFTER GETTING CONFIRMATION, WE TURN IT OVER TO SECTIONS 1 OR 2.
WE'RE THE ONES WHO INVESTIGATED ALL THE BASIC FACTS OF ALL THE CASES YOU'VE BEEN WORKING ON.
THE ADDRESS THAT CALL CAME FROM WAS BLACKLISTED AS HARASSMENT LONG AGO.
Meguro-ward, Aobadai 1-chome 1-1 03(33[redacted])[redacted]
Meguro-ward, Aobadai 1-chome 1-2 03(33[redacted])[redacted]
Meguro-ward, Aobadai 1-chome 1-3 03(33[redacted])[redacted]
Meguro-ward, Aobadai 1-chome 1-4 03(33[redacted])[redacted]
Meguro-ward, Aobadai 1-chome 1-5 03(33[redacted])[redacted]
KREEK
KREEK
KREEK
AAH...
MM...

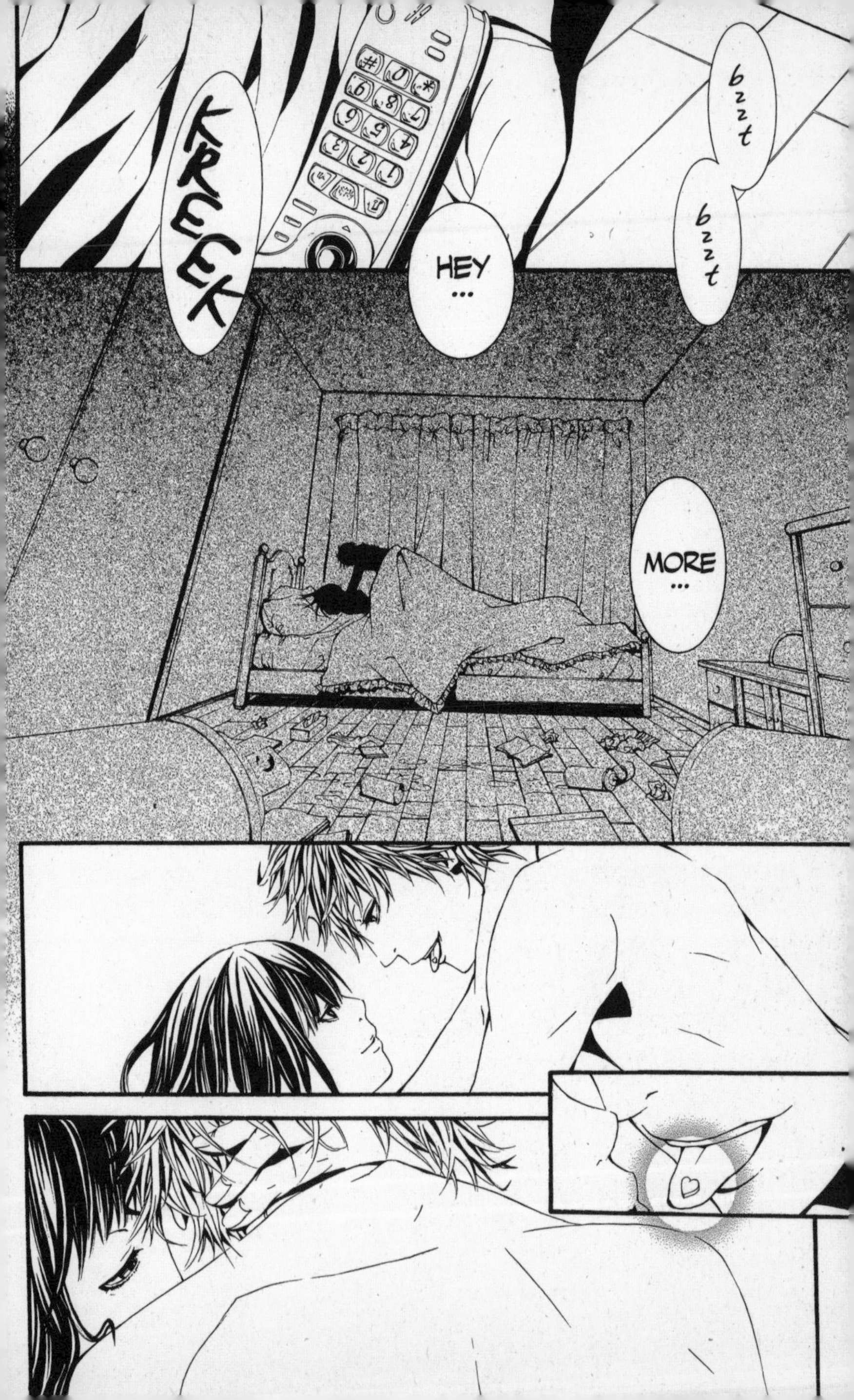
bzzt
bzzt
HEY ...
KREEK
MORE ...

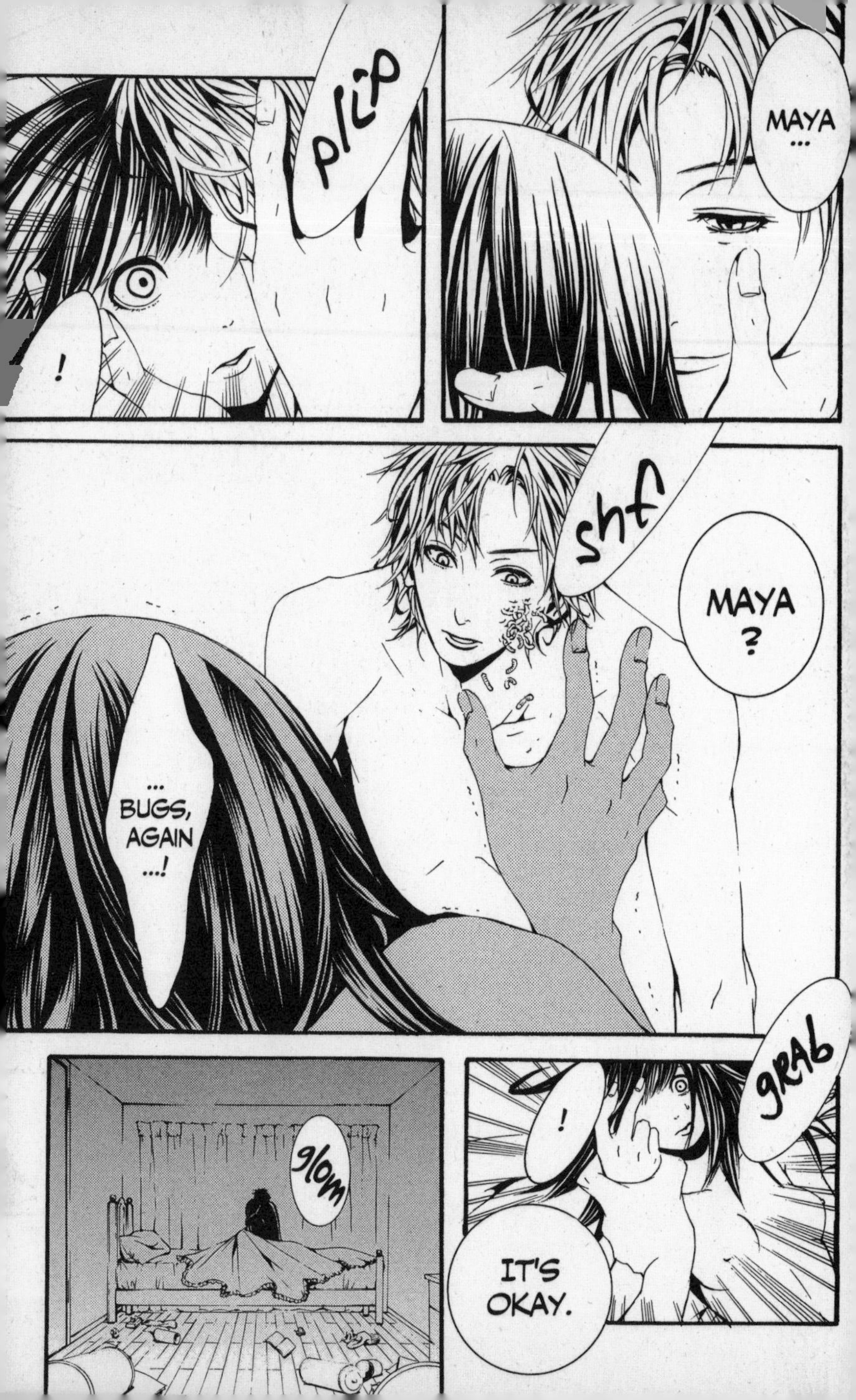
MAYA ...
plip
!
shf
MAYA ?
... BUGS, AGAIN ...!
grab
!
IT'S OKAY.
glom

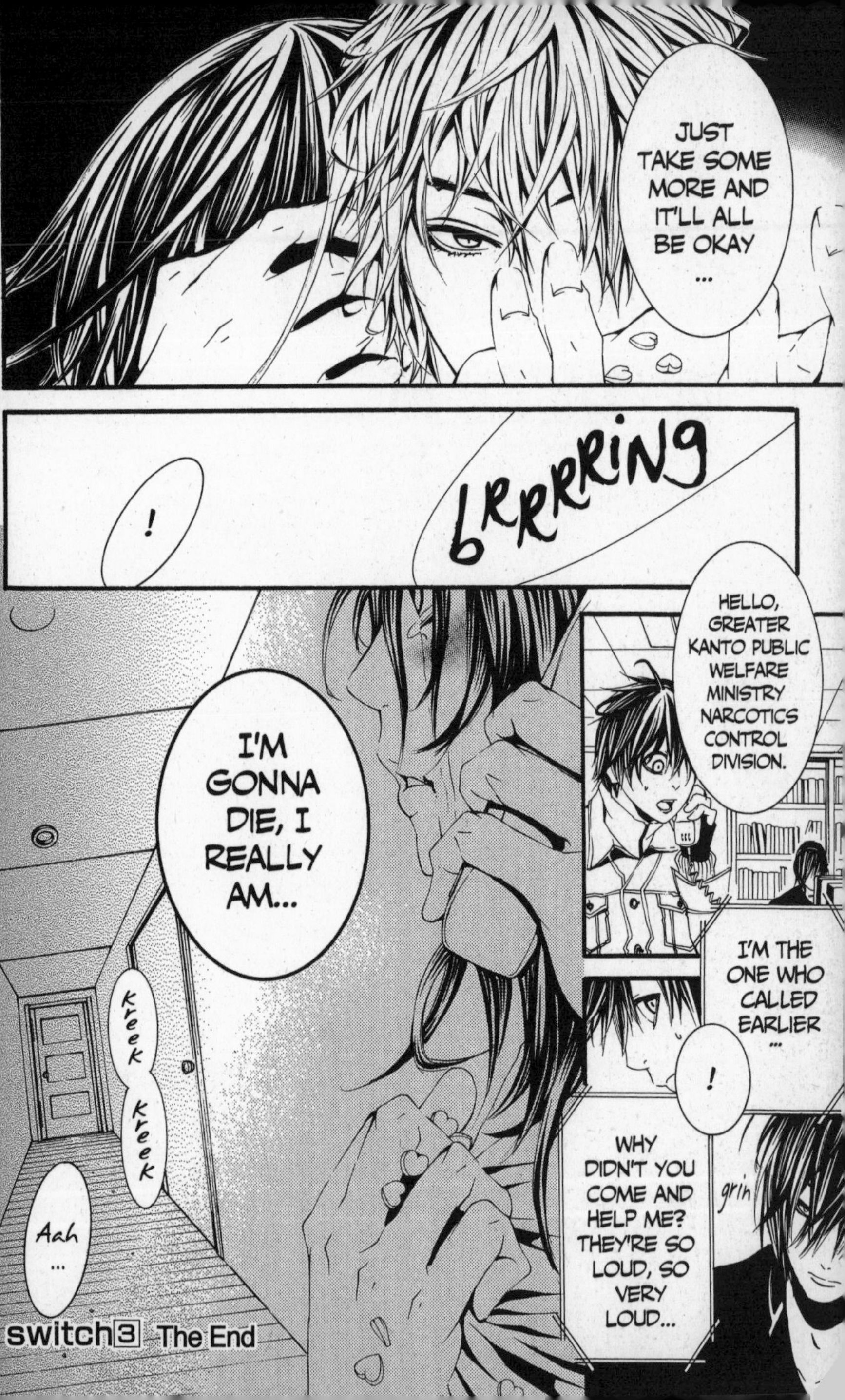
JUST TAKE SOME MORE AND IT'LL ALL BE OKAY ...
brrRRing
!
HELLO, GREATER KANTO PUBLIC WELFARE MINISTRY NARCOTICS CONTROL DIVISION.
I'M THE ONE WHO CALLED EARLIER ...
!
WHY DIDN'T YOU COME AND HELP ME? THEY'RE SO LOUD, SO VERY LOUD...
grin
I'M GONNA DIE, I REALLY AM...
Kreek
Kreek
Aah ...

switch3 The End

naked ape.s

http://naked-ape.net/

Visit the naked ape website (Japanese)
for more switch art and information.

Presented by naked ape
webmaster. otoh saki

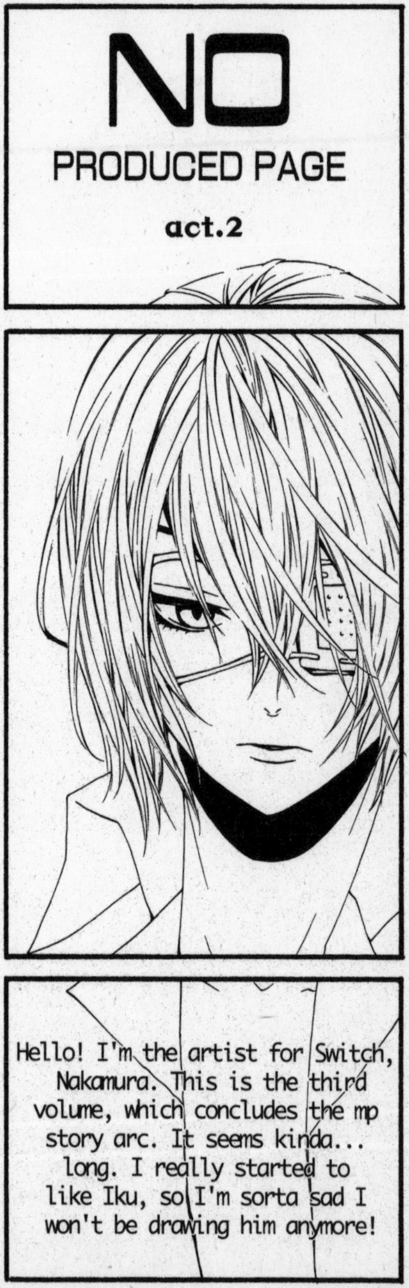
NO
PRODUCED PAGE
act.2
Hello! I'm the artist for Switch, Nakamura. This is the third volume, which concludes the mp story arc. It seems kinda... long. I really started to like Iku, so I'm sorta sad I won't be drawing him anymore!

(I) Sniper (part I)

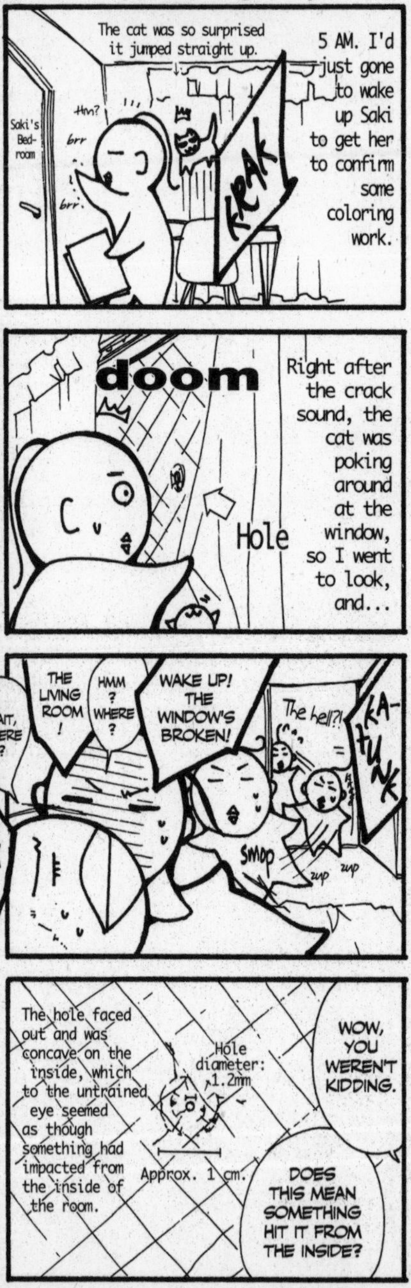
5 AM. I'd just gone to wake up Saki to get her to confirm some coloring work.
The cat was so surprised it jumped straight up.
KRAK
Hm?
brr
Saki's Bed-room
brr
Right after the crack sound, the cat was poking around at the window, so I went to look, and...
doom
Hole
KA-TUNK
The hell?!
WAKE UP! THE WINDOW'S BROKEN!
HMM ? WHERE ?
THE LIVING ROOM !
SMOP
zup zup
WOW, YOU WEREN'T KIDDING.
DOES THIS MEAN SOMETHING HIT IT FROM THE INSIDE?
Hole diameter: 1.2mm
Approx. 1 cm.
The hole faced out and was concave on the inside, which to the untrained eye seemed as though something had impacted from the inside of the room.

(2) Sniper (part II)

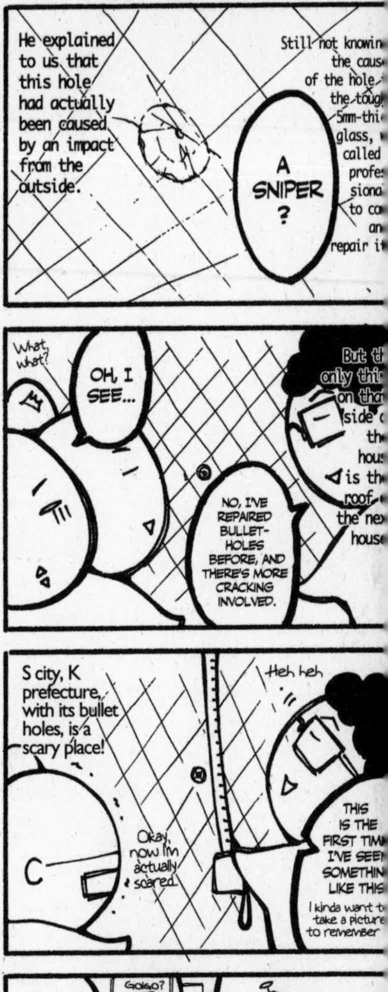
Still not knowin the caus of the hole the tougl 5mm-thi glass, called profes siona to co an repair it
A SNIPER?
He explained to us that this hole had actually been caused by an impact from the outside.
But th only thi on tha side o th hous is th roof the ne house
OH, I SEE...
What, what?
NO, I'VE REPAIRED BULLET-HOLES BEFORE, AND THERE'S MORE CRACKING INVOLVED.
Heh heh
THIS IS THE FIRST TIM I'VE SEE SOMETHIN LIKE THIS
I kinda want t take a picture to remember
S city, K prefecture, with its bullet holes, is a scary place!
Okay, now I'm actually scared.
Even now the hole is-a mystery
An agent?
GOLGO?
Maybe an agent?

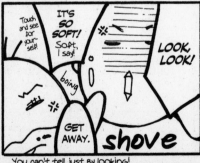

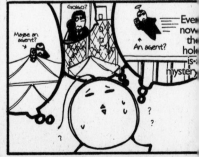

There is another apartment building past the house next door, but that still doesn't explain why the hole was so small. So many mysteries...

(3) Touch me, please...

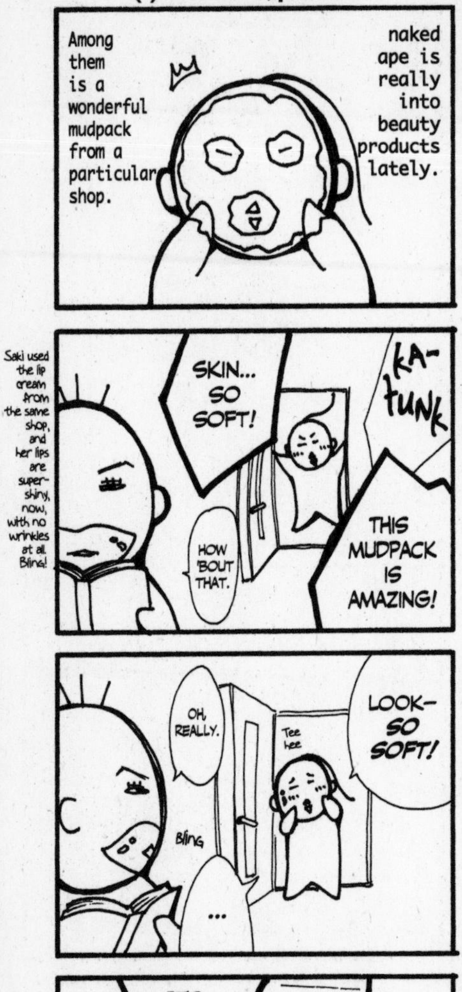
naked ape is really into beauty products lately.
Among them is a wonderful mudpack from a particular shop.
KA-TUNK
THIS MUDPACK IS AMAZING!
SKIN... SO SOFT!
HOW 'BOUT THAT.
Saki used the lip cream from the same shop, and her lips are super-shiny, now, with no wrinkles at all. Bling!
LOOK—SO SOFT!
Tee hee
OH, REALLY.
Bling
...
LOOK, LOOK!
IT'S SO SOFT! Soft, I say!
Touch and see for your-self!
boing
GET AWAY.
shove

You can't tell just by looking!

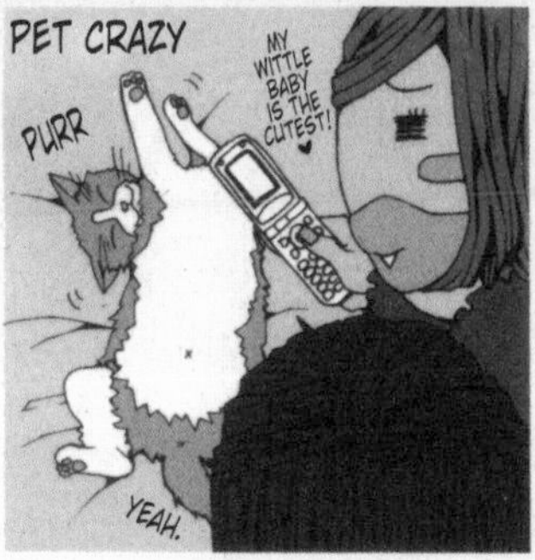
PET CRAZY
MY WITTLE BABY IS THE CUTEST!
PURR
YEAH.

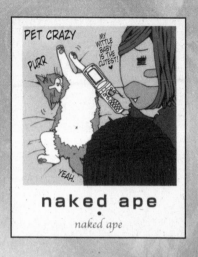

naked ape

naked ape

Recent events: I've been up late at night so my pores are staying open. My window was mysteriously broken. Doing deep breathing excercises several times a day for a headache. Stiff shoulders. Chronic insomnia. Every time I open my mouth I say, "I need a vacation." Such is the life of a manga artist. Hah!

Naked ape is the collaboration of Tomomi Nakamura and Otoh Saki, who were born just three months apart. Nakamura, the artist, takes things at her own pace and feels no guilt for missing deadlines. Saki, the writer, also does cover design and inking and is called President by the assistants. Naked ape's other works include *Black tar* and the ongoing futuristic crime thriller *DOLLS*.

SWITCH
Vol. 3

Story and Art by naked ape

Translation & English Adaptation/Paul Tuttle Starr,
Translation by Design
Touch-up Art & Lettering/Evan Waldinger
Design/Sean Lee
Editor/Pancha Diaz

Editor in Chief, Books/Alvin Lu
Editor in Chief, Magazines/Marc Weidenbaum
VP of Publishing Licensing/Rika Inouye
VP of Sales/Gonzalo Ferreyra
Sr. VP of Marketing/Liza Coppola
Publisher/Hyoe Narita

Published by VIZ Media, LLC
P.O. Box 77010
San Francisco, CA 94107

VIZ Media Edition
10 9 8 7 6 5 4 3 2 1
First printing, July 2008

www.viz.com store.viz.com

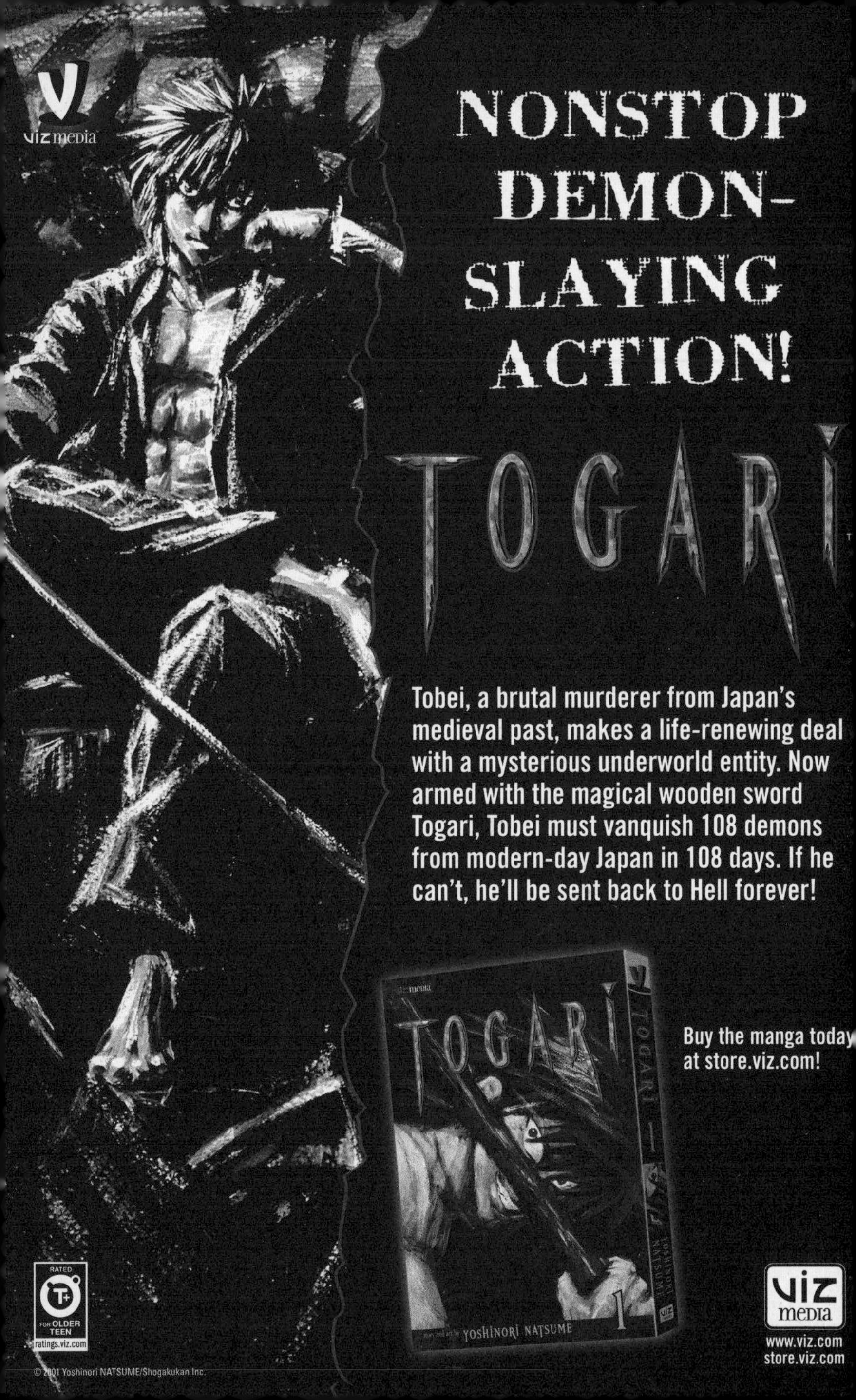
VIZ media
NONSTOP DEMON-SLAYING ACTION!
TOGARI™
Tobei, a brutal murderer from Japan's medieval past, makes a life-renewing deal with a mysterious underworld entity. Now armed with the magical wooden sword Togari, Tobei must vanquish 108 demons from modern-day Japan in 108 days. If he can't, he'll be sent back to Hell forever!
TOGARI 1
story and art by YOSHINORI NATSUME
Buy the manga today at store.viz.com!
RATED T+ FOR OLDER TEEN
ratings.viz.com
VIZ media
www.viz.com
store.viz.com
© 2001 Yoshinori NATSUME/Shogakukan Inc.

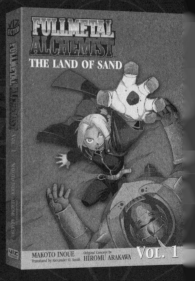